India's Revolution

India's Revolution
Gandhi
and the
Quit India
Movement

Francis G. Hutchins

Harvard University Press, Cambridge, Massachusetts 1973

For Anne, William, and Robert

Preface

This book focuses on a little-known episode of the Indian nationalist movement, the Quit India movement of 1942. In it Gandhi climaxed a lifetime of struggle with British imperialism in a totally unexpected way. The exponent of controlled nonviolent struggle presided over a chaotic violent movement at a critical period of World War II when Japanese troops stood poised for an invasion of Indian soil. The fact that at this crucial moment Gandhi sanctioned a violent uprising must be taken into account in any assessment of his total strategy of revolutionary action.

The Quit India movement is also an event of critical significance in Indian history generally. An analysis of the movement, and Britain's response to it, demonstrates that the events of 1942 persuaded the British to leave India without having established the safeguards which had previously been demanded as a condition of withdrawal. India, it can thus be argued, attained independence by revolution, by an act of Indian defiance and not, as is often asserted, through a process of gradual constitutional evolution.

The importance of the Quit India movement in revealing the full measure of Gandhi's revolutionary technique and in determining the way in which India attained independence has rarely been recognized because war censorship prevented publication of contemporary accounts. The magnitude which the movement attained despite the blackout of news coverage is in fact one of its most notable features, but the absence of adequate coverage at the time has made the task of historical reconstruction difficult. The prospect of prosecution for illegal activities, moreover, induced most underground workers to destroy all private papers pertaining to their activities, and consequently there is very little unpublished documentary evidence in the possession of survivors to make up for this deficiency. After the movement had ended and government controls had been relaxed fol-

lowing the war, the crises of independence left little time to participants to draw up their memoirs—and many, furthermore, were
doubtful whether they should divulge the role they had played in the
secret movement. The analysis of the movement presented here has
thus had to be based primarily on interviews with surviving participants and on the secret records of the British government, which have
only recently become available. These records reveal for the first time
the extent of the movement, as well as the nature of the plans the
British were making at this time to cope with the movement and
thereby mold India's future. No other regime has left such careful
documentation of its strategies or compiled such extensive records
revealing the way in which it was overthrown.

I wish to express my appreciation to the scores of former
revolutionaries who were kind enough to relive with me the events
of 1942. I hope that I have been able to record their recollections accurately. This study has also drawn heavily on the holdings of the
National Archives of India, New Delhi, to whose staff I am indebted.
I have made use of private papers in the possession of the Gandhi
Memorial Museum and the Nehru Memorial Museum and Library,
both in New Delhi, and of the India Office Library, London, and am
grateful to their staffs for courtesy and cooperation. Mr. Viswanath
Verma of New Delhi kindly arranged access to the papers of Rajendra
Prasad. I have profited in many ways from the sympathetic guidance
of the Nehru Museum's director, B. R. Nanda. Permission to use
material in the Linlithgow Papers has been kindly accorded by the
present Lord Linlithgow and the Trustees of the Hopetoun Papers
Trust. Unpublished Crown copyright material in the India Office
Records reproduced in this book appears by permission of the Con-
troller of Her Majesty's Stationery Office. For provocative advice I am
indebted to P. N. Chopra, Pamela Daniels, Carolyn Elliott, Ramesh
Jain, D. G. Keswani, James Kurth, Jürgen Lütt, Ian Martin, Thomas
Metcalf, Frances Pritchett, Dietmar Rothermund, Lloyd and Susanne
Rudolph, and Judith Shklar. None of these people expected that this
book would assume its present form. The editors of *Public Policy* have
kindly given permission to reprint material which first appeared in
Public Policy in a somewhat different form. An earlier version of this
book was published in India in 1971 under the title *Spontaneous Revolu-
tion: The Quit India Movement* by Manohar Book Service, Delhi. The
American Institute of Indian Studies has contributed generously to

the support of my research, and Harvard University has provided me with leave and assistance from the University's Ford Foundation Grant for International Studies. The zealous commitment of my research assistant Devinder Singh made possible completion of the book on schedule.

F.G.H.

Boston, Massachusetts
February 1973

Contents

1. Introduction   1
2. The Imperialist's Dilemma: Unequal
   Partners   6
3. The Imperialist's Dilemma: The Limits
   of Liberalization   21
4. The Nationalist's Dilemma: Coping
   with the West   50
5. The Revolutionary Solution: Defining
   and Distinguishing Revolutions   74
6. Gandhi as a Revolutionary Leader   105
7. Quit India: Official Violence   139
8. Quit India: Gandhi's Answer   180
9. Spontaneous Revolution: August 1942   217
10. Aftermath   282
11. Gandhi's Future   290
     Selected Bibliography   299
     Notes   305
     Index   321

India's Revolution

1   Introduction

The dismantling of European empires in Asia after World War II is frequently explained as the consequence of a weakening of European power caused by the war itself. Britain, one is often told, was no longer strong enough to hold India and withdrew as an act of political precaution. In reality, British withdrawal was the result of pressure exerted from within India. Following the war, the French returned to Indochina, the Dutch to Indonesia, and the British to Malaya, Singapore, and Burma. The British showed sufficient will in repressing a guerrilla insurgency in Malaya that was limited to one section of the population, and the French and Dutch did their best to hold onto Indochina and Indonesia. The imperial regimes were forced out of Indochina, Indonesia, Burma, and India because local pressures had become uncontrollable. What happened after the war was a result of what Asians had experienced during the war, not of what Europeans had lost by the war.

The transformations which occurred in many countries during World War II are only now beginning to come into focus. During the war momentous changes were taking place. Awareness of these changes came with startling suddenness following 1945 because of the prior monopolization of public attention by war news. In India, the war's end led to independence for India and the creation of the new state of Pakistan—events so unexpected as to lead observers naturally to attribute them vaguely to an undefined postwar exhaustion. Reconstruction of the social history of the war years is now beginning to make sense of these events, as it becomes clear that Indian independence and the creation of Pakistan were the direct results of a confrontation of social forces within India during the war years. The British left India because Indians had made it impossible for them to stay.

India attained independence through revolution. The midwar Quit India movement climaxed India's nationalist revolution, which overthrew a powerful, effective political regime. Yet the revolutionary nature of Indian nationalism might not have been recognized even if its triumphs had not been obscured by the World War. The reluctance to consider nationalisms such as India's as revolutionary stems from a pooling of partial perceptions, those of many nationalists combined with those of liberal imperialists and many social scientists. Revolutionaries need not be consciously so; they may conceive of themselves and their goals much more modestly or vaguely. Liberal imperialists in turn often portray the attainment of independence as the "fulfillment" of colonial rule. From the earliest period of British dominance in India, Englishmen had proclaimed their hopes that India would some day be ripe for independence, though it was usually assumed that this referred to an irrelevantly remote eventuality. After the fact, however, India's independence could be described as the fulfillment of British policy by reference to these frequently reiterated hopes. This impression was reinforced by the fact that the Labour party happened to be in power when India became independent. The Labour party had been associated with the enactment of several latter-day imperial experiments with political liberalization. Depicted as methods by which the imperial regime was laying the groundwork — consciously or unconsciously — for its departure, these experiments were in fact efforts to forestall independence by neutralizing grievances. The British Labour party was committed only to independence on British terms. To win independence on their own terms, Indians had to defy their liberal well-wishers no less than their conservative detractors. Only when independence became inevitable following the Quit India movement of 1942 did both parties switch to efforts to insure that the attainment of formal independence would not affect vested interests adversely.

Some imperial regimes did take action before this had become inevitable. By conceding independence at an early date, the United States in the Philippines and Britain and France in Africa and elsewhere were able to exert greater influence on postindependence national development. In such instances it is more accurate to speak of the "granting" of independence. Not surprisingly, national elites who have been given independence have often had difficulty holding their nations together. Some countries, such as China, have resisted imperialism in a clearly revolutionary manner. Other countries have been given independence and not known what to do with it. India stands in between, having attained independence through a movement which must be called revolutionary, but which has not usually been recognized as such because of certain formal resemblances to movements which did not attain independence through their own efforts.

Social scientists have customarily reinforced the liberal imperial vision of benign tutelage by stressing continuities rather than discontinuities in analyzing political development, producing an impression of linear progress in "underdeveloped regions," possibly highlighted by events such as the achievement of national independence, but not created or determined by such events. Many feel that crises associated with radical nationalism have actually delayed independence by disrupting the even flow of political development. Many social scientists think of all revolutions as disasters for political development. Revolutions are described variously as "breakdowns," "virus infections," and the like. If an event is judged to be revolutionary or not on such negative criteria—depending upon its degree of disruptiveness—naturally there will be a tendency to hope that colonial nationalism is not revolutionary and to piece together fragmentary evidence of continuity before and after independence.

It is easy to downgrade the creative potential of revolutionary events by pointing to the superficial similarities between even the most revolutionary new regime and its predecessor. It has seemed both incongruous and reassuring to see nationalist judges dispensing justice from beneath powdered wigs, to see judges or parliamentarians or bureaucrats perpetuate details of colonial usage. Now, it appears, things are returning to normal and stable progress may recommence after the unfortunate bitterness preceding independence. "Nation-building" may now proceed on the foundation left by colonial rule, under the guidance of colonialism's most apt students of John Stuart Mill and *Roberts' Rules of Order*. Yet only insofar as it has been revolutionary has colonial nationalism become self-sustaining. The revolution itself makes possible the retention of colonial vestiges, the revolution alone makes such vestiges legitimate and integral aspects of national development. Alexis de Tocqueville has noted that in destroying the French *ancien régime*, the French Revolution was also enlarging on its work. The policies which the French monarchy had employed to save itself from bankruptcy and the clutches of the nobility were often the same policies which revolutionaries introduced as the birthrights of free men. Because legitimacy had been revived through revolution basic reforms could be accepted.[1]

The assumption that development following independence is continuous with the past usually implies that national progress will be not only linear but unrestricted. Any of the nation's handicaps can presumably be overcome with time and talent. Such an attitude obscures the extent to which an irreversible event may set boundaries to national development, the limits within which change can take place. While the heritage of revolution may be acknowledged to have molded much of the subsequent history of France, it is considered uncharitable and unscientific to contend that nationalism may have left a similar imprint on currently developing societies. Presumably, the sky is the limit as long as one takes one step at a time. An unlimited optimism breeds the hope that, for instance, a deeply divided society can evolve into an integrated democracy, or that the revolutions in Cuba and China, being mere interruptions of development, can be simply nullified by invasion. Such cosmic optimism, which has from time to time been incorporated into official government policy in the United States, has as its obverse side an obsession at the level of policy application with matters of technique and detail. If things are presumed to be proceeding in the right direction, one can decide pragmatically on a basis of immediate convenience which of the elements of the desired social end-product to press for first. Any one good thing will lead to all the others. Economic development today, for example, means in this view a better hope of political democracy tomorrow.

Such an attitude toward development prospects elsewhere mirrors, not the American experience, but common perceptions of it. America's Revolution has also been allowed to fade into relative insignificance as a moment in a connected chain of development. In fact, both sides of the debate over the contemporary relevance or irrelevance of America's experience as a "new nation" have overlooked the effect of the Revolution. Samuel Huntington has argued that there was no revolution, and that the nation founded in 1776 was not new. Seymour Martin Lipset has found world-wide relevance in the early years of America's experience as *The First New Nation*, but he neglects the Revolution's effect as a possible area of meaningful comparison, beginning his analysis only when the new American nation had already come into existence.[2] Yet, in America no less than in other countries, it was revolution itself which solved many of the nation's problems and created others. The failure to perceive the effect of the American Revolution on the position of black Americans, for instance, has crippled efforts to cope with this heritage of revolution.

The nature of an *ancien régime* defines the problems with which revolutionaries have to cope. It also provides inadvertently many of the resources, intellectual and material, with which the new order is constructed, and sets a practical limit to the fulfillment of revolutionary aspirations. As Tocqueville set out to study the French Revolution by studying the French *ancien régime*, so, with regard to formerly colonial societies, one must study the nature of the prerevolutionary regime in order to understand the course of events following its downfall. The ambiguous term "neocolonialism" has been coined in an effort to cope with one consequence of interrelatedness, the fact that imperialism is not so alien and formal as to disappear with the pronouncing of a verbal exorcism. Imperialism lives on, not simply in the ghost of allegations past, but in a variety of institutional embodiments. Imperialism was a social and political system as well as an ideology. It had an alien appearance because its top administrative and military officials were foreigners, but it was also a domestic regime, supported by vested interests and supporting in turn institutions relating directly or indirectly to its perpetuation. While alien administrators could be removed with relative rapidity once it had been decided to withdraw, the domestic system at the head of which they stood could not be so readily dismantled. It is often said that India was fortunate in its inheritance of a "developed" society. India was perhaps fortunate in having materials to work with, but the claim of the nationalist movement was to revolution, not simply to succession, and its inheritance represented a gauge of the remaining challenge to the revolution rather than a guarantee of its easy success.

The British had a plan for India's future and helped develop India with this end in mind. This could not provide the foundation for the independent India nationalists had in mind. To attain this end, British rule and the type of development for which it stood had to be terminated by a revolutionary redirection of the nation's energies and resources. Indian independence meant the rejection of Britain's plan for India and the fulfillment of a plan of revolution.

2   The Imperialist's Dilemma:

Unequal Partners

Cultural Innovation

British rule in India had to be overthrown because even benevolent British intentions with respect to India's development had pernicious consequences. All social experimentation is hazardous. The desire of a dominant class to innovate in itself sets them apart from the object of their concern, making it difficult for them to anticipate what the response to innovation will be. When reformers are foreigners the difficulty is compounded. The problem of inadequate information about potential response—which any innovator would face—has added to it the problem of inexact translation. The cultural meaning of a given gesture or the likely effect of a given reform may be accurately perceived in relation to one's own society, but inappropriately extended by analogy, with unforeseen consequences. A society's resiliency is rarely apparent on the surface, but readily discovered if it is assumed not to exist. It is simpler to destroy a country's physical infrastructure than to build it up, but it is easier to add to a society's social infrastructure than it is to tear it down. The application of external pressure can level buildings, but it tends to compress and consolidate social structures.

Foreign influence may be applied negatively or positively and at the top or at the side of a society. An indiscriminate attack on a society from outside—negative pressure at the top—usually provokes an energetic effort at self-defense, which may result in a strengthening of the social position of the traditionally dominant social class. A hated or parasitic class may in fact be saved from dying a natural death by a peremptory challenge shocking it into new energy or arousing new sympathy. The workers of the world have tended to unite behind national leadership when efforts to "liberate" them from without are made.

Violence applied to the side of a society involves an effort to be more discriminating by causing injury only to selected classes, with presumptive benefit to others. This may be combined with an effort to provide positive incentives to other classes. Violence directed against a nonelite class may succeed in causing injury but is unlikely to achieve the intended goal of furthering social well-being. The injured class will be driven underground or overseas and may in the end, like the French Huguenots, prosper more than the classes which sought their exclusion.

When an effort is made to innovate positively in a foreign society in a context of peaceful development through foreign aid or under direct imperial control, the approach may also be from above or from the side. The availability of foreign aid introduces a new stake into a self-contained society. Such aid will act like a magnet. If the magnet is applied from above, the society is likely to become artificially rigidified. Resources are concentrated at the top, the society becomes top-heavy, and the position of the dominant elite is reinforced. When sustained by foreign aid, an elite will have more resources available than their native wit or powers of extortion would otherwise provide. This will permit a comfortable life with slackened oppression and greater ease in the manipulation of less privileged classes. The normal struggle between exploiters and exploited may consequently be paralyzed. The class system will be kept intact because its normal costs are waived.

If the magnet of foreign aid is set at the side of the social hierarchy, it will attract certain persons, a few from every level of the old hierarchy, the majority from a particular level, depending upon the nature of the magnet. The old structure will be sapped of some of its vitality, but remain basically unaltered. A new class of interpreters—in a literal or figurative sense—will have been added which is capable of interacting with the external force but which may not be an effective part of the original society.

Positive innovation from the top as well as from the side of Indian society characterized much of British Indian policy. The effects of these differing approaches were well exemplified by the results of British educational policy, which passed through several distinct stages. In the eighteenth century, the British had begun cautiously at the top. While trying to maintain Indian society as a whole intact, the British artificially bolstered the position of a traditional elite at the expense of the rest of the society. Aid administered at the top did not trickle down, though its effect was felt indirectly in the enhanced arrogance of a favored class.

The British at this time drew an analogy from the eighteenth century British situation in which learning was closely associated with a class of clerical specialists and consisted largely of close study of Europe's classical texts. Efforts to promote learning in India reflected an attempt to translate the British into the Indian situation by supporting the traditional learned classes among Hindus and Muslims, respectively, in the study of their own classical texts. This was logical enough but had the effect of giving an artificial stimulus to orthodoxy. The British gave ancient textual prescriptions a renewed mandate and reversed the "corrupting" trend of later centuries. By subsidizing the study of the ancient texts in government-fostered institutions, the British accorded the priestly classes a strategic position within the governing structure which was hardly comparable to the position of Anglican clerics within English society.[1]

When British liberals gained control of Indian educational policy in the first half of the nineteenth century, they abandoned the illusory conservative effort to preserve the old culture intact and frankly planned its replacement by rational Western ways. The liberals were not averse to employing negative pressure to obstructive elements by withdrawing government patronage from the traditional learned classes. By and large, however, the liberals felt that the ambitious changes they envisioned could be achieved by positive incentives, by simply moving the magnet from the top to the side of Indian society.

The conviction that Indian tradition could be painlessly replaced by merely making available a Western alternative was a reflection of liberal faith in the superiority of Western civilization and in the capacity of non-Western peoples to appreciate its superiority. The adoption of Western civilization was to be essentially a simple process, involving the substitution of one set of customs for another. Traditional Indian social arrangements were not accorded the dignity of a logic or coherence of their own, but were thought of as ill-assorted and haphazard, just as traditional ideas and thought processes seemed inconsistent and illogical. The reform program which Benthamite liberals sought to introduce into India in the early nineteenth century proposed the substitution of reason for custom as the source and vindication of law. Custom, of course, has its own reasonableness, and "reason" in Benthamite usage a customary connotation, but Benthamites chose to consider customs discrete and dispensable. Traditional customs would be voluntarily abandoned when Indians were informed of the availability of rational alternatives. Burkean conservatives had once warned of the dangers of tinkering with, and imperialists had once extolled the advantages of exploiting, Indian prejudice. Unlike Benthamite liberals, both these conservative groups had seen Indian society as an organic whole and had sensed the possibility that small reforms might set off chain reactions whose ultimate consequences could not be estimated, that "if one finger brings oil it soils the others."[2] The liberal Benthamites, however, conceived of chain reactions only in optimistic terms, referring to the rapid spread of new ideas rather than the reaction of the old; tradition, being inert, did not react. While the intentions of reformers might be misunderstood, their efforts could not be objectively destructive; the spread of reason, by disarming ignorant suspicion, would be sufficient to clear the way for progress. The magnet of English education placed at its side would gradually draw over the entire society, still intact while progressively adopting Western attributes. The traditional elite's better elements, allied with the best of the new men produced by new educational opportunities, would, it was thought, stimulate a thoroughgoing social transformation.

The elation with which liberal reformers greeted the willingness of Indians to adopt small signs of Western life into their speech or dress was a logical application of their theory of the nature of change. One thing would lead to another. The person who became Westernized in small things would no doubt become Westernized in large things; on this point British reformers and orthodox Indian revivalists were agreed.

A small number of fully Westernized Indians might by the same token be expected to have a revolutionary impact on Indian society as a whole. There was a tendency to lionize individual Indians who "responded" to the West, who repeated appropriate sentiments, memorized Shakespeare, and spoke admiringly of London Bridge. The "good Indian" was quickly seized upon and paraded as indicative of the wave of the future. The result was an extraordinary monopolization of British awareness of India by a tiny handful who were in effect self-appointed spokesmen to the West. When Westernized Indians some decades later began to show signs of radicalization, they were ridiculed by conservative British administrators as "representing only the anomaly of their own position." Earlier, while docile but much less representative, they were made much of as representatives of what India might soon become.

It was assumed that as the effects of English education spread, Western ways would be gratefully adopted and Western goods as gratefully purchased. A little English education was expected to raise an individual's moral tone and stimulate his ambition to improve his material condition. Knowledge would make the Chinaman want a more sober life, and thus a longer shirttail. Englishmen were frankly incorporating underdeveloped regions into an economic system in which it was understood that they would be at the bottom. It was understood that countries might or might not advance, just as it was known that some members of the English lower class would probably never be more than vagrants. But it was held that insofar as countries could advance it would be only in response to the challenge offered by free market competition. The "diffusion of knowledge" would encourage the spread of understanding of this fact and develop capacity to respond creatively to this challenge.

Under the terms of the liberal educational policy for India, formulated between the 1820's and the 1850's, the British government in India was requested to sponsor, with all its persuasive power, the type of moral and social revolution which had occurred in England as a result of the effort of reformers working against the entrenched power structure of British society. In England, the reformers were circumscribed by their position as subordinate members of a larger society. In India the radical creed of a disadvantaged group became the official creed of an autocratic government. When a member of England's lower middle class preached self-reliance to his fellows it had an effect different from that when self-reliance was preached at Indians by inadequately paid teachers in a half-understood language, on orders from Olympian British officials.

Indian policy was formulated at this period by liberals who believed that a society advanced through individual initiative but who could not resist the opportunity which the possession of arbitrary power provided to force people to help themselves. This was justified on the grounds that the resources of government might be utilized in an *exemplary* fashion, stimulating and initiating activity which might then be emulated by private individuals acting on their own. The government might be made the leading sector of the society in a transitional period until independent initiative was sufficiently developed to carry on unaided. The purpose of government would be to stimulate, not to limit or control, and the ultimate object of government would be a free and competitive society.

British liberal imperialists hoped to employ liberal illiberality to encourage a three-fold revolution: to improve Indian moral character, to increase social mobility, and to stimulate material advance. It was expected that all these things could be accomplished by the study of English literature, to which Indians would be attracted by the magnet of prospective government employment.

Government employment was held out as a possible reward of English education to a vastly wider circle of students than could in the end be actually offered employment because it was assumed that the education a person received while motivated by the prospect of securing a government job would be useful to him in private life even if he failed to secure employment under the government. Education, the liberal presumed, was a substance which might be diluted but could not be debased; however small the quantity one received, one would be to that extent proportionately and permanently edified. Education, being directed at the accomplishment of an essentially moral improvement, was not designed to equip its recipient with technical skills. A single element from the lifelong influences to which a middle class Englishman was subjected was isolated and charged with the task of re-creating in its entirety a middle class morality among Indians, though the study of a foreign language, at a low level of proficiency, did not in the end prove a promising medium for the transmission of an alien morality. That the recipient of such an education, whose only practical utility was to enable one to find employment under the English government, failing to secure such employment, would be equally well equipped for a useful career in private life also proved to be an unfounded hypothesis. Middle class morality was not automatically transmitted by literary studies at any level of sophistication, nor was English middle class morality a universal currency capable of insuring that those who possessed it would succeed in any calling in any society.

The liberal reformers imagined that they were offering India the distilled lessons of their own experience. It was a matter of necessity that official government programs not directly sponsor Christian instruction which might give offense to Indian sensibilities. More important, the liberals found themselves more comfortable with the morality without the religion, "the fruit without the root." No longer fully committed to the literal truth of Christian dogma, the reformers preferred to dissociate Christian morality from the specific dogmas of Christianity, hoping that by learning "everything but" the specifically doctrinal part of Christian English education it would be possible for Indians to achieve the condition the reformers envisioned for themselves as cultured moral men unhampered by cant.

As members of England's educated middle class, the liberal reformers were reluctant to draw a clear line between the middle and upper classes. Education, they knew, might facilitate the rise of "new men," but they saw this as a process which would gradually expand the existing upper class through liberalization, not one involving the creation of a new, different, incompatible class. India's chief educational planner, Thomas Macaulay, a bright product of a middle class, rose to become Lord Macaulay. Middle class Englishmen before Macaulay were often inspired by an animus against all privilege, Indian as well as English. In the 1830's, forties, and fifties, the term "respectable classes" could be employed to combine what once had seemed—and what would subsequently seem again—the incompatible qualities of hereditary eminence and intellectual ability.

The Education Despatch of 1854 from the East India Company's Court of Directors proposed the establishment of universities which would be examining rather than teaching institutions. It was stated that standards should not be rigorous for otherwise graduates would be "naturally disinclined to accept such employment as persons who intend to make the public service their profession must necessarily commence with." The directors were eager to see the emergence of a larger class of poorer students prepared to take ill-paid jobs. They deplored the previous policy, involving "too exclusive a direction of the efforts of Government towards providing the means of acquiring a very high degree of education for a small number of natives of India, drawn, for the most part, from what we should here call the higher classes." They advocated that "different classes of colleges and schools . . . should be maintained in simultaneous operation in order to place within the reach of all classes of the natives of India the means of obtaining improved knowledge suited to their several conditions of life."

The directors regretted the fact that government support for education had tended to go to the "higher classes," not because they were antagonistic to them, but because "the higher classes are both able and willing in many cases to bear a considerable part at least of the cost of their education."[3] The directors hoped that financial support might be channeled toward those who would have difficulty securing an education without it, not to create a class antagonistic to the already existing "higher classes," but to broaden the base of and ease the route of access into the higher classes. The privileged classes could not be permitted to survive as parasites, but they had the means to save themselves if they wished by taking advantage of educational opportunities. In England the worthless members of the nobility had not been exterminated; the institutions and privileges associated with the nobility were extended to new groups. This had been good for the nobility by giving them an incentive to maintain their position in a wider world, and had set limits to the radicalism of new groups by channeling their aspirations in traditional directions. A parallel fusing of classes was anticipated in India.

The disruptive effect of the liberals' educational policy was a result of that feature which seemed to Englishmen most unexceptionable—its magnet-like impartiality. Schools and competitive examinations were opened to all on the basis of merit, and the use of the English language seemed to have liquidated the traditional advantages enjoyed by those who were conversant with the older languages of law and administration; the use of Persian for administrative communications was discriminatory in favor of Muslims, as was the use of Sanskrit in applying Hindu personal law discriminatory in favor of Brahmin pandits. And yet, employing the magnet of impartiality was itself a form of partiality. Impartiality favored those who were most strategically placed to take advantage of its terms of competition. British liberals rewarded impartially the possession of certain qualities which the British admired—but which were not uniformly possessed or admired by India's varying communities. Individuals and groups had to decide for themselves whether to respond to the magnet which opportunities for involvement in British rule had placed at their side. It would have been possible to anticipate who would respond to the provision of comparable opportunities within England: the "middle class," which in nineteenth century English usage referred more to a state of mind than a level of income or type of occupation. The middle class were those people embarked on independent careers in business or the professions who were, if not self-employed, certainly self-improving, mobile, and ambitious, but also sober and disciplined—professionals, whatever their calling happened to be. The extension of opportunities for all was implicitly understood to be intended for those already most able to grasp opportunities, and the moral qualities and social background of most such people were also well understood.

In England at this time political power and traditional status were relatively united in a single pyramid whose base could be safely broadened. In India, the British recognized a class of landlords as the traditional heads of Indian society, but retained political power to themselves. The British monopoly of positions in the higher echelons of the official pyramid meant that no one at the top of the traditional status pyramid was inclined to acquire the type of education which would prepare him for a position at the bottom of the official pyramid. Those who responded to the opportunities for English education were persons who hoped to better their worldly position. English education offered no prospect that it could help make one a better Hindu or Muslim. The moral consequences of the decision to educate their sons in English were a source of the greatest trepidation in Indian families and were overcome only by the calculation of compensating worldly advantage through employment within the structure of British rule. Families with a comfortable income from land or trade were little inclined to take the risks involved, to jeopardize their sons' assured prospects and their own social position in return for a speculative advantage. Thus, while established families held back, families with less to lose pushed forward to explore the new possibilities. The British soon discovered that the people they were educating were not the traditional leaders of society, who could use their respected social positions to diffuse Western values widely; the educational magnet had created an entirely new class without traditional standing, without substantial resources.

Those disadvantaged individuals who did entertain an interest in English education, to the extent that they successfully assimilated its ethos, to the same extent found themselves unimpressed by those at the top of the traditional status pyramid. The result, predictably, came to resemble more the eighteenth century French situation than the nineteenth century English situation. A secure but somewhat superfluous privileged class found themselves at odds with a new class with radical ideas and limited prospects, in a society presided over by an autocratic power for which neither class had great affection.

The British bestowed upon India the cheapest, most expedient educational system conceivable. A large class of relatively impoverished Indians with a moderate English language competence insured the government of a supply of lower level clerks, making it easier for Englishmen to run India in their own language while saving the cost of importing numerous clerks from England. By providing a university system which incorporated the many existing independent teaching units established over the years by private initiative and encouraging the establishment of new independent units, the British gave a license to mediocrity; under such a system standards could not be adequately supervised and the pull was inevitably in the direction of the lowest common denominator. This was all done with the most liberal intentions, through nonviolent positive innovation, by placing an impartial magnet by the side of Indian society. In fact, as the British did become more calculating in later years, they instinctively moved to the establishment of schools in India and in Africa on an exclusive, elitist model. As a basis for social organization they then substituted upper-class manners for universal principle.

In this later period, the magnet was moved back to the top of Indian society, but this time to the benefit of landlords rather than priests. A diluted commitment to Indian moral betterment survived, but now the touchstone of moral improvement was assumed to be games. The feat of assimilating an alien ethic was moreover now perceived to be a complicated task, feasible only for men of aristocratic background. Those who were successfully assimilated were henceforth stuffy, rather than bright, more stylish than enterprising. Schools were established explicitly for the sons of princes and landlords, with admission limited by nomination and reservation. The British effort to Anglicize the nobility, however, proved as unsuccessful as their effort to produce a replica of the English middle class. British rule guaranteed the position of the aristocrats but in doing so deprived them of incentives to alter their way of life. The public schools that were provided for the princes, such as Mayo College at Ajmer, failed to achieve the remarkable feats of character-building with which their public school prototypes in England were credited. In England games were supposed to mold character, so games were provided for the princes. In India, games were considered one among many princely indulgences. The Victorian public school boy and the Indian prince both became great sportsmen, but each took from his sport what he put into it; the Englishman returned from the field, his sense of moral well-being bolstered, while the Indian prince returned from the field only to turn to some alternative diversion.

The British by 1900 had experimented with three types of positive innovation which employed, respectively, a clerical, middle class, and aristocratic Indian class ally. Each of these attempts failed to achieve its intended goal, though each achieved some superficial success. Each demonstrated that positive incentives could mold a class to order, but could not make it work.

British education was a success, but the student failed. This was not entirely because of misconceived educational policies. Training was a simple, philanthropic activity; employing responsibly and working as colleagues with Indians involved an entirely different set of reflexes which the British found much more difficult to develop. English-educated Indians gravitated into marginal employment under the British, or lived by their wits as lawyers; the princes drifted back to the tedium of sham rule, plagued by meddling British officials. What effect British education might have had was not reinforced, but vitiated, as Indians were caught between the unfulfilled promise of British education and the pressure of Indian social tradition.

The Englishman in India never escaped the patron's dilemma that in sponsoring change he is also entering into an entangling relationship. What is intended to be a temporary stimulant leading to "takeoff" often becomes a permanent obligation to maintain a dependent. It is natural to suppose that a class supported or rewarded from outside has come to prefer the embrace of the foreigner to the respect of their fellow countrymen. Instead of assisting a class in becoming a leading sector, foreign patronage may atrophy their will or confirm their social irrelevance. At best it may make incidentally available — as Western education did to middle class Indians — some ammunition which will prove useful in overthrowing the tyranny of beneficence.

Positive innovation by outsiders is, in sum, as disorienting as it is nonviolent. Some have felt that the solution to the curious effects of such half-measures lies in a unified approach, combining the violent eradication of obstructions with the energetic encouragement of alternatives. The implication of such an approach is that desirable change can actually be externally stimulated, if it is only properly managed. While it is true that an aggressive foreign involvement may derange a society by pressing an old equilibrium beyond the point of possible resurrection, it is difficult to say what will grow up in its place. The temptation persists nonetheless to explain failure as a failure of technique, and to ignore the inherent unpredictability in efforts at positive cultural innovation, no matter how carefully the plans are made and the ground prepared.

Structural Innovation

The fate of British efforts to stimulate the acquisition of traits by individuals of one class or another suggests the parallel fate of efforts to introduce institutions and structures. Just as Western customs were thought of by many Britishers as discrete and universally useful, so structures were thought of as tools that could be used with equal efficacy in different settings and by different groups. Structures were neutral, a safe common denominator which could be introduced while the debate over control and application was being resolved in the messy political arena.

The stimulation of railroad construction by the government was, for instance, welcomed as self-evidently desirable for the development of India. Criticism was rained on the government for the terms it granted private railway companies and there was much suspicion that solicitude for the British investor outweighed commitment to Indian development in planning for expansion. The effect of the railways, as distinct from the motives attendant upon their creation, was held to be largely beneficial.[4]

What was ignored in focusing on the self-enrichment of the British investor was that British planners might be capable of bending the institutions they had created in ways antagonistic to progressive development. The purpose of railway construction went beyond the provision of profitable investment opportunities. Railways were also intended to facilitate the control and exploitation of Indian resources by the existing social structure, based in England. Railways fanned out from the ports into the countryside; they were valuable in encouraging trade in and out of the country, but less useful in encouraging trade between different parts of India. Railways also linked the plains with British hill-stations, facilitating the movement of troops and civilian government personnel from salubrious retreats to trouble spots below. The railway system inherited by India upon the attainment of independence represented a capital investment not simply in tools, but in a social system. The infrastructure built up by imperialists was not readily adaptable to nationalist purposes. India had paid for an infrastructure which, in the old view, only needed new management; but the investment had been made in ways which, while exhausting resources, have made it difficult to redirect the structures created to new social ends.[5]

Structures such as the railways served larger social ends; their staffing also had social implications. One problem with the British commitment to the peaceful termination of their control of India was that the more likely it seemed on the basis of the criterion of "development," the more difficult it became in political terms. As India was transformed, as rail lines were put down and factories and schools put up, as India became more technologically complex and professionally specialized, ever more experts were needed to fill the jobs thus created. India's social transformation became institutionalized, like a top-heavy department of welfare. "Helping India" became a vested interest, a form of outdoor relief for the middle classes. The difficulties produced by an influx of Englishmen into lower and lower echelons of the bureaucracy were frequently pointed out, but the inexorable logic that there was always room for one more nephew continued to prevail. Marginal people with small prospects elsewhere would be the first to be displaced once "competent Indians" became available. The consequent inclination was to shove into the future the day when Indians would be competent enough.

The total number of Englishmen in India rose steeply immediately following the Rebellion of 1857, as British troop strength went from about 40,000 to about 70,000, but remained remarkably constant thereafter. In 1883–1884 the total number of "British-born and other Europeans" in India was 143,000; in 1931 the figure had risen to only 168,000. The increase, small as it is, can be accounted for largely by the increased numbers of women and children, as the disproportionately male population of the earlier years were more frequently joined by their families. The size of the community variously described in the census as "Eurasian" or "Anglo-Indian," however, grew steadily, from 62,000 in 1883 to 138,000 in 1931. If one includes this community of mixed British and Indian blood in the European category, the picture takes on a strikingly different appearance, indicating an increase in the size of the European community of 50 per cent, from approximately 200,000 to approximately 300,000 between the years 1883 and 1931.

The Anglo-Indian community stood in a peculiarly vulnerable position within the racially founded society of British India. In the American

South the problem posed by the existence of persons of mixed blood was officially ignored, and such persons were routinely classified as members of the subordinate race. Such a policy was not possible in British India for several reasons. In the first place, the majority of the Anglo-Indian community were the product of legitimate marriages contracted between lower class Englishmen, often army enlisted men who could not easily afford to import a wife from England, and Indian women. Anglo-Indians inherited their fathers' names, their language, and their religion, all of which marked them off decisively from the majority of Indians. Having as a community such a degree of cultural distinctness, Anglo-Indians were insistent that such factors not be outweighed in the determination of their identity and place in the social hierarchy by mere physical similarities to other Indians. Their self-respect and career prospects rested on their ability to identify themselves with the dominant racial community. Since Englishmen in the nature of the case were unable to ignore their claims, they tried to find ways to use them to advantage.

The British thus created an area of reserved employment for Anglo-Indians at the lower, technical levels of British government, most notably in the railroads. The status level was appropriately marginal, but respectable, and such a reservation served the further purpose of lodging the strategic technical services in compulsively loyal hands. The result was the exclusion of Indians from participation in an important sector of India's development.

Structures such as the railways adjust to a society's ends as old wineskins to old wine, becoming subtly inseparable. Means and ends, tools and products, structures and social values are intimately connected, acting and reacting on one another in a mutually supportive relationship which makes it difficult to predict how one would function without the other. When institutions are introduced from outside, they may serve outside interests, as in the case of the Indian railways. They may, alternatively, serve no purpose, and simply remain standing in picturesque juxtaposition to the unchanging traditional society surrounding them. The plains of many countries are strewn with majestic wrecks, machines abandoned as useless after a season for want of a simple replacement part, and perhaps retained proudly as nonfunctioning monuments. The imported tools which prove most durable are those most readily adaptable to old-fashioned uses. Imported institutions cannot create purposes to serve them, but they may interact with existing purposes and produce a new synthesis which is different but effective. The producer of the first Indian "mythological" film portraying the exploits of Hindu deities was inspired by a filmed *Life of Christ* distributed under missionary auspices.[6] In a vastly more complex fashion, the success of democratic institutions in postindependence India reflects the same process. Their success does not flow from a preliminary internalization of the values associated with Western democracy, but from the fact that they have proved adaptable to the purposes—old and new—which Indians at many levels of sophistication wish to pursue.

For over a century, the British experimented with methods of stimulating India's social and economic development. They promoted the spread of character traits —which made Indians cultural misfits. They built up institutions which employed Indians —at the lower levels. Good intentions were neutralized by the fact that a close association between unequal partners if intended to be enduring must in time become exploitative and debilitating. Whatever benefit a junior partner may derive will be only that which enables him to move quickly to dispense with the services of his benefactor by the selective acquisition of tools to serve his own purposes.

The history of the British in India is a history of efforts to find a solid basis for permanent exploitation which might be accepted as mutually beneficial. The British deranged Indian society while trying to develop it, leaving India with huge problems and an array of institutions designed to serve discredited purposes. The British stirred up Indian energies by disorienting Indian society, and ultimately provoked a concerted Indian effort to end British rule.

3   The Imperialist's Dilemma:

The Limits of Liberalization

During most of the nineteenth century the British were able to experiment with different approaches to cultural and structural innovation in India without worrying overmuch about what Indians thought of their activities. The opposition that did surface, as in the Rebellion of 1857, was easy to label reactionary and destined to wane. In the twentieth century the British were increasingly obliged to respond to Indian pressure, which had grown and altered in nature. The *political* innovations of the decades preceding Indian independence are often likened to the optimistic cultural and structural innovations of the earlier years. The process is called political liberalization and is retrospectively viewed as a preparation for independence. In fact, these political innovations were defensive and involved initially efforts to forestall India's independence. When these seemed doomed to fail, the British shifted to an effort to purge India of dangerous elements to insure that India after independence would continue to be acquiescent. Political liberalization in India was an effort to control political challenges and thereby to break the back of the nationalist revolution. In the twentieth century, British innovations were efforts to cope with Indian challenges in order to conserve the position in India the British had built for themselves in the name of India's advancement.

Political liberalization, in other words, is a process whose consequences depend upon the context in which it occurs and the purposes which it is hoped it will serve. A "liberalizing" reform cannot be viewed as patently desirable on its merits; it must be considered in relation to the motives of its movers and the role it is expected to play vis-à-vis existing structures. A reform justified on one basis may have a different intent—and an effect different from either justification or intent.

Institutional liberalization involves the devolution of new rights and powers to new groups or the encouragement of increased popular participation in the processes of government. Whether such reforms actually have a "liberalizing" effect and whether liberalization is or is not conducive to the stability of government depends upon many factors. In a competitive polity liberalization may involve the gradual, haphazard expansion of existing privileges, a process characterized by unpredictable anomalies, arbitrary distinctions drawn, for instance, between £ 9 and £ 10 freeholders, and ad hoc responses to pressure group demands from, for instance, suffragettes. Parties who hope to gain advantages from the inclusion of new groups of voters will press for electoral expansion. The English reforms of 1832 and 1867 reflected this calculation, as did the admission of additional states to the American Union. Expansion initiated in this manner by competitive politics promises slow progress and the indefinite perpetuation of inequities as well as orderly integration, as the parties concerned will be prepared to organize the new voters and tie them into old alliances.

Under an autocratic government, the effect of liberalization depends in large part upon whether the initiative comes from below or above. When liberalization of an autocratic system results from a process initiated from below, to which the government responds positively, even though reluctantly, the effect may be stabilizing. When liberalization is initiated by energetic rulers as a technique for consolidating and legitimizing their rule, its effect may also be stabilizing, in that it reinforces autocracy. Bismarck and the Bolsheviks both strengthened their regimes in this manner. Regimes which establish predictable plebiscites may succeed in impressing foreign opinion as well as in intimidating domestic critics by a show of hands. Where the electoral process is used in this way as a cloak for autocracy it will have little appeal for intellectuals as a potential bulwark of liberty or vehicle for significant peaceful change. By taking the initiative, however, an autocracy may neutralize its opponents, or drive them underground.

When, alternatively, liberalization is undertaken by an autocracy halfheartedly under foreign pressure, or through inherent feebleness, the action of government may well be perfunctory and the effect divisive. The inclination will be to hire agents, to serve the government as a form of liberal window-dressing, and to perform the onerous tasks of organizing factions and fighting the enemies of government. A frontal attack by government on internal forces is risky. An attack through specially recruited intermediaries is, however, even more dangerous, as the British government of India discovered.

When an insecure autocracy attempts in this fashion to strengthen its position vis-à-vis external forces and weaken the position of its internal opponents, the government becomes a partisan, offering rewards for loyal service to those who will combat the government's foes. The stakes will be higher than when parties seek to gain marginal advantages within a stable competitive system through electoral expansion. If the tactic succeeds, domestic opposition may be bottled up indefinitely. If it fails, as happened in India, the government may fall. The government may gamble that an expanded electorate will be docile or capable of being made so. An autocratic government instinctively claims to speak for all whose voices cannot be heard and views its political opponents as self-seeking and unrepresentative. It is safer to speak for the voiceless masses, however, than to ask them to speak. If a restricted electorate has become dominated by unmanageable intellectuals, the only alternatives are the termination of elections or the expansion of the electorate in search of a wider mandate undercutting entrenched spokesmen. The first course invites revolution; the second may forestall it, for a time. Expanding the electorate may force the troublesome beneficiaries of the former restricted electorate into the position of defenders of privilege; or it may induce them to alter their habits and appeal for the support of the new voters, in competition with the regime's favored agents.

In British India political liberalization involved the recruiting of favored Indian agents and the expansion of electorates to undercut troublemakers. These tactics failed because the structure of government that was to be liberalized was inherently weak; its legitimacy had never been adequately established.

Every stable system of government, even the most autocratic, rests on a theory of representation. Any ruler considered legitimate is ultimately accepted as God's representative on earth, or the virtual representative of all the people. One or both of these assumptions underlies whatever mechanism of selection is deemed necessary to insure that rulers are in fact genuine representatives of God or the people. The British monarch—in Britain—for example, has never ceased to be God's representative in form, though the locus of power has shifted to the crown's "ministers," whose method of selection is popular, not appointive. Practical legitimacy in Britain springs from the people, though power is still exercised formally as if derived from God.

In Britain the shift from God-derived to man-derived authority was the most lasting accomplishment of the revolution that beheaded Charles I. The period of Tudor and Stuart ascendancy before the revolution may be contrasted with the postrevolutionary period extending through the eighteenth century in terms of differing theories of representation which reflect this change. Samuel Beer has noted that the prerevolutionary "Old Tory" theory of representation stressed hierarchy, with differing ranks in society having a justly greater voice in the affairs of the kingdom as they approached more closely the royal fount of authority. The "Old Whig" view which dominated in the eighteenth century, while retaining the monarchical, hierarchical form and the form of deference to the divine will, implied in fact political control by an aristocracy of wealth and talent operating through the Houses of Parliament, justified on secular grounds of social convenience and prosperity. Parliament ruled as the representative of the people. Its claim to be a genuine representative rested upon the presumption that it was an epitome of the nation, which it exemplified and represented virtually if not directly. An irregular system of election was considered a blessing in that it tended to insure that the nation's diversity would be faithfully reflected. Interests, classes, estates — the land, the law, the church, as well as that numerous class the common people — were represented in their capacity as constituent elements of the nation. Men were represented by virtue of their membership in a class. While individual members of Parliament might be more closely identified with some classes than with others, and moreover the representation even of classes was often not direct but virtual, Parliament as a whole presumably represented the nation as a whole. Unenfranchized towns and individuals could still anticipate that their interests would be taken into account, because individual M.P.'s acted as trustees, not merely as advocates of narrow interests.[1]

A theory of democratic territorial representation such as that prevailing with modifications in the United States presumes that individuals should be represented as individuals, and that as individual citizens they have equal and similar interests in the operation of the polity except for those interests stemming from their residence in a particular locality. Individuals are directly represented, and can express directly their private interests, whatever they happen to be at any given time.

To this extent, the theory acknowledges the validity of change; the community's individual members change constantly, and may be expected to have different individual desires. The Old Whig theory in contrast recognizes the validity only of constituted estates whose interests remain despite changes in their individual composition. Acts of government, furthermore, are summations of national will. Not simply expressions of the majority's current inclinations, they are expressions of the fused interests of all the nation's permanent constituent parts. Unity is achieved before action is taken and is exemplified in the action taken. Conflict as a form of purposeful action is excluded; conflict has to be muted before purposeful action is possible. The Old Whig theory, thus, like the Old Tory theory, has an essentially static bias. According to both theories changes in national interests are unlikely, actions in response to particular desires unacceptable. Whether acting, as in the Old Tory theory, through a single representative, or, as in the Old Whig theory, through a collective body, the sovereign is supposed to act for the nation, conceived of as an entity with permanent collective interests.

The British in India started from a traditional Indian premise in the early period of their rule: they were only agents of the Moghul emperor in form. Very quickly, however, ideas of British origin asserted themselves. The Benthamite tradition contributed material for a modernized version of Old Toryism. The new autocrat ruled in the name of a higher dispensation—that of science—on behalf of his subjects. After 1857 the more traditional form of Old Toryism was revived, with an effort to associate British rule with a class of Indian nobles and to conceive of Indian society as composed of stable ranks all of which looked up to a sovereign authority established by a dispensation from afar; Queen Victoria performed the function for the British viceroy which God had performed for James I. British rule presumably acted in the interest of all, though the acts of British authority were self-sufficient and authoritative without Indian sanction.

British government in this period was formally a judicious dispensation of Queen Victoria's beneficence. It was thus not a political regime in the usual sense; it did not have to indulge in bargaining and compromise to maintain itself. There was however, in rational bureaucratic fashion, a Political Department. India's foreign affairs were handled by the Foreign Department. British India was dealt with by administrative departments: in addition a realm of politics was recognized in British India's delicate relationship with the Indian princes, a relationship of control which had to be exercised *politically* through a mixture of persuasion, threats, and flattery.

Toward the end of the nineteenth century, the British began to move, in response to conflicting pressures, toward the adoption of elements of the Old Whig position. The basic dilemma of India's political development, as seen by the British at the beginning of the twentieth century, was how to move from an Old Tory to an Old Whig position without the intervening stage of revolution, and in the face of demands for movement to a political condition much more advanced than one which promised only to bring India abreast of the eighteenth century. The British were reluctant to abandon their claim to ultimate authority with its reserves of discretionary power, but they hoped to gain the advantages stemming from greater Indian identification with the regime by establishing popular legitimacy without popular power. In opening the processes of government to greater participation and pressure, the British employed the Old Whig model because of its premise of a basic social stability. Communities, not individuals, were represented; communities were easier to consult without empowering than the people as a whole, who could logically only be asked for a mandate—and that the British claimed not to need. Communities presumably had interests that were permanent and distinct, which made it easier to treat them separately and to prevent their combining. The British alone would continue to perform the function of the Old Whig Parliament, of fusing together into a national will the varying interests of all classes.

The Aitchison Commission of 1888 recommended that representation in the expanded Legislative Councils be determined on the basis of "classes and interests." In the Executive Council special skills would be represented—by the military member, the finance and law members, and so forth. In the Legislative Council classes and interests would be represented. This was a logical extension of the older Legislative Council, which was simply the Executive Council sitting as a Legislative Council. Members heading various administrative departments represented the interests of their own departments; widening the Legislative Council on the same basic principle would bring in representatives of other constituted interests: university graduates, the chamber of commerce, landlords, and others.

One subtly significant feature of representation under the reforms introduced in 1893 was the provision that those elected by the designated constituent elements of society were technically nominees who had to be accepted by the viceroy before they became members of the Legislative Council. Representation implicitly consisted of an opportunity to send delegates as petitioners to the viceroy, who reserved the right to accept or reject them. Lord Minto and his predecessor as viceroy Lord Curzon expressed dismay when Lord Morley, as secretary of state for India, informed them that he did not intend to retain this distinction under the 1909 reforms, but at this time the communal right of nominal representation by a person of the community's own choice was recognized.

In instituting communal representation, the British had no notion that they were establishing a system on the basis of which India's democratization would proceed. The improved Old Tory system was designed to last indefinitely and to place the empire on an even firmer footing.

The result of the reforms of 1893 and 1909 was a concretization of the implicit functioning of the eighteenth century Parliament. Classes and communities had only been presumed to have de facto representation in the eighteenth century Parliament, beneath the façade of confusing anachronisms, inequities, rotten boroughs, and the like, which were the accretions of centuries of haphazard development. In India communal representation was formal and scientific. This had the effect of turning a once workable system into an intractable monstrosity. The Old Whig model presumed the existence of stable interests behind a disorderly façade; the fact of real change in interests could be accommodated in practice without being acknowledged in theory. In India, the presumption of stability was formalized and legislated. Factions were transformed into vested interests and no longer had to continue strong in order to be influential. Whereas in England the presumption of stability had permitted constructive change, in India it prevented it; the theory of virtual representation had been transformed into a formal recognition by the government of separate group interests, and the consolidating function of representation was left unperformed in a society undergoing rapid change.

The institutions of a well-functioning society perform three types of functions: maintaining, in other words supplying law and order and goods and services; representing, in other words expressing popular desires; and educating, in other words developing analytic ability. Individual institutions usually perform only one of these functions directly but ordinarily facilitate others as well. In fact, institutions must tacitly support one another if stability is to be preserved. Separate institutions cannot beneficially check and balance one another if they are fundamentally at odds concerning basic values instead of competing over priorities within an ordered context.

In a stable society all these functions will be fused in a balanced fashion. Institutions performing separate functions will be autonomous, jealous of their perogatives, but not basically opposed to the functioning of other institutions. Institutions, however, frequently become corrupt. A corrupt institution is one which is no longer performing its constituted function, but rather some other function, at the behest of others, or in response to its own dynamic development. Some institutions are corrupted by others; some are corrupted by their own success in performing the wrong function.[2] A corrupt institution may be quite healthy and independent as an institution, while not performing the function associated with its founding. An institution's new function may be legitimated by making it official, formally abandoning the original purpose. A major cause of the disintegration of societies, however, is the perpetuation of institutions, superficially strong and developed, which are erroneously thought to be devoting their strength to their constituted purposes.

Any one type of institution may evolve into one of the other two types. Institutions concerned with maintenance — the police, the army, the bureaucracy in government and industry, and so forth — may be corrupted into representative institutions by, for example, a process of recruitment reflecting popular demands for reserved places for different communities. In this case, the process of sharing, the distributive function, will preoccupy officials and corrupt their ability to maintain order and increase productivity. Representative and educational institutions may in turn evolve into maintenance institutions — institutions designed to control people on behalf of governing institutions, rather than to serve the public's own interests by expressing their desires and providing them with a type of education in their own interest.

The natural tendency of healthy institutions is to expand the scope of their control over social resources. It is difficult, if not impossible, for an institution of one sort to create an institution of another which will consequently be in competition with it. The more natural tendency is for an institution to create another which nominally serves a separate purpose, but which in fact is an extension of the purposes of the original institution. When a guerrilla army—an educational institution—creates a government—a maintenance institution—the government will normally be expected to extend the educational aims of the guerrillas by indoctrinating the society at large at the expense of strictly bureaucratic instincts. The purpose of establishing a government will be to strengthen the educational purpose of the revolutionary army. When a maintenance institution establishes a representative or educational institution, the purpose will normally be to strengthen the maintenance institution by extending its powers of control or increasing its reserves of useful manpower. An institution established to serve another's purpose may develop an independent life of its own, but there is no necessary reason why this should happen. If an institution is designed especially to serve the purpose of another institution, rather than established as a concession to external demands, it is likely to continue under the control of its founding influence.

In British India, both the educational institutions and the representative institutions were created by a maintenance institution—the British government. While they thus possessed some superficial similarity to the genuine educational and representative institutions of Great Britain, they were in fact maintenance institutions, designed to extend the government's control. The educational institutions did not educate; they trained clerks. The representative institutions did not represent; they served as connecting links between the government and various sections of the society. Being specially designed by the government, the links were intended to bind these sections of society to government, not to open up the government to the play of popular pressures. Their purpose was to give people experience in dealing with the government, and thereby to increase its acceptability.

These institutions could not contribute to the stabilization of society by introducing missing institutional components. Order customarily begets more order as representativeness begets more representativeness unless actively opposed by competing interests. Strengthening one institution of a society on the assumption that this will be beneficial to the entire society is misconceived. Improving the army improves the army; this is likely to serve as a "precondition" for nothing except an expansion of military control over the rest of the society. It is wrong to assume that improved maintenance or improved representativeness or improved education will automatically further the development of competing social institutions. If one institution is substantially stronger

than others, it is likely that this institution will feel impelled to rule
society on behalf of the others. By taking the initiative in establishing
nominally representative and educational institutions, the British government had only extended their control, and the true functions of
representation and education were still left unperformed. These functions began slowly to be undertaken under independent Indian
auspices. The formulation of a type of education which would be meaningful to Indians and the exploration of political methods by which
Indians could attain their own purposes were the bases upon which
the nationalist movement was built.

These developments took place outside the official structures nominally devoted to the purposes Indians had in mind. The result was
a type of development which was initially scattered and erratic, and
ultimately revolutionary. If educational institutions are concerned exclusively with maintenance, they may fail to educate—or even attract—
students. If, on the other hand, educational institutions do not have
maintenance implications—if the type of education students receive
is antagonistic to society as it exists—students may assimilate social
values but society may not assimilate students.

With established channels proven to be unsatisfactory, Indians
examined alternatives. In a convulsive crisis of rejection, as in the Great
Rebellion of 1857, the instinct was to fall back upon familiar alternatives.
Hindu soldiers raised the standard of the Muslim Moghul emperor,
much to his consternation. The traditionally constituted leaders of all
faiths were the beneficiaries of popular trust and cooperated together
against the common British enemy. The failure of coordination and
leadership which brought the Rebellion down had nothing to do with
the religious allegiances of those involved.

The failure of the Great Rebellion taught Indians the futility—at any
rate the extreme difficulty—of carrying through a successful armed
insurrection. The alternatives were infiltration of the British regime
through assimilation or organization for agitation. Both of these
techniques involved new patterns of action, and resources for innovation came normally from one's family or kinship group. One might
be prepared to tolerate and cooperate with other groups, but self-
advancement and innovation taxed the mutual ties of obligation which
extended beyond the security of family and caste. The logic of British
impartiality, and of the kind of response which Indians could make
to the British regime, forced communities back into themselves.

As it turned out the theoretical goal of opposition to the British often evolved into the applied tactic of opposing the other community. When Bankim Chandra Chatterjee wrote a "nationalist" novel, *Ananda Math*, intended to arouse Bengalis to return to their former glory and throw off the foreign oppressors, he employed the literary device of depicting the foreign oppressors as the Muslims who ruled Bengal before the British and concluded the novel with a deft tribute to British rule, portrayed as establishing the conditions for Hindu resurgence. Bankim Chandra identified nationalism with Hinduism and distinguished between the good British foreigners and the bad Muslim foreigners. The point of the novel was a call for nationalist resurgence against foreign denationalization; the symbol of nationality was Hinduism, that of foreign oppression, Islam. Whether Bankim Chandra actually intended to indict British rule while only ostensibly describing Muslim rulers, in the manner of Montesquieu employing *Persian Letters* to criticize the French monarchy, or whether he sincerely thought of Muslims as greater enemies of Hinduism than were the British seems less important than the fact that Bankim Chandra recognized the need for organization and regeneration; given the conditions in which Bengal found itself, this could only be on a basis of established social units. The Hindus had to organize themselves as Hindus, which meant that he might as well use Islam; it was safer to do so under a British government.[3]

Exploratory reactions to British rule produced a revival of factional feeling. This was not a result of the fact that the British sought to introduce a system of representation based on classes and interests, but of the failure of this system of representation to represent anything. Real representation developed on the basis of isolated communities, outside the structure of formal representation. This isolation permitted community feeling to develop on sectional lines which true representative institutions would have been able to mute. A truly political government would have permitted the articulation and resolution of sectional grievances within recognized structures. The British failure to involve Indians politically with established institutions resulted in the phenomenon with which the British next attempted to cope: the development of radical political consciousness on factional lines.

A further round of Indian reform was precipitated by the crisis of the First World War. In 1914 at the outset of the war, the empire still seemed magnificent and durable. The sun never set on it; the image

frankly encompassed both space and time. The war put the Victorian
parade of Indian loyalty, affirmed at jubilees and durbars, to the test.
The initial response was impressive. India's princes vied with one
another with offers of men and money. Hundreds of thousands of
Indians were fighting in Europe and the Middle East to save the empire.
But the war continued. By the summer of 1917 Britain's fortunes had
reached a low ebb, and a constant effort was required to keep the
empire from buckling under the strain. The Russian imperial government, allied with Britain, did buckle and Russia was forced to withdraw
from the war. The United States had declared war on Germany in
April 1917, but it was uncertain whether American military forces could
be mobilized in time to save the situation. The British government
felt under pressure to marshal all the military and political forces at
their disposal to hold the empire and the alliance together until the
Americans arrived in strength. In the Middle East, the Arab nationalist
revolt against the Turkish imperial government, allied with Germany,
was actively encouraged by T. E. Lawrence with the full support of
British authorities. In November 1917 the historic Balfour declaration
was made, expressing British support for the Zionist goal of a "national
home" for the Jews, though what and where a "national home" would
be were left deliberately vague. On August 20, 1917, an equally historic
declaration was made by Edwin Montagu, secretary of state for India,
formally affirming Britain's commitment to the goal of "self-governing
institutions" for India. The statement moved sinuously between the
Scylla of the left and the Charibdys of the right:

> The policy of H.M. Government, with which the Government of
> India are in complete accord, is that of the increasing association
> of Indians in every branch of the administration, and the gradual
> development of self-governing institutions, with a view to the pro-
> gressive realisation of responsible government in India as an integral
> part of the Empire.[4]

The statement implied that a new policy would be followed without
admitting that this had not always been the policy in the past, spoke
of "self-governing institutions" without clarifying whether this meant
"self-government," and included for purposes of ambiguity the words
"increasing," "gradual," "progressive," and "responsible." The statement thus ranked with the Balfour declaration in calculated evasiveness
as well as historic importance.

Montagu followed up the announcement of proposed reforms with
a six-month visit to India during the cold weather of 1917–1918. Montagu

noted three times in his *Indian Diary* his satisfaction that his visit had served to keep "India quiet for six months at a critical period of the War."[5] His trip could also be said to reflect a new awareness of the relevance of forces within India to the determination of India's fate. Lord Morley had presided over the passage of the Morley-Minto reform of 1909 from London, and in doing so had seriously miscalculated the nature of the situation for which he was legislating. He had failed to perceive that the growing volatility of the Indian situation would make British policy on such a point as communal electorates difficult to reverse. Morley's reforms had not been intended as the prototypes of self-governing institutions but necessarily became so.

By coming to India, Montagu exposed himself to radical political pressures, but he had an equally vivid encounter with forces opposed to change. Though the subsequent reforms were devised in a less rarefied atmosphere, they represented a complicated compromise with a divisive potential as great as those of 1909.

The initial statement of British intentions of August 20, 1917, had originated with the government in India, where the greatest anxiety about Indian restiveness was combined with the greatest reluctance to rock the boat. The viceroy, Lord Chelmsford, had pressed for a statement of postwar intentions in order to placate Indian opinion, but also shared the concern of his conservative counselors about doing anything which might undermine British authority. The viceroy's Executive Council approved a draft statement for submission to the British cabinet promising "the largest measure of Self-Government compatible with the maintenance of the supremacy of British rule."[6] This clear-cut if uninspiring assertion was transformed in London into a seamless web of masterly subtlety, apparently largely the work not of Montagu, newly installed at the India Office, but of the former viceroy Lord Curzon. Chelmsford and Curzon both had the same objects in mind, but Curzon stated them more precisely. What had only been instinct with Chelmsford was transformed into a practical policy by Curzon. The immediate purpose of mollifying Indian opinion while leaving room to maneuver once peace returned remained uppermost; in addition, there was an explicit if unelaborated indication of the long-range intent of British policy. This was not simply the "whatever is possible" of Chelmsford's statement, but the promise to inaugurate a new kind of government: responsible government. Curzon felt that he had devised a more satisfactory answer to the demand for self-government than the temporizing "Yes, but not now," or "Yes, but not much." The formula of responsible government was thought to represent a synthesis of nationalist demand and British necessity. The formula by implication ruled out irresponsible self-government; there was no intention of permitting Indians to determine for themselves the difference between a rash and rational action. The projected government was to be responsible, in other words dependable and conscientious. It was also to be responsible in the sense of answerable and culpable. The first meaning, with its implicit limitations on Indian initiative, was familiar; the second represented a change. The intent was, in the words used somewhat later by Lord Chelmsford, to "fix responsibility on Indians," rather than to *give* responsibility to Indians. [7]

World War I had brought to an end the era in which British officials felt that they could control India by themselves, on their own terms. Until the shattering experiences of World War I and its immediate aftermath, the government had thought of its alliances with sectors of Indian society as emanating from the charitable condescension of secure authority. The government might honor the Maharajahs, or express sympathy for the aspirations of the organizers of the Muslim League, but these gestures were seen as signs of governmental strength, as demonstrations of its capacity to help its friends, live up to its treaty obligations, and encourage the underprivileged. Following the Montagu-Chelmsford reforms the government became frankly partisan. No longer holding aloof from direct involvement in internal politics, the government took the initiative in propagandizing on its own behalf and actively promoting the political fortunes of groups disinclined to radical change. The government sought to "rally the moderates" and to place itself at the head of a political faction which explicitly excluded many elements of Indian public life. After 1919, the British attempted to establish a regime which would respond to independent and increasingly powerful political forces, and which might conceivably evolve toward full Indian self-government by disciplining political forces to such an extent that they might be trusted to carry on by themselves in a fashion compatible with British purposes. The autocracy sought to strengthen its base through liberalization.

The Montagu-Chelmsford reforms were intended to be a modernized version of the ancient British policy of securing useful Indian allies. In the eighteenth century, friendly despots who sought to use the British in pursuing their own rivalries were supported. In the middle years of the nineteenth century the products of Western education seemed the most promising intermediaries. The later years saw a return to the now-domesticated Indian princes. By 1917 the need for a new tactic was fully evident. The princes could no longer be palmed off as adequate spokesmen for all Indians. Unsavory though they might seem, at least the more moderate Indian agitators had to be reckoned with. British rule had shifted its base from refractory traditional to docile Westernized, then to docile traditional Indians; now the dangerous decision was made to approach refractory Westernized Indians. The hope was to involve them in government, so that they might be held responsible in the public eye. A responsible, blameable, but limited popular government was to serve as a buffer, as had other Indian groups in the past.

British decisions on India during this period of England's — successful — domestic political liberalization were arrived at in a pragmatic fashion through compromise among influential interested parties. The result was a judicious blending of conservative and liberal viewpoints. Liberals were willing to compromise on principle in order to win tangible concessions; conservatives were prepared to be flexible on details if this permitted the retention of essentials.

Typically, it was the liberals who undertook to push through each new advance, and to believe in the promise it contained. If optimism is seen as good in itself as a precondition of active commitment, dwelling on contingencies may seem morbid. It is known that a task which would not have been undertaken if all its drawbacks were perceived in advance often proves valuable. Starting blind as a matter of policy may be justified by the assumption that events have a momentum of their own, in the right direction. Putting a premium on attitude, the liberal believed that if men came together as individuals they could solve their differences, transcending their backgrounds and objective interests. There were no irreconcilable conflicts, only misunderstandings. People associating together constituted the essence of government. If a government faltered, the remedy was looked for through new or extended association between rulers and ruled.

This instinct lay behind both the Morley-Minto and the Montagu-Chelmsford reforms of 1909 and 1919. The two liberal secretaries of state for India, Morley and Montagu, were determined to implement reforms which they defined simply as greater association of Indians with government, ignoring for the present "what this all might lead to." The two conservative viceroys, Minto and Chelmsford, accepting the reforms with difficulty, struggled hard to mute their impact. Morley dismissed the possible objections which might be raised to the reforms of 1909 with the confident prediction that their defects could be safely left to later modification. "Some may be shocked at the idea of a religious register at all," he noted. "We may wish, we do wish—certainly I do—that it were otherwise. We hope that time, with careful and impartial statesmanship, will make things otherwise."[8] Ten years later, Montagu expressed a similar optimism in dismissing the possible implications of Curzon's higher logic. "For some reason that I am absolutely unable to understand," he wrote, "people prefer 'responsible government' to 'self-government.' I do not know the difference."[9] More Indian participation was insured, whatever the label, and to Montagu this seemed the crucial distinction. Once the system was in practical operation, the hostilities and suspicions which lay behind the conservative's machinations and the radical's posturings would be easily overcome. Montagu let the conservatives have their verbal distinctions; he was eager to devote his own energies to getting things moving. "I must try and bring the Government of India with me," he wrote. "I myself would go very much further."[10] It was Lord Morley who perhaps best summed up the working philosophy of liberalism when he noted in 1907 that "When you are at the top of a house and want to get to the bottom there are two ways of doing so. You can throw yourself out of a window, or you can go downstairs. I prefer to go downstairs."[11] The liberal believed in gradualism, justified because things were moving in the right direction any way; pragmatism, because once a reform took hold it would evolve on its own, working out the kinks; and institutionalism, because once structures were established which brought people together, misunderstandings could be easily resolved.

The reforms of 1919 had two main features: "responsible government" for the politicians and a Chamber of Princes for the princes. The estimable loyalty of the princes was too valuable an asset to be scorned, and it was thought that assembling the princes might increase their relevance to modern Indian politics. In accepting the necessity of a more politicized government, the instinct of British liberals was to bring more English-educated Indians into government service, as civil servants or public officials in Legislative and Executive Councils. The instinct of British conservatives was to strengthen the posture of the existing power structure by demonstrating its adequacy and popularity. The compromise arrived at was to accommodate English-educated Indians, but to contain and counter them by princely representation.

The Indian princes before 1919 had served as decorative appendages to power, lending a shred of Indianness to the British presence. This involved their acquiescing in the pretense that they were independent rulers of ancient semisovereign states, allies of the British, despite the evident contradiction between this posture and the necessity to take orders from junior British officers. Secure in their states and incomes, through British protection, and having little autonomy in the administration of their states, through British interference, the bulk of their attention was diverted to a competition with other princes for precedence and to efforts to persuade themselves that they were what they were told they were. The position of the princes was peculiarly demoralizing because they were alternately lionized and treated with arrogant condescension. An incident "which excited much hostile comment and created a great stir" occurred when the Gaekwar of Baroda "made a very inadequate obeisance" to their Majesties King George V and Queen Mary at the Delhi Durbar in 1911. [12] The Maharaja Scindhia of Gwalior told Montagu "that once when he was in Delhi he was severely reprimanded for taking his pugaree off after the Viceroy had left. He is not allowed to appear at dinner without his head cover. This, he says, is quite right, because in the presence of his superiors an Indian ought to have his head covered; but why does this not apply to British Indians like Sankaran Nair and only to Indian princes? He says that now whenever somebody like Chelmsford, or a Governor, or myself, comes to shoot with him he has to wear a pugaree to shoot in, although he risks sun-stroke by doing so." [13]

The princes were encouraged to play the role of titled innkeeper and caterer to hunting parties for prominent officials. A good prince was also expected to have a decorous concern for the improvement of his state, and normally had a model enterprise or school to show to his visitors. The princes nevertheless knew that they were playing someone else's game and, Montagu noted, "had all been to me with their stories of the scandalous interference by Residents, and I wanted them to make a clean breast of it. They tried to hedge . . . I told them that they were our allies, of whom the King-Emperor was proud, and we wanted them to be happy, and they ought to state their case." [14] Such counsel missed the point because the substance of princely complaints was a sense of embarrassment rather than a sense of injustice. The princes could not make a clean breast of their grievances without making themselves ridiculous in their own as well as others' eyes.

The prospect of taking more constructive advantage of princely loyalty had been contemplated by conservatives for some time. A second upper house containing "the more stable elements of the community" as a supplement to the existing Legislative Councils, Lord Minto suggested in 1907, would "furnish the heads of local Government with a useful counterpoise against the body of advanced opinion which tends to obtain undue prominence in the Provincial Legislative Councils."[15] These sentiments were echoed in a letter from Secretary of State Austen Chamberlain to Lord Chelmsford on November 24, 1916, in which he wrote that "I wish I saw my way clear to a somewhat closer association of the Ruling Chiefs with the Government of India. If that were possible they might be a great conservative force and afford a valuable counterpoise to the pseudo-democratic movement. But so far I can see no means to this desired end."[16]

A number of princes had been growing restive over their future prospects under an Indianized government, but the main impetus for the new Chamber came from the British, interested in using the princes as a make-weight. The differing perspectives of the princes and the British doomed to sterility the Chamber which thrashed out a pitiful existence until it expired in 1935. The princes, supposed to act as a political force, became only a pressure group, lobbying to enhance and guarantee their personal perogatives as princes. They did not pretend to act as spokesmen for the public interest. The Chamber of Princes was not a hard-won concession, from which the public expected great things. It was created as an act of imperial policy. Princely attendance was in fact a command performance. The princes were required to construct expensive official residences decorously down hill from the viceroy's palace in New Delhi for their occasional visits to the capital. They felt under no pressure to air representative grievances, and confined themselves to special pleading. Being a representative institution created by a maintenance institution, the Chamber of Princes had nothing to represent.

While conservatives were eager to establish the Chamber of Princes as a make-weight against the "pseudo-democratic movement," liberals accepted the idea in the confidence that India's political development toward self-government would be furthered by bringing all the relevant parties together and involving them in the complexities of parliamentary procedure. Liberals overlooked the underlying purpose which these institutions were designed to serve—to balance factions off against one another and insulate the British government from criticism—out of confidence that small details of parliamentary functioning would inevitably lead on to the establishment of healthy, integrated governing institutions. The institutions were held to have a life of their own and, it was thought, would quickly evolve into institutions serving the purposes of all, not simply those of their conservative designers. Liberals welcomed the reforms of 1919, as they had the development of railways in the nineteenth century, with the confidence that institutions were neutral and, even if built to serve conservative purposes, could easily be turned to liberal ends.

The Montagu-Chelmsford proposal combined minute technicalities of obscure British origin with a very un-British demarcation of authority in rigid spheres. Where many things were implicitly understood, decisions could be reached quickly and then legitimized through hoary rituals. In the exported version, the same routinely circumvented rituals assumed a forbidding intransigence—became idols, not tools. Englishmen expected a more long-faced solemnity from their colonial initiates than they observed among themselves. While shared implicit values made the cumbersome structure move in England, in India it was expected to move of its own accord, despite the fact that each element of the government would be acting with independent motives. The British liberals hoped that India would reap "the advantages of being second." The difficulty was that the forms which Britain bestowed upon India and many other colonies were introduced from outside, not imported by indigenous enterpreneurs of political development. The purposes served were external, and the structures reflected this fact. It was assumed, however, by both British and Indian liberals that India's political development would be marked by a gradual maturation of colonial assemblies which at some point would lead to an almost effortless attainment of full Indian independence involving no necessary defiance of Britain.

And yet, while representative institutions may reflect or disguise social forces, they cannot shape them. If differences are thought to stem from misunderstanding, it is natural to assume that they can be removed by the close association of different people working together. But while individuals may forget their interests, groups cannot ignore them. And values, when widely shared and sincerely believed, will not give way because of a recognition of individual compatibility between isolated representatives. It was thus the British conservative concentrating on essentials, not the liberal emphasizing future evolution, who accurately perceived the nature of the 1919 reforms. The conservative was nonetheless equally deluded in assuming that the reforms, by strengthening British authority, would solve the long-range political problem. The conservatives finessed the liberals in devising institutions which could not evolve; the liberals, however, best understood the need for evolution, and the fact that Indian political demands would not disappear through the strengthening of the structure of British authority. Lord Willingdon once observed that the retention of strategic powers in British hands was feasible because the oriental understood the *hukm* or royal command and consequently would not object to a system involving an active use of reserved powers and executive vetoes. [17] His reasoning implied that Indians would retain their oriental instincts while mastering British procedure, and consequently would not ask for anything better than the system then arranged. Inevitably, reserved power, arbitrarily wielded by an impartial governor without the political means of backing up his resolve, spread chaos. While the reforms of 1919 did succeed in fixing responsibility on Indians willing to cooperate with the government, thereby discrediting them, the use of the *hukm* spurred hostility by underscoring the distrust which underlay the cumbersome machinery of this attempt at political manipulation. Coopting some politicians, and parading loyal retainers, recognizing social forces in ways which set them at odds, the newly aggressive government of British India in liberalizing its structure had set itself adrift on a perilous sea.

British India in 1919 was not a promising candidate for political liberalization. Social and governmental factions had become strong and self-confident and insulated from one another. The political system had little capacity for evolution in a liberal direction because the different factions felt no fondness for one another and resented outside efforts to bring them together. The Lords who were appointed to the highest Indian positions, and the bureaucrats who formed the government's "steel frame," were, moreover, ill-suited to manage a politically liberalized government. The government was controlled by men whose background and conditions of life reinforced values which put them at odds with rapidly evolving political forces.

In any society the person who possesses one of three things —power, status, or wealth—will have tremendous advantages if he attempts to acquire the other two. In a society capable of significant evolution it is nonetheless possible to make distinctions among the elite in terms of their relative identification with one or the other of these attributes.

It will be possible to conceive of a person who is more powerful than he is rich, more rich than he is powerful, and so forth. In the rigid colonial society, in contrast, such distinctions would have been difficult to make because these attributes were automatically allied. The person with the highest status, the colonial civil servant, was assured of the possession of the greatest power and the greatest wealth, and such graded equivalences were made all the way up and down the social hierarchy. In such a society it was possible to enforce ideologies, because everyone at a given level was equal in so many respects. The members of each class were also more prepared to cooperate with others in their class than would have been the case in a society where a person's social rank depends on so many things that he can easily fancy himself superior to those most similar to him. The expatriate colonial society was in many respects a perfect example of class rigidification, and class consciousness.

The positions of viceroy and presidency governor were customarily reserved for a class of professional aristocrats who might have had some political experience in England before their Indian appointments, but only of a certain type. In 1942, for example, Winston Churchill proposed Sir Cyril Asquith for the viceroyalty. The secretary of state for India, L. S. Amery, noted of Asquith that "He has got ability and character and a very nice wife, but he is most decidedly a dark horse, with no political experience and unknown to the public. On the other hand, he comes from a stable where both political knowledge and intellectual ability have characterised all turned out by it."[18]

The customary reservation of the highest Indian offices for such men underscored the fact that ornamental qualities were considered as crucial as executive or political ability. British India was still ruled according to a modernized version of the Old Tory world view, which held that legitimacy stemmed from God and descended by degrees through the several ranks of the nobility. Only men of "blood," it was assumed, could command the respect of the Indian people in general, and of the Indian princes in particular. Viceroys believed that their prime function was to act as surrogate kings maintaining dignity and observing precedence. Trained to appreciate the social importance of ceremony, they were easily persuaded that this was the central pillar of British power in India.

When the new viceroy, Lord Hardinge, arrived in Calcutta in November of 1910 to relieve Lord Minto, he noted that the Mintos "did not leave Calcutta till two days later, which was uncomfortable both for them and for me, for although I was not actually Viceroy until I had been sworn in, it was only natural that I should be treated on all sides as the rising and not the setting sun. I made a mental resolution that when my turn came I would arrange otherwise."[19] Embarrassment also plagued Hardinge at the time of his departure, however, because the government named as his successor Lord Chelmsford, "who was serving as a Captain in the Territorials, and with his company was guarding the wireless station at Chitogh, near Simla. He ought to have been recalled to England before the offer was made to him as naturally the Indians could not understand how the post of Viceroy could be offered to a Captain of Territorials out in India."[20]

Lord Chelmsford in turn stimulated some salient reflections on the nature of viceregal government from Montagu. Speaking generally of people of Lord Chelmsford's "class" he noted, "Informal discussion, informal conversation they do not know. Political instinct they have none. The wooing of constituents is beneath their idea; the coaxing of the Press is not their *métier* . . . Everything is prescribed; everything is printed. Well, this may be all right for a Court, it is all wrong when the Court is not Royal and is also the Prime Minister of the place."[21] Twenty-five years later, in 1942, the then viceroy could still voice his opposition to the suggestion that he might hold news conferences by contending that this would be beneath the accepted dignity of a viceroy: "We are dealing here with a vast and politically unsophisticated population," wrote Lord Linlithgow with satisfaction, "which, despite the trend of the times, continues to regard the Viceroyalty with something of superstitious awe."[22]

The viceroy was the ceremonial head of a structure which he often encountered for the first time upon assuming command of it. Even if he had not conceived of his role in static terms, he would have had great difficulties acting independently of the permanent bureaucracy over which he presided, which was prepared to denounce any fresh departure as evidence of inexperience. The Indian Civil Service was often proudly called a steel frame. The image was intended in a positive sense, to suggest that the service held India together; the image could suggest equally the qualities of inflexibility and unresponsiveness, or a dignified irrelevance equivalent to that of the French national toy, the Eiffel Tower. All these connotations hint at parts of the truth.

Bureaucracies may be distinguished according to the ethos which governs them as primarily servile, status-conscious, or efficient. A servile bureaucracy is one which is motivated to please a master—royal or popular. Those who rise within it will be those best at pleasing the master, whatever may be their standing with other bureaucrats or their record of efficiency. A servile bureaucracy stands below the source of authority in a society.

A status-conscious bureaucracy will be closely identified with the larger society. Status in the bureaucracy will be determined much as it is in other parts of the society, and the same sort of men will be found at equivalent statuses inside and outside of the bureaucracy because society will reflect rather than act upon or for society. Such a bureaucracy will have little incentive to work hard, not even that which might be instilled by a royal master.

An efficient bureaucracy will stand above society, with status distinctions of its own devising, based upon effectiveness in achieving goals which the bureaucracy sets for itself. An efficient bureaucracy will serve no master—directly. Yet there must be a reason why an efficient bureaucracy is tolerated. An external authority for reasons of its own will tolerate or encourage efficiency because what the bureaucracy sincerely desires to do if left alone is acceptable to the external authority. While any one bureaucracy will combine some concern for servility and status and efficiency, some bureaucracies closely approximate pure types. The Indian Civil Service, as a singularly pure example of an efficient bureaucracy, reveals the merits and constraints of such an entity.[23]

Members of the Indian Civil Service were secure in an elite status guaranteed for life in a society in which they were unwilling to involve themselves, in which few took an interest except as aloof patrons. The Civil Service, like the princes who were captives of privilege and position, were also primarily preoccupied with their relations with one another, though these relations involved the serious business of governing in addition to concern with the maintenance of relative status. Members of the Civil Service might improve their status by hard work, while the princes could only accomplish this, if at all, by wheedling and bickering over trivialities. The disregard for the necessity of maintaining by political means the status of their class within the broader society, and the consequent concentration on internal rivalries, however, made the Civil Service in many respects similar to the princes.

Indian Civil Servants have been likened to an Indian caste and to Chinese mandarins. The description of I.C.S. officers as "New Kshatriyas," a new martial, ruling caste, so appealing because of its paradoxical quality, suggests the social exclusiveness of British officials who could be called a caste in the sense of a group which limits its social contact with the rest of the society in which it is located. They were never, however, part of a caste *system*, a social arrangement of ritually sanctioned interdependence. The specific content of the Kshatriya ethic moreover had only a superficial resemblance to the Victorian ethic of service. It might result in comparable actions, but it sprang from a radically different inspiration.

In comparing the training and selection of Chinese and British scholar-bureaucrats, Rupert Wilkinson notes that both were selected by competitive examinations heavily weighted toward familiarity with literary classics.[24] The service ethos in the two countries seems to have been quite different, however, suggesting that the content of training and type of selection employed—ostensibly open to all, but stressing the type of learning ordinarily available to those with aristocratic connections—served a similar purpose in each case: to provide a civil service which combined moderate ability with aristocratic class ties, or at least pretensions, but had little relevance to molding the character of the civil servants, which was a product of social conditioning in each case, rather than of the scholastic content of the syllabus.

A third parallel, which seems in some respects more valid, might be drawn. In the Tokugawa period the Japanese samurai were a dominant social class—a class which, though hereditary, were sternly disciplined and entirely absorbed in the tasks of administration. "A cross between a feudal warrior and a man of letters, [the samurai] somehow reconciled the rough heritage of qualities required in the field with the humane values of the Confucian system. He was confined throughout his life to official service. He could not own rice fields or participate in commercial ventures. His sole rewards were favours from his lord; his sole temptation, the abuse of political power."[25] With appropriate modifications, this description could apply equally to the British official in India. Though selected in a manner more closely resembling that employed in China, the British official in the field at the beginning of the twentieth century exemplified more the spirit of the samurai than that of the mandarin.

The Indian Civil Service, though saddled with a system of recruitment by competitive examinations, was concerned that its members should be imbued with the requisite character. The character training dispensed at the public schools, where one officially studied only the classics, was felt to be more important than the formal academic fare; the Civil Service supplemented its examinations with a riding test and, in the twentieth century, instituted a required "probationary" year at Oxford or Cambridge where character training was presumably advanced. Significantly, those who qualified for the Service by passing the examinations in India were required to take *two* years at one of the English universities. The examination system as originally envisaged in the 1840's and 1850's had assumed the presence of moral strength and sought to test the additional variable, ability; the appearance of Indian and lower class English competitors, whose moral dependability aristocratic Englishmen were reluctant to acknowledge, forced a more overt emphasis upon racial differentiation and character training. The result was a partial return to the policy of the beginning of the nineteenth century, when Haileybury was established to improve the character of upper and middle class English recruits, in the years before the evangelical moral revival had worked its leaven in the higher levels of English society.

In both China and Japan, the ruling class maintained its monopoly of social eminence and administrative power by adoption. Powerful families would adopt the promising sons of less well connected families, leading lineages being preserved intact while talented aspirants were attached to the aristocracy. The British ruling class in India functioned on somewhat similar lines. The competitive system permitted the recruitment of talented Englishmen from modest family backgrounds who, once "adopted" by the Civil Service, rapidly acquired its implicitly aristocratic mentality. In all three of these countries, however, there were practical limits beyond which the tactic of assimilation became difficult. In China there was no formal proscription of specific social classes, and the circle within which adoption and advancement might take place was circumscribed only by the natural constraints of an inegalitarian society. In Japan, formal recognition of the samurai as a hereditary social class for whom all higher administrative posts were reserved limited opportunity for advancement to this rather large class —though other social classes, such as merchants, might find satisfactory reward and honor within their own spheres. British India stood in a somewhat unstable intermediate position. Administrative opportunity was theoretically open to all, and the rewards of alternative occupations were not stressed; the service nevertheless was for all practical purposes a closed social unit. As the service in Japan was open to all samurai and to no others, so the I.C.S. was open to all Britishers but almost inaccessible to Indians, who were relegated to a position of permanent social inferiority. The Indian who aspired to membership in the service had to demonstrate not a high level of competence in the recognized classics of his country, as in China, but his understanding of the ethos of a class not naturally his own. One could not become a samurai by passing an examination; one could not become a Civil Servant, with all of the implications of that term, simply by demonstrating that one was "clever at examinations." When an Indian did make it into the Service, he would be dogged throughout his life by a suspicious aloofness, the conviction among his colleagues that he probably was not a "real" Civil Servant. A pardonable foible in an Englishman would be "just like an Indian" in the eyes of Englishmen alert for confirmation of a preconceived stereotype.

British India failed to attain the stability of either the Chinese or the Japanese system, since it rested of necessity upon an unrealistic ideology of opportunity for all. The Chinese made an ideology of opportunity work because it had some relationship to reality; the Japanese made a system of restricted opportunity work by legitimating it within the context of an acknowledged tradition and by ascribing other types of honorable status to those to whom administrative occupations were not available. Englishmen were unable to find a rationale for restricting opportunity which would be acceptable to Indians and liberal Englishmen, and were unable to make a system of equal opportunity work in a society so sharply divided as was British India.

The Indian Civil Service has occasionally been compared to another ruling order—Plato's Guardians.[26] The Guardians described in *The Republic* had an effective ideology for the permanent monopolization of power, in the association of different social classes with different metals, and a presumptive adequacy of knowledge and virtue to rule in a disinterested fashion. An analogy between Plato's Guardians and the Indian Civil Service tells very little about the actual character of the Civil Service, but a great deal about the way in which they viewed themselves. The conditions in which they worked permitted British officials to imagine that government consisted of acting as a remote but all-powerful arbiter between competing social groups. The most common arguments against Indian independence were that the minorities would be handed over to exploitation by the majority, or alternatively, that the majority would be handed over to exploitation by a minority. Both arguments were heard with almost interchangeable regularity, depending upon whether one wished to warn against Brahman domination of other Hindus, or Hindu domination of Muslims, Sikhs, Untouchables, and others. Every class was not identical with every other class and consequently any given Indian could not "speak for" all classes. Classes pursued their own interests, and representatives of classes were captives of their constituencies.

All these arguments had an element of credibility, but only as arguments against all politics. The type of administrative government which had been developed in British India permitted officials to imagine that they exercised a type of impartial justice, measured against which any political regime would have been found wanting. Ironically, the unmitigated antagonisms within Indian society which the British felt only their impartiality could restrain were themselves aggravated by that very impartiality. A nonpolitical government could only act as an arbiter after the fact; it could not lead the society in ways which would forestall the emergence of murderous factionalism in the first place.

The British Civil Servant's self-image involved the assumption that England's objectivity made it unusually easy for Britishers to acquire knowledge concerning, and to act to alleviate, India's problems. Any Indian would be hampered by considerations of community: the demands of his own and the distrust of others. Such a view, however, could only be advanced by a person with a very exalted notion of his own impartiality and a very formalistic conception of the nature of the governmental process. Lord Curzon's "disinterested" decision to partition Bengal, in order to "improve administration," could not avoid being a pro-Muslim, anti-Hindu gesture; his effort to "raise the standards" of university education was inevitably directed toward a political object. Significantly, neither of these Curzon policies could be sustained, though the partition of Bengal came ultimately at the insistence of Indians and Curzon's educational proposals anticipated many of the suggestions made by official commissions of independent India. The British posture ignored the relevance of trust to governmental activity; the "handicap" of political involvement with the people whose fate one is deciding was ultimately demonstrated to be less onerous than the handicap of their distrust.

The government could have avoided partiality only by total inaction.

And they were no more immune to pressure than they were impartial. Efforts to increase the extent of participation of Indians in the government of their own country and the degree of equality of treatment with Englishmen which Indians might be accorded were greeted with consistent hostility from the majority of Englishmen resident in India. Macaulay's proposal in the 1830's for equal legal treatment was shelved in deference to British protests. Lord Canning's appointment in 1857 of a Muslim to a position which might have been given to an Englishman was strongly criticized. Lord Ripon's renewal in 1883 of Macaulay's efforts to extend legal equality was soundly defeated, following strong public and official objections. It was clear as early as the 1830's that a major order of business for anyone interested in liberalizing the treatment of Indians was the necessity of coming to terms with the English community in India. Until Indians organized themselves into an effective countervailing pressure group, efforts at liberalization had behind them only the weight of good intentions.

The British government of India, its presumptions notwithstanding, was like every other government, subject to pressure from its constituents. Fitzjames Stephen, as law member of the viceroy's Council from 1869 to 1872, had gloried in his seeming freedom to legislate as his conscience and expert advice dictated, aloof from expedient compromise. Such a view of the nature of Indian government was possible only because Stephen did nothing to arouse the British community, and because Indian opinion was not yet effectively organized. When Curzon (whose interest in India was first kindled by a talk which he heard Stephen give while at Eton) attempted to act in the manner which Stephen mistakenly thought he had successfully exemplified, he antagonized everyone. The British community denounced his punishment of a British regiment guilty of anti-Indian atrocities, as Indians denounced his Olympian partition of Bengal and "enlightened" university reform.

Even if the British had been as disinterested as they thought they were, they would not have been in a stronger position. Good government is not self-legitimating and good government without legitimacy is self-defeating. Good government, in fact, is the usual prerevolutionary condition, one in which things are being done, issues are being articulated, and a type of progress advantageous to certain groups is occurring, which only makes matters worse in the eyes of many because it seems that the government and its allied classes are prospering and entrenching themselves and thereby confirming their insulation from the popular will.

By 1917, British India had developed into a large and increasingly unwieldy system of vested interests, at odds with a hostile Indian intelligentsia. Such was the system Montagu sought to liberalize by bringing Indians in and by making British rulers more self-consciously political. As a liberal, Montagu was alert to the need to be popular in order to be effective. Petulant sermons on the importance of law and order and evasive references to the "complexity" of altering the status quo were inadequate expedients for a government which aspired to lead an aroused citizenry. As a liberal, Montagu was also hopeful that bringing rulers and ruled together would make the government more responsive and agitators more understanding. As a liberal, Montagu was satisfied that he was making a step toward Indian "self-government" by accepting the formula of "responsible government," by which conservatives meant the establishment of a new equilibrium in which vested interests would be safe and which would leave the British holding the balance between conflicting forces.

As a liberal, Montagu assumed that by fudging the issue of sovereignty, it would simply disappear. If people first learned to get along well together, the technicality of which person wielded ultimate authority would be no more important than which of two gentlemen preceded the other through a door. And yet, whether or not it is only a matter of courtesy, sovereignty is indivisible. You either have it or you don't. It cannot be passed from one to another gradually. Nor can it be shared between two prospective heirs. To withhold sovereignty until an agreement has been reached between two or more claimants to sovereignty—politicians and princes, British planters and Indian peasants, Muslims and Hindus—is simply a way of retaining sovereignty. Of two claimants, one must wield sovereignty over the other. The fate of submission to a new unwanted sovereignty may not be disastrous but it can hardly be voluntary. The political system of British India could not evolve; it had to be overthrown.

4   The Nationalist's Dilemma:

Coping with the West

Each time the British reached an impasse in India, they came up with a policy designed to deal with the problem. The British responded to Indian needs and demands in ways which they considered constructive—in other words, in ways intended to alleviate grievances with the least damage to British interests. But what did Indians think of this? At what point did the latest promise to alleviate the latest problem cease to be reassuring? On what basis did Indians conclude that it would be necessary to take matters into their own hands? It was not an easy decision for Indians to dismiss British good intentions. It was a decision arrived at after a lengthy and circuitous intellectual journey.

The effort to cope with the established fact of Western dominance, though agonizing and protracted and often abortive, has actually followed a remarkably uniform course throughout the colonial world. Under the variety of forms which this response took in India and other countries, it is possible to distinguish several phases, representing an ascending scale of self-confidence, sophistication, and aggressiveness. These were not chronologically distinct stages, but layers added on consecutively. Individuals experimenting with earlier approaches could be found at any later time. In general terms, however, an evolution can be seen from manipulation to assimilation to rebellion to revolution.

Manipulation

The manipulative stage is one in which individuals welcome the power of the West because they desire to manipulate its power for their own ends. In this spirit Indian despots sought to direct British power to the embarrassment of their hereditary enemies. Indians who responded to the West in this manner were in intention exploiters or collaborators. They were interested in the ways in which British rule, or individual Englishmen, might be bent to their own advantage. This calculation motivated the moneylenders who assisted the newly arrived Englishman in his early struggles to live aristocratically, as well as the personal servants of the Englishman who used their positions to impress and intimidate other Indians.[1] The subordinate officials of the British government were also men of this type, in the days before an attempt was made to turn Indian officials into model moral Englishmen.[2] They were men who looked upon British rule as providing an enhanced opportunity for the employment of their traditional abilities in traditional ways. British rule confirmed their sense of the suitability of these conventions of behavior by offering them new scope to pursue ancient aspirations while not challenging basic values. The orthodox Muslim, Lutfullah, for example, taught himself English in the early nineteenth century to secure employment with the British, but took pains to guard himself against too close association with the Christian infidel. He once put up at an English hotel in Ceylon, but "Early in the morning, to our great astonishment and disgust, we beheld a herd of unclean animals running, grunting, snorting, and roaring about our rooms. This abominable sight at once made us anxious to quit the Christian roof as soon as possible."[3]

Many Christian converts similarly adopted Christianity and learned Western languages without a perception that these acts might have implications beyond the possibility of improving their worldly position. There was no crisis of conscience, no perceived conflict, no conscious rejection of former values, because this was not understood to be required. What was desired from the West was secret knowledge, to enrich one's traditional lore and enable one to acquire further power, with the help of the West, in the context of one's own society.[4]

Conversion, in fact, might be the result of a calculation made not by the individual concerned but on his behalf by his family or community. The desire of families to advance their corporate interests induced many Indians to depute a son to acquire the skill necessary for advancement within the hierarchy of British rule. Lal Behari Dey describes the reasoning his father used to justify placing him in a British missionary college in Calcutta in 1834 as follows:

> A knowledge of English education, he said, was necessary to enable a man to earn a competence in life. People ignorant of English no doubt got berths, but berths to which only paltry salaries were attached. He felt his want of English every day and was therefore resolved to remedy that defect in the education of his son. He did

not wish to give me what is called high education — that he considered
to be useless; for, in his opinion, real wisdom was not to be found
within the range of English literature, it being confined to the Sanskrit
alone, which is the language of the gods. But for secular purposes,
for gaining a decent livelihood, a knowledge of the English language
was absolutely necessary, as that was the language of the rulers
of the land.[5]

The deputation of individual family members in this way normally
strengthened the traditional family unit. That son who demonstrated
the greatest promise of acquiring the particular attributes which won
promotion from the British would be designated for training in English
while his brothers continued to pursue more traditional careers. In
a parallel fashion, Hindu families might direct one of their sons to
grow a beard, sport a turban, and join the British army as a Sikh
soldier. If the British, because they thought Sikhs were good soldiers,
insisted on recruiting Sikhs in preference to equally qualified Hindus,
then the Hindus were prepared to become Sikhs in order to join the
army. A similar policy had been followed by families in premodern
Europe who sacrificed one of their number to the church in the hope
that he might rise and prosper within the church, and thereby extend
and consolidate the power of the other members of his family who
continued to follow mundane pursuits. There was always the possibility
that in adapting himself to his new organizational loyalties he might
spurn embarrassing ties and refuse to reciprocate in the manner
intended by his family in originally underwriting his preparations for
assimilation; but often he would retain clan loyalties while advancing
within the system, turning the system in ways advantageous to his
family, acting as an ambassador and intermediary, conversant with
both cultural settings.

The acquisition by an Indian of a position in the British hierarchy
was rarely the result of independent effort because of the social constraints operating to limit the egalitarian potentialities of recruitment
by examination in India, no less than in China. In both China and
India the most scholastically promising youth within a given clan or
extended family group would be deputed for the arduous task of preparation and supported during long years of specialized study. The
need for extended preparation meant that the opportunities for the
bright son of a poor family were limited unless he was adopted by
a rich family without bright sons, thereby acquiring social obligations
in advance of the acquisition of official power. The availability of

scholarships and missionary educational institutions in India may have loosened the hold of such preexisting social obligations in some cases, but it would be difficult to find many such instances, especially at the level of the elite Indian Civil Service. The type of preparation required for passing into the I.C.S. was as remote from normal concerns as the scholastic exercises required of those appearing for the Chinese examinations. A long residence in Great Britain mastering the conventional elite subjects of the English curriculum was not likely to be covered by a missionary scholarship, and those few who were selected and funded for this enterprise were emissaries of family units who could not be expected to look with total disinterestedness upon their investment. K. P. S. Menon recorded with gratitude the fact that his elder brother spent much more money on his education than he did on the education of his own sons; the soundness of an investment was a greater consideration than questions of loyalty to one's immediate offspring. Menon was grateful for his elder brother's interest in his prospects, but less appreciative of the attempts his brother subsequently made to cash in on the success of the investment following his admission to the I.C.S.[6]

Subhas Chandra Bose records that "One evening, when my father was in Calcutta, he suddenly sent for me. I found him closeted with my second brother, Sarat. He asked me if I would like to go to England to study for the Indian Civil Service. If I agreed I should start as soon as possible. I was given twenty-four hours to make up my mind . . . All my plans about researches in psychology were put aside." Bose ultimately did pass into the service, but resigned before signing the covenant pledging loyalty to a government to which he was opposed. Interestingly enough, in proposing the resignation to his family, he retained the analogy of family representation. He proposed that, rather than serving as the family emissary to the British power structure, he should be the family sacrifice in the cause of voluntary national service. "Each family if not each individual," he wrote in a letter to his elder brother on February 23, 1921, "should now bring forward its offering to the feet of the mother."[7]

Sardar Patel, in his early life, upheld the other end of a comparable family arrangement. The Sardar's brother Vithalbhai, who was accustomed to presume rather heavily upon his rights as the elder brother, entered into an arrangement with the Sardar which would permit him to devote himself to public life unembarrassed by the requirement of having to support himself. "We, therefore, decided," explained the

Sardar in a speech delivered in 1921, "that one of us should serve the country and the other, the family. My brother gave up his flourishing practice and started on a career of public service, while I bore the burden of maintaining the household. I had, thus, to commit all the sins and he performed all the good deeds, but I reconciled myself by the thought that I could claim at least a share in his good works!"[8]

Assimilation

The purpose of family councils in sending a member to a Western school was manipulative: to enable an individual to gain useful knowledge to supplement the basic traditional values which he would presumably retain. The alienness of the experience of subjection to Western culture meant, however, that the result was not always that intended. A young student designated for Western training by a manipulative family might be so successfully trained as to develop a desire to become fully assimilated. The purpose of manipulators was intentionally to stay in two worlds. A young assimilationist was a person who wanted to move fully into the new world. When he also found himself stuck in between, he felt less satisfied, since this was not the limit of his ambitions.

A student's encounter with the West had elements of comedy and excitement, as when Bipin Chandra Pal went with a group of student friends to dine at the Great Eastern Hotel in Calcutta. They ordered a private room to cover their embarrassment and ordered "the best in the house" to disguise their unfamiliarity with the menu. While their waiter was in the room they played idly with their knives and forks, but when he left "we commenced to attack the victuals on our plate vigorously with hand and teeth."[9]

Such embarrassing moments reflected the wide range of uncertainties which could afflict the neophyte assimilationist. The British school system in fact might be said to have created Indian adolescence. Traditional Indian society had so managed the process of coming of age that the anxieties a Westerner normally associates with this period rarely found expression. The crises an Indian boy or girl had to face—notably the arranged marriage—were confronted almost before any real comprehension of their consequences was possible. What was agonized about even in regard to such a crisis was essentially one's luck: whether one's designated spouse would fulfil one's dreams.

The normal problems of maturing—marrying and establishing a family, choosing a profession, one's relationship to his parents—were muted by dispersal over time. Marriage was an event of childhood, following which one remained firmly within the family. The bride was ordinarily "adopted" into a new family; the groom remained at home, a son. One's professional identity was similarly anticipated from an early age. A son normally followed in his father's occupation and was involved in professional activities at his father's side while still a child. This in turn eased the third crisis, the problem of one's relation to his parents. A son was treated by his father with great fondness and permissiveness in his first years, and shortly thereafter as a companion and co-worker. There were good practical reasons why both parents should be grateful for the existence of a son. Only a son could guarantee to his father that his memory would be satisfactorily served; only a son could reassure a mother that she would not be discarded by her husband in his pursuit of an heir. A son's situation in a closed group-oriented society, moreover, did not provide him with a band of contemporaries from differing backgrounds from whom he might have drawn inspiration for a collective revolt against old age.

A son thus had neither incentive nor encouragement to revolt against the stringent restrictions which accompanied his favored treatment. Though an increasing acquiescence to family pressures and lifelong deference to one's father was demanded of an Indian son, he nonetheless was not treated, as in the typical Western case, as a rival. The Indian father treated his son as an extension of himself. The strong emotional ties between mother and son were not resented by the father, because he expected only deference, not love, from the mother of his son. The sexual relationship between husband and wife was viewed as one initiated and desired by the wife, which a man should fulfil but strive ultimately to renounce. The father, though he expected formal deference from his son, was not a vindictive presence. The deference expected of a son was something which he could scarcely blame his father for; it was expected in almost equal measure by all the elders of his clan.

Gandhi, in his *Autobiography*, describes the extraordinary impression made upon him when as a boy he witnessed a performance of the story of Harischandra by a traveling theatrical company. The point of the story was that a person should obey even the most irrational demands made by sanctioned authority. In the same vein, Gandhi notes the "indelible impression" made upon him by another troupe who illustrated their dramatization of Shravana's devotion to his parents by holding up a picture of "Shravana carrying, by means of slings fitted for his shoulders, his blind parents on a pilgrimage.''[10] Such service was not demeaning or threatening to one's integrity because it did not challenge one's self-respect. One served one's father as an elder, as one respected all other elders, as the Maharajah Harischandra respected a Brahman priest.

The Indian father was neither an exclusive source of authority nor an exclusive model for emulation. Society sanctioned a man's formal control over his son's external conduct. A son's inner life was relatively ignored, and to that extent free. There was, in fact, a common understanding that a person might choose a model for himself outside his immediate family. A person was expected to serve his parents, whether they were good or bad, whether he admired them or not, because they were his parents. If he wished, he could seek out an entirely different person as a source of ethical inspiration. One inherited one's parents, but one chose one's own guru. The Western father typically treats his son as a rival while at the same time expecting him to follow his moral example; the Western son is thus virtually forced to oppose him as a threatening authority and in opposing unconsciously to emulate him. This paradox was avoided in India by the limitation of parental demands, and the substitution of an external model of virtue which one was free to choose without incurring parental resentment. A person's inner life was consigned to the charge of an adopted spiritual father who had more coercive control over his pupil than either a Western father or a Western teacher. Submission to the direction of a particular teacher was an act of free choice. A teacher might require strict obedience over many years from his student, yet because this was essentially voluntary the authority was not resented. Swami Dayanand wandered throughout India for years before associating himself with a teacher at the age of thirty-six. Gandhi adopted Gokhale as his ''political guru'' after meeting him for the first time at the age of twenty-seven. The adoption of a guru was an action not taken lightly, and once taken was likely to be permanent. An Indian did not have an adolescent rebellion forced upon him; nor was one necessary in order to establish an independent identity.

The British school system consequently represented a major innovation in the manner in which Indian youth were brought into contact with society's expectations. Going to school now meant studying in a foreign language with a succession of foreign teachers and English-educated Indian teachers who were selected by the school attended rather than by personal choice. The purpose of schooling was to enable one to progress further away from the home setting into an alien hierarchy. A setting was established outside of the control of either the student or his parents. The preferred new pattern prescribed delaying marriage until after education, altering the traditionally rapid transition from child to parent. And just as the new school system created the setting for adolescence, the English teacher became the logical focus of adolescent ambivalence toward authority. The teacher stood for a generalized authority which made moral demands, which seemed to exemplify all that was desirable, intellectually and materially, and yet was alien and reproving.

The British teacher and—in due course—the British administrator made themselves the targets of feelings which their counterparts in the West shared with a much more salient parental authority. In the West there has been a considerable overlapping of the role of parent and that of teacher. There might have been disagreement as to the point at which spheres of authority should be divided, whether morality, for instance, should be the responsibility of the school or the home, but there has usually been agreement as to what should be taught. In such a setting it was easy for a student to transfer his feelings from one authority to another. The British Indian school system, in contrast, was patronized by ambitious Indian parents, but could not rely upon their moral support. In traditional India the roles of teacher and parent were understood to be noncompetitive. A student's relationship to his teacher was a specialized one wherein he learned principles which did not interfere with his capacity to perform his filial obligations. The alienness of the British school situation aroused new anxieties in Indian parents and placed students in the midst of a delicate struggle.

Gandhi describes in his *Autobiography* the dilemma of a boy from a traditional family exposed to Western influence. Gandhi's most important "school" was the anonymous city of London where he went for legal training. Gandhi's mother was reluctant to permit her son to travel to England where, report had it, it was impossible to live without violating Indian custom. Her objections were only overcome when Gandhi took a solemn vow not to touch wine, meat, or women while in England. Gandhi kept his word, at the cost of severe embarrassment and, at times, near starvation, despite the worldly advice of well-meaning friends that a vow to "an illiterate mother" was of no account. Gandhi kept his vow, but only, he observes, out of loyalty. He saw no intrinsic merit or logic in his mother's request not to eat meat. He assumed that he would begin to eat meat as soon as his parents died, releasing him from his vow, and that ultimately all Indians would follow suit. It was only when he chanced upon a pamphlet justifying vegetarianism in a London restaurant that, as he says, he became a vegetarian "from conviction." Later he was shamed when a Western friend asked for assistance in understanding the *Bhagavad Gita*; Gandhi had never read it.

Like many other students, Gandhi had been exposed primarily to the conventional level of his own culture. Tradition was associated with one's "illiterate mother," who piously observed established rituals, not comprehending the logic of Western culture any more than that of her own. Such a mother perceived the effect of Western education as a potential change in externals, in eating habits and apparel, which to her mind were the substance of tradition. The son, in the course of his Western education, might come to appreciate the "essence" of Western customs, while perceiving his traditional observances as sustained only by unthinking convention.

Some students like Gandhi lived up to the spirit and the letter of their promises because they could not contemplate the prospect of lying to their parents, even if they had no personal objection to the habits they had promised to avoid. Others observed the letter if not the spirit of their promises. A student colleague of B. C. Pal, a Brahman, refused to take rice from the hands of his Kayastha classmates, but readily accepted much more polluting curries because at home he would be asked if he had accepted *rice* from non-Brahmans, it not occurring to his parents to inquire more particularly about other foods.[11] Gandhi recounts that shortly after he first left home for England, he began collecting "chits" of good behavior, signed testimonials that he had abstained from meat, to present to his mother on his return; he soon abandoned this practice when he discovered that others were cynically collecting similar statements which bore no relation to the truth. A statement could be falsified and so, he concluded, even a true statement would be meaningless if his own words were not believed.

The majority of students sought to preserve at least a façade of deference to parental desires, but there were some who, like Gandhi, felt that honesty demanded the rejection of a double standard and took the opposite course, pursuing unorthodox conduct even while at home. Conscious defiance of one's parents was an extreme step because of the virtual impossibility of starting life on one's own in a society in which so much of one's life was controlled by one's family. B. C. Pal took this step, refusing to observe food restrictions at home, and was disinherited. He lived an extremely marginal existence thereafter, supporting himself as a journalist and arranging his own marriage to a child widow who had been married at eight and widowed at nine.[12] A compartmentalization of life, however rationalized, could be relatively satisfying, and relatively successful. It was not difficult to combine Western conduct at school, at work, and in the West with decorous orthodoxy in the home. For a well-adjusted person such inconsistency was almost impossible to avoid. The decision to Westernize one's private life was so wrenching, entailed so severe a break with one's family, that it was a highly unattractive prospect for anyone without fiercely independent ideals, unless he was already at odds with his family and happy for an excuse to break with them completely.

One part of the youthful experiment with Westernization which was ordinarily only feasible for those actually in the West was romance. This was a common experience at the level of experimentation; Gandhi, though married and a father, engaged in a passing flirtation with an English girl.[13] A much more complicated mental process was brought into play if one attempted to marry a Westerner, or a fellow Indian of a different background met in the freer atmosphere of England. Then, it was no longer an episode and entailed, like eating meat at home, a firm decision to alter permanently one's private style of life.

If one committed oneself to Anglicization wholeheartedly, setting aside the pressures of tradition, the struggle was still not at an end. No one could have seemed more successfully Anglicized than the young Surendranath Banerjea, yet his very success seems to have contributed to the resentment his English superiors felt toward him, which led ultimately to his expulsion from the Indian Civil Service. B. C. Pal recalls the effect made upon him as a schoolboy by Banerjea when posted to Pal's home town of Sylhet. Banerjea at this time, about 1872, "was dressed up as a *pucca Saheb* and talked to us [fellow Bengalis] in English. I have, however, a more vivid mental picture of Mrs. Banerjea, who, riding, after the fashion of those days, on a high pony, with flowing skirts and veil that covered her hat, was the wonder of the town."[14]

Surendranath's expulsion from the Civil Service demonstrated that an Indian who Anglicized himself might find himself thereby no better off in British eyes, and hopelessly alienated from his traditional base of strength and influence in his own community into the bargain. Surendranath records in his autobiography that it was the realization that he was defenseless to redress what he considered his unjust expulsion, and that his helplessness was typical of the condition of all his countrymen, which launched him on his public career.[15] It was clearly a gamble to attempt to follow what was proclaimed to be an unobstructed route of advancement. More than one Indian took the gamble, did all the specified things, only to find themselves disqualified from the deserved prize on a technicality. Of the tiny handful of Indians who actually managed to qualify for the Indian Civil Service, a number were excluded on minor pretexts, with the face-saving formula that "an I.C.S. man must be above suspicion."[16]

It is doubtful that even the most Anglicized Victorian moderates felt completely at home in British society. One views them today across the Gandhian divide, and one's picture of them is drawn largely from their speeches and writings, which sound very British whether denouncing or extolling British rule. The ridicule they received from imperialists, however, suggests another portion of the truth. The imperialist image of the moderate was of an opportunist, mouthing British principles in a British accent in order to embarrass his benefactors, but who either misunderstood these principles or cynically exploited them. In truth, the moderates were more Indian than British, and the elements of British style they displayed did give a deceptive impression. It was once said of an eminent Indian nationalist that he spoke to his servants in Bengali, but addressed his dog in English; an Englishman would have done so unself-consciously, but not a Bengali.

The cultural expression of the Anglicized Victorian Indian reflected the basic ambiguity of an essentially imitative enterprise. Even the noblest literary outpourings were judged good "for a native" and accurately likened to the derivativeness of a schoolboy oration. What was once called the Bengal Renaissance, for example, was not a spontaneous borrowing from one's own ancient traditions seen in a vital perspective, but the result of an attempt by a dominant elite to encourage imitation among its dependents. Bengalis were admired for demonstrating an ability to write sentimental novels and turgid verse. While the subject matter of Renaissance writers might be nominally Indian, the treatment and effect were Victorian. The achievements of the Bengal Renaissance were primarily feats of dexterity, like a demonstration of an ability to walk on one's hands, not monuments which have continued to provide inspiration to later generations.[17]

Families ambitious for worldly advancement had launched individuals into contact with Western culture and unintentionally produced some persons so fully assimilated that they had internalized values which put them at odds with their own families. When such individuals aspired beyond the securing of immediate advantages for themselves or their families, and considered their responsibilities to their society as a whole as persons in a unique position to act as intermediaries, they might take one of a number of routes. The aspiring member of a subordinate community may choose to concern himself exclusively with his own career prospects, in which case he will probably justify his actions to himself as useful to his community as an example of what any one of them could do if he applied himself. If he is more of an activist he may devote himself to the task of helping others along the path he has pioneered, helping them master the skills necessary for achieving fuller acceptance. In either case he will be acting as an accomplice of the dominant society. He will have internalized its values, and will judge himself and other members of his community by them. His purpose will be to conserve the structure of power through extension—by inclusion of those who lie outside it.

The aspiring individual may, on the other hand, attempt to serve as the leader of a backward group because he is from it but not of it, because he personally is advanced above the level of other members of his community and therefore better able to deal in their name with the dominant elite. He then has an argument for immediate action. He is prepared to contend that his community should act as a separate force now, whether or not they can now or ever will pass muster according to the prevailing standard of acceptability. He may consequently be ridiculed for "representing only the anomaly of his own position" by those contending that he has no special claim to the leadership of the community from which he happens to be accidentally sprung. To the claim of leadership based upon charity anyone may aspire. If he is recognized as the effective leader of his community, he only trades one set of problems for another. If his attention has been devoted to securing recognition from the dominant community as the leader of the subordinate community, he may be unacquainted with the real nature and needs of his community and unable to control the community politically. To the extent that he expects deference from his community because of his recognition as their representative by the dominant community, he will be vulnerable to challenges from within. His bluff may be called. He may propose to lead his people, but the people may decide not to follow.

If a Victorian moderate became convinced that his difficulties in advancing politically stemmed more from the nature of the system in which he was forced to operate than from his own shortcomings or those of his community and consequently attempted to alter that system, his instinct was to appeal to sympathy or to reason, to enlist the energies of the ruling elite's better elements in the cause of reform. The would-be assimilationist and the liberal representative of the dominant culture entered into a conspiracy of sympathy. The one confessed his embarrassment at what he had been, the other sympathized with him and encouraged his efforts to become something different, deploring the sarcasm of those who would scoff at the attempt. In her *Letters of a Javanese Princess*, Raden Adjeng Kartini, writing in Dutch to her Dutch friends, expressed her desire to become Hollandized: "To go to Europe! Till my last breath that shall always be my ideal. If I could only make myself small enough to slip into an envelope." Kartini, as a patriot, hoped to see her people advance and resented Dutch conservatism. "The Hollanders laugh and make fun of our stupidity, but if we strive for enlightenment, then they assume a defiant attitude . . . Why do many Hollanders find it unpleasant to converse with us in their own language? Oh, yes, now I understand; Dutch is too beautiful to be spoken by a brown mouth."[18]

It was not thought necessary to rely on pity alone. A persistent article of the assimilationist creed is the belief that when rulers falter it is a result of bad advice or inaccurate information. A major effort of Indian moderates was thus directed to the task of setting the facts straight. Had India, for instance, grown richer or poorer under British control? This question was heatedly debated by nationalists and imperialists because of the nationalist assumption that an argument based upon facts could not fail to be persuasive. In reality, the issue was too nebulous, too susceptible of subjective definition and special pleading to be conclusively resolved, and nationalists and imperialists continued to argue to their own satisfaction that India was growing progressively poorer or richer as the case might be.[19] When British Indian administrators proved indifferent to the "facts," it was decided to resort directly to Parliament in England; when this failed, a further effort was made to reach British public opinion, at which point disillusionment finally had to be faced. Moderates appealed to sympathy and reason; in return they received sympathy—and reasons.

The belief that well-informed rulers will act in the interests of all disregards the fact that rulers have interests and perspectives of their own. The British were satisfied with the justness of their policy of holding Indian aspirations in line. The British sat in skeptical judgment on the Indian's attempt to pass as a person culturally assimilated, taking note of shortfalls, gaucheries large and small, as well as of the "inconsistencies" represented by reversions to traditional behavior when Indians returned to the society of friends and family. The difficulties inherent in the attempt to maneuver within several contexts were little appreciated; the tendency was to take inadequacies and contradictions as proof of inferiority and depravity. Indians were considered hypocrites with a double standard of morality because they were modern enough at the office while still caste-ridden in their private lives, though the nature of British rule encouraged Indians to compartmentalize their lives from an early age to meet the demands of a Western schoolteacher during the day and a conservative mother at home. The "impractical, inconsistent" Indian was making a very practical, very consistent adaptation to a situation which was itself disjointed. In fact, many of the traits which Englishmen derided as typically Indian were strongly reinforced, if not created altogether, by British policy. Educated Indians were considered verbally dexterous but impractical; the nature of the education provided by the British was primarily literary and untechnical, as was the nature of subsequent employment opportunities. The fact that educated Indians were to be seen in jobs and professions stressing verbal skills—as clerks, teachers, lawyers, and so forth—was a reflection of the limited employment opportunities available to the product of British–Indian education.

The British had assumed that a direct transfer of values would occur, by a process resembling that involved in producing a rubbing of a brass relief. The visage would remain the same, though transferred to a new medium, flattened out, and deprived of some felicity of detail. Whenever cultural contact failed to produce a faithful copy, Britishers reacted with irritation—or amusement. The impression that unpredictable non-Westerners put together a jerry-built intellectual house constructed of whatever pieces they happen to stumble across is a composite of two images of the non-Westerner—as a mendicant who has to make do with whatever happens to be given to him, and as a tabula rasa on which impressions are randomly recorded in the order of their reception. One's visual image of a non-Western city with its colorful juxtaposition of Western and non-Western artifacts may be an accurate reflection of an indiscriminate mental condition, but one should not overlook the possibility that the confusion may be in the eyes of the beholder. A perfect copy may be accidental and lifeless, and an incongruous mixture deliberate and volatile.

Lord Mountbatten once commented following a garden party that "the Indian had a good sense of humour, or at least the good manners to laugh at the right time."[20] The Englishman who contended that an Indian "had no sense of humour," as well as Mountbatten in gallantly doubting the contention, had in mind a highly specialized definition of humor, the sense of humor of an English gentleman.

If full social acceptance is premised upon the attainment of a certain standard, two questions arise: What level of attainment is to be designated as fully qualifying? Who is to judge? In the American South, black college graduates often "failed" literacy tests used to qualify voters. Literacy, like any other desirable quality, is never of as high a standard as it might be. The standard of acceptability need only be steadily advanced, like a mechanical hare leading a pack of greyhounds, and the effort to succeed will keep people straining ahead indefinitely. Individual Indians such as G. K. Gokhale might deliver speeches in council of Burkean grandeur and comprehensiveness, demonstrating a mastery of all the several skills required for parliamentary self-government, but the perfection of example was readily dismissed as irrelevant because of the unrepresentativeness of such talented individuals. When would India be ready for self-government? When had England been ready? The very notion that political independence should be made dependent upon tangible criteria was misconceived. India would never be ready for independence so long as she conceded the need for conditions adjudged by others. "I have said—and I say it again," said Flora Annie Steel in 1918, "that when I see a Brahmin gentleman teaching in a sweepers' school I will consider responsible government."[21] Presumably, if Miss Steel's stipulation had in fact been fulfilled, she would have been able to devise a new test of fitness. The argument that India should be "prepared" for independence readily became an infinitely receding dead end. So long as Indians sought only to demonstrate a passive merit, to appear worthy of trust, so long might Englishmen set new conditions. In 1905 the future George V, then Prince of Wales, paid a visit to India during which he is reported to have had the following conversation with Gokhale:

> Prince: I have been reading your speech at Benares, in which you said that it would be better for India if the Indians had a much larger part in the administration. I have now been travelling for some months in India . . . and I have never seen a happier-looking people . . . Would the people of India be happier if you ran the country?
>
> Gokhale: No, Sir, I do not say they would be happier, but they would have more self-respect.
>
> Prince: That may be, but I cannot see how there can be real self-respect while the Indians treat their women as they do now.
>
> Gokhale: Yes, that is a great blot.[22]

The Prince of Wales was asking Gokhale a question to which any answer was incriminating. If Gokhale denied that Indians mistreated their wives, he was a fool or a liar; if he admitted the fact, the absurdity of independence under these circumstances seemed self-evident. In England in 1905 no woman could vote, and the condition of English match girls was undoubtedly a "blot," but this had not induced anyone to propose that England submit herself to an impartial despotism until this state of affairs was remedied. In the reckoning of Indian moderates, the granting of independence was to be the climactic act of benevolent governance. Recognizing the futility of this hope involved acceptance of the inevitability of self-interest in politics.

It was delusory to hope that the British would give India independence simply because Indians were judged ready. If the British gave India independence, it would be for reasons of their own. Nor was it correct to assume that those individuals who seemed most "ready" to rule would prove most fit to rule. A class which has responded dutifully to Western requirements has on occasion been the beneficiary of Western withdrawal from captured territories; it has been a class with outward attributes which suggest acceptability as successor to the retreating imperialists, and one that sincerely aspires to be a worthy successor, imbued with a bourgeois mentality without being bourgeois. Frantz Fanon has argued in *The Wretched of the Earth* that the indigenous elite which took power when the colonial states of Africa gained their independence were by and large such a would-be bourgeoisie. They were a class composed on the basis of an educational qualification, well suited to act as interpreters before independence, and thereafter as administrators of an inherited status quo. They were skilled imitators of foreign elegance but incapable of performing the bourgeoisie's classic historical task of industrializing the country. Their claim to a right to rule was based only on a superficial resemblance to the Western middle class. They were not emblematic of a social transformation comparable to that which brought social ascendancy to the Western bourgeoisie. They were committed to values with class connotations in the West which they did not have in Africa. Ideas were transmitted to and internalized by a group whose objective position was not comparable to that of the class from which these ideas originally emanated. African leaders were bourgeois in thought, without being in a position to produce a bourgeois revolution in practice, and they lacked the independence of perspective which might have led them to new indigenous solutions. Foreign sponsorship had produced a class which could function effectively only under foreign sponsorship.

Rebellion

Assimilation, whether as a family plan, an internalized need, or a political program, is an engine of social control. The myth of equal opportunity in India, like the myth of the American melting pot, served to channel the energies of men seeking to rise in the direction of emulation of those who set the tone and controlled the commanding heights of the existing society. An elite are always equipped to manage those who seek only to join them, for even if submerged they will not feel that they have been supplanted.

Among engines of social control, an assimilationist myth has much to recommend it. In the absence of serious social divisions, it is capable of providing a valid aspiration for all. The decision to ignore its promise is arbitrary, and must be taken in the name of an alternative idea; mere frustration is never reason to abandon hope. No policy is given up simply because it fails. Technique and tactics may be taken up and dropped on this basis but it takes more than failure to convince a person of the futility of his basic strategy; there are too many conveniently accessible explanations for failure which stop short of an arraignment of one's basic orientation. No policy ever has a "fair" test of how it might do under optimum conditions, and the inclination to try again and hope for better results next time is always tantalizing. There is always the prospect that success will come if one holds out a little longer, and the discouraging fear that those who revolt are only seeking an excuse for failure.

Where a lifetime of socialization guides an individual's aspirations, backing away from expectations is complicated and likely to cause severe anxiety. If a person has a physical handicap, he may spend a lifetime indulging in self-pity, or feel challenged to exert the extra effort necessary to succeed in competition with more favored individuals. The same options often seem to be the only ones open to those with socially-imposed handicaps. The natural response is to attempt to make it, despite the recognition of adverse odds. Some may consider such odds a stimulating challenge. If the black American realizes that he has to be twice as good to get half as far, he may think of this as an opportunity to demonstrate that he really is twice as good.[23] If hope is not borne out for an individual, it may be transferred to his children's prospects. Such an approach might be followed for centuries without effecting significant change in the lives of any but a handful in each generation.

The devotee of moderate constitutionalism in certain intractable situations may become like a middle-aged infant perpetually straining for signs that an oft-deferred recognition of maturity may eventually be granted by kindly but still skeptical parents. A son is never fully mature in the eyes of his parents and never will be mature so long as he is dependent upon his parents' suggestions. The act which demonstrates a person's maturity—the making of an intelligent decision independently—often seems an act of immaturity in the eyes of his elders. Waiting for one's parents to determine when one will be sufficiently mature to exercise one's own discretion may become a lifelong obligation.

The parent-child analogy suggests an obvious conclusion—that the solution may lie in adolescent rebellion. Whether or not a rejection of assimilation is similar to adolescent rebellion, it is certain to *seem* adolescent to those against whom it is directed.

Rebellion by adolescents was a new phenomenon in India, and was related to the nationalist movement in that the setting of rebellion was the British school and its target the British teacher. Certain mature acts of nationalists involved a working out on a larger stage of the pattern set by school rebellion. Erik Erikson has suggested that Martin Luther's defiance of the Pope recalled his earlier defiance of his own father. When Subhas Bose passed the Civil Service Examination and then renounced his position in an alien bureaucracy he too was recalling the style of his earlier rebellion in school.[24] Adolescent rebellion in the literal sense, however, implies only a desire to replace a hated father. If an act has revolutionary connotations, it will involve intellectual originality more important to its definition as a mature act than a coincidence of style with youthful rebellion. If a person continues in adolescent defiance in later life he will never be able to improve upon his father's example.

To make adolescent rebellion more than the beginning of a new cycle, alternative sources of inspiration are required. A rebellion on the grounds of unfairness may serve to sustain the system by accepting its potential fairness. A rebellion against the *system* will not be possible unless something very basic is felt to have been left out. This is likely to be suggested to the young aspirant for assimilation, not by any number of failures in efforts to assimilate, but by the continued existence of people totally indifferent to assimilation. The more assimilated can bury their resentment against ill-treatment by congratulating themselves on their superiority to the less assimilated. But how to cope with those who will not envy their success? The young Westernized Bengali students of the nineteenth century streamed out to gaze in fascination at the illiterate saint Ramakrishna. The young Subhas Bose, educated from childhood in a missionary school, left home secretly on an extended tour of Hindu holy places in search of a traditional guru. As a university student, Bose was fascinated by the saint Aurobindo, who grew up in England and spoke no Indian language on his return to India, but nonetheless had identified himself completely with the Hindu tradition.[25] Westernized Indians could not avoid asking themselves if their Anglicized gymnastics had not made them ridiculous.

Neither manipulators nor assimilationists had made a serious attempt to correlate Indian and Western principles. Manipulators kept their traditional principles unsullied in seeking the West's useful knowledge; assimilationists were unaware or contemptuous of the intellectual component of their traditions. As assimilated Indians became more self-conscious, they grew increasingly fascinated by the example of those who had made intellectual efforts to relate East and West. This enterprise had been fostered initially by expropriationists, men such as Raja Ram Mohan Roy and Sir Syed Ahmed Khan, who attempted to demonstrate that their inherited traditions were *potentially as good* as those of the West. The terms of judgment were expropriated from the West; the need to be rational and scientific was acknowledged, as was the necessity of transforming their traditional society and received learning on Western lines. An informed elite from within traditional society who conceived of themselves as spokesmen for their society undertook to address the West and to propose reforms, breaking with the irresponsible opportunism of earlier emissaries of tradition, while endeavoring to maintain a stance within tradition which had been spurned by assimilationists.

The activities of such spokesmen produced a response to the West which many Westerners thought would lead to a full conversion equivalent to that of the assimilationists. Actually the motivation of such traditional intellectuals in acquainting themselves with Western learning was to make tradition equivalent to the West, so that no conversion would be necessary. Was Hinduism thought to be debased polytheism? Raja Ram Mohan Roy could demonstrate that it could also be chaste monotheism. Was Hinduism thought to have many good teachings, but to lack the central figure of Christ? Krishna could be depicted as possessing all the desired attributes. If the problem appeared to be that the caste system inhibited individual mobility, the caste system could be depicted as anciently and hence potentially a system open to talents. Missionaries were hard-pressed to deny the logic of this position, but its exponents were equally hard-pressed by the more orthodox elements in their own communities.

The presumption of apologists for tradition to a special position as intermediaries with the West, no less than the parallel presumption of those who were most fully assimilated, was highly vulnerable to challenge by more traditional figures. Those with a vested interest in, or a strong idealistic commitment to, the preservation of traditions may devote themselves initially to simple defiance of the infidel barbarians. Protracted contact, however, is likely to stimulate an interest in new forms of conflict. Traditionalists may then attempt to demonstrate that their tradition is *already as good* as the West, by the West's own standards. This effort may have a high degree of intellectual integrity. Sophisticated Western medical experiments have demonstrated the efficacy of ancient herb remedies. Careful archaeological investigations have often verified supposedly fanciful historical chronicles. The scientific verification of tradition may, however, be transformed into an effort to vindicate tradition by expropriating science. The effort to save whatever in tradition is compatible with a modern outlook is different from an effort to save tradition by maintaining its scientific credibility through any convenient means. It is tempting, for example, to discern scientific reasons of health or economy for practices which are not open to acceptance or rejection on these grounds, being matters of religious faith. Rituals may thereby be preserved without the embarrassment of seeming to be superstitious.

Somewhat more ambitious than an expropriation of arguments is the expropriation of artifacts. For all its seeming improbability, the attempt to envision the distant past as endowed with all the latest inventions of Western science has been remarkably widespread. The "cargo cults" of Southeast Asia, which consist of the attempt by various ritual means to secure the "cargo" of Western ships and airplanes, were often premised upon such a rationalization. An impression would spread abroad that the local people had once known how to secure cargo directly from the deity, but that the secret had been stolen from them by the foreigner. Manufactured goods were considered gifts of the deity, which had always been available and which had been available first exclusively to them.[26]

The argument employed was that all the accomplishments for which the West was honored were in fact the accomplishments of one's traditional society in ages past. The seeming absurdity of such a claim obscures its psychological aptness. A traditional conception of knowledge as divine revelation, which may be lost and then rediscovered, makes it logical to view Western accomplishments as the result of such a rediscovery, and the conviction of the superiority of one's own tradition makes it equally logical to suspect that a scientific revelation in one's own past has been made and then lost, or stolen by foreigners.

The most sweeping of expropriational efforts to counter the West were the attempts to expropriate, not bits and pieces, but Western legitimacy itself. A substantial number of messianic movements arose which made a direct claim on the spiritual foundation of the West. If Christianity seemed the West's ultimate weapon, this too could be wrested away. Movements arose claiming a new and immediate relationship to Christ which did away with the necessity of missionary mediation. In India the Ahmadiya movement and that of Birsa Munda, among others, made special claims to direct Christian inspiration.[27] The most extensive and convulsive of such movements, however, was the Chinese Taiping Rebellion, which survived as the government of large regions of China from 1851 to 1864, and nearly brought down the Manchu Empire altogether. Hung Hsiu-ch'üan, who failed the imperial examinations three times, and who had received some instruction from an American Southern Baptist missionary, proclaimed himself the younger brother of Jesus Christ and evolved a revolutionary program including abstention from opium, alcohol, and tobacco, the segregation and equality of the sexes, and community ownership of property.

In proclaiming himself the younger brother of Jesus Christ, Hung

Hsiu-ch'üan established a direct line of inspiration excluding missionaries. What was attractive in Christian teachings to Chinese restive under Manchu oppression was expropriated and designated rightfully Chinese. Thus, the term for God used by the missionaries Hung encountered was Shang-ti, a concept evocative of ancient Chinese usage. In the Taiping "Book of Heavenly Precepts" it was asserted that the God in question was in fact the God of China's Golden Age:

> Another absurd statement says that to worship the August God is to follow the barbarians. It is not known that the historical annals of China refute this. From Pan Ku to the Three Dynasties, rulers and people did all reverently worship the same August God. [28]

Messianic movements such as the Taiping Rebellion often have very clear notions about the nature of the malaise in the larger society around them, and equally clear ideas about the nature of a society in which these ills would be remedied. In the absence of adequate information, or in despair of a quick practical solution, fantasies may develop regarding the method of moving from the one state to the other. It was tantalizing for Bengalis to imagine, for example, that the Partition of Bengal of 1905 might be reversed by a march of holy men through the gates of Fort William: "Sannyasis or fakirs with blankets on their shoulders would enter the fort. The British troops would stand stockstill, unable to move or fight, and power would pass into the hands of the people." [29] Messianic movements are not so much symptoms of a disease, as of a desire for cure, for a future state which seems powerless to be born.

Messianism appears in situations of impossible odds or disorienting social change. If expropriated or paranoiac it may not survive. It is possible, however, that it may evolve into a viable form of revivalism, the classic response of a system in crisis. Revivalism is not a response to the West, though the Western challenge is one of many causes which may provoke the crisis which produces a revivalist response. Revivalism is a movement of traditional men using traditional means. Its leaders are unimpressed with the need for expropriating anything; all that is needed can be found in the past of their own society. The urge for a restoration, for a classical revolution permitting a return to a purer age, may be a creative and adequate impulse, if social malaise is in fact the result of cyclical decline. Even if such a restoration proves impossible, the exploration of ancient alternatives, as in Machiavelli's studies of republican Rome, may stimulate an understanding of what is wrong and what is to be done.

One of India's leading exponents of classic revolution was Swami Dayanand Saraswati. Dayanand's mission originated in an effort to test the validity of the accepted practices of his religion. What was so awesome about a piece of stone? he asked his father. His father explained that the graven image was not actually being worshipped, but served as an aid to faltering worshipers "in this Kali Yug—the age of mental darkness . . . But this explanation fell short of satisfying me. I could not, young as I was, help suspecting misinterpretation and sophistry in all this."

Disillusioned with conventional practice, Dayanand proceeded to investigate the pretensions of conventional priestly and textual authority. His faith in priests was shaken on a visit to the "mountain ascetics" of the Himalayas when he discovered in an interior room "a large company of pandits seated with a pyramid of flesh, rump-steaks and dressed up heads of animals before them." His faith in conventional textual authority was broken when, while wandering alone beside the Ganges,

> I chanced to meet a corpse floating down the river. There was the opportunity, and it remained with me to satisfy myself as to the correctness of the statements contained in the books about anatomy and man's inner organs. Ridding myself of the books which I laid near by, and taking off my clothes, I resolutely entered the river and soon brought the dead body out and laid it on the bank. I then proceeded to cut it open with a large knife in the best manner I could. I took out and examined the Kamal (the heart) and cutting it from the navel to the ribs, and a portion of the head and neck, I carefully examined and compared them with the descriptions in the books. Finding that they did not tally at all, I tore the books to pieces and threw them into the river after the corpse. From that time gradually I came to the conclusion that with the exception of the *Vedas, Upanisada, Patanjali* and *Sankhya* all other works upon Science and Yoga were false.[30]

Dayanand, in short, arrived at the conclusion that his society was decadent. His recourse was to look into his own inherited tradition in search of a purer dispensation, following a pattern stretching at least as far back as Akhnaton's effort to sweep away the accretions of Pharonic religion in the second millenium *B.C.* Dayanand felt the need for an unmediated revelation and swept away the decorated idols of unconsidered evolution. Dayanand's searching was carried out within the Hindu tradition and within a geographic region beyond the reaches of British cultural penetration, in India's Northwest in the middle years of the nineteenth century. Dayanand's confrontation with Western civilization was a consequence, not a cause, of his reformulation of the Hindu tradition; if the British had not existed, they would not have had to be created.

In the course of his struggles Dayanand employed a number of expropriationist arguments, claiming utility for cow-preservation and modern scientific genius for Vedic society. Such claims were, however, incidental to his basic commitment to the Vedas and not directly inspired by admiration for Western accomplishments. Dayanand is sometimes said to have asserted that airplanes are mentioned in the Vedas. Dayanand's "airplanes" were not meant in a literal modern sense; the Vedas were held to contain only the germs of modern scientific knowledge. Inferences in Vedic hymns suggested that railways, steamships, and airplanes were destined for ultimate creation. Dayanand was not claiming that archaeologists might some day find remnants of ancient railway systems or the wings of long-lost aircraft; he was simply stating that modern scientific advances were in the spirit of the Vedas, and that if Indians had retained a Vedic mentality they would have developed all that the West held dear—and more.

The confidence as well as the solid evidence with which Dayanand assaulted the West suggests the advantages of his position in contrast to that of either an assimilationist or an expropriationist. The one sought to see himself as something he was not; the other, to see his tradition as something it was not. Dayanand was proud of his tradition and possessed a reasonable strategy for its reinvigoration.

Dayanand's limitations stemmed from his inadequate appreciation of the uniqueness of the challenge his society faced. Assimilated Indians had greater problems but also greater prospects. Assimilated Indians might indeed go on endlessly walking the treadmill of deferred acceptance. If they sought to return to their traditions, the shock of reentry was painful and their ability to communicate with traditional people difficult to reestablish. The opportunity which attended this anguish, however, was the chance to transcend the cycle of purifying restorations within which Dayanand was bound and to transform their reaction into a revolution.

5   The Revolutionary Solution:

Defining and Distinguishing

Revolutions

What, then, is a revolution? What are its causes and effects? A revolution's causes may be classified, following Aristotle, as referring to the general conditions which are conducive to revolution or to specific precipitants.[1] The latter are almost always accidents, unique and unpredictable; the former, however, can be described with some certainty.

A revolution may occur when autonomous alienated groups become powerful in a society because of changes in the mode of production or the system of education or representation or because of governmental failure, or when a new society is formed of previously unrelated groups, in which one group asserts its dominance and disadvantaged groups resist dependence and prefer to fight for control of the whole society rather than for independence from it.

A revolution may be defined as the sequence of events which occurs when a government's constitution — as distinct from its temporary composition—becomes identified with the interests of a single group, causing others to attempt to establish a new constitutional order, altering both the nature and the locus of governmental legitimacy, both the rationale and the agency of government, by an arbitrary act of will that is thought to be its own justification, that disregards accepted conventions of thought and behavior, and that usually involves the use of violence. From first to last, revolutions are intellectual events, involving perceptions, decisions and acts of will. A revolution's sound and fury signify nothing apart from the meaning given them by the conscious intentions of revolutionaries. As John Adams said of the events of 1776, "But what do we mean by the American Revolution? Do we mean the American War? The Revolution was effected before the war commenced. The Revolution was in the minds and hearts of the people; a change in their religious sentiments, of their duties and obligations."[2]

Revolutions are usually violent, but they are not revolutions because they are violent; they are violent, if they are, because they are revolutions. The meaning of an instance of violence is not determined by its scope or intensity but by the use to which it is put. Revolutions do entail a major degree of psychic exhaustion; they are experiences which societies cannot soon repeat. Such exhaustion can result from prolonged warfare or revolution, phenomena which sometimes are intertwined and sometimes occur separately. An inconclusive civil war may exhaust a society's capacity to take new initiatives without resolving social divisions. A successful revolution, on the other hand, may resolve societal divisions with little or no violence.

De Tocqueville observed that the United States was fortunate in never having experienced—or needed—a democratic revolution. France had obviously had a democratic revolution, and French society, as de Tocqueville well knew, had been polarized ever since. De Tocqueville recognized the true distinctiveness of American society: it was postrevolutionary, but without unreconciled divisions at the heart of the society. This was not, however, because America had never endured a democratic revolution, not because Americans were "born equal without having to become so," but because America's revolution had been unusually successful. The American Revolution achieved its objectives so fully that the eye is fooled into calling the result of contrivance natural.

Many of the American characteristics which de Tocqueville criticized are also traceable to the Revolution. The position of black Americans and the American Indian, the prevalence of lawyers, the fondness for generalizations, the intellectual narrowness reflecting the tyranny of legitimated majority opinion, phenomena which de Tocqueville carefully dissected, all reflect the experience of revolution. The true distinction between American and French development concerns the relative degree of success of the two revolutions; they are not different in kind. The American Revolution succeeded in removing all obstacles to its permanent enthronement, whereas the French Revolution, facing much greater resistance, was less thorough, less democratic in its lasting effect, and left vestiges of opposition to plague the subsequent history of

France. De Tocqueville recognized the differences between the French
and American situations but attributed America's distinctiveness to
evolutionary trends, seeing America as a forcing house of democratizing
modernization where the inexorable course of egalitarianism had moved
ahead of Europe. De Tocqueville was right, but for the wrong reasons.
America's characteristics were the result of an American revolution,
not the wave of Europe's future.

Just as revolutions are best defined in intellectual terms, as arbitrary
acts of will, so are they best distinguished one from another in intellectual terms. Many efforts have been made to classify revolutions in
other ways, according to their degree of success, or the amount of
violence which accompanies them, or whether they are "limited" or
"unlimited," or "social" rather than "political." Such efforts have been
either accurate but of limited utility, because they dwell on superficial
characteristics, or misleading, as with the distinction between "social"
and "political" revolutions, because every revolution is both social and
political. A more illuminating distinction, referring to revolutionary
self-awareness and purpose, can be made between revolutions which
are predominantly self-fulfilling and those which are predominantly
plan-fulfilling. Plan-fulfilling revolutions are part of long-range, clearly
thought out plans for the reconstruction of society; they are instigated
in order to establish the political instruments recognized as necessary
to accomplish this reconstruction. In a self-fulfilling revolution, basic
changes also occur, but in an accidental, unpremeditated fashion.

This distinction between two basic—slightly idealized—types of
revolution corresponds in part to Samuel Huntington's distinction
between what he calls the Eastern and Western models of revolution.[3]
In the Western model, he suggests, the revolution begins when the
revolutionaries take the capital; in the Eastern model, this ends the
revolution. The two models would be typified by the French and Russian
Revolutions on the one hand, and the Chinese Communist Revolution
in its later phases on the other. The Western revolution begins accidentally and proceeds unpredictably and from the top down; the Eastern
revolution devises its character and institutions and trains its cadres
in the rural areas where it first gains control, and simply extends this
control progressively until it finally topples the capital. These two models suggest important distinctions, though the distinctions are obviously
in no sense a function of hemispheric determinism. Chronology,
technology, and the internal contours of geography and society largely

determine whether a particular revolution more closely approximates one or the other of these models. Chronology is important because the Eastern model has become the increasingly necessary technique of revolution because of the great difficulty of accidental conquest of the capital by a revolutionary coup. The formidable difficulties of concerting a revolutionary effort from rural areas were not readily conquered, but now the experience can be studied and adapted more easily elsewhere. Technology is always important in determining strategy, although relative access to current technology is more important than its absolute level of sophistication. Social and political organization and simple topography also obviously condition whether the capital or the countryside is more vulnerable.

The distinction between Eastern and Western revolution relates essentially to whether revolution originates near the center of a society or at its periphery. This fact determines much of a revolution's character, but primarily at the level of military strategy; what is omitted is the question of political intent. Guerrilla wars—identified by Huntington with the Eastern model of revolution—may actually have restorational social goals, or limited revolutionary goals as in the American Revolution, a limited guerrilla war. For this reason it seems preferable to use the largely but not entirely coterminous categories of plan-fulfilling and self-fulfilling revolutions. Most—not all—Eastern revolutions, starting from the periphery and with plenty of time to plan for the future, are plan-fulfilling; many Western revolutions, starting from near the center, are self-fulfilling. The Russian Revolution was anomalous in this as in other ways, being a plan-fulfilling revolution launched unexpectedly from near the center.

The paradigm of self-fulfilling revolution would prescribe a slow gathering of grievances throughout a country, a gradual growth of a network of alliances, at length stimulated into action by accidental factors. Plan-fulfilling revolutionaries expect to confront an amorphous unradicalized society, and to assume simultaneously the tasks of prerevolutionary preparation and postrevolutionary consolidation. This process normally can begin on only a small scale in remote areas. It was a historical accident which permitted plan-fulfilling revolutionaries allied with the urban working class to gain political power in Russia in 1917; the crude approximation of the Marxist model of revolution which occurred in Russia in 1917 can only be explained as a result of governmental collapse aggravated by a disastrous war and the strategic

flexibility of the Bolsheviks in making expedient appeals to the countryside.

Revolutions in the twentieth century have become more often plan-
fulfilling as revolutionaries have grown more self-conscious about their
goals and the obstacles to their attainment. Both goals and obstacles
have grown larger, and the confrontation more total. Revolutionaries,
sobered by the failure or premature waning of other revolutions, plot
to perpetuate their own past the point of formal success; counter-
revolutionaries, more powerful and more sensitive to the threat of
revolution, know better how to forestall it. The self-fulfilling revolution
remains nonetheless a much more frequent phenomenon. Nationalist
revolutions, though occasionally plan-fulfilling, are most often self-
fulfilling revolutions.

A self-fulfilling revolution can be defined in part by what it lacks.
It is less specific about its postrevolutionary goals; its emphasis is more
negative and revivalistic. The mission of revolutionaries is not permanent, or world-historical, but ad hoc: to remove a certain regime. After
the revolution it is assumed that things will settle into a new equilibrium
somewhat but not altogether different from what had been experienced
—at least in imagination—in happier periods in the past. A self-
fulfilling revolution aims at the restoration of balance and order. The
evils of the *ancien régime* are limited and specific; so are the remedies.

A self-fulfilling revolution can also be defined in part by what it
fails to perceive about its own nature and achievement. A self-fulfilling
revolution accomplishes more than it intends or realizes. There is not
only no desire, there is no need for a permanent revolution. The purpose
of the revolution is to remove a specific evil; among its unintended
side effects is a societal revolution which, if completed, insures that
the revolution will be automatically enshrined and sustained. The relation between the revolution and its effect is somewhat similar to that
between the individual's pursuit of happiness and its attainment, as
described by John Stuart Mill. "Ask yourself whether you are happy,
and you cease to be so," Mill observed.

> The only chance is to treat, not happiness, but some end external
> to it, as the purpose of life. Let your self-consciousness, your scrutiny,
> your self-interrogation, exhaust themselves on that; and if otherwise
> fortunately circumstanced, you will inhale happiness with the air
> you breathe, without dwelling on it or thinking about it, without

either forestalling it in imagination, or putting it to flight by fatal questioning.[4]

Mill suggested that an individual might achieve happiness by pursuing an unrelated concrete end; by reverse analogy, a society by organizing to pursue an abstract goal such as peace or happiness may accomplish an unanticipated concrete result. By pursuing a limited political objective a society may achieve a different, more important social result. In a self-fulfilling revolution a society is transformed in spite of itself by the pursuit of an end external to itself. By bluff or luck, by not being overly self-conscious about the motives and consequences of their actions, by being simply righteous extremists, revolutionaries may find that they have carried the day, and that the pieces are falling into place almost of their own accord. A limited political revolution becomes unexpectedly a sweeping societal revolution. One demand, one gesture brings down the whole structure. Such an accidental result may be more permanently—because spontaneously—transformative than a self-conscious effort to impose a blueprint on society from above.

The unpremeditated quality of a self-fulfilling revolution is a mixed blessing, for the chance of failure is high, and an uncompleted revolution may be worse than none at all. The English and French Revolutions, for instance, were unsuccessful self-fulfilling revolutions, revolutions which faltered because the problems confronted were greater than the revolution's potential for self-fulfilment. The revolutionary techniques used — exhortations for the general citizenry, punishments for individual recalcitrants — were the techniques of self-fulfilling revolution, in which specific evils are combatted by limited means. These revolutions failed, however, to generate their own complete fulfillment because the extent of reform desired and the intransigence of those opposed to the revolution were too great for the resources of the revolutionary leadership. A more moderate revolution might have produced more sweeping and stable results. The ambitious uncompleted revolutions in England and France created seriously divided societies. Here, self-fulfilling revolution became self-defeating.

The American and Indian Revolutions combined two conditions of success for a self-fulfilling revolution lacking in England and France: a mild superficial tyranny which permitted, as well as facilitated by repression, combination and agitation to overthrow it, which permitted revolution to begin close to the throne under partially assimilated and moderate leadership; and continuity of revolutionary leadership and goals. There was no progressive escalation of ambition or radicalization of leadership in the course of the revolution, and the postrevolutionary regime was constructed by the men who had first articulated the evils of the old regime.

In America, the revolutionary opposition to tyranny survived as a hostility to centralized authority in any new government. There were, concurrently, many with an almost equal fear of democracy. The result was the creation of a system of checks and balances which, as Samuel Huntington has argued, works only because it is based upon a false assumption: "Their Constitution was successful only because their view of American society was erroneous."[5] The Constitution was designed to check and balance factional extremism and the excesses of democracy and tyranny. Such a system would have proved unworkable had the society been in fact riven by faction and torn between monarchists and democrats. The assumption that such dangers needed to be guarded against in the new government was wrong, however, not because searing cleavages had never existed in America, but because of the fact and effect of the Revolution itself. The Revolution solved the problems which the Founding Fathers sought to solve in the structure of government, and what had once been divisive factionalism evolved into limited party competition. Inevitably, this long-range effect of the Revolution could not have been presumed at the time the Constitution was formulated; the Founding Fathers were forced to confront this fortunately redundant task.

The colonial American assemblies often had two chambers, like the new Congress; the royal governor stood in relation to them somewhat as the President does to the Congress. The formal parallel is striking, so much so as to disguise the critical differences in what went on inside these forms. The colonial assemblies before the Revolution did not work; the later institutions did. If the nature of the society and of governmental legitimacy had not been altered, what happened after the revolution might have looked just as bad as what went before. As it turned out, the changes wrought by the experience of revolution made the new-old system workable. Post-revolutionary American society was "simplified" by partition and emigration, and the new homogeneous dominant class was given full power to establish conditions for citizenship for the minorities who remained. The issue of governmental legitimacy was firmly settled on a popular basis, royal sovereignty being replaced by popular legitimacy traceable to a revolutionary act of creation.

The combination of these two factors—a simplified society and strongly reinforced popular legitimacy—provided the critical difference in the functioning of the seemingly similar institutions before and after the Revolution. Samuel Huntington has compared the American presidency to the Tudor monarchy, concluding that "Today America still has a king, Britain only a Crown."[6] The argument is illuminating as an indication of the sources of American practice and the relationship between the executive authority and a higher law; the difference between the Tudor monarchy and the American presidency stems from the revolutionary basis on which the presidency rests. The American President exercises a legitimate unified popular mandate. Structurally, he is a Tudor monarch, but he operates in and on behalf of a post-revolutionary society.

Britain ruled the American colonies through emissaries sent from England, who had the assistance and support of elements in the indigenous society. There were British settlers who thought of themselves as displaced Englishmen. There were Anglicans committed to religious loyalty. There were placemen who had or sought employment as agents of British government. The bulk of British support, however, came from ethnic minorities and backward sectors. The dominant English-derived stratum of indigenous American society was revolutionary; orthodox or alien minorities who had much less in common with Great Britain proved most loyal to her. Less assimilated sectors were more likely to be loyalist. Germans, Dutch, French Catholics, Quakers, Appalachian frontiersmen, and American Indians all resisted revolutionary involvement.

In America, "Adherents of religious groups that were in a local minority were everywhere inclined towards Loyalism . . . The loyalty of the Indians is well known, and contemporary opinion held that the Negroes were dangerously Toryified . . . Taking all the groups and factions, sects, classes and inhabitants of regions that seem to have been Tory, they have but one thing in common: they represented conscious minorities, people who felt weak and threatened."[7]

Where economic interests played a part, dependent or defensive sectors were allied with Britain:

In the West and in the tidal region of the Middle Colonies Loyalists and neutrals may have formed a majority of the population . . . All that the Tory regions, the mountain and maritime frontiers, had in common was that both suffered or were threatened with economic and political subjugation by richer adjoining areas . . . The Appalachian frontiersmen—hunters, trappers, and fur traders—feared the advance of close settlement which would destroy their economy. Like the Indians of the region, many of the frontiersmen were loyal to Britain because the British government was the only force they could rely on to check the rapid advance of agricultural settlement . . . [In addition] the truly maritime regions seem to have been less than enthusiastic in their support of the Revolution. Newport lacked zeal; Nantucket and Martha's Vineyard were opportunist or neutral . . . wherever regions newly or thinly settled touched the sea, there the Revolution was weakest: in Quebec, in Nova Scotia, in Georgia and in New York where the Hudson carried the Atlantic world into the mountains.[8]

Colonial America, in other words, was a social and political system with which a great many people were well satisfied and in whose fall they could only see dangers for the preservationof their own culture and livelihood. Groups already strong and self-sufficient could afford to gamble on being able to hold their own under new conditions. The settled rich and the weak and isolated anticipated little profit for themselves in basic alterations. The patrons and the patronized preferred the stability of a colonial *ancien régime* which opposed the ambitions of rising classes.

Into such an inherently volatile situation was sent a royal governor, a man, like the Indian viceroy, without local connections, appointed for a term only. The governor did not have the sources of influence available to the prime minister in England, having no patronage to provide in return for the revenue he required. He was incapable of exercising any continuous control over a coherent faction of "governor's men," and the colonial assemblies were disorderly and obstructive, adept at opposing, in fact chronically uncompliant.

The Revolution retrieved the colonies from political confusion. The United States did not attain independence through a "maturing" of the colonial assemblies leading to a final severing of ties with the parent body. As Bernard Bailyn notes, the pre-Revolutionary assemblies were scarcely promising prototypes.[9] At the time of the Revolution, America was developing into a stalemated society, in which ineffective rulers feuded vainly with chaotic representative assemblies.

It has often been argued that democratic government and popular sovereignty were ancient traditions in America even before the Revolution, stemming from the foundation of Puritan New England. This statement is true, but it is also true that this foundation was being eroded in the years preceding the Revolution. New immigrant groups were joining the Puritan nucleus. American society was growing more prosperous and diversified, and the hierarchical class system of England was being rapidly duplicated; even an established church was feared in the offing. American society was being developed, the tightly-knit society of the Puritans transformed into a cosmopolitan welter of groups which the British hoped could be held together by appointed autocrats.

The Revolution, far from being a culmination of eighteenth century constitutional evolution, actually saved the United States from being cut off entirely from its Puritan roots by providing the conditions for the perpetuation on a large scale of many of the qualities which had characterized the primitive communities of the early settlers. These groups had been protorevolutionary in origin, offshoots from the upheaval which produced the seventeenth century English Revolution. In the more worldly eighteenth century America they were no longer dominant. The distinctive "ideological definition of citizenship" which Louis Hartz has demonstrated to be critical in American development, in contrast to the definition of citizenship in other countries by residence alone, was indeed a Puritan hallmark, and again a hallmark of post-revolutionary America.[10] The establishment of such a definition is the achievement of a successful revolution, and this was precisely what was in danger of being lost in eighteenth century America. Such a definition is not natural; its establishment first by the Puritans, then by the revolutionaries, was an act of will. To paraphrase Perry Miller, America has *twice* been founded by an act of will.[11]

A strikingly similar social transformation was accomplished by the revolution which made India an independent country. The Indian equivalent of eighteenth century American factionalism was "casteism, linguism, and communalism," a litany often heard in India before and after independence. It referred to divisions within British Indian society which literally tore the country apart; the partition was viewed by India's leadership as a great defeat for their own ideals, a great victory for communalism. After independence, the nationalist leadership, now the legitimate rulers of an independent country, tried with every new resource at their disposal to stem "fissiparous tendencies." Nehru opposed the demand for linguistic states, and constantly lamented the prevalence of caste rivalries in politics. Before independence they had torn the country apart; how could they be permitted to continue, be permitted to tear the country apart again? It was difficult to understand the argument which some people began to make a few years after independence that such divisions might be benign, even compatible with and supportive of democratic functioning. [12] Weren't they the same old divisions? And yet, when linguistic states were reluctantly conceded, the nation was strengthened, and agitation abated. When caste associations participated in politics, the political system was reinforced. India's leaders, like America's Founding Fathers, looked upon the acquisition of independence as an opportunity to redouble their efforts to combat the evils of the society of the *ancien régime*; not surprisingly, they too failed to perceive the extent of the transformation which the revolution had wrought. The old divisions no longer needed to be checked and balanced because revolutionary legitimation had made them neutralized, contained, and channeled. The most intransigent counter-revolutionaries had been eliminated by partition, and those who remained were willing to obey the new rules of the game. The "impartial" British rule of India, like the intrusive rule of eighteenth century American colonial governors, had set factions at one another's throats; the new structures were less impartial and more stable.

Where continuity with India's past was feared—in the operation of divisive factionalism—there was very little. Where continuity was perceived and planned—in the operation of structures and institutions—there was also very little. In both instances the effect of the revolution was underestimated. The old-fashioned institutions which survived into the new regime—legislatures based on colonial models, the military and civil services—were successfully assimilated because they were redirected to serve revolutionary ends. As with America's Tudor institutions, so in India these institutions have proved serviceable only because they were compatible with the revolution's priorities, and made subordinate to them.

Revolutionary Morality

Revolutions reflect individual intentions, even if in paradoxical and inverted ways. Revolutions happen only when some people want them to happen. In fact, the central impetus of a revolution is moral; every revolution is a "revolution of the saints." The sole cause for which the unusual exertions required to sustain a revolution will be pledged is that of virtue.

The distinctive moral purpose of revolution explains many seeming paradoxes in revolutionary policy and alliances. It is often treated as an irony that revolutionaries, once in power, continue and even intensify the very developments they find most sinister in the *ancien régime*. The outcome is ironical, but it is also logical, because the critical issue in a revolution is validation. Who does a thing and for what reason can make all the difference in the morality of an act, although the result may seem no different to an outsider.

A further irony is seen in the coalescence of extremists of the right and left. The affinity of reaction and revolution is treated by spokesmen of the center as an ironic confirmation of extremist irrationality, if not expediency, but the affinity is logical, for it is moral. Revolutionaries and reactionaries both agree that things are now more dangerous for virtue than they were.

If one asks what constitutes revolutionary morality, what makes people want revolutions and what they want from them, it is possible to discern certain widely shared, roughly comparable moral impulses. The revolutionary is almost invariably motivated by a vision which juxtaposes the past against the present and the country against the capital.

In the era of the nation-state, revolutions have usually been the result of organized efforts by the provinces to take control of the capital. Urban insurrections may topple governments but usually cannot replace them. Rebellions, primitive rural insurrections, and millennial secessionist movements are efforts by elements in the countryside to escape the city's control. A coup is an all-urban affair, although it may begin in the provinces with forces raised there by dissident generals, as often happened in the Roman Empire, or when insurrections play into the hands of antigovernment conspirators. A corporatist or fascist movement involves an effort by the city to dominate the provincial countryside, to control it in order to exploit it. A revolution, in contrast, is typically an effort by the provinces, conceived of as a largely self-sufficient social system including small-town merchants, peasants, and nonelite intellectuals, to take over and transform the capital. Successful revolutions enlist recruits from the capital, just as fascist movements enlist recruits from the countryside, but the great revolutionary leaders have usually been reared away from major urban centers. Mao was from rural Hunan and never left China until 1949, unlike his deputy Chou En-lai who was educated in cosmopolitan Shanghai and traveled as a student to France. Robespierre was from a small town. Talleyrand was a Parisian. Both Lenin and Stalin were from provincial towns. Gandhi was from the rural frontier region of Gujarat; Nehru was from Allahabad, the premier city of northern India, and was educated from early youth in England. Much of what a revolution means can be traced to the confrontation of the provincial intellectual with the capital's opulence and self-satisfaction: Luther in Rome, Rousseau and Ho Chi Minh in Paris, Hitler in Vienna, Mao in Peking, Lenin in St. Petersburg, Gandhi in London. The revolutionary, from some combination of incapacity and revulsion, cannot join the urbanites; he must beat them.

The sole basis upon which the provinces feel confident of their superiority over the capital is that of virtue. The sole school in which the moral leadership for revolution can be nurtured is provincial life. The provinces, in fact, are always fearful of the city's moral influence; what makes a revolutionary situation is an added sense of power, of the ability to do more than guard oneself and one's community against excessive contamination, the ability to take the offensive and conquer the city by combining with allies from other regions and other classes. The crucial questions for revolution thus become: How do the provinces become aware of their strength, and how do they organize that strength for effective coercion? In certain circumstances the awareness may come spontaneously, from a hastily arranged meeting of people who suddenly realize there are others who share their feelings. In other circumstances, it may result from systematic propagandizing by committed devotees.

The capacity of the provinces to organize for the purpose of coercing the city presupposes some degree of dependence and some degree of independence; it requires some degree of educated indigenous leadership unintimidated by the city's world and a sense of the potential value of participating in the larger political community — a feeling that the city is worth conquering. The provinces learn to care about the city when their traditional leaders — the landlords — disappear or are discredited and can no longer defend the countryside from, or sell the countryside to, the city. In cases where a landlord class has not existed to provide a connecting link, the incorporation of previously self-sufficient areas into the city's cultural and economic sphere produces a similar result. The countryside learns to cope with the city when the city's system of education is opened to it.

The United States is unusual in that the countryside became aware of its strength and mounted a successful revolution before cities had even come into existence on American soil. Americans were forewarned; they knew enough at second hand about the cities of Europe. The provincial capitals of Boston and Philadelphia led the American provinces in opposing the influence of London. It was because America's traditional democracy was essentially agrarian rather than essentially of the city, as in Athens and Rome, that it was able to survive a vast expansion in size and complexity; American democracy was post-revolutionary before it became traditional. The provinces were firmly organized to handle the city when it emerged. Attacks of the organized countryside on the incipient immorality of the American city were mounted periodically, with easy success: the Jacksonian seizure of power and the Prohibition movement were events which would have required another revolution to achieve in most other countries. In the United States, from the beginning the city was taught that it must be prepared to be punished as a condition of its survival. In the Civil War, the national government acted as the agent of the countryside in imposing moral reform on the South. The abolitionist was preeminently a representative of the moral world view of the small town. The capitalist of the northern city was willing to be led. Since the Civil War, the city has grown powerful, and has at times dominated, but the countryside still feels that it is possible to utilize institutions of the national government to pursue moral reforms.

When things are getting better in some fashion for some people the quality of a society's life will be changed in a way which may seem to other people to be destructive of important values. Signs of progress heralded by optimists from the city seem to a revolutionary — as to a reactionary — only to make true virtue more difficult, to tighten the grip on society of a sinister, debilitating prosperity. If the Roman Church had announced a new record in income from the sale of indulgences, Martin Luther would not have been favorably impressed. The British in India did announce gains in Indian exports, which Indians feared as signs of creeping parasitism, devoid of value to India and Indians because the manufacture and shipping of India's exports were in British hands. To hail such announcements appreciatively, observed Lokamanya Tilak in 1897, would be equivalent to "decorating another's wife."[13]

The eighteenth century was a period of rapid economic growth in England and France. In both countries this was destabilizing. New wealth was introduced into society, tripping off anxieties about its control. Bernard Bailyn has shown the crucial role played by such a preoccupation in the background of the American Revolution.[14] He suggests the extent to which the American Revolution was an English revolution, fought in terms of issues originally formulated in England to protest the course of development that English government seemed to be taking.

As Bailyn points out, the American Revolution was fostered by the force of circumstances in a new land where much needed to be done and by the ideas of opposition elements—left and right—in English political life. The colonies had retained the archaic notion of local interest representation which had been supplanted in England by the new concept of virtual representation, of Parliament as a body governing in the interest of the entire nation, rather than an assemblage of representatives of competing localities. The waning of local representation in England had contributed to an increase in corruption, as members of Parliament were free from constituent pressure, free to sell themselves as they chose. The colonies retained the old system with its greater stress on local control and autonomy, and at the same time developed a standard of public honesty not attained in England for another century. Where vested interests were few, the purpose of government could be portrayed as the provision of vital public services rather than the maintenance of lords and royalty in their accustomed dignity. Americans thus responded sympathetically to the arguments of disaffected Englishmen who had denounced the growing wealth, corruption, and tyranny of eighteenth century England.

Things were thought to be getting rapidly worse in England as money flowed from the hands of Walpole and then George III to subvert parliamentary liberty. While the colonists required ever-increasing services from government to provide public facilities in a new land, the current structure of government seemed to be strengthening only its capacity for extortion. The American Revolution was thus, like the French Revolution, initially conceived as an effort to accomplish new purposes and save old values. The advantages of a new society are hypothetical until realized; the ideals of reaction have a much more powerful appeal. It is not surprising, then, that persons who are purely reactionary in intent should provide the intellectual weapons for revolution; the Viscount Bolingbroke and the Baron de Montesquieu are improbable, but legitimate, parents of the American and French Revolutions.

A revolution is ordinarily first nurtured by reactionaries. Reaction is always potentially revolutionary, and is the antithesis of conservatism. What Lord Melbourne said about a gentleman's religion — that every gentleman held the same opinions about religion, but that no gentleman would express them — could be said equally of the political philosophy of the true conservative. The true conservative realizes that articulating his philosophy will undermine his position. If he is a politician, therefore, he will, whatever his party, confine himself to routinized utterances. If he is a philosopher he will probably dwell on the preferability of undirected change. He will presume the desirability and functionality of apparent abuses and anomalies, while avoiding a too detailed discussion thereof which might place an embarrassing strain on credulity by conveying an impression either of obtuseness or of special pleading. The reactionary is restrained by no such scruples. On the contrary, the reactionary is plagued by a terrifying clarity of vision, a vision of "fearful symmetry." He feels compelled to speak with searing logic whenever he perceives disparities between presumption and practice, regardless of the effect on personal relations or intellectual propriety. In the process he may develop revolutionary ideas as he gropes for ways to dispose of the conventional pieties of the day. Jonathan Swift was a classic reactionary: sarcastic, accurate, cruelly rational. No one could have been more bitingly critical of current political practice in eighteenth century Europe than the Christian pessimist Swift. The puzzling disparities in the writings of Machiavelli can also be explained as an exemplification of the kinship of reaction and revolution. Machiavelli wrote in his *Discourses* as a classical revolutionary, yearning for the return of primitive democracy; in *The Prince*, however, he wrote as a reactionary. He reacted against medieval Christian literature dealing with the good prince, taking as a model the conventional pious tract and turning it inside out; the good prince, says Machiavelli, is a bad prince. Only later was *raison d'état* presented in its own terms as a positive doctrine. The reactionary rejects contemporary values but fails to make a positive statement of his position which might be capable of appealing to those who are comfortable with convention. Reaction has no program and seeks no converts; it can only serve to draw the disaffected more closely together. Satire is its finest expression.

As Machiavelli anticipated Hobbes, so did Bernard de Mandeville anticipate the shift of thinking positively articulated by Adam Smith and Jeremy Bentham in a negative, reactionary formulation in his *Fable of the Bees*. Taking for granted the terminology of his conventional antagonists, he argued that vice was better than virtue because vice stimulated industry and commerce. He preferred, he said, a prosperous corruption to the tedious virtue of Sparta, with its iron money. Later, the same argument was phrased in the attractive jargon of free enterprise and individual initiative, but Mandeville failed to make his preference —and insight—sound like anything more than perversity.

The reactionary is a person whose contribution may be larger and more original than he himself can guess. He is content to employ the language of paradox and the politics of harassment, defying the disapproval of conventional men. India's most flamboyant opponent of social reform, Lokamanya Tilak, seemed to most liberals to be pandering to the worst forms of orthodoxy and gratuitously drumming up opposition to the most beneficial and innocuous of reforms, such as those concerned with health measures to prevent plague and smallpox. Tilak performed a major service to Indian nationalism by arousing pride in India's past and suspicion of British intentions, but he was unable to transcend the ambiguity of his position, to present himself to his antagonists in any more positive light than that of troublemaker. He could defy and arouse, bait and irritate, in the usual reactionary manner, but produced the usual result of seeming to be irresponsible and perverse. Placing the smallpox vaccination in context—depicting it as the jewel on the head of a snake—required Gandhi's synthesizing genius.

Almost all the ideas and agitational methods subsequently employed by Gandhi were first suggested by reactionary extremists such as Tilak. The limitation of the extremist technique was that it was impossible to weld it into a coherent program of action. Energies were aroused, but not directed. The extremists were rebels with a cause but without a program. There was a restless, haphazard quality in their activities. They performed an invaluable service by daring to do and say the unthinkable. They spoke of self-government and experimented with boycotts. Tilak specialized in the veiled threat, skirting the edge of legality, keeping the British guessing by ambiguous oracular utterances. He was consciously enigmatic; he was not eager to help the British convict him of treason. He moved opportunistically from point to point, exploiting whatever resources came to hand for embarrassing the British. He preached sermons on Hindu religious texts and defended himself in British courts with a virtuosic exploitation of legalistic technicalities. Tilak claimed innocence of sedition on technical legal grounds, unlike Gandhi whose invariable plea of guilty challenged the very basis of the legal structure Tilak sought to exploit to his advantage. Tilak's fellow reactionary Veer Savarkar significantly explained his intention to study law in England by noting that "The study of law shows the vital points in the system of Government and accurate base where to strike at an advantage."[15]

The reactionary takes his challenge and terms of reference from the dominant pieties of his age. His opponents suggest his direction. Savarkar, for example, while studying the uses of British law, was suddenly prompted to devote eighteen months to the composition of his influential reinterpretation of what Englishmen called the Great Indian Mutiny, which Savarkar designated *The First Indian War of Independence*, by the commemorative activities in honor of British "heroes and martyrs of the Mutiny" conducted in London in 1907; Savarkar wanted to prove that the Indians, not the British, were the true martyrs of 1857.[16]

A reactionary's strength is his willingness to do anything; his weakness stems from the fact that, taking his cue from his enemies, his direction is uncertain, and the relative significance of his many methods of opposing undefined. Typically, the exact nature of the connection, if any, which Tilak, Savarkar, Sri Aurobindo, and Sister Nivedita had with the assassinations and bombings which broke out sporadically in India in the early years of the twentieth century is hard to determine because it was kept intentionally ambiguous. When the Chapekar brothers murdered the hated Plague Commissioner Rand in Poona in 1897, Tilak wrote an article defending in abstract terms the occasional justness of killing in a virtuous cause, drawing his text from the *Gita* and his nominal inspiration from Shivaji's killing of his opponent Afzul Khan. A similarly indirect endorsement followed the bomb explosion which killed two English women in 1908. Whether or not Tilak had a more direct link to the assassins has been as impossible for historians to prove as it was for British judges at the time. Tilak's normal technique was to cause the British as much anxiety as possible by leaving his real intentions unspecified. He sought the role of Nemesis, terrifying but elusive.

As Gandhi's political tactics were drawn from those of political reactionaries — the extremists — so were his philosophical concepts modified versions of ideas first elaborated by philosophical reactionaries. Nineteenth century Indian reformers had argued that Indian civilization *could become* as good as that of the West; Indian expropriationists argued that Indian civilization *had once been* as good. The philosophical reactionaries disparaged such a competition as demeaning, arguing that Indian civilization had always been different, and superior. Why ape or expropriate the accomplishments of the West? Why not make a direct claim of superiority for Indian civilization on its own merits? Why was Western rationality considered an absolute value? Was it defensible to rank civilizations on the basis of their material wealth? Wealth might be vulgar, science mean and trivial in contrast to the profundity of spirit of Eastern philosophy.

Rabindranath Tagore, who often expressed his anti-Victorian ideas in an eminently Victorian way, was the greatest of India's philosophical reactionaries. Tagore's answer to the positive statement of the superiority of Western material civilization was an assertion that spirit is more important than matter. The official British valuations had become the reverse of those against which Mandeville had reacted. Material progress, wealth, unfettered individualism, all the things which had seemed so corrupting in Mandeville's day, were now presumed to be the true gauge of moral health. Tagore, however, depicted the triumphs of Western materialism as a dehumanizing tyranny which India would be wise to ignore:

> The teaching and example of the West have entirely run counter to what we think was given to India to accomplish. In the West the national machinery of commerce and politics turns out neatly compressed bales of humanity which have their use and high market value; but they are bound in iron hoops . . . [in contrast] here is India . . . This is the remote portion of humanity, childlike in its manner, with the wisdom of the old.

Tagore concludes his essay on "Nationalism in the West" with the following peroration:

> And we . . . whose heads have been bowed to the dust, will know that this dust is more sacred than the bricks which build the pride of power. For their dust is fertile of life, and of beauty and worship . . . And we can still cherish the hope, that, when power becomes ashamed to occupy its throne and it is ready to make way for love, when the morning comes for cleansing the blood-stained steps of the Nation along the high road of humanity, we shall be called upon to bring our own vessel of sacred water—the water of worship—to sweeten the history of man into purity, and with its sprinkling make the trampled dust of the centuries blessed with fruitfulness.[17]

Turning Western valuations on their heads, Tagore depicted the source of Western pride as an evil, and the Western proof of Indian inadequacy as a proof of her actual superiority.

Such a commitment lay behind the magnificent artistic creativity of Tagore. As a philosophy for average men, it could easily degenerate into sterile escapism, a comforting excuse for inaction. If Indians were already so much better than Westerners, why bestir oneself? The argument on behalf of India's greater spirituality also served to attract to India's cause Westerners who were reacting just as unimaginatively to Western materialism. Admiring the East because of its presumed immunity to Westernization, they were able to gratify their own distaste for aspects of their own civilization and to indulge in a type of condescending admiration for a sensitive East which they could mother but which they were hopeful would never grow up into a distasteful Western crassness.

It is illuminating to compare Tagore with another poet-artist who stood on the borderline of reaction and revolution — William Blake. Blake despised the conventional conservative wisdom of his day — the aesthetics of "Sir Joshua & his Gang of Cunning Hired Knaves," the religion of the Church of England, and the politics of Burke.

> I wander thro' each charter'd street,
> Near where the charter'd Thames does flow,
> And mark in every face I meet
> Marks of weakness, marks of woe.
>
> In every cry of every Man,
> In every infant's cry of fear,
> In every voice, in every ban,
> The mind-forg'd manacles I hear.
>
> How the Chimney sweeper's cry
> Every black'ning Church appalls;
> And the hapless Soldier's sigh
> Runs in blood down Palace walls.

Blake also grew to despise the progressive forces of his time — Deism, Science, Industrialization, and Rationality as exemplified by Voltaire, Locke, and Newton.

> I turn my eyes to the Schools & Universities of Europe
> And there behold the Loom of Locke, whose Woof rages dire,
> Wash'd by the Waterwheels of Newton: black the cloth
> In heavy wreathes folds over every Nation.

Blake devised a myth of an heroic past, and depicted all the advances that his own age was most proud of as pollution, destruction, confinement, death. These were mind-forg'd manacles; Newton, exegete of the Book of Revelations, was himself Anti-Christ. Blake cast himself in the role of prophet of a new age in which England would become again the home of spontaneity and beauty — the Jerusalem of his imagining. "Rouse up, O Young Men of the New Age!" he exhorted, "set your foreheads against the ignorant Hirelings! For we have Hirelings in the Camp, the Court & the University, who would, if they could, for ever depress Mental & prolong Corporeal War." This, however, was the dream of a poet and prophet — majestic but powerless to be born outside the realm of artistic vision; not simply reaction, but neither the stuff of political revolution.[18]

The line which separates the reactionary from the revolutionary is thin. They share common values and differ only in the extent to which they have dealt with the practical aspects of relating their desires to modern ideological and organizational necessities. Even that highly forward-looking and scientific revolutionary Frederick Engels admitted that the best revolutionary is often a good reactionary. In his book *The Peasant War in Germany* Engels explains his great admiration for the "budding revolutionary spirit" of the radical sixteenth century evangelist Thomas Münzer. Münzer's "programme demanded the immediate establishment of the kingdom of God, the prophesied millennium," Engels notes, "by restoring the Church to its original status and abolishing all the institutions that conflicted with this allegedly early-Christian, but, in fact, very much novel church."[19]

Reaction takes a necessary step backward from politics-as-usual but remains trapped by the logic of the situation against which it reacts. Modern political revolution transforms the instincts of reaction into a positive statement designed to recreate old values in an institutional setting which it is recognized must be new. Modern society in all its complexity is not repudiated in the name of an idyllic utopia. New, complex institutions are devised to guarantee old-fashioned virutes in the new context. The prototype of the modern political revolutionary ideologue, Rousseau, began by rejecting the refinement of civilization in the name of an idealized past simplicity, and ended by projecting into the future the hope that what had once been natural might be artificially restored through institutions. Gandhi followed a parallel course rejecting Western civilization as Rousseau rejected eighteenth century refinement, and then going beyond reaction to the statement of a positive program to establish the old virtues in terms of the realities of contemporary politics.

Social Effects of Revolution

Revolutions aim at the creation of new societies and result in a redistribution of society's spoils. Some stand to gain more than others, some feel the success of the revolution will be so disastrous to their prospects that they are prepared to leave the country; every revolution produces émigrés. The new order presumes a new uniformity reinforced by new allegiances, because revolution is first and foremost a moral and intellectual affair. And yet, if a revolution is going to happen anyway, some people will start figuring out how to take advantage of it, for the true bourgeois mentality can live with the status quo, just as it can live, or will try to live, even in Communist China, with revolution. A revolutionary may find backers to fund him, but it would be difficult for investors to create a revolutionary to order. The bourgeoisie invest in revolution as they would in anything else, spreading risk and covering all options by backing all promising political movements.

Some recent accounts have shifted from an emphasis on the bourgeoisie as a revolutionary class to an emphasis on the role of another class—the peasantry. While the revolutionary leadership associated with the bourgeoisie is depicted as a vehicle of the bourgeoisie, however, the revolutionary leadership associated with the peasantry is usually depicted as autonomous and exploitative. In neither case is this an accurate picture of the nature of revolution as a social force. Class interest is as inadequate an explanation of bourgeois participation in a revolution as is the hunger for land for rural participation. An anarchic rural upheaval may have relatively clear-cut causes, as is true of an urban strike; the kind of sustained commitment evidenced in a revolution, however, requires a moral vision and organization which can only be supplied by indigenous leaders. In a revolution, the specific class interests of rich peasants in securing the title to their land is usually merged in a broader social movement of the entire countryside.

Those who have argued that peasants play a crucial, yet limited and negative, role have called peasants the "swing factor" in revolutions, and indeed in the day-to-day politics of predominantly rural societies. Unable to take command themselves and interested only in preserving their own position on the land, they can nonetheless, it has been argued, make or break governments and revolutions. This argument tends to coincide with an exaggerated impression of the social uniformity of rural life, identified with a class of peasants, who may be large and small but who are still at least as much like one another as a small potato is like a large potato. Even where a relative equality of social conditions exists in a rural society, there is likely to be a fairly complex social system, including religious figures, moneylenders, merchants, schoolteachers, and so forth. Within the agricultural sector itself—and this is especially true of the densely settled rural areas of Asia—there is usually an intricate social hierarchy, ranging from rich peasants through sharecroppers to landless laborers. The countryside as a social system contains much more than peasants, and "the peasantry" includes people with divergent status and interests.

The class interest of rich peasants may figure prominently in a revolution. A revolution, although couched in terms of equality for all, usually involves the devolution of power only one step, from the aristocracy to the bourgeoisie in the city, from landlord to rich peasant on the land. The rich peasants, like the bourgeoisie, are in a position to reap the most immediate material rewards of revolution. A revolution, however, not being born of material interests, is not bound by them. Rich peasants who have sought material advantage through participation in revolution may find that the revolution has passed over and beyond them, as Barrington Moore argues.[20] But the provinces include a wider social range with wider economic interests than those of a single class of rich peasants, and in this wider sense the countryside contributes leadership and legitimacy to revolution, as well as specific class grievances. The revolution belongs to the countryside, whatever direction it may take.

Postrevolutionary societies dominated by the countryside—such as the United States—combine intense energy with intense conservatism, enormous talent for political organization, coalition, and compromise with great moral rigidity. This pattern permits considerable ease of social mobility within accepted channels, but it also means that the full weight of organized majority hostility will be directed against unacceptable groups. The treatment of the Irish by the seventeenth century English Puritans, for example, or of black Americans and Indians in the United States clearly reflects the problem of post-revolutionary exclusion. The background of social feeling which lay behind these actions was not created by revolution, but the revolution in destroying the mediating institutions of the old regime made it necessary to confront long-evaded issues. The revolution's mandate of universality forces it to confront the reality of incompatibility.

In a successful revolution a nation is born anew in a state of holy innocence. Legitimacy ends and begins; no subsequent act need or can be justified on anterior grounds. The fact of revolution is a self-sufficient act of creation. The revolution's agents are unanswerable to any law higher than revolutionary necessity. All extant rights, foreign and domestic, are subject to challenge. The manner in which America has followed its Manifest Destiny across America and more recently across the world is unparallelled except by the course taken by other postrevolutionary societies — for example republican France and Soviet Russia.

Purity begins at home; the revolutionary society cannot be a beacon for humanity if it harbors every variety of person, good and bad. Enemies of the revolution cannot be tolerated; they must be expelled, or at least neutralized, dispossessed, and disenfranchised. The process, of course, is not as pure as its justification. Revolutionaries, reluctant to disown their own rhetoric, and equally reluctant to offer every specimen who calls himself a man the rights they have claimed as the due of all mankind, disqualify unacceptable groups by presuming them to be enemies of the revolution — by deciding that they ought to be, or probably secretly already are, enemies of the revolution. Traitors have no rights merely as men and are expected to demonstrate their innocence if they wish to escape the wrath of the just. Americans helped to justify the exclusion of black Americans from postrevolutionary social rights by the argument that they had probably been pro-Tory. Indians have expressed parallel suspicions about the loyalty of Indian Muslims. Following every revolution there are some born traitors; some have treachery thrust upon them.

Whether groups who sit out the revolution become disadvantaged minorities within the new state, or elect or are forced into exile, or manage to salvage a state for themselves depends upon accidents of foreign intervention and geography. Many revolutions produce groups who suffer variously all of these fates. Those who are submerged or exiled may suffer greatly and remain problem minorities at home or in their country of exile, but their problems are largely their own, not initially those of the newly established revolutionary state. For the revolutionaries, such minorities are sources of profit and plunder. The formation of salvaged societies, in contrast, means the persistence for many years of serious military and political problems. A hostile adjacent state is created by the division of what may have been a natural geographic unit, making the defense of artificial boundaries necessary; moreover, the bitterness of displaced exiles, the intensity resulting from the division of friends and families puts the relations between two such states in a special category. The common memory of having participated in the larger political community of the past may encourage on both sides a yearning to set back the clock by incorporating the one state into the other. The result is often a series of wars which are ideologically unlimited, no matter how localized or stalemated they may prove to be. At least a generation is required before totalistic perspectives wane; divergent evolution, suspicion, and animosity may never disappear.

The main factors determining whether a salvaged society can be formed are the geographic concentration of loyalists and the role played by external powers. Canada contained a variety of groups hostile to the American Revolution for different reasons and offered a commodious new home for exiles from the United States. Taiwan provided a convenient — if less commodious — place of exile for the Nationalist Chinese, having been under Japanese control until 1945, and therefore isolated from the revolution on the mainland. Protestant Northern Ireland was a logical nucleus for the division of Ireland on Protestant-Catholic lines. Contiguous areas of India with Muslim majorities initially proved a viable basis for the state of Pakistan. Many of South Vietnam's difficulties have stemmed from the lack of such a contiguous area of consolidated control; throughout South Vietnam areas exist which have long been under the control of Communist revolutionaries. Germany and Korea were divided following foreign conquests rather than as an outgrowth of the dynamic of indigenous revolution, although "revolutions from above" were subsequently sponsored in the Communist-controlled halves of these two formerly unified areas. Whether or not these divisions are irreversible is still an open question and depends upon the success of the officially-sponsored revolutions.

States salvaged from the path of revolution show a distinctive course of development traceable to the manner in which they were founded. This outcome has been well demonstrated in the case of Canada.[21] Typically such societies have difficulty establishing unity because the diverse groups within the society have little in common except accidental proximity and antagonism to the dominant revolutionary force. Anomalies, bizarre social fossils, may also survive out of the mainstream in a postrevolutionary society, but in a salvaged society they are likely to be much more prominent. On Taiwan a full structure of government is maintained as if the Nationalist regime still controlled all of mainland China, with representatives in the legislature nominally representing the different regions of the Communist-controlled mainland. In Canada ethnic communities of all descriptions—including the dominant British—have remained much closer to their country of origin and less assimilated to a positive national identity than in the United States. Pakistan had an advantage in having Islam as an organizing principle, but even this bond proved in the end a frail link between two areas so disparate and distant as East and West Pakistan, and the Islamic nation finally became two nations when revolutionary nationalism led to the creation of Bangladesh in what had been East Pakistan. Significantly, princely states retained their autonomy much longer in Pakistan than in India, where they were almost instantly swept away.[22] South Vietnam has also found it difficult to develop a positive national identity, given the division of the population among Buddhist, Catholic, and Confucian faiths, and given the fact that most of its leaders have been refugees from North Vietnam. The southern regime with its largely northern personnel sits on top of an assemblage of internally cohesive minority groups who have common enemies but few common goals.

America, South Asia, China, and Vietnam illustrate clearly the contrasting patterns of development in societies partitioned into revolutionary and salvaged segments. There are in addition several partly comparable international situations, for example the division of areas of the old Ottoman Empire into the modern states of Turkey and Greece, and the establishment of Israel as a postrevolutionary state and the consequent transformation of Jordan into a partially salvaged society. In these two cases, as to a lesser degree with India-Pakistan, the pure type of revolution-stimulated change verges on a situation of competing nationalisms; opposition to revolutionary nationalism is focused around a competing nationalism rather than a simple preference for the *ancien régime*. The relative intensity of the two nationalisms, however, has left Jordan and Greece with more characteristics of salvaged societies, Israel and Turkey with more characteristics of postrevolutionary societies.

Foreign sponsorship has usually been available to salvaged societies. This support may come from the defeated colonial power—Britain in the case of Canada, Northern Ireland, and Pakistan—or from other interested world powers. An accessibility to outside aid, whether or not it actually materializes, is a critical aspect of the strategic geography of a salvaged society. The American West was loyal but boxed in. India's large Muslim-ruled princely state of Hyderabad flirted with ideas of independence or alliance with Pakistan, but its geographic location, landlocked and surrounded by Indian territory, doomed it to inclusion within India.

Groups who are unable to escape during the course of a revolution ordinarily have little luck in defying revolutionary orthodoxy in subsequent years. The ultimate fate of plundered, exploited minorities in postrevolutionary societies is still an open question, as in the United States, for example, with reference to black Americans.

The plight of black Americans is sometimes viewed, not as the heritage of a revolution, but as the future cause of one. Black Americans are thus sometimes referred to as a "colonial nation," and black activism is compared to nationalist revolution in India and elsewhere. The parallel between Gandhi and Martin Luther King, Jr., strikes many people as particularly apt; King acknowledged his debt to Gandhi, patterned his agitational techniques upon Gandhi's, and ultimately met like Gandhi a martyr's death. Alexis de Tocqueville, moreover, once predicted that "If America ever undergoes great revolutions, they will be produced by the presence of Negroes on its soil."[23] Recent events seem to suggest that the black revolution, following the lead of India and colonial nations, will soon occur.

The position of the black community does bear many similarities to that of a colonial nation. Blacks were fitted into an exploitatively maintained social structure, in much the way that Indians were fitted into the structure of British India. Inoperative platitudes about prospects for advancement forestalled recognition of the closed nature of the society, by concerned whites no less than by blacks.

The parallel between Gandhi and King is, however, limited. King's debt to Gandhi was in the realm of tactics rather than of strategy. Both employed the tactics of nonviolent confrontation to demand that formal promises long since made be fulfilled. In Gandhi's case the promise was for the termination of British rule; keeping the promise entailed the dismemberment of one society and the construction of another. In King's case what was promised was presumably available in the society as it then existed.

King understood his mission as Gandhi understood his in South Africa: to agitate for full acceptance by the existing society. Gandhi actually suggested a parallel between the situation of Indians in South Africa and of blacks in America. In America, Gandhi noted, "a man like Booker T. Washington who has received the best Western education, is a Christian of high character and has fully assimilated Western civilization, was not considered fit for admission to the court of President Roosevelt."[21] Gandhi claimed that Indians were fit for admission to South African white society. While his efforts were valuable in arousing Indian self-respect, little lasting improvement resulted, and Gandhi moved on to India, where the situation was ripe for a much more radical movement. King's movement seems to have been valuable in a similarly limited sphere, being more successful in stirring black pride than in altering white conduct.

The courses taken by the Indian Muslim and Untouchable communities in their dealings with the Indian majority pose the alternatives confronting black Americans. These alternative routes were determined in great measure by the supreme leaders of these two communities, Dr. B. R. Ambedkar and Mohammed Ali Jinnah. Dr. Ambedkar bears a greater resemblance to Martin Luther King, Jr., in many respects than does Gandhi. Ambedkar was a highly educated leader of a highly depressed community, a scholarly man who earned a Ph.D. from Columbia University. He remained outside of the Congress party, wary and critical of Gandhi, but still hopeful about the future of Untouchables within India. He agreed to become law member of the Nehru cabinet, and guided the drafting of India's constitution, which gave legal equality to all. Only after independence, toward the end of his life, did he dissociate himself from the government. He, like King, had a dream that legal promises might be made into social reality, that Untouchables might find a place in Indian society. He, like King, founded a distinctive, religiously-oriented protest movement, whose prospects remained inconclusive at the time of his death.

Jinnah, by contrast, achieved the ultimate goal of separate national independence for the Muslim minority in British India. The Muslim community, like the American black community today, was divided between city and country. Its leadership was urban and presumed to speak for the voiceless rural sections of the community without bothering to organize them—although the Muslim League did eventually accomplish this task in a hasty and tardy fashion. The urban leadership in both the Muslim and black communities at first dissociated themselves from direct, violent outbursts of resentment by the less educated sections of the community, such as the Muslim Mopla uprising, but later attempted to use such occurrences by identifying with the violent sections of the community, as in Jinnah's willingness to play with fire in issuing a call for "Direct Action" to strengthen his hand in the final bargaining for partition. Jinnah's remarkable achievement in actually carving out a separate Muslim state might not have been accomplished, however, had he attempted it in a stable polity. He was able to capitalize upon the uncertainty attendant upon Britain's departure to create a sense of urgency and opportunity. This situation permitted him at the last moment to bring the diverse sections of his community together and gave him strategic leverage in a moment of transition, securing the partition of the country from the retreating British elite.

It is conceivable that black separatists might similarly succeed in partitioning the United States. The establishment of a separate black nation on American soil is logically no more impossible than was the creation of a separate Muslim nation on Indian soil. A black nation, however, would have to be established by the much more difficult process of secession, unlike Pakistan where partition came with a change of regime. A more likely prospect might be the emergence of a black state within the American union, on the model of the Indian state of Punjab, which was recently divided to create a region in which Sikhs would have a clear majority. This would serve most of the purposes of the black separatists without making revolution or civil war inevitable.

Whether enough blacks will unite behind a separatist movement is still not clear. Unanimity would not be necessary—many Muslims opposed partition of India, as many Sikhs opposed division of Punjab. If a sufficient number—perhaps not even a majority—want a separate state there is no power which can prevent them from securing it—as Gandhi observed with reference to the Muslim demand for Pakistan. Victimized by one revolution, black Americans are still undecided whether another revolution will be necessary to set matters right. It is possible, however, that most black Americans will remain interested in some form of membership in American society. There is even a chance that the majority community can ultimately be persuaded to take black advances in stride.

Whatever may be the institutional implications of the contemporary black movement, its consequences are certain to be revolutionary in a psychological sense. Political revolutions are major events; radical movements advocating revolution, even if unsuccessful, often have a comparably liberating effect on individuals. Every successful revolution, like every successful business venture, spawns a host of imitators who are loath to focus upon the handicaps or disabilities they possess which may prevent them from becoming an equal success. For this reason successful and even partially successful revolutions tend to become world-historical whether or not they set themselves up consciously as exemplars for the rest of humanity. The American, French, Russian, Chinese, Indian, and Cuban Revolutions have provoked imitative efforts which have rarely succeeded, and which have succeeded—as in Vietnam—only when adapted to local conditions, when the local conditions duplicate the main ingredients which made for success in the first place. The chain of revolutions which spread across Latin America in the years following the American and French Revolutions proved abortive because they were superficial and imitative; so have many of the nationalist revolutions in Africa and Asia which arose in the wake of events in India and China. The plan-fulfilling revolution of Che Guevara in Bolivia failed to find local roots; the self-fulfilling revolutions of Ghana, Nigeria, Burma, and Indonesia, among others, were too hasty and disorganized to produce a unified postrevolutionary society.

A great revolution can nonetheless be usefully analyzed in relation to many nonrevolutionary situations and to the psychological liberation of groups or individuals if the lack of full comparability is understood, because a revolution is an epitome of national experience, as a play can be of human experience. Revolutions usually do not occur; individual lives are usually more inconclusive than tragic, but the lessons are relevant even when the analogy is not complete. When governmental rigidity is combined with national polarization resulting from destabilizing developments in society and economy, and exploited by creative leadership, a revolution may occur, if favored by accidental circumstances. Revolutions may be accompanied by civil war. They may fail. If they succeed, they draw larger and sharper circles around the effective national community, expanding the active citizenry while decisively excluding some groups. Revolutions determine the course of national development for an indefinite period, establishing its myths, shaping its institutional prospects, and exhausting the national capacity for new initiatives. The heightened creativity of a revolutionary era builds, ill or well, for many years to come.

6 Gandhi as a Revolutionary Leader

I said to myself there is no state run by Nero or Mussolini which has not good points about it, but we have to reject the whole once we decide to non-co-operate with the system . . . The beneficent institutions of the British Government are like the fabled snake with a brilliant jewel on its head, but which has fangs full of poison.

Mahatma Gandhi[1]

Origins and Goals

Gandhi arrived in London in 1888 to take up an undirected course of study for the bar. For many months he led an aimless existence, experimenting with diverse books, diets, and time schedules, in a manner somewhat reminiscent of the youthful Mao Tse-tung's rapid fluctuations in career ambitions. In a short space of time in Changsha, Mao signed up for professional training in police work, soap-making, commerce, and teaching, and informally explored other possibilities.[2] Gandhi spent hours walking around London by himself, shifted his lodging numerous times, experimented with elocution, dancing, and violin lessons, and even his discovery of his first vegetarian restaurant was by chance. He accepted any advice offered him and dutifully read any book recommended to him. Toward the end of his years in London he went to call on Mr. Frederick Pincutt for advice. "When I acquainted him with my little stock of reading," Gandhi wrote, "he was, as I could see, rather disappointed." Mr. Pincutt recommended that Gandhi read Kaye and Malleson's *History of the Indian Mutiny* of 1857, and "Lavator's and Shemmelpennick's books on physiognomy." Gandhi was "extremely grateful" for this advice and immediately went out in search of these volumes which he found "scarcely interesting," concluding that "Mr. Pincutt's advice did me very little direct service."[3] Even Gandhi's discovery of the New Testament was something of an accident; he almost abandoned the Bible before he got to the New Testament, finding the Book of Numbers hard going.[4]

Gandhi's youthful acquaintance with Western society was limited to landladies, a curious fringe of vegetarians and religious fellow-travelers of the East, and an occasional interview with a great man, such as Cardinal Manning. He read for and passed his bar examination, but typically he found the social side of his preparation useless. As a candidate for the bar he was expected to take a certain number of meals with his fellow students. "I could not see then, nor have I seen since, how these dinners qualified the students better for the bar." He was a popular dinner companion because he left his quota of wine untouched.[5]

It is not surprising that Gandhi took a cautious approach to the adoption of Western ways, or that he ultimately launched a series of experiments covering the range of issues raised by the contradictions between Western science and the inclusive social conventions of Hinduism. Gandhi knew the West only as a problem to be solved.

Gandhi's method was haphazard but his instinct was not. Gandhi was searching for—and found—a revolutionary ideology amidst the peculiar books he ran across.

Before it has run much of its course a revolution must evolve an ideology. Ideologies do not always exist before the outbreak of revolutions. The existence of conscious purpose is a major distinguishing mark of the plan-fulfilling revolution, but even self-fulfilling revolutions evolve ideologies in due course. Ideologies extemporized after the fact may prove perfectly serviceable. India's revolution—thanks to Gandhi—had an ideology early in its development.

Revolutionaries frequently borrow their ideas, but they do so in a very distinctive way. Reactionaries permit themselves to be controlled by the ideas against which they react; the traditional expropriationist borrows only what he can ascribe to the past of his own society. Revolutionaries borrow for the future and are not burdened by a desire to attribute the achievements of Western science to a past golden age. Their borrowing has a calculation of its own, and constraints imposed by revolutionary concerns and objectives.

Reactionaries carry their society's inherited precepts to their logical extremes. Revolutionaries often carry precepts borrowed from other

societies to logical, but radically unorthodox, extremes. The opportunities for creative distortion often inhere in marginal, or even
mediocre, thinkers of foreign societies, or marginal aspects of thinkers
best known in their own countries for other contributions. In a foreign
context conscious hyperbole may not exhaust itself against the expected
wall of deprecation, but plunge forward to unintended consequences.

Borrowing from abroad equips revolutionaries with weapons their
domestic opponents do not possess, weapons which revolutionaries
have the freedom to manipulate as they wish. Revolutionaries respond to ideas they can use, which make sense in terms of problems
which already concern them, and which are capable of adaptation to
meet local requirements. A marginal writer from one culture may develop an entirely unexpected following in another. No prophet is honored in his own country; there he is just another intellectual. A writer
who, because of lack of subtlety or extreme unorthodoxy, has met
ridicule in his own country may well find himself lionized in another.
Shakespeare, Milton, and John Stuart Mill were the favorite authors
of Indians who sought to emulate Victorian Englishmen; the list of
men who fascinated the more innovative subjects of nineteenth century imperialism included such lesser figures as August Comte and
Herbert Spencer. Each of these men preached a doctrine which was
capable of simplification but which was sufficiently embracing to form
the basis of a way of life representing a clear alternative to existing
conditions in subject countries. Each was action-oriented and man-
centered, qualities which appealed to disaffected members of societies
circumscribed by social and religious conventions.

Importation of a theory into an alien context permits the elaboration
of implications which may not seem significant in its original setting,
because they are common to other theories as well, or wrong or exaggerated with reference to the subject to which the theory was originally
applied. A writer may thus be taken as typical of his age and find
ascribed to his "system" values he shares with others and himself
takes for granted. This explains much of the appeal of Herbert Spencer
in places as remote as China and Latin America, where he was taken
as representative of certain values typical of Western civilization as
a whole, and consequently associated with values quite different from
those associated with his name in England and America, where he
was known for what was unique in his writings, not what was typical.[6]
Marx is the classic example of a writer who was wrong in many par-

ticulars with reference to the societies he analyzed—wrong in his analysis of both Western and Eastern societies—but who provided material which could be applied in different arrangements by others with revolutionary results. Marxism has been successful when imaginatively applied to the specific problems of individual societies; where Marxists have been "faithful" they have failed.

Marxism makes it possible to find scapegoats, to lament an idealized past, and to look confidently to a certain future whose main contours are known. The traditional society offers the glamour of luxurious handicrafts, the pathos of the irreversibly doomed, and the fascination of evil personified by the exploiting class which patronized the handicrafts industries. The capitalist class supplies a dynamic villain, the proletariat an exploited orphan finally coming into his just inheritance. Insofar as a Marxist interpretation is made realistic as well as dramatic, is intelligently related to the dramatic material at hand, it may prove a malleable revolutionary ideology.

Marxism, unimaginatively applied by those more impressed by its irreverence than by its relevance, may supply only the inspiration for reaction, arguments by which one may expose bland pieties cloaking ruthless exploitation, mouthed by parasites who profit from the maintenance of the status quo. Marxism, so long as it supplies only the thrill of tough talk, will not transcend the categories of its opponents. Matching the violence of exploitation with the violence of liberation is simply reactionary. Without a positive vision within which violence is only an incidental element, if it persists at all, Marxism will do nothing more than gratify the disgruntled. In India, where Marxism remained the preserve of such literalists, Gandhi and Ruskin led the way.

Gandhi was dining in a vegetarian restaurant one evening in South Africa when a young man named Polak introduced himself. They chatted; several days later Mr. Polak "came to see me off at the station, and left me with a book to read during the journey, which he said I was sure to like. It was Ruskin's *Unto This Last.*" Gandhi found the book "impossible to lay aside . . . I determined to change my life in accordance with the ideals of the book." It was "the one [book] that brought about an instantaneous and practical transformation in my life." Why? As Gandhi put it, "I believe that I discovered some of my deepest convictions reflected in this great book of Ruskin, and that is why it so captured me and made me transform my life."[7]

When he first encountered Ruskin, Gandhi was already a mature man successfully launched on a radical career. Decisive intellectual events of the type Gandhi describes occur when a book crystallizes speculations of one's own, though the book itself may be addressed to a totally unrelated subject. Such moments are not the result of an author's genius or a reader's susceptibility, but of a meeting of two minds, both active, both with special preoccupations of their own.

Ruskin's *Unto This Last* is a plea for an appreciation of the social value of sentiment. Ruskin attacks the "scientific" approach of political economists, and urges that nothing can ever be solved so long as everyone is only pursuing his own selfish interest. Without social affections, he suggests, society would simply fly apart, with employers and employees at one another's throats.

Ruskin advocates a socialism of the heart, a society in which all work will be considered holy, and every occupation a vocation, that of the laborer no less than that of the priest. A laborer would then be paid as are priests, regularly and with a generous assumption that he will always do the best he can, being motivated to serve, not simply to earn.

The socialism of the heart does not require a leveling of social ranks. Affection in fact may flow most freely between persons of divergent stations. Ruskin proposes as a suitable model for factory relations the relations between a master and his devoted domestic servants. The employer should certainly feel a strong bond of obligation to his employees, and, like a ship's captain, suffer with his men in the storms of economic depression. He should, as a servant of society, be content with a decent salary and a sense of fulfillment in ministering to the material needs of his fellow men, but the making holy of all callings would not make ranks and degree any less relevant. Leaders would be crucial, for "if we once can get a sufficient quantity of honesty in our captains, the organization of labour is easy, and will develop itself without quarrel or difficulty; but if we cannot get honesty in our captains, the organization of labour is for evermore impossible."[8]

The purpose of life, Ruskin insists, is not competition, but service. A luxurious life enjoyed at the expense of others would be empty, a simple life of service full. Ruskin, like Thoreau, eulogizes rustic pleasures and derides the sophisticated man's servitude to his material desires.

Some readers of Ruskin might view his argument as an effort to spiritualize the status quo: if employers retain a fondness for simple pleasures and treat their employees like family retainers, all will be well. Gandhi, however, took Ruskin literally. He was indifferent to the ease with which Victorian readers could interpret Ruskin's homilies in self-serving ways. His own eyes were on Indian society, where the application of these ideas would have a quite different effect. They were attractive in that they resonated with the ancient Hindu ideal of a society in which every individual was genuinely dependent upon others for the performance of essential services, and in which the welfare of all was dependent upon the virtue of the ruler. Ruskin's ideas were also potentially revolutionary in that what was required to overturn British rule in India was the unification of Indians among themselves. The spiritual bond which Ruskin saw as saving English society from disintegration, Gandhi saw as uniting Indian society in such a way as to make British rule superfluous. Ruskin's scorn for luxury, innocuous enough in an English context, formed for Gandhi the basis for an attack on the economic foundations of British rule. Ruskin developed his theories to neutralize a sinister selfishness; Gandhi employed them to overturn a political order. The religion of simplicity, and the spiritualization of the lowliest callings, was intended in England to help the humblest tolerate their lot. In India, Gandhi made it an argument for Indians to do without the services of the mighty.

One day, putting Ruskin into practice, Gandhi broke the law by picking up a bit of salt. He dramatized the act by announcing his intention well in advance, and then walking the 241 miles to the sea, taking almost a month—from March 12 to April 6, 1930—to arrive, allowing public excitement to gather momentum in anticipation, and permitting thousands to join the march along the way. By focusing on British taxation and monopolization of the manufacture of salt Gandhi threw British rule into the worst possible light; far from being a servant of India, British rule was a parasite on the backs of the poor. By taking natural salt from the seashore Gandhi emphasized that Indians were being prevented by law from reaping the bounty of nature. Gandhi sought to demonstrate that Indians could be happy because they were human beings, that they did not have to wait for happiness until their country had been fully developed by foreigners. Gandhi was making a declaration of economic independence, defying the need for industrial conditions for English withdrawal, just as he defied the relevance of educational and political conditions. Englishmen made and sold Indians salt and called that economic development. Englishmen sold Indians machine-made cloth from Manchester and called that progress. Gandhi refused to consider "development" healthy when it served the interests of an alien rule.

When Gandhi advocated village autonomy, he meant in the first instance every village, but he also thought of India itself as a village which must be autonomous from the city of London and its trading outposts clutching India's coast. Indians who had tied their fortunes to British rule were only facilitating the country's despoliation: "Little do they know that their miserable comfort represents the brokerage they get for the work they do for the foreign exploiter, that the profits and the brokerage are sucked from the masses. Little do they realize that the Government established by law in British India is carried on for this exploitation of the masses."[9]

Machinery was to be resisted as long as it remained in the control of the exploiting classes. "Today machinery merely helps a few to ride on the back of millions. The impetus behind it all is not the philanthropy to save labour, but greed."[10] The good society free of exploitation which Gandhi envisioned was comparable to that envisioned by Marx in which the machine serves man, not man the machine. In their idealized humanism and emphasis on the power of the machine, both Marx and Gandhi were eminently Victorian. Accepting the Victorian view that machinery had the power to transform social relations, they went beyond the prevailing Victorian self-satisfaction to premise the beneficence of machinery upon a requisite social transformation. Without such a revolution, machinery could only intensify the exploitation and inequalities of the preindustrial age. Put in its place, as a servant of human convenience, machinery was welcome. Gandhi once offered a ride in a car to a man who inquired how an exponent of the simple life could justify using such a contraption. Smiling, Gandhi said to his guest, "If you don't like it, you can get out."[11]

Until a social transformation had occurred which could guarantee its socially advantageous utilization, India's development would have to be stopped at its source. Smooth rails to facilitate movement should be shunned until it was clear that good, not evil, would be riding the rails. Before one gratefully accepted beneficent institutions, one would have to be certain that they were not simply palliatives designed to reconcile one to permanent servility. One should not be taken in by the British promise to alleviate sufferings caused by their advances, after the fact. The British intruder offered temptations and exemption from the traditional cost of indulgence. Being victimized was to be both pleasureful and painless. "Doctors induce us to indulge," Gandhi argued in *Hind Swaraj*. Under British rule, "Hospitals are institutions for propagating sin. Men take less care of their bodies and immorality increases." Western medicine stood ready to drug Indians into a stupor-like indifference to the agony of exploitation by Western capitalists by promising exemption from nature's admonitory retribution for over-indulgence. Under present conditions, doctors, like lawyers, were a sinister influence because British rule made it profitable for them to encourage Indians to yield to their passions. A person who sought to ease the anguish of India's transition to the bottom of the Western heap was like a man piously offering to sell pills to the victims of a plague he has knowingly brought himself. The proper goal of a doctor in a justly ordered society would be to forestall profitable diseases by helping the individual strengthen himself, just as the proper goal for a lawyer would be to forestall litigation by reconciling antagonists. This would involve Ruskinian service and sharing, not an exploitative brokerage.

Gandhi opposed the spread of Western civilization under the auspices of the unequal partnership which made a mockery of the pretense of mutual benefit in an unfettered relationship of free trade. Civilization's emissaries brought fire-water to the American Indian, and rum to Africa to barter for slaves, and opium to China, where Englishmen fought valiantly for the rights of Chinese citizens to buy opium which the Chinese government sought to restrict. Civilization, once ensconced in India, licensed and taxed the production and sale of liquor to Indians. Gandhi advocated prohibition because he saw in government promotion of the liquor traffic an effort to enhance government revenues by corrupting the morals of their subjects. Abstention from alcohol was seen as an act of self-restraint at once morally edifying and politically effective against British intentions.

Gandhi tied together the personal and the national, the ethical and the political, the emotional and the rational, the physical and the spiritual into a coherent world view. The individual Indian learned to connect his personal anxieties with national humiliation, his personal solutions with national hope. Every Indian could defy the British and be a better man for having done so. Alcoholic beverages, devices for controlling births artificially, and the presence of British administrators were concessions to weakness, admissions of inadequacy. India's development under the auspices of British science and British civilization meant deracination, assimilation, and incorporation. Gandhi persuaded Indians that this meant as well devitalization, the loss of virility and integrity, and that every Indian must strengthen himself before India could be strong. Gandhi sought to free individuals from a dread-filled distance from their natural selves. Once freed, an individual's embarrassing habit might become an unmatchable strength. Gandhi sought to free individuals from a dread-filled distance from one another; once freed, their common strength would make British rule superfluous. If Indians pulled themselves together, they could pull out of the British imperial system.

Revolutions are rooted in the commitment of individuals to embark on a new life. In Dostoevski's *The Possessed* the anarchist conspirator Shatov attempts to turn his small band of idealistic followers into disciplined revolutionary cadres by implicating them in a murder. They would then presumably be freed from ordinary moral inhibitions and unable to back out because they would be treated as ordinary criminals in an unreconstructed society. Communist discipline in certain areas has developed a similar technique, in which the test of a guerrilla's emancipation is the performance of an assigned task in his home district, or against friends or relatives, demonstrating an irrevocable commitment to his new comrades and a new order of society which has not yet been brought into existence. The old Indian society kept Indians apart by making them contemptuous of the occupations of others. Indians could not work together while handicapped by deference and disdain. Social solidarity required social familiarity, as well as trust and respect reinforced by the experience of shared labor. Gandhi made Ruskin the basis of a revolutionary conversion experience for Indians by interpreting Ruskin's belief in the equality of all professions to mean logically the interchangeability of all professions. Instead of exhorting Brahmans to treat latrine sweepers like equals, Gandhi gave the Brahman a broom and told him to sweep. There was an irreversibility about doing what one had always been taught to avoid, whether this meant committing a murder or sweeping a latrine. A public act set one apart from family and friends and from the entire apparatus of habit and reflex, just as one's inhibitions were made up of perhaps equal proportions of internalized dread of wrong-doing and anxiety about incurring the disapproval of others.

In sending the Brahman nationalist Pundalik off to Sabarmati Ashram, Gandhi informed him that it would be good preparation for a possible jail sentence, since "you will get all the experience of jail routine at Sabarmati." Training for the rigors of a prison schedule was one reason for the uncompromising regularity of the *ashram* schedule. More significantly, Gandhi's stress on punctuality was directed at a cultural trait typical of a status-conscious society in which a person's importance is reflected in the liberty he can take with other people's time.

On arrival at the *ashram*, Pundalik was assigned to cleaning latrines.

I went to my room and sad thoughts came to my mind. "Oh! that patriotism should have brought this scavenger's work to me . . . How can they assign such menial work to a person who was sent to Gandhiji's *ashram* by a noted and respected patriot like Gangadharrao Despande? . . .

Four or five days later, while I was accompanying Gandhiji on his evening walk, he asked me, "Well, what work are you doing nowadays?" I looked down and answered, "Latrine cleaning." He replied, "That is your great good fortune!" I did not even utter a single syllable to indicate my agreement with him, but he continued, "What valuable service our brothers the scavengers are rendering to society! And society treats them as untouchables. If the work is dirty or involves unsanitary conditions, we must introduce improvements in it."

"Oh! That must be done," I blurted out, "and how long must I continue to do it?"

"Not very long, just one lifetime," he replied . . .

After another four or five days, Gandhiji asked me of his own accord, "Well, how are you getting along with your work?"

"It is all right now. I don't mind the bad smell so much now and also do not have such a feeling of disgust."

When the evening walk was over that night and we were about to part, Gandhiji said, "Change your work tomorrow. You must get experience for some other kind of work."[12]

Style

Gandhi's influence on his immediate followers as well as on Indians as a whole was such that it is conventional to speak of Gandhi as an example of modern charismatic leadership. Gandhi's unique style, his passionately devoted entourage, and his remarkable mass appeal all correspond to the common impression. The idea of a modern charismatic leader would, however, have been considered almost a contradiction in terms by Max Weber, who first expounded the concept of charismatic leadership. Weber's charismatic leader was typically a phenomenon of the distant past, in the present scarcely more than an anachronism. Current usage has long since inflated the concept, because something obviously connects the phenomenon of which Weber spoke and developments in the contemporary world.

Weber sought to distinguish three opposing types of actions — rational, traditional, and charismatic. Weber assumed that mankind was moving in the direction of ever greater rationality and away from "prerationalistic periods [when] tradition and charisma between them have almost exhausted the whole of the orientation of action." In prerationalistic periods, Weber acknowledged that "charisma is the greatest revolutionary force . . . Charisma . . . may involve a subjective or internal reorientation born out of suffering, conflicts, or enthusiasm. It may then result in a radical alteration of the central system of attitudes toward the different problems and structures of the 'world.'" Weber, however, contrasted revolution through charisma unfavorably with revolution through reason, which "works from without by altering the situations of action, and hence, its problems finally in this way changing men's attitudes toward them; or it intellectualizes the individual." Weber used the concept of rationality in both an institutional and an individual sense; a society might become rational through an orderly arrangement of its functions as an individual might become rational through an orderly analysis of his situation. Charisma, however, was prerational, incompatible with social or intellectual order. Emotions were an interruption of, not the subject matter of, rationality. As man evolved, he would become a more abstract, nonemotional being in a functionally-specific society. Revolution through charisma, which had its origins in emotion, was held to be capable of disrupting traditional societies but incapable of producing a rational society. Rational elements could only be introduced after the fact, through routinization.[13]

By describing charisma as specifically antitraditional as well as prerational, Weber hoped to devise a conception of charisma which was value-free and free of particularistic traditions. His definition stressed the unmediated personal authority of the charismatic individual which was thought to be self-sufficient, hostile to received forms. Weber concentrated his attention on the supposedly insulated internal dimensions of charismatic movements, stressing the leader's capacity, as a result of intangible personal qualities, to inspire selfless devotion in his immediate circle. And yet every cultural tradition instills certain expectations about the nature of a genuine leader which facilitate the process of recognition of the person who excels in this traditionally understood manner. In this sense, all charisma must be routinized before it is charismatic. Long before Muhammad the Arabs had come to place a high valuation on oral poetry; Muhammad's mastery of this traditional accomplishment served as proof of his divine mission to his Arab followers. In a parallel fashion, Mao Tse-tung's poetry, written in the classic Chinese tradition, serves to legitimate his claim to be the authentic voice of modern China.

Significantly, in neither the Islamic nor the Chinese tradition was there a special association between asceticism and capacity for leadership. In India this association was made and related to an ancient tradition which held that the conservation of sexual energies increased spiritual power. What might seem eccentricity in another culture was here related in a concrete and logical fashion to the requirements for leadership. Through fasting and sexual restraint, Gandhi was meeting minimal conditions for leadership.

As a boy Gandhi once refused to eat mangoes as a way of punishing his mother, who knew of his fondness for the fruit. As a national leader Gandhi engaged in fasts for a variety of purposes, at times as an act of penance and self-purification, at others to induce his associates to accept his viewpoint. Gandhi's refusal of his mother's mangoes was a childish act. A fast performed for selfish reasons is not likely to impress anyone—even a mother—as admirable, and a fast directed against an implacable antagonist is unlikely to succeed in bringing about a change of heart. As a leader Gandhi fasted only in carefully defined circumstances.

The accomplishment of Gandhi's leadership lay in such rational modifications of tradition. He redeployed and applied to new ends the traditionally acknowledged resources of leadership. As an entrepreneur would, Gandhi amassed his reserves, winning followers and wide respect by meeting the criteria of conventional prowess, and then steadily and creatively applied these resources to new purposes. Fasting, sexual abstinence, vows of silence, retreats for meditation to the holy *ashram* were all familiar enough, but not in their Gandhian incarnation. Normally associated with self-cultivation, with the individual's quest for personal spiritual power, they were transformed by Gandhi into techniques for social action.

An illustration of the pointedness with which this was done is contained in the autobiography of Pundalik. Pundalik was assigned by Gandhi to work among the villagers of Champaran, to follow up Gandhi's campaign there in 1917. He tried to apply some of Gandhi's techniques, and at one stage decided to undertake a fast against hookah-smoking among the villagers. When he wrote Gandhi an account of the affair, he received a detailed critique of the entire operation, which suggests much of the planning which Gandhi devoted to his own efforts. As Pundalik summarized them, Gandhi's criticisms were:

(a) This *satyagraha* dealt with a problem much beyond the scope of the field of my service. It should have been confined to the boys and girls in the school;

(b) Notice of the *satyagraha* was not given to the villagers in a proper manner, and so two or three days were wasted;

(c) That I went repeatedly to the window to see if anybody from the village was coming for a compromise proposal showed that I had not the true spirit of *satyagraha*;

(d) The final compromise was arrived at in too great a hurry.[14]

Pundalik had not understood the careful calculations and long preparations which underlay Gandhi's fasts. Only when fasting seems a rational act, is performed by a man of stature, and is directed against those under an obligation of sympathy is it likely to prove successful.

Charismatic leadership, as exemplified by Gandhi, was rooted in tradition and motivated by rationality. The qualities which Weber tried to set at odds become meaningful only when related to one another. According to Weber's isolated definition, a charismatic leader is anyone who is viewed as one; the "signs" of charisma—ability to perform miracles, the appearance of a special superhuman authority—are unrelated to social needs and superficially similar in the charlatan self-seeker and the genuine idealist. For this reason, Weber's definition is inadequate to a full understanding of the potential importance of charismatic leadership. If a charismatic leader is anyone who is thought by some group to be one, to ask whether or not a person is a charismatic leader becomes a secondary issue. The crucial question is: What makes charismatic authority more than a historical diversion? What, in the nature of the leader, what, in the nature of his followers, what, in the nature of the cultural and historical context, combine to make charismatic authority a decisive factor in furthering social change?

An individual is recognized as potentially a charismatic leader largely because of his mastery of a traditional idiom of greatness. He becomes a modern charismatic leader if in addition he has an ability to focus upon and solve successfully basic social problems. By fulfilling traditional expectations he is in a position to go beyond them. Gandhi broke laws, defied customs, ignored family claims in ways which confirmed rather than compromised his claim to a traditionally recognized status. Disruption led to a new synthesis by a person who had inter-

nalized the old and understood which of its external manifestations
could be discarded.

Gandhi's charisma reflected a widespread popular recognition of the
radical rationality of what he proposed. When what he proposed did
not seem rational, Gandhi's charisma sagged badly. On the heels of
a successful agrarian agitation in Gujarat in 1917, Gandhi returned to
the same district to recruit troops for the British war effort. In doing
so, Gandhi was motivated by a sense of personal obligation to keep
his word to British authorities and was not responding to a genuine
Indian need. "I used to walk miles in the hot burning sun in order
to collect recruits and make an impression on the people about the
urgency of it. But I could not." In the small village of Navagam,
recounted Indulal Yajnik, where the "hardy peasants . . . had stood
up bravely against the threats of forfeiture of their lands . . . not a
soul would stir out, even to pay his respects to the Great Mahatma . . . And Mr. Gandhi and Mr. Patel had the mortifying consolation
of sitting on the outskirts of the village for about three days, and living
on food which they cooked themselves without evoking the slightest
response to their appeal for recruitment." "You will see, therefore,"
Gandhi concluded, "that my influence, great as it may appear to outsiders, is strictly limited. I may have considerable influence to conduct
a campaign for the redress of popular grievances because people are
ready and need a helper. But I have no influence to direct people's
energy in a channel in which they have no interest."[15]

A charismatic innovator does not invent problems; he suggests solutions. The materials exist; creativity lies in synthesis. All greatly creative
thinkers are, paradoxically, accused of lack of originality out of envy
but more significantly in indirect tribute to the profoundness of their
achievement. A fundamental insight seems so self-evidently true that
one is struck with a sense of having heard it before. It ties together
so succinctly the loose ends existing in one's own mind that, not being
aware of having been coerced into accepting the validity of a compelling
idea, one may have an insecure sense of uneasiness that one's gullibility
is being played upon to pay a high price in praise for an insight which
one already possessed. A self-evident truth seizes minds which are
ready for it. One is incredulous that so total a solution could have
so completely eluded discovery before. Once embarrassment is overcome, a person may be overwhelmed by the sheer relevance of what
has been said—by awe acknowledging a major rational contribution.

Robert Tucker, elaborating upon ideas of Erik Erikson, has described the importance which a rational response to the anxiety caused by the breakdown of a traditional village society can have. Tucker notes that "The leader who at such a juncture can make national identity meaningful and thereby give the people of his country a sense of belonging to a new and greater community, and who at the same time can help them find their way to a new life-style, a new ritualization of existence, will certainly acquire great charisma in the eyes of very many."[16]

Charisma can thus be intelligently therapeutic in ways which are socially significant. Gandhi, moreover, challenged false complacency as well as responding to anxiety. He sought to aggravate anxiety among those who clung to the status quo by exposing hidden psychological costs. Certain emotions in every member of a society and certain social groups as groups bear a disproportionate burden for the maintenance of any society's value structure. Anglicized Indians bore such a disproportionate burden in British India, as did youth in Confucian China. To preserve the social structure, they were required to suppress certain natural desires; idealizations of the good native and the dutiful son did not always succeed in making them find pleasure in self-denial. A charismatic leader with a revolutionary vision can track down repression and turn this wasted energy in a creative direction.

Weber held that a charismatic leader was one who could inspire worship and induce others to depend upon him by demonstrations of supernatural power. Gandhi commanded the attention of Indians by the power of example, the ability to suggest things — large and small, from chastity to hand spinning — which every Indian could do himself, according to capacity. Most were simple acts which made sense in terms of the personal experience of most Indians and made a difference when most Indians voluntarily performed them.

Gandhi's style exemplified the liberation he urged on others. Gandhi's style in dress, as in speaking and writing, was the plain style of the authentic revolutionary. He was outlandish. He discarded English tophat and spats for peasant dress. He ignored English conventions of elegance and reserve, insisting on painting himself as his fellow-revolutionary Oliver Cromwell insisted that he be painted, with the warts left in.

Gandhi was informal because he was in deadly earnest. He said in his Benares Hindu University speech of February 4, 1916, after Mrs.

Annie Besant had interrupted to say, "Please stop it," that he was only saying out loud what people were saying every day in the privacy of their homes. "I consider that it is much better that we talk these things openly . . . Let us frankly and openly say whatever we want to say to our rulers and face the consequences."[17] It is indeed better for the cause of revolution if the formal rhetoric of public propriety and the irreverent bitterness of the back room are merged into a single reckless public style. A double standard effectively preserves the status quo. It is better to say it "to our rulers and face the consequences" only if an open breach has been decided upon.

Rousseau realized that clothes could make the man if the man made his clothes a sign of his internal condition. Rousseau advised Polish patriots to revive the use of traditional Polish peasant costumes in order to throw off the enslavement of Poland to French culture. A Pole who attempted to keep up with Paris fashions, Rousseau contended, only proclaimed his abasement, his lack of self-reliance, his shame in his own condition, the fate of being a Pole. An Indian who similarly prided himself on the cut of his English clothes would not think it a simple thing to appear in public in the *dhoti* of an Indian peasant. Nor would he think the spinning and weaving of the cloth he wore a trivial task if he did it himself. Gandhi once required that Congress dues be paid in kind, in cloth spun and woven by each individual.

Gandhi's radicalism was reflected in the very fact that he customarily spoke in Indian languages. The English language, like Western clothes, was something most Indians put on with a certain self-consciousness. It was an affair, like eating at the Great Eastern Hotel with forks and knives. Gandhi did the most embarrassing thing in the most embarrassing circumstances when he addressed public meetings in India in the vernacular. Public meetings were a British activity, designed to demontrate Indian capacity to perform in a British idiom, to orate with Gladstonian floridness in English. Gandhi, while sharing a platform with India's great English-language orators, spoke in direct and businesslike Hindi or Gujarati.

Gandhi's style, reflected in these individual gestures, was the expression of an inflexible commitment. In each of his campaigns Gandhi sought to exhaust established channels before resorting to organized protest; his life taken as a whole also reflects a movement from a moderate to an adamant stance. Gandhi began his public career as a reformer in South Africa. Here, the Indian community was a small minority, situated between white Europeans and black Africans. Indians could aspire only to full rights as British subjects in this country to which they came as immigrants. There was never a question of establishing a new form of government; Indians sought only to live in peace with and with the respect of the country's ruling elements. Gandhi's program for improvement thus involved making Indians more acceptable according to the prevailing white norms. The Europeans "argued that the Indians were very dirty and close-fisted . . . Lectures were therefore delivered, debates held, and suggestions made at Congress meetings on subjects such as domestic sanitation, personal hygiene, the necessity of having separate buildings for houses and shops and for well-to-do traders of living in a style befitting their position." Gandhi wished to demonstrate that Indians were full citizens of the society and were not interested in acting "like worms which settle inside wood and eat it up hollow."[18] At its most militant, Gandhi's South African campaign involved the burning of identity cards and mass courting of arrest, but with no object other than the protesting of discrimination and the securing of equal rights in the existing society.

Even in South Africa, however, Gandhi had been only tactically loyal. An underlying purpose of Gandhi's work in South Africa and in India until his final break with the empire in the wake of World War I was an effort to overwhelm the British with loyal service in order to test British willingness to reward even the best-behaved "good boy," as he later described himself in the role of "recruiting sergeant" during World War I. Such a test was necessary to ascertain the inevitability of a revolution to attain the goals he outlined in 1909 in his book *Hind Swaraj*.

The way in which India's services in World War I were rewarded constituted in Gandhi's mind adequate proof of the futility of further loyalty. The rapidity with which Gandhi turned to revolution upon his return to India also reflected the fact that here revolution made sense, here Gandhi's eccentricities could become a national rallying point, rather than grounds for ridicule from those whom Indians were anxious to impress. The Congress in India had itself been a moderate movement, dedicated to securing for Indians their rights as British subjects. Gandhi sensed an incongruity in the fact that the Congress in India — which could claim to speak for an entire nation — conducted itself no differently from the small organization he had put together to advance the welfare of an immigrant minority. Gandhi quickly insisted that the Congress drop some of the tactics he had himself employed in South Africa. There, he had busily sought to promote the Indian cause in Britain, knowing that this was where ultimate decisions were made. In 1920, he insisted that the Indian Congress terminate its ancient practice of propaganda in Great Britain, as a necessary part of revolutionary noncooperation. Older Congressmen pleaded strenuously against this proposal, but "eventually Mr. Gandhi's resolution was passed by an overwhelming majority, to the great chagrin and discomfiture, of course, of our British guests."[19]

In moving from moderation to militance, Gandhi exchanged mediation for partisanship. Early in his career Gandhi had failed as a trial lawyer, and he subsequently rejected advocate proceedings in favor of mediation as the proper role for a lawyer. Gandhi employed the ancient Indian technique of third-party mediation as an effective method of settling disputes and as a role which provided great satisfaction to the mediator in bringing opponents together. Gandhi was concerned about the tendency of partisan proceedings to exacerbate tensions in a country without a tradition of cordial competition, and he found that he could mediate with all his enthusiasm, while the role of legal contestant left him tongue-tied. He had also been impressed with the hazards of partisanship when he visited Poona to publicize his activities in South Africa. He visited both Tilak and Gokhale and discovered that a meeting chaired by one would be boycotted by the followers of the other; they both advised him to request a distinguished neutral, Professor Bhandarkar, to chair his meeting, thereby making it possible for both factions to attend.[20]

Gandhi tried to combine the roles of agitator and mediator either in sequence, or simultaneously if possible. He found, however, that mediation and agitation could not always be successfully combined, and he was ultimately compelled to appeal to others to act as mediators on his behalf. The mediator could not launch a movement, and Gandhi's love of mediation finally had to give way to his greater commitment to innovation.

Tactics

Gandhi embodied revolution, exemplifying the style of a man who had already freed himself. Gandhi also devised the intellectual tools and the agitational techniques which turned his message into a successful revolutionary movement.

Gandhi suggested that citizens of India were needlessly humbling themselves in accepting the status of second-class British subjects. If they would stop trying to be Englishmen, Indians would discover that they were much better at being Indians, and that furthermore Indianness included some remarkably effective tools for social action. Gandhi summed up an Indian technique of struggle in the linked concepts of *Satya* and *Ahimsa*: truth and nonviolence. These concepts formed the nexus of an unmediated inspiration for Indians. No foreign aid was necessary to expound or apply them. When applied, *Satyagraha*, holding fast to the truth, shook the hold on Indians of British rule. *Satyagraha* led ultimately to *Swaraj*—self-government—an old term which Gandhi pointedly defined in both a personal and a national sense. If Indians could control themselves, the British would not control India.

National *Swaraj* would be attained through "noncooperation." The term was less crisp than a variety of fighting words Gandhi might have chosen, but he did not want a fighting word. He avoided the trap of direct confrontation, realizing that it is more potent to ignore than to oppose. Many of his followers thought it peculiar that Gandhi should have insisted on boycotting "foreign cloth" rather than simply "British cloth." The point as they saw it was to oppose the British. The point as Gandhi saw it was to develop Indian self-sufficiency. Gandhi urged Indians to leave British schools, renounce their degrees and titles and career prospects as kept men, and attend the new free universities, where Indians devised their own curricula and bestowed their own degrees. And why should Indians take their disputes to British-sponsored courts when they could settle disputes more quickly and cheaply on their own? In declaring in 1921 that India could be free within a year if noncooperation were practiced with sufficient determination, Gandhi was stressing the fact that independence was not something which Britain could give to India. "Independence Day" was celebrated on January 26, 1930, without the cooperation of the British.

Gandhi's placing of women at the center of his movements typified his method. Women were perhaps the most oppressed class of Indian society; they consequently had developed a capacity for enduring suffering which, if properly employed, could lead to their deliverance. Indian women epitomized the plight of Indians as a whole and exemplified the technique of turning apparent liabilities into assets which Gandhi recommended to Indians as a whole. The British, however, had their own interpretation of what Gandhi was up to in sending defenseless women to attack the burly British. In a letter to the chief secretaries of all provincial governments, dated December 20, 1940, the central government warned that "the next move of Mr. Gandhi may be to employ a large number of women Satyagrahis. If such a move were made, it would clearly be inspired by an unworthy motive, namely to exploit the weaker sex in order to advertise the movement . . . and to excite odium by making the most of the 'harsh' treatment to which the ladies would be exposed by breaking the law." The government, the letter stated, were considering "whether Government should not issue a Communique hinting at the motives referred to above announcing that they would in consequence refrain from arresting ladies who merely uttered the slogans put into their mouths."[21]

An elite is always tempted to see the unorthodoxy of a revolutionary movement as a sign of weakness. It is gratifying to imagine that one's opponent is resorting to unfair expedients because he cannot measure up in the customary competition. Just as individual revolutionaries are often held responsible for unwanted social movements, so hidden motives are often blamed for the actions of revolutionaries. As Henry Kissinger has noted, "The refusal to believe in irreconcilable antagonism is the reverse side of a state of mind to which basic transformations have become inconceivable. Hence, revolutionaries are often given the benefit of every doubt. Even when they lay down a fundamental theoretical challenge, they are thought to be overstating their case for bargaining purposes; they are believed to remain subject to the 'normal' preferences for compromise."[22] The British in India tried to trivialize such a basic challenge. The crank and the revolutionary look the same to those who think only cranks talk of revolution.

The British tried to visualize Gandhi's nonviolent revolution in terms compatible with the preservation of their rule by equating nonviolence with ineffectuality. British responses to Gandhi's ever-changing positions thus often reflected the spirit of a person trying to keep another to the terms of a bet. It was argued that Gandhi had promised to act nonviolently and hence as a result of some putative misstep could be treated as a person who had failed to do what he undertook to dare. "He has always used the language of warfare in describing his mass movements," observed the Viceroy Lord Linlithgow in a telegram to the secretary of state for India. "But this is exactly what the prime exponent of *Ahimsa* has no right to do."[23] Gandhi, however, could not let others define what he meant by his own terminology. Gandhi was not playing games or engaging in ritualized political contests. Gandhi proposed to act "in a spirit of nonviolence," not to perform some prearranged feat of moral acrobatics. Gandhi frequently stated that he would willingly abandon everything except truth and nonviolence. By this he meant that truth and nonviolence would inevitably dictate different actions in different circumstances.

Truth and nonviolence were inseparable. There was no such thing as a violent truth. Gandhi consequently spoke on occasion in an "unrealistic" fashion, expressing hope for conversion of high officials or nonviolent conduct by riotous mobs. Gandhi practiced positive speaking because he believed that truth could not be identified with accuracy, which might be cruel and aggressive. Gandhi would express supreme confidence in the purity of his own motives, the justness of his opponents, and the discipline of his followers before each critical confrontation, thereby suggesting how all ought to act and implying that if they did not act that way, the consequences for all might be very serious. After each crisis Gandhi quickly pointed out the reasons for the failure of all to realize his high hopes. Gandhi's disappointment with himself and others then became an urgent argument for the need to start all over again. During World War I, Gandhi announced, for example, that he "knew" that if India offered "all her able-bodied sons as a sacrifice to the Empire . . . India by this very act would become the most favoured partner in the Empire and racial distinctions would become a thing of the past."[24] This was Gandhi's way of saying that if India's provocatively dutiful sacrifices during World War I were not amply rewarded, he would be compelled to resort to drastic sanctions. A strong man's praise is always challenging; a strong man's disappointment always potent.

While Gandhi frequently engaged in positive speaking, he was not a positive *thinker*. In fact, Gandhi's preference for positive formulations which sound negative—nonkilling, nonviolence—reflected his normally pessimistic expectations; for man to act violently was so predictable that the very idea of *non*violence contained an element of wonder and mysterious power. "We have an ancient proverb," Gandhi wrote in *Hind Swaraj*, "which literally means: 'One negative cures thirty-six diseases.'"

Truth and nonviolence summed up the spirit in which Gandhi examined each new situation; they were the touchstones of a dichotomized world view. Gandhi described the proposed partition of India as not simply ill-advised, but as "an untruth." Because the Congress was nonviolent it was the "most truly democratic organization in the world—not because of its numerical strength, but because its only sanction deliberately adopted is non-violence."[25] The British Indian government, or as Gandhi put it, "the system of Government in vogue here," was nondemocratic and therefore violent.

Any untruth, as a violation of plain speaking about reality, was violent. The orderly, duly constituted proceedings of Lord Hunter's commission appointed to inquire into the Jallianwallah Bagh Massacre of 1919 Gandhi called "official violence . . . by reason of their grievous condonation of these acts."[26] In contrast, he wrote that "Non-violence works in a most mysterious manner. Often a man's actions defy analysis in terms of Non-violence; equally often his actions may wear the appearance of violence when he is absolutely non-violent in the highest sense of the term, and is subsequently found so to be."[27] What appears to be orderly may be violent; what appears to be violent may be nonviolent. In such clear terms Gandhi declared his refusal to be trapped into legalistic definitions of his own terminology.

Truth and nonviolence in fact required compromises with violence and untruth because truth could not be imposed by violence. In the name of truth, Gandhi accepted the errors of others, having once exhausted nonviolent methods of persuading them that they were in error. Gandhi held that a society should embody truth freely accepted by all. Whenever this was unattainable Gandhi endorsed in the name of truth and nonviolence acceptance of violence and falsehood in whatever form would do least harm. His goal was a consensual society animated by positive bonds of sentiment, but this by definition could not be coercively created. Gandhi assumed that society would be held together by force and falsehood until better means had been spontaneously accepted.

Gandhi's nonviolence had much in common with Freudian psychotherapy, as Erik Erikson has observed. Freud held that mental illness could only be conquered by self-knowledge. Therapy could thus work only in the form of a nonviolent struggle through which a doctor hoped that a patient might come to a realization of the nature of his problems and thereby gain the capacity to resolve them himself. Mental illness, furthermore, consisted in being violent to a part of one's nature; Freud taught that mental health consisted in a nonviolent acceptance of the contradictory facets of one's own personality. Gandhi developed for the relations between social groups many of the same insights Freud applied to private relationships and the relationship between different parts of a single personality.[28]

Gandhi's acceptance of contradictions was, however, tactical rather than an end in itself. Gandhi wished not only to relieve tensions but to instill values. Gandhi sought not only self-knowledge, but knowledge of truth. Gandhi was not a therapist, but a partisan.

In the name of nonviolence, Gandhi supported the right of others to do what he thought was wrong. At the same time, Gandhi continually besieged the emotions of even his closest associates. Opinions might change, and might be considered private matters. One's underlying moral disposition, however, was of public importance, for a society could not be healthy if its citizens were not morally strong. Moral strength had public utility, and its cultivation was a public responsibility. A commitment to truth and nonviolence was not a passive quality; nor was it likely to thrive if cultivated in isolation. Exercise was necessary to develop the strength to hold fast to the truth, exercise gained in struggling with oneself and with others. While men were naturally violent, nonviolence might be achieved by determined effort to control and redirect natural impulses. By wrestling with one another, nonviolent warriors might acquire the alertness necessary to keep man's natural inclinations under control.

Gandhi considered the strength generated by a struggle of wills more important than agreement on issues because issues were aspects of the material world, with its confusing, deluding changeability. Combining a Victorian emphasis on the realization of faith in action with the *Gita*'s advocacy of engagement with reality with an indifference to consequences, Gandhi stressed the training of basic moral character, trusting the seasoned warrior to engage in the battles of the moment in whatever way he wished. Figthing in a wrong cause, making mistakes, and experiencing setbacks could be beneficial if done with an indifference to consequences reflecting adherence to a truth beyond consequences. Gandhi's *Gita*-inspired recklessness induced him to tackle anything with a confidence that he could profit from failure, as long as he retained sufficient independence to acknowledge failure. Statesmen who attempt to maintain a façade of infallibility are enslaved by their own past. Gandhi made every mistake a lesson in public morality, and was not afraid to commit, or admit, mistakes. "There is no defeat for Satyagrahis," Gandhi remarked, "till they give up Truth."[29] Without a pure heart, moreover, no victory had value. The British viceroy's skill in repressing his opponents would avail him nothing if he lacked purity of heart. Gandhi's final letter to the departing viceroy Lord Linlithgow, dated September 27, 1943, expressed sorrow that the viceroy had "countenanced untruth."[30] For Gandhi the sorrow—no less than the censure—was genuine; Linlithgow, having countenanced untruth, was the very definition of a defeated man.

Gandhi sought to provoke in every individual an intensification of moral purity, with the confidence that this would result in a spontaneous recognition of the importance of truth in the individual's own life. Within the limits of his methods imposed by the nature of his goals— since truth could not be imposed by force—Gandhi attempted to achieve a revolutionary moral transformation, to make India a nation of disciplined truth-seekers. Through Gandhi's most casual gesture ran an undercurrent of moral assault. Millie Polak was once asked by Gandhi to decide whether her husband should undertake a difficult assignment. "But he would not consent to Henry's going unless I first gave my consent. He did not wish to influence this in any way, but I was to do just what I thought right myself, and he would agree with me, and Henry should agree also! This letter was so characteristic of Mr. Gandhi, because in it he had done as he always did, put the moral obligation for decision upon the other person concerned, but at the same time conveyed a feeling, rather than a direct suggestion, that if one came to a different decision from his one would place oneself in the wrong."[31] Gandhi told others to do what they thought was right and also suggested what he thought was right. Gandhi even dealt with his "political guru" Gokhale in a singularly determined way. Gandhi frequently sought Gokhale's guidance during his struggles in South Africa, but their relationship seems to have been understood by Gandhi as meaning primarily that he should always try to persuade Gokhale that his conduct was correct. When Gokhale succumbed on one occasion to Gandhi's insistence that Gokhale speak in Marathi rather than in English, he said good-naturedly, "You will always have your own way."[32] It was an unusual "guru" who could make such a statement, and an unusual "chela" who could later report this remark with satisfaction.

Gandhi made his demands on others with the expectation that if they had moral grounds for objection, they would be aroused to express them. While it required two wrestlers to have a struggle to develop

moral strength, someone had to start the fight. If Gandhi's attack provoked only acquiescence, this could be taken as evidence that his
demand was not a demand made in his personal capacity, but in his
capacity as a Satyagrahi—one holding fast to truth. Obedience would
then not be personal service, but service of truth. Gandhi could not
have acted so imperiously had he believed he spoke only for himself.
Even a suspicion that weakness might seduce him into an identification
of vanity with truth, a suspicion that he might have been deluded
into demanding personal service for selfish reasons, was enough to
rouse Gandhi to undertake new austerities. Gandhi destroyed letters
which contained "no more than praise for his work," for fear that
he might be led astray by depending for strength upon the admiration
of others. "Truth had to stand on its own strength; and so he had
burnt the letters."[33]

The intensity of the relations Gandhi sought to have with others
nonetheless posed a constant danger of distorted judgment. Despite
his precautions, Gandhi never rid himself of the tendency to treat submission to his requests as a sign that they were not selfishly motivated,
or the tendency to seek confirmation of the rightness of his personal
course in the reflected experience of others. While a consciousness
of violence must precede an effort to transcend it, Gandhi believed
that a person was never too young to start learning to recognize and
control his naturally violent nature. There was already enough evil in
human nature; evil did not need to be cultivated before it was controlled.
Moral strength came from wrestling with violence, not experimenting with it. Gandhi felt that no one would be missing anything by
being taught self-control at an early age. Gandhi's consequent attempt
to regulate the lives of others in their own interest was motivated by
a solicitude stemming from the equation of his personal needs with
the needs of others. Gandhi tolerated differences of opinion, but did
not accept the validity of differing moral orientations. Gandhi actually
put into practice what Rousseau, in *Emile*, had only envisioned. Gandhi
subjected the children in his care to an intensive indoctrination in virtue
to prepare them for the world before they knew it. For Rousseau,
however, the dangers to be guarded against were in the world at large;
for Gandhi, the dangers were already present in the newborn child.

Ironically, Gandhi subjected others to his will while intending only
to accost them as potential equals. Gandhi wrote to N. K. Bose that
he was "amazed at your assumption that my experiment [of sleeping

beside his grandniece to test the purity of their feelings for one another]
implied any assumption of woman's inferiority. She would be, if I
looked upon her with lust with or without her consent . . . My wife
was 'inferior' when she was the instrument of my lust. She ceased
to be that when she lay with me naked as my sister. If she and I
were not lustfully agitated in our minds and bodies, the contact raised
both of us. Should there be difference if it was not my wife, as she
once was, but some other sister?" Gandhi failed to see why others
should have any more difficulty in controlling their emotions than he
had himself and hence did not think of such experiments as unequal
contests which might be harmful to the weaker party. Gandhi invariably
expected too much of others; too much good, and consequently too
much evil from their failure to be as good as he would have wished.
Gandhi reacted to shortcomings in others with the same anxiety with
which he would have greeted a similar shortcoming in himself. Gandhi
characteristically softened his censures of others by confessing that
he had the same trouble. He was all too sincere in thinking that he
was as much a sinner as others and hoping that others might be as
virtuous as he. His generous assumption that others were like himself,
at times a disarming didactic device, at other times inspired a repressive
rejection of innocent desires. Gandhi could be destructive of the
individuality of average persons close to him, who could not reasonably
be expected to fight back with the same moral energy with which he
attacked, and who succumbed to worship or vices worse still. Idealiza-
tion may become a way of avoiding hating what is feared.

Despite these difficulties Gandhi continued with ruthless rigor —
some would say with a compulsiveness which was itself a form of
violence — to help guard those closest to him against their own violent
selves. Violence connoted what Western moralists used to be able to
convey by the concept of sin. Violence was pervasive in the human
condition—even, perhaps especially, in the most intimate relationships, between friends, between parent and child, between
husband and wife. Such relationships subjected one to terrible temptations. Friendship encouraged favoritism, and physical attraction encouraged the selfish imposition of one's desires on others. The only form
of friendship which would not lead to the clouding of judgment was
one between persons of equally high character; then, neither party
would be compelled to choose between honor and kindness. Even
with family members, Gandhi permitted himself only a didactic intimacy

until it was clear that he was dealing with a moral equal—as his wife Kasturba proved to be. "You who are trying to make *Sadhus* of my boys from today!" Kasturba exclaimed.[35]

Sexual love, Gandhi believed, could never transcend the violence of lust any more than beneficent institutions could grow from greed. Marital relations governed by sexual desire, like industrialization under the auspices of capitalism, involved not mutual service, but exploitation. Gandhi's views reflected the intensity of his determination to purify himself, which in turn was rooted in Gandhi's personal and national experience of forms of human relationship which had been permitted to deteriorate to such an extent that they contained much of the violence Gandhi saw as inherent in such relationships. A society which enveloped a young man in a steaming atmosphere of personalism, in which all advancement seemed dependent upon favoritism, naturally encouraged a tendency to feel that entangling emotional alliances would have to be cut completely before an ennobling friendship could develop. A society which by an arranged marriage forced a young man into sexual contact with a person who had no interest for him initially except as a sexual object naturally encouraged the impression that a sexual basis for marriage forestalled the growth of a higher mutuality.

Sex was intrinsically violent, as was preference for one's family; Gandhi did not believe that social conditions would ever alter sufficiently so that marital sex and friendship between unequals might survive purified from the violence which had infected them in the society in which Gandhi grew up. Violence was natural and only by an arduous abstention from violence could one make possible the emergence of a human relationship of an entirely different kind. Such a conviction drove Gandhi to undertake a life of unremitting austerity and made him reluctant to believe that a less austere life for normal people in normal times could ever be wholly satisfactory. A machine or an institution, being neutral, might be given a new direction; human drives were not neutral, were not capable of positive or negative effects in different settings. The reformation of natural instincts could alter the effect of institutions; a mere change in institutions could not alter the effect of natural instincts.

Gandhi did not believe that revolutionary ardor was desirable only so long as it might come in handy to achieve a political object. The heightening of moral intensity which he sought was not seen as simply strategic—necessary until bad social conditions changed. Gandhi believed that heroic effort was always possible and would always be necessary. The compelling intensity which drove Gandhi throughout his life and which provoked complex conversion experiences in others could hardly have been sustained in pursuit of a limited end. It is difficult to develop a revolutionary commitment while acknowledging—even to oneself—that comparable moral exaltation may not always be needed. Revolutionaries may hope that their sacrifices will make the attainment of purity by others easier; they will not imagine that their sacrifices will make purity any less necessary.

And yet, while every revolution seeks a universal solution, it is provoked by a concrete situation which suggests the direction in which the solution is sought. Gandhi, like all revolutionaries, believed in the universality of his particularistic solution, although he also accurately predicted that his "message" for those confronted with other kinds of problems would lie in his manner of tackling problems, rather than in the details of his schemes of reform. Gandhi's abstract awareness that some of his values might some day be dated did not affect the determination with which he propagated them. Gandhi was more generous than most other revolutionary moralists only in his willingness to wait until others accepted his values voluntarily. The ultimate austerity of Gandhi's aspirations was modified by the pragmatic way in which he was willing to pursue them. Though not adopted for circumstances, Gandhi's moral intensity was adapted to circumstances. Gandhi always made it clear that his campaigns for limited political ends—such as mere "parliamentary Swaraj"—were only the most basic training for the final triumph of virtue. The potential for oppression in Gandhi's saintly revolution was, however, minimized by his willingness to let others become saints by installments.

The most difficult test of revolutionary leadership may well concern a leader's relations, not with the mass of the general public, nor with his immediate circle of devotees, but with other political activists and organized interests. A leader may attempt to eliminate potential rivals, or indoctrinate them, thus reflecting anxiety about the outcome of an unfettered competition. Gandhi actively encouraged others to criticize him. When N. K. Bose left Gandhi to protest, among other things, Gandhi's decision to test his continence by sleeping beside his grandniece, Gandhi wrote to Bose: "Of course you are at liberty to discuss the whole of me and my writings with anybody you like. This applies equally to the three letters" concerning Bose's reasons for leaving

Gandhi's service.[36] While Gandhi's leadership was profoundly dismaying to many, Gandhi, by his willingness to consider carefully all objections, achieved substantial success in winning over skeptics whose natural preference was for a different kind of politics. Gandhi's technique was well suited for struggles with strong rivals.

Gandhi succeeded in harnessing leftists by welcoming them and asking of them only a change of heart, not of mind. They in turn saw much that was compatible with their own program in his social reform objectives. Whatever they might think in the abstract about the feasibility of social reform through moral exhortation, Gandhi's method so obviously worked, when employed by Gandhi, that it was difficult to fault him on this score, even if they considered him only an exception to the working of normal social laws. Under the circumstances it was not illogical to oppose almost everything Gandhi stood for and yet follow him.

The radical who gave Gandhi the greatest difficulty was Subhas Bose. Bose describes his first encounter with Gandhi following his patriotic resignation from the Indian Civil Service in 1921 as follows:

> I was ushered into a room covered with Indian carpets. Almost in the centre, facing the door, sat the Mahatma surrounded by some of his closest followers. All were clad in homemade Khadi. As I entered the room, I felt somewhat out of place in my foreign costume and could not help apologizing for it. The Mahatma received me with his characteristic hearty smile and soon put me at ease and the conversation started at once. I desired to obtain a clear understanding of the details—the successive stages—of his plan, leading on step by step to the ultimate seizure of power from the foreign bureaucracy.[37]

Gandhi failed to satisfy Bose on these points, but he knew what to do with him. He sent Bose to C. R. Das and the two became inseparable almost overnight, and Bose was launched on the career which led him ultimately into open conflict with Gandhi and then into armed conflict with Great Britain. For almost twenty years, Gandhi kept Bose within the Congress movement and even in opposition Bose never lost his high esteem for Gandhi's accomplishments.

The conservative was as impressed by Gandhi's efficient management of his resources as was the leftist by his ability to get results. Sardar Patel was probably the greatest of the conservatives who served with Gandhi. In early life Patel was a successful careerist, an arrogantly

Anglicized lawyer and clubman. When Gandhi first spoke at the Ahmedabad club of which Patel was a member, Patel did not bother to interrupt his card game to stroll into the adjoining room to listen. This was not out of indolence; Patel was eminently successful and energetic in his early efforts to press home the logic of British liberalism. Patel at this time had already entered into a notable confrontation with the British authorities in Ahmedabad over the appointment of a less qualified British engineer in preference to better qualified Indians. He was clearly a rising lawyer, moving into public life, determined to make the British practice what they preached. Gandhi's message to Patel was that the successful pursuit of such a policy might humiliate the British and gratify his own vanity, but provided no way out of the impasse.[38]

Gandhi hoped that all groups might join his revolution. But Gandhi also knew who were most likely to join and went after them. Just as he fashioned special appeals for different types of intellectuals, so he sensed the appropriate method of appealing to groups with specific desires or grievances. When Indian groups were in conflict, he sought to mediate; when a conflict had an antigovernment slant, he sought to use it. He championed the cause of laborers on British-owned plantations in Bihar and Ceylon. He urged peasants in Gujarat to withhold rent when the government attempted to collect in a bad season. In appealing to Muslims, he stressed respect for religious traditions. In appealing to untouchables, he stressed the need for reform. Gandhi had a place in his movement for barristers and failed B.A.'s. Marginal men, drifters, those with grievances over just-missed positions in the British hierarchy, school drop-outs were all welcome in Gandhi's movement. Capitalists anticipated benefits from protective tariffs. Middle class intellectuals hoped to move into jobs vacated by Britishers. Many Congressmen of all types thought in terms of deferred gratification for sufferings rendered.

Gandhi's plea for solidarity among Indians in opposing British rule naturally appealed most to those in a position to wield influence in an independent Indian nation and was viewed with suspicion by those who felt that solidarity meant their own incorporation at the bottom of the new social order. Gandhi's good intentions could not obscure the fact that pious Hindus and big businessmen remained, as suggested by the title of G. D. Birla's memoir, *In the Shadow of the Mahatma*. Gandhi was relatively unsuccessful with groups who suspected that their position within British India was more secure than that offered them in a new order: with landlords, princes, untouchables, Anglo-Indians, Sikhs, and Muslims.

Gandhi's success, moreover, was only limited in the regions in which militant nationalism had taken root before Gandhi took control of the Congress. Before Gandhi, most leaders of all-India stature had been men with limited appeal — the moderates. Popular nationalism had been sparked by regional figures in Bengal, Maharashtra, and Punjab. Gandhi's emergence coincided with the ascendance of the Indian heartland, where Gandhi was the first militant leader to establish himself. In the regions where militant nationalism had already got underway under other leaders, Gandhi was resented by many who felt cheated of rightful leadership and who were skeptical of Gandhi's strategy.

Through it all, Gandhi never gave in. His indifference to consequences left him unshaken when he was denounced and sober when he triumphed. Shortly after his return to India in 1915, he had remarked that he was "not very much worried about securing a large following. That will come in due course. But I do anticipate that a time may come when my large following may throw me overboard . . . and it may be that I shall almost be turned out on the streets and have to beg for a piece of bread from door to door."[39]

Gandhi made this prediction to Indulal Yajnik, an ardent young nationalist who attached himself to Gandhi shortly after his return from South Africa. Yajnik at this time was trying to make Gandhi into the fiery national savior he felt India needed. Gandhi, Yajnik hoped, would pick up the sword and sweep the British into the sea, by pressing every advantage and exploiting every weakness. Yajnik followed Gandhi loyally through the turmoil of the years 1916–1922, and served as his cellmate and secretary during their imprisonment from 1922 to 1924. Then, Gandhi picked up, not the sword, but the spinning wheel. Yajnik, the rational young radical, denounced Gandhi as a counter-revolutionary, and composed a long, bitter, intimate book entitled *Gandhi As I Know Him*. The years of loyal service had turned sour. Gandhi's former cellmate now advertised the irritation he had felt at Gandhi's habit of clattering around the cobblestone prison courtyard in wooden sandals. In subsequent years, Yajnik devoted himself to praising violent nationalism and organizing the peasantry, inspired by Ireland's agrarian struggles. In 1942, he denounced the Quit India movement, fearing that it would harm Britain's war effort, and thus also Britain's ally, socialist Russia. In 1943, Yajnik at last decided that Gandhi had been right all along, and dedicated the rest of his life to Gandhian service. As soon as Gandhi was released from prison, Yajnik went to him to report that his twenty-year rebellion had ended. He came to Gandhi on a day when Gandhi was observing a vow of silence. When Gandhi noticed Yajnik sitting quietly in the crowd, he scribbled out a note. "How many changes will you make in your life?" it read. "As many as I have made?"[40]

Gandhi and the Quit India Movement

Gandhi's confessional style, reflected in his note to Indulal Yajnik as well as in his *Autobiography*, has misled many people into concluding that Gandhi was compulsive or unsure of himself. Actually Gandhi's continual deflation of himself and inflation of others was possible only because of an indomitable confidence that he was acting in the name of a higher dispensation. Gandhi portrayed himself as a struggling pilgrim to help others just beginning to walk.

Gandhi's hortatory praise of British officials has similarly misled many people into concluding he was ambivalent toward or dependent upon generous British officials. In fact, Gandhi portrayed himself as a slave of officials to force his way into their consciences. Gandhi's technique called for a change of heart on the part of those in authority who might be brought to a willing acceptance of the justice of the demands made upon them. This did not mean, however, that Gandhi's technique could work only against unusually disinterested gentlemen. In the Quit India movement, Gandhi had to contend with a government which disliked and misunderstood him, and which made strenuous efforts to destroy his influence and defeat his purposes. Gandhi's refusal to abandon his emphasis on the possibility of a change of heart by even the most incorrigible imperialist did not stem from a conviction that such a change of heart was likely. Gandhi's stance was assumed with the hope of avoiding unnecessary bitterness, giving the vanquished a chance to escape by suggesting those elements in their own perspective which might make retreat seem a generous act. Finding scapegoats cannot alter structures; plaguing individuals unnecessarily is a sign of weakness. Gandhi realized that even the most evil of men cherish their self-respect, and that a defeated man does not enjoy feeling defeated. Gandhi's final accomplishment was his success in making his victims look like heroes. Gandhi did not begrudge the British an opportunity to find self-justification in defeat. The British were permitted to withdraw to compose their memoirs.

It is also often thought that Gandhi was not only dependent upon the generosity of his opponents, but also considerate of their convenience, that Gandhi opposed authority only in ineffectual ways designed to touch the heart but leave the sinner free to continue his affairs until such time as his change of heart had occurred. This too ignores the firmness of Gandhi's technique. Gandhi stayed his hand, not out of concern for his opponent's convenience, but to avoid a premature confrontation. Gandhi's restraint was meant for those in his own movement because the revolution he intended would not succeed with the removal of the imperial regime if the masses were not yet ready to take command.

In the Quit India movement, Gandhi did not stay his hand. The restraint he exercised was strategic, to build the movement's momentum. The young radicals spearheaded by Subhas Bose were ready for a final showdown even before war with Germany was officially declared in September 1939. A struggle with the British government of India inaugurated at this time would, however, have been a factional affair launched in defiance of the inclinations of many congressmen and would, incidentally, have fallen into the government's trap, laid in anticipation of a premature assault. By 1942 Gandhi had pulled together the generations split in 1939. When he now adopted the course advocated earlier by youthful radicals, he did so with confidence that he had demonstrated its inevitability by exhausting other routes. Gandhi then watched grimly as mass fury toppled the pillars on which the regime rested. The movement, Gandhi had concluded, was as ready as it would ever be. The British were then no longer the accidental beneficiaries of Gandhi's restraint.

The Quit India movement is often called the low point of Gandhi's career as a revolutionary leader. Gandhi, it is said, attempted to launch a movement only to be arrested. And Gandhi "countenanced violence" in a momentary abandonment of his own principles. The events of the war years are consequently often passed over in polite silence by Gandhian chroniclers. In reality, Gandhi's personal removal from the scene and his conditional acquiescence in violence suggest the reasons for considering this crisis Gandhi's toughest test. Gandhi's technique is best observed, not under laboratory or hothouse conditions, but in circumstances in which everything seems to militate against any chance of success. The climax of Gandhi's career was the achievement which made him dispensable. With a united movement ready to do or die, ready to accept responsibility and take initiatives — if necessary, by violence — Gandhi's physical removal from the scene only intensified the determination of others to act for themselves.

Gandhi neither asked nor gave favors. Gandhi's technique of struggle presupposed nothing more than a common humanity. Gandhi required no preconditions because he expected no easy victory. Dying might well be good for the cause. Anarchy might well presage a purified resurgence. Gandhi presumed only that the import of heroism could not be ultimately suppressed. As a nonviolent revolutionary, Gandhi was intent on revolution, by nonviolence if possible, by violence if necessary and possible. He disdained violence as a blunt weapon, ill-suited to accomplish the social transformation which alone justified revolution. But he did not shun violence when the revolution was ready and the regime was not.

Quit India:

Official Violence

Lord Linlithgow announced on September 3, 1939, that India had decided to go to the defense of the Poles. "Confronted with the demand that she should accept the dictation of foreign power in relation to her own subjects, Poland has elected to stand firm," noted the viceroy. In Poland the principles of international justice and morality were at war with "the law of the jungle . . . Nowhere do these great principles mean more than in India."[1]

When a government decides that it is necessary to defend liberty in some very remote corner of the world—as Poland seemed in Indian eyes—it must presume upon a reservoir of trust. Linlithgow made this presumption in 1939. The slowness with which the war began would have allowed time for building a preparedness for commitment, a concern which kept the United States leadership on the sidelines until after Pearl Harbor. This was not done by the British Indian administration, despite the existence of popular Indian ministries in the different provinces which had been exercising substantial powers for over two years and which might have been readily consulted. Three hundred million Indians were told they were at war by an official appointed by a foreign government.

The British viceroy was not acting in ignorance of the likely response; the Congress had frequently stated in previous months opposition to Indian involvement in an "imperialist" war. The viceroy knew that consulations would be frustrating and might end in deadlock. The viceroy acted with the knowledge that he would arouse widespread opposition but in the hope that, once the decision had been announced, some opponents could be roped in and the remainder isolated. The tedious process of waiting for public commitment to build up brought the United States into the war with substantial unity; the efficient use of surprise by the British viceroy got the war effort off on the wrong foot and led to a confrontation which crippled the war effort and paralyzed the government. Several weeks after the declaration of war, the provincial Congress ministries resigned in protest; the Indian nation was officially at war, and its largest organized political body was united in opposition to the nation's war effort. In the midst of war, the stage had been set for total war between a government and a mass-based political party.

At the outbreak of war, British officials in India shared the determination of their countrymen elsewhere to make England's response to the Axis challenge her finest hour. Englishmen were convinced that the decision whether or not India should go to war was too elemental to make contingent upon discussion. The press was soon full of war news, and war advertisements. The British, officials and nonofficials, had all swung into the routine of voluntary service in the war effort with an instinctive sense of national solidarity. Domestic news was shoved off the front page, and pictures of smiling British soldiers replaced the faces of Indian politicians.

The times required heroism, risk, and sacrifice. British officials were in a mood for heroism, after decades of strain, defiance, and bickering. Throughout their official lives they had known nothing but retreat, the "melancholy, long, withdrawing roar" of the system to which they had devoted their careers. The war emergency seemed to provide a mandate as well as an opportunity to regain the initiative, to return to the masterly mold of their predecessors. The resignations of the Congress ministries were viewed hopefully, as opening up new opportunities for the government at a time when bold initiatives would be easy to justify.

The central government in particular welcomed the new challenge as an opportunity to reassert their control over policy formulation. With India faced with an external threat, All-India coordination took on a new urgency, and the central government quickly resumed some of the powers which had devolved to the provinces. In recent decades, the role of the central government had been steadily shrinking. First under British administrators acting alone, then after the Montagu-Chelmsford reforms under British administrators acting in collaboration with Indian politicians, the provinces had developed a self-confident autonomy. Fully immersed in the complexities of provincial affairs, local officials had increasingly come to treat policy directives from Simla with benign indifference. The type of "coordination" which the central government attempted seemed characterized by a rarefied irrelevance. Whatever general principles might be communicated "did not apply" to the unique situation in any one province, as perceived by the men on the spot. Some governors even neglected central requests for information on local matters which the center considered necessary for the formulation of All-India policy. The central government knew the way they were viewed, but now felt that strong central leadership would be accepted as essential.

The war emergency was recognized as perhaps the last opportunity the government would have to make bold provision for the future course of Indian politics. The British Indian government were eager to seize this last chance to affect India's future development by decisively arresting the drift of events which appeared to make the Congress the inevitable beneficiary of British withdrawal.

In 1931, Gandhi had had difficulty persuading his followers that he had not gone too far in entering into the Gandhi-Irwin pact. Lord Irwin had similar difficulties, "as most European officials thought he had given Mr. Gandhi unnecessary rope," in the words of Sir Arthur Lothian. Sir Arthur, in retrospect, however, "doubted whether Lord Willingdon would have recovered the ground he did unless Lord Irwin had first gone to the limit of human patience in dealing with Mr. Gandhi's intransigence."[2] The stiffening of the government's position under Willingdon and Linlithgow from 1932 to 1937 had been temporarily reversed by the introduction of provincial autonomy under the Government of India Act of 1935, whose passage served as a warning sign to British Indian officials of changing opinion at home. The reforms approved by Parliament in 1935 permitted the Congress to gain real political power through electoral victories in a number of provinces, which placed them in power from 1937 to 1939. The declaration of war, and Congress' resignation of office in protest to it, provided the Indian government with a welcome opportunity to return to the offensive in a final attempt to stem the Congress tide.

The increased democratization of India had been settled as an issue of British domestic politics during the debates leading to the approval of the Government of India Act of 1935. The imperial die-hards, led by Winston Churchill, had been defeated within their own Conservative party, and the failure of their efforts to arouse popular opposition to retreat was acknowledged by the die-hards themselves. The popular Congress ministries of 1937-1939 were the result of the British Parliament's decision, and a national Congress government appeared to be the logical beneficiary of complete democratization.

The accident of war took the Congress out of power and brought Churchill into power. Churchill had identified himself in the thirties with two "extremist" positions, warning against the dire consequences of appeasement of the Nazis and of Indian agitators. This gamble paid off politically with his elevation to the office of prime minister in 1940 when his warnings regarding Nazi intentions proved correct. He had not won office because of his views on Indian nationalism, but neither had he changed his views. His romanticization of empire and derisive contempt for Indian politicians were matched only by his candid admission of the practical necessity of keeping India to ward off the fate of England's becoming a depleted minor power. Churchill retained the shamelessly self-satisfied candor of the nineteenth century imperialist, spurning the muting of tone which had been adopted by others newly aware that their words were now overheard by Indians as well as fellow Englishmen. When Churchill spoke on Indian subjects as prime minister, his views were not even representative of his own party, let alone his Labour colleagues in the war cabinet. Churchill nonetheless made every effort to portray his views on Indian subjects as national policy, proclaiming, for example, after his speech of September 10, 1942, in which he had revived almost every imaginable imperialist argument, that he had been up late the night before conferring with Clement Attlee about it.[3]

Churchill normally did not force his personal preferences in crucial cabinet discussions. On the other hand, Churchill gave full rein to his imagination in public statements made in his official capacity as prime minister, and indulged in even more vigorous polemic in confidential correspondence with other world leaders. "We are fighting to defend this vast mass of helpless Indians from imminent invasion," Churchill wrote to Harry Hopkins on May 31, 1942, suggesting that Roosevelt should therefore cease meddling in Indian affairs. On July 31, 1942, Churchill wrote Roosevelt, who was eager for a compromise with the Congress, that "Congress represents mainly the intelligentsia of non-fighting Hindu elements, and can neither defend India nor raise a revolt. The military classes on whom everything depends are thoroughly loyal." On August 27, Churchill wrote to Chiang Kai-shek, who was even more pro-Congress than Roosevelt, that "I do not consider that Congress in any way represents India . . . If at any time in the future as a result of the constitutional process to which we are committed the British withdraw their troops from India the Hindu Parliamentarians would be rapidly dominated by the Moslem warriors. If Mr. Gandhi could get a compact and adequate Japanese army placed at the disposal of the Congress for the purpose of holding down the Moslems, other non-Hindu elements and the States, furnished to him in return for assistance to the Japanese in making a free passage through India to try to join hands with the Germans, then and then only would he be able to set up Hindu ascendancy all over India . . . The Japanese would . . . have to lend him an army or he and his friends would speedily be overthrown by the martial races."[4]

Reacting to the Quit India demand on November 10, 1942, Churchill said publicly, "We intend to remain the effective rulers of India for a long and indefinite period . . . We mean to hold our own. I have not become the King's First Minister in order to preside over the liquidation of the British Empire . . . Here we are, and here we stand, a veritable rock of salvation in this drifting world." Churchill had not been made the king's first minister in order to hold India in perpetual subjection, but it was difficult for Churchill's colleagues to make this point. Under the pressure of war, Labour had been brought into the cabinet, and even communists—following Russia's entry into the war—found themselves allied with die-hard imperialists determined to "hold their own."

The government in New Delhi thus felt reasonably confident that strong measures could be taken in India for the duration of the war without stirring up a storm in Parliament. Accepting the possibility that there might be renewed experiments with democratization following the war and confronted with a political body which claimed to be the nation-in-waiting, the British administration undertook to insure that an Indianized India would not mean Congress Raj.

British administrators acknowledged that India might some day be free. Preparation for independence in official eyes had initially involved insuring that India was "ready," that India had experienced, pragmatic leadership familiar with the advantages of preserving the status quo and possessing the stamina necessary to preserve it in defiance of popular pressure. But Britain's tentative experiments with Indian democratization had not proved reassuring. In the hope of furthering

orderly development, the institutional structure had been liberalized
in 1919, and moderate Indians had been encouraged to fight the government's battle against extremists in the new electoral context. The moderates had, however, not fared well. Moderate forces, it seemed, could
not carry the day singlehandedly, so long as they had to contend with
parties such as the Congress which were dedicated to intimidation
and fundamentally opposed to the working of democratic institutions.
Descriptions of the Congress as a "totalitarian dictatorship" were com-
monplaces of British official correspondence. On the evening of August
8, 1942, for example, scarcely minutes after the All-India Congress Committee in Bombay had passed the Quit India Resolution, the governor-
general in council issued a resolution decreeing that "The Congress
Party is not India's mouthpiece, yet in the interests of securing their
own dominance and in pursuit of their totalitarian policy, its leaders
have consistently impeded the efforts made to bring India to full
nationhood."[5]

If India were ever to attain "full nationhood," she would first have
to find a method of neutralizing the destructive fever of party emotional-
ism, with its tendency to totalitarian excess. The problem with the
whole process of democratization in India, as viewed by British officials,
was that it tended to produce parties led by men with inflated notions
of their own importance and ability, stemming from their success in
attracting an ignorant following. The Congress, Lord Linlithgow
admitted, was "a great political party which, misguided and malevolent
as it may be, still has a first-class electoral machine and commands
the votes (however obtained) of an immense preponderance of the Hindu
population of this country." This only seemed to increase the inclination
of the Congress toward "naughtiness," to "misbehave."[6] The process
of democratization had been designed originally to permit party men
to come close to the viceroy, where they might hope to influence his
decisions. In practice, however, party men demonstrated their lack
of "seriousness" by viewing with contempt "access to the viceroy"
and demanding instead complete power for themselves. Sir Stafford
Cripps, bitter over his failure during the Cripps Mission of 1942 to
induce the Congress to enter the viceroy's Executive Council, complained that the skepticism of Congress leaders was childish. "I stated
that I was sure the Viceroy had in mind—if representative Indians
were on his executive—to treat it more as a cabinet than as an executive
council." And moreover, "I further pointed out that . . . they would

always have the power to resign, which would put them in a strong position to press their point of view."[7] Secretary of state for India L. S. Amery agreed in a letter to Linlithgow that "If these Congress folk had any real intention of sharing responsibility they would have known quite well the extent to which the unwritten convention of your working with your Executive on all ordinary issues has grown and is inevitably growing."[8]

One "totalitarian" party was bad enough; the difficulty was compounded by the fact that when it became evident that the government took Congress leaders seriously, all sorts of others also wanted to get into the act. The British government were firmly convinced, for example, of the "impossibility of Pakistan."[9] The apparent success of the Congress in pursuing unreasonable antics had nonetheless induced Mohammed Ali Jinnah to conjure up this most unreasonable antic of all. One would have expected better of Mr. Jinnah; the fact that a person of Jinnah's caliber was also toying with popularity was a sad tribute to Gandhi's success in transforming the tone of Indian political discourse.

The British imperial rationale had long assumed that a small class of Indians, properly educated and fully Anglicized, might absorb the spirit of Western civilization and consequently serve as a link with the bulk of India's population, which remained in the grip of immemorial tradition and divided into irreconcilable factions. Jinnah was a highly Westernized spokesman of a religious community, and as such fit the British stereotype of an acceptable political leader.

Once a Congressman himself, Jinnah broke with Gandhi and the Congress in 1920 because Jinnah objected to Gandhi's political style and opposed his determination to turn the Congress into a mass movement. A mass movement could only mean one thing: bringing to bear on political decision-making the religious fanaticism of the bulk of the population. Jinnah objected to the popular and demagogic elements in Gandhi's program and his desertion of the tradition of polite and reasonable discussion with the British. Jinnah during this period was a prominent Muslim, but at the same time a member of the sophisticated elite of Bombay, living on fashionable Malabar Hill, a brilliant and successful lawyer. Jinnah epitomized the Anglicized professional class which wholeheartedly accepted the structure of British rule as one in which their interests could be pursued. Jinnah was a master of the skills which won acclaim from the British. He could always be counted upon to give a speech in Council which was unemotional, clear, and in English. He shared Gandhi's admiration for the great Hindu constitutionalist Gokhale; unlike Gandhi he also emulated him. Any trace of religious bigotry was alien to Jinnah for it would have inhibited his movement among the elite of British India. He numbered among his close friends men of Hindu, Parsi, and Christian faith.

In 1929 an English lady wrote to her mother after dining with Jinnah at the Viceregal Lodge at Simla, praising his elegance and eloquence and concluding by designating him "a future Viceroy if the present system of gradually Indianizing all the services continues."[10] She was thoroughly accurate in her prediction and in her qualifying statement. Gandhi's redirection of Indian nationalism meant that the "present system" of demission of power was no longer acceptable to the Congress. Jinnah was in truth in 1929 a future viceroy whose prospects were dampened by the change in the style of Indian politics.[11]

Jinnah continued to espouse the values of the generation of constitutionalists who had dominated Indian nationalist politics from 1885 to 1920. Characteristically when it seemed that politics had gone irreversibly beyond him, he became a voluntary exile practicing law in England. Jinnah returned to India in answer to a "call" from the Muslim League and conducted himself initially like a good advocate who had accepted the brief of a religious community. He thus became the most eminent remaining representative of the age of constitutionalism, of the tradition of Naoroji and Gokhale, who was able to survive the Gandhian revolution because of the independent base of power supplied him by the increasingly apprehensive Muslim community. He did not, like Gandhi, create a mass movement; he represented one.

In the 1940's, Jinnah spearheaded the drive for Pakistan. Jinnah retained his aristocratic personal style, but he was now firmly committed to the ending of British rule and the politics of pressure and mass consolidation. The British, however, treated the Muslim League simply as an anti-Congress force, a reaction against Gandhi which would subside with Gandhi's disappearance. Mr. Jinnah, having once been a reasonable man, might then be expected to become reasonable once again. The Muslim League appeared useful in the short run and manageable in the long run.

It has been alleged that the British fostered Jinnah's plan to establish Pakistan and alternatively that the British were opposed to Pakistan. Both allegations are true. The British fostered Pakistan as a bargaining ploy whose use they confidently expected would forestall the necessity of dividing the country they had worked so hard to unite. Amery stated the basic British approach succinctly when he wrote to Linlithgow that "we have always made it clear that in our opinion some sort of unity for India is essential and that the freedom to stand out has been conceded, not in order to encourage division, but to encourage give and take and ensure a really agreed settlement." Linlithgow, for his part, took a certain morbid delight in giving prominence to Jinnah's claims. He saw them as a sort of parody of Congress claims; by treating Mr. Jinnah seriously, he could simultaneously deride and balance the Congress. "I am glad to say that Jinnah, at any rate, has now been moved to express himself," Linlithgow wrote to L. S. Amery on June 23, 1942. "While, as you will see, he too is delighted to think that the country should be rid of our obnoxious presence, he accompanies that progressive suggestion with a clear indication that the Muslim League are going to stand no nonsense from Congress, from His Majesty's Government or from any one else. It is just as well that he has come out with this, for it is a useful counterblast to the Congress." Unfortunately, Congress seemed unable to appreciate the joke involved in the government's lionization of Jinnah. "The Hindus," Linlithgow complained on another occasion, "have made the mistake of taking Jinnah seriously about Pakistan, and as a result they have given substance to a shadow." In giving encouragement to "Jinnah's game of Poker," the British wished to be understood as doing so to humiliate the Congress, not because they saw any merit in Jinnah's claims. "Somebody put the general position in Indian politics at the moment rather well to me the other day," Linlithgow wrote to Amery, "by saying that the Congress were blackmailing His Majesty's Government, and the Muslim League were blackmailing Congress!"[12]

Parties like the Congress, in short, begot more such parties. Irrational claims by one faction stimulated more irrational claims by other factions. One might as a sovereign balance blackmail against blackmail, but it was a dangerous game, and one which was inconceivable without the maintenance of a strong reserve of discretionary power in British hands. "I am now quite sure," Linlithgow declared, "that self-government along with the removal of British influence is incompatible with unity, and I have little doubt that Indians themselves will gradually come to realise that this is the case."[13]

From the perspective of Linlithgow and his advisers, the Congress, the Muslim League, the Hindu Mahasabha, and the Communist party were all "equal." They were all parties which drew their power from a substantial degree of public support. The fact that one party was more successful in pursuing this essentially dubious enterprise did not make it more persuasive in Linlithgow's eyes. Parties of pressure were all equally bad, however big or small they might be. The issue in Linlithgow's mind was therefore not what kind of party regime India should have, and certainly not whether the largest party should have complete sway, but rather, whether or not a party regime was inevitable at all. The involvement of "politicians" of any stripe in the exercise of power was in itself a step backward. Mere popularity might vault a man into office where he might prove squeamish and incompetent. But, after all, government often required compromises with the less than best. If, for purposes of show, politicians were to be brought in, one should approach this with optimism. Politicians might shape up under the challenge. "It may be that the elements we encourage now may not be reliable in the future: but they may be influenced in a better direction in the sunshine of official favour."[14] Such optimism was of course much easier to sustain in contemplating dealings with the smaller parties. The leaders of large parties would be more likely to let popularity intoxicate them; leaders of small parties would be more realistic and willing to compromise. In 1942 Linlithgow toyed with the idea of calling in the Muslim League, the Hindu Mahasabha, and even the Communists. They might shape up; if they didn't they could be disposed of without difficulty or embarrassment to the government. Linlithgow had no greater fondness for these parties, however, than for the Congress, and thought of dealings with them primarily as a way of humiliating the Congress and making Congress leaders envious and possibly even of making them sufficiently malleable to consider appointing in their individual capacity as Congress moderates. The prospect of party men in the Executive Council was also a convenient lever for use against the Indians already in the Council. Linlithgow periodically sought to encourage his councilors to become more publicly assertive by hinting that they might be supplanted by party representatives.

If necessary, Linlithgow would put up with an Executive Council made up of persons from "the parties"; his preference, however, was to demonstrate the superiority of a strong authoritarian government in which the viceroy was at liberty to choose the best men to serve as his advisers. Parties appealed to men's baser instincts; Linlithgow was equally convinced that it was possible to appeal to their higher instincts by demonstrating mastery and eliciting willing cooperation.

Linlithgow felt that a strong, benevolent regime was even more desirable in India than elsewhere because of the nature of the Indian character. Linlithgow noted with interest the impression he had garnered from his Hindu councilors that they seemed to prefer a strong central government of the sort he had reinstituted in 1939 and were contemptuous of the pre-war experiment with provincial autonomy. "Hindus" seemed to understand strong central authority and accept it without qualms. And, if the Indian masses responded to firm direction, Indian dignitaries were equally receptive to personal attention. Linlithgow felt that being "friendly and easy" were "qualities which, whether displayed in public or in private, are even more valuable in India than elsewhere in the world." "No Indian minds being hauled over the coals so long as the operation is performed by someone who loves him and in private."[15] If Indians were recruited and handled gingerly, they would be loyal and also useful. Amery wrote that "I have always held the view that, in India, office in very large measure helps to make the man and give him status, whether he was originally elected or can command an electoral following."[16]

In view of the unsuitability of India for democratic institutions, experiments with democratization probably should never have been started in the first place. Fortunately, however, democratization was a curable malady, for its excesses could be dealt with effectively in ways which would progressively show up the entire procedure. The British had no one to blame but themselves for the extent to which parties had monopolized the center of the political stage. What Amery called a game of "cat-and-mouse" could be quickly halted by a firm display of power by the cat. Amery commented that he was "not really surprised that Nehru . . . should be so bitter about myself. After all, though wholeheartedly in sympathy with Indian nationalist aspirations, I have been mainly responsible for confronting Congress with the hateful fact that it cannot step directly into the shoes of the British Government and run India through its party executive, but has got to begin at the beginning and conciliate the other elements by some form of new constitutional settlement which may very well preclude anything in the nature of Congress Party control."[17]

The process of democratization had been permitted to go rather far, but the ease with which it could be halted at any time suggested that India's long-range future might lie in an entirely different direction. Democratization was not inevitable, and as it became increasingly clear that democratization had been given a full and fair trial and been found wanting, it would be reasonable to expect greater public support for the policy which administrators had always privately hoped would win out in the end. Democratization would lead to partition—in other words, chaos. Some British liberals were apparently unconcerned by this prospect. Sir Reginal Coupland, argued Linlithgow, "would regard it as no disaster to ourselves if within ten years [after the British departed] all had fallen into chaos."[18] In Linlithgow's view, in contrast, the British had an obligation to make sure that India continued to have strong rulers, even if this meant that the British had to rule themselves. If the British were to be responsible, they must retain ultimate power. Linlithgow found the suggestion that the British hand over power to Indians, and continue to serve under them in a subordinate capacity, totally unacceptable. "This assumption that the British will be found ready to put up with such conditions is touching."[19]

Linlithgow attempted to build up his appointive Council into a viable Indianized government. He devoted enormous effort to the task of coaxing his councilors along in the hope of strengthening their mettle and encouraging popular Indian recognition of his Indian advisers as an adequate guarantee that Indian interests would not be overlooked by the British. "I think my Council deserve full marks for the way in which they stood up to a most unpopular decision,"—to arrest Gandhi and other congressmen—Linlithgow wrote to Amery on August 11, 1942. "I was quite ready to take the decision myself if it had to be taken, but realising how great would be the value to Council as an education in responsibility, and equally how great would be the propaganda value outside of a unanimous vote by them, I strained every nerve to secure that result."[20]

The Council seemed to be learning, but this, India's best hope, was still not much of a hope. Linlithgow complained that his councilors were "morbidly sensitive" and "unduly touchy." On September 1, 1942, Linlithgow wrote that "the sensitiveness of some of my Hindu colleagues may be gauged from the fact that when I discussed the business of a fast [by Gandhi] the other day in Council, and made it clear that I contemplated the old man dying if he wanted to, one of them burst into tears at the table." What could one hope from an independent India managed by such men, seemingly incapable of taking tough decisions? On August 31, 1942, Linlithgow noted that several councilors were "in mortal terror of the possible consequences to themselves of their having supported me in arresting Gandhi."[21]

Linlithgow expected his advisers to be both deferential and self-confident; when they proved to be only deferential and self-conscious, Linlithgow was "disillusioned" and led on to conclude that even the best Indians were men of straw. Having been set an impossible task, the viceroy's councilors were now to be blamed for failure—and if these men failed, what could one hope from others? For all the pains he devoted to the Indian members of his Council, the viceroy despaired of ever seeing them become full colleagues. At the height of the Quit India movement, Linlithgow complained that he was compelled to "spend a disproportionate amount of time . . . listening to discussion by my Council on matters falling outside their own sphere and on which individual speakers have occasionally shown some lack of appreciation of what is practicable as well as of the proper constitutional boundaries of the Council's functions." These developments confirmed Linlithgow "in my view of intolerable burden that would fall on GG [governor-general] in present circumstances without a European element in the Council."[22]

The "increasing association of Indians" in the government of their own country was not leading to a magic moment when Indian influence suddenly became more decisive than British. The process of democratization encouraged by the British promised Indians "everything but" the final power to take decisions which might be offensive to the position of the British in India. The Labourite Sir Stafford Cripps envisioned only that the viceroy would "treat his Council more like a Cabinet." Linlithgow made every effort to bring his Council along—but would have gone along without them if he had to. Commenting on the powers of the viceroy's Executive Council of which he was a member, Sir Mahomed Usman remarked, "If the Governor-General consults his Executive Council, he gets its opinion."[23] Indians were appointed to ceremonially high positions, but the result was the establishment of new lines of communication within the government, so that Indians continued to be effectively excluded from sensitive decisions. Perhaps the deepest irony in the British effort to identify Indians with the government of their own country was in the treatment of the Indians sent to represent India in the war cabinet in London. Churchill agreed to accept them, caustically commenting, "We shall have to take the Albert Hall for our War Cabinet meetings." But Churchill had the last word, directing that the Indian representatives His Highness the Maharaja Jam Sahib of Nawanagar and the Honourable Sir Ramaswami Mudaliar not be given the most sensitive cabinet papers, and noting that "it must not be assumed that I shall feel able to invite them to Meetings when Indian affairs are to be discussed."[24]

The British were committed to "orderly Indianization." Formally, the only obstacle preventing them from leaving was Indian disagreement. Yet the viceroy was appalled by the suggestion from several of his councilors that he simply declare himself the ruler of India, thereby freeing India and maintaining the continuity he felt was so important. Then the viceroy was forced to concede that solicitude for formal continuity and institutional efficiency were not the ultimate reasons for British reluctance to leave. "The answer was that all these powers should be vested in the Viceroy. It does not seem to have occurred to them that you and I as Secretary of State and Viceroy are no more than the channels through which Parliamentary control is exercised . . . it would be out of the question for any Viceroy to control or hold such a position; and . . . the burden put on him of adjudicating between the communities, of reconciling the attitudes of British India and the Indian States where they conflicted, and of trying to keep the peace between the new Government of India and His Majesty's Government would be quite impossible."[25] The viceroy ruled because he was backed by British power, and the viceroy was backed by British power because he safeguarded British interests. As often as Indians politely pressed the British to go, so often did the British find reasons to consider this an impossibility. Indians were not ready; Indians might never be ready. Chaos would come after ten years. It would be "irresponsible" for the British to sanction a political rule of which they could not honestly approve. The British rightly recognized that only one agency could wield sovereignty at a time, and they were not prepared to relinquish sovereignty, however far the "increasing association of Indians" with the government of their own country proceeded. Given this fact, Linlithgow felt that it might be just as well to begin reversing the process of "association."

In the future Indian government, as Linlithgow conceived it, a continuing core of British administrators would be necessary, with, in addition, adequate backing from a British military force. Indians might be permitted to fill the majority of posts in the viceroy's Executive Council, with the exception of Home and Finance, because this body was little more than an exercise in public relations anyway. The Indian princes would be encouraged to continue their efforts at cooperation and to foster reforms in the administration of their states. Much effort would be needed, however, to bring India back to the standard of performance attained before the drift toward democratization set in. The matter was delicate: "Were we dealing with this country in the happy conditions of 70 years ago, when it was our business to clean up a mess into which India had got itself, and we were in a position to do so without any interference that mattered, things would be very different. At a moment when our energies are devoted to finding someone to take over our own burdens from us, and to convince the world that we are anxious to make over those burdens . . . one has . . . to walk a little more delicately, and we are, I fear, not the free agents that we were, say, after the Mutiny!" But one should not despair altogether. "I would not, as I said in a recent telegram, exclude, either, the possibility that at the end of a successful war circumstances here may make it impossible for us to give effect to our anxiety to see India a Dominion. But I am equally clear (though of this you are a much better judge than I can be) that however deep and serious the cracks that are beginning to reveal themselves in the façade of a possible Indian Dominion, the signs of disintegration must become more manifest and the dangers more apparent, both at home and here, before we can well admit that the democratic experiment may have failed, and that we must retrace our steps."[26]

What the world and public opinion would come to appreciate in time was all too clear to Linlithgow: "The more I watch this Indian situation develop the more ground one sees for pessimism. There is little if any sign of personnel of the requisite quality; there is precious little indication of any desire to face unpopular decisions or to carry responsibility; and I have not the least doubt that progressive Indianisation is leading, whether in the educational world, in archaeology, in the field of agriculture, in science, or in the services, to a substantial deterioration in quality, which acquires momentum every year." When a Parsi second lieutenant "refused to undertake duties which involved taking an active part against Congress," Lord Linlithgow exclaimed, "These Parsees are a nuisance . . . Their educational and social standing being high, but unfortunately a great deal higher than their military capacity, they are excessively touchy . . . and extremely bitter whenever any question arises of disciplinary action being taken against them on grounds of inefficiency or the like."[27]

Linlithgow proposed the total abandonment of recruitment for the Indian Civil Service for the duration of the war; at the end of the war, vacancies could be filled by British military officers, and in the meantime the "over-Indianisation" of the services would have been prevented.[28]

The path to the reestablishment of British rule on a solid new footing was clearly demarcated, but was obstructed by the unpredictability of Parliament on the one hand, and the presumably related intransigence of the Congress on the other. During the war, parliamentary intervention had been to some extent neutralized, and this fact had induced the Indian government to move ahead with their plans for eliminating the other major obstacle to Indian progress. For almost a year following the British declaration of war on September 3, 1939, and the Congress declaration of opposition, the government plotted their strategy. By the summer of 1940, this had taken final shape in the form of a Revolutionary Movement Ordinance and an accompanying manifesto.

The manifesto was prepared for issuance in conjunction with the Revolutionary Movement Ordinance as a way of clarifying the government's position and future intentions. The manifesto asserted that the intention of Congress leaders in launching a campaign of active opposition to government was to

> take concerted action in an endeavor to obstruct the war effort of the country and to overthrow or change the present form of government in India by deliberately defying its laws . . . Their decision is thus not only a depressing commentary on the value of their professions, nor merely and simply a political blunder of the first magnitude. It is an act of treachery to their own ideals and the interests of their own country to which it would be hard to find a parallel.
>
> The Government of India have never accepted the claim of the Indian National Congress to speak for the people of India as a whole . . . they have always held it to be their duty to respect also the views, and to protect impartially the interests, of those—and they are many—who disagree with Congress as a political party and have an equal right to call themselves Indians.
>
> Now, if ever, the rightness of this attitude on the part of the Government is vindicated. There must be countless Indians who will condemn or disown the decision of the leaders of the Congress and who will feel that, whatever the future may hold in store, India can now best fulfill her destiny and take her due place among the nations of the world only after the total extinction of the political party which, at this vital juncture, has seen fit to betray them . . .
>
> Those . . . who are supporters of constituted authority have nothing to fear. To law abiding citizens and men of true patriotism and goodwill throughout India the Government guarantee, not only their protection so long as the movement lasts, but also, when it

has been defeated, due recognition of their loyal support. It is for them now to demonstrate, by word and deed, that they are at one with the Government in holding that the entire energies of the country in war time must be devoted wholeheartedly to the defeat of its enemies, whether outside or within the gates.[29]

In the space of a few lines in this draft document, the viceroy had impugned the judgment and patriotism of the Congress, decreed its total extinction, and called for its active denunciation by loyal Indians who would be duly rewarded for their services in a manner which would be reminiscent of the aftermath of the Great Rebellion of 1857.

The Revolutionary Movement Ordinance and the accompanying manifesto were attempts to pronounce decisively on the issues which had been troubling officials since the outbreak of war and the break with Congress in the fall of 1939. In a series of letters exchanged with the provincial governments, and in conferences at Simla and elsewhere, views had been gathered, anxieties assessed, and reactions to proposed remedies collected. Summing up the results of these consultations, the home member of the viceroy's Executive Council, Sir Reginald Maxwell, recommended action "before the public have too far forgotten their grievances against the Congress Ministry." Sir Reginald proposed "not merely to reduce the Congress to a condition in which they will be prepared to make terms but to crush the Congress finally as a political organisation."[30]

Such a measure had first been discussed in 1937 when it was thought that Congress might refuse to cooperate with the reforms inaugurated under the Government of India Act of 1935. The resignation of Congress ministries in 1939 quickly stimulated the round of consultations which produced the updated package plan communicated to selected provincial officials in August 1940. In a personal letter to governors dated August 8, the viceroy explained that despite the studied vagueness of the phrase "revolutionary movement," "of course, the situation primarily envisaged is still a clash with Congress." He also drew their attention to the significance of the decision reflected in the wording of the ordinance declaring the Congress as a whole an unlawful association. The proposed language had "the merit of simplicity." More important, wrote the viceroy, "I feel very strongly that the only possible answer to a 'declaration of war' by any section of Congress in present circumstances must be a declared determination to crush the organisation as a whole."

The plan envisaged the wholesale arrest of Congress leaders, the dismissal of officials considered disloyal, the closing of educational institutions, and the seizure of bank accounts and party premises. Collective fines were to be imposed on troublesome areas, and wealthy supporters of Congress were to be assaulted by what the government called "economic warfare." The government would have preferred to deny government contracts to all Congress contributors categorically, but it was decided that this would be impracticable in instances in which Congress contributors were major suppliers of materials necessary for the war effort. The vagueness of the ordinance is suggested by its prohibition of "signs . . . rumour or report which is likely to cause fear or alarm to the public or to any section of the public or to defame Government or any servant of the Crown or to further any revolutionary activity or any revolutionary movement." The legal question of what constituted a revolutionary movement was resolved simply by the statement that any movement declared to be a revolutionary movement by the viceroy was to be legally considered such. As Sir Richard Tottenham observed, a peculiar virtue of the ordinance was that it declared that it was a "revolutionary activity" to "encourage or incite any persons to combine in any concerted action with a view, by reason of the concerted nature of the action, to exert pressure on Government or on the public or any section or member of the public or to interfere with the lawful actions of any persons. It would thus enable us to proceed . . . against a wide range of activities which may not, in themselves, involve a breach of any particular law, but which become actionable merely because they are designed to exert concerted pressure on the Government."

After the initial distribution of the draft ordinance some officials expressed concern that the title of the Revolutionary Movement Ordinance "might produce an unfortunate impression in America and also give a handle to the German broadcasts." Linlithgow's proposed solution to this problem was to change the name to the Subversive Movement Ordinance, with the intention of making Congress leaders feel ashamed of themselves. "'Probably,'" he wrote, "because they do not understand the meaning of the word 'subversive' there are, I suspect, a number of people who would think it rather fine to be 'revolutionary,' but who would be a little ashamed of being dubbed *subversive*. The first smacks of the Bastille; the second of Vine Street!" Home Member Sir Reginald Maxwell opposed this suggestion because he thought "revolutionary" a stronger term, and to employ the word "subversive" "would involve watering down to some extent the impression likely to be caused" within India. The solution finally arrived at was to retain the ordinance as drafted, with its references to a revolutionary movement, to insure a proper appreciation of the government's thinking within India, but to change the short title to "Emergency Powers Ordinance" to reduce the impact likely to be caused abroad since "It is the short title that will, presumably, be broadcast to the outer world . . . and the actual clauses of the Ordinance will not be available for study, at any rate for some time, in countries like America or Germany."

Since the proposed ordinance did not significantly increase the powers the government already possessed under the Defence of India Rules, there was some discussion, sparked by Sir Maurice Hallett, governor of the United Provinces, about the desirability of dealing with the Congress as a "revolutionary movement" rather than as a defense menace. Sir Maurice, while expecting trouble from Gandhi, advocated dealing with the Congress under the Defence of India Rules for the duration of the war because "in these days of total war I can see no distinction between the man who attacks the frontier of my country and the man who, for whatever purpose, starts an internal revolution in it and so hampers my war effort." Sir Maurice considered the Revolutionary Movement Ordinance "administratively unnecessary and confusing and politically a mistake." Politically it was a mistake because "if we are out to smash the Congress as a political party in this country, we alienate all the support we might get from its half-hearted supporters. I do not question the desirability of smashing the Congress, but I submit that that is not the way to do it . . . Having said that the future constitution of India will, subject to certain safeguards, be decided by Indians themselves, it seems anomalous for us to go out and smash the Congress on any other ground but that they are interfering in the war." Sir Maurice felt that there were "a great many Hindus who are not Congressmen, or not rabidly so [who] have a regard for the Congress and a great regard for Gandhi in internal politics. But these people are very strongly anti-Nazi and pro-war . . . and they will have to admit the justice of our action if we deal with any movement started by Congress as an anti-war movement."[34]

The Simla government, in reply, rejected Sir Maurice's analysis as too pessimistic. In the government's view, there was no cause for concern that overt repression might backfire, for public opinion was already irreversibly alienated from Congress leadership. Sir Maurice had addressed his protest to the home member, Sir Reginald Maxwell, with a request that his letter be shown to the viceroy. Sir Reginald replied in a letter whose "general lines" had the "concurrence" of the viceroy contesting Sir Maurice's apparent assumption "that Congress does in fact represent the Indian people as a whole. We deny this; we see no reason why the Congress Working Committee should be allowed to set themselves up as the political dictators of India; and we think that on the wider view the time may be approaching when it may be possible to expose the insincerity and opportunism of its political leaders and give the people of India a chance of deciding their future constitution in some other way than under the domination of a political party which has led them badly since the beginning of the war and no longer represents their views correctly." Sir Reginald then added a further argument, stating that "even if the Congress were the only people we had to deal with in shaping the political future of India," he would not "be deterred from resisting such a movement by the amount of support which Congress might be able to enlist by methods known to you as well as to me." Sir Reginald contended that Congress had already lost public support, but that even if it still had public support, direct resistance was the only honorable course. Pursuing Congress on the pretext of its interference in the war was an unnecessary subterfuge; even if it might be a convenient subterfuge, an open and manly defiance seemed the worthier course. Sir Reginald concluded by stressing that the government's decision had been reached only after "full consideration," and "so far as I know no other governor . . . is dissatisfied with the policy which we wish to pursue." He consequently hoped that Sir Maurice would agree that a common front was essential under the circumstances.[35]

The government preferred a separate Revolutionary Movement Ordinance for two main reasons: the possibility that the Congress movement might not be fully suppressed until some time after the cessation of hostilities resulted in a lapsing of the Defence Rules and the desirability of making known the government's long-range intentions to those who might otherwise be inclined to hedge their actions in anticipation of an eventual Congress return to power. Sir Maurice Hallett himself admitted that the end of the second war might repeat the experience of the first. "If and when the war is over and we are all war weary and there are the inevitable post-war economic difficulties," the Congress, Sir Maurice acknowledged, might seize the occasion to blackmail Government into conceding the Congress demand . . . Gandhi has no doubt not overlooked the fact that the first non-co-operation movement owed its success largely to war weariness and post-war difficulties; he may hope that a Rowlatt Bill or a Jallianwalla Bagh incident may give him the desired opportunity."[36]

At a conference of provincial officials responsible for home affairs, held at Simla on August 29 and 30, 1940, "Discussion showed that the view that the Ordinance was unnecessary was based on the assumption that the Defence of India Rules would remain in force and could (along with certain provisions of the ordinary law) be used to deal satisfactorily with a Civil Disobedience Movement. The home member explained that neither of these assumptions was entirely justified."[37]

More urgent than the concern with postwar prospects was the government's desire to reassure their more timorous supporters. A forthright statement of intention seemed the only way to communicate to waverers the long-range thinking of the government. Sir Reginald Maxwell, following a discussion with officials in Bombay, reported that he had been "a good deal impressed by the tendency which I observed to discuss all questions on the assumption that either Congress or a Hindu Government consisting largely of friends of Congress would ultimately return to power and would be in a position to undo whatever Government had done . . . It is evident that not only are Government officers thoroughly permeated with this idea but that the general public will watch their steps on some such assumption."[38] Sir Maurice Hallett went even further, suggesting that some officers might even want Congress to return to power for diverse motives of their own. He insisted that "we must never lose sight of the fact that at the back of the minds in particular of every Hindu officer is the anticipation, and possibly the hope, that a Congress Ministry will return to power."[39]

Pro-British officials were naturally anxious about the prospect that actions taken in pursuance of British orders would result in future victimization. Consequently, reported Sir Reginald, "Bombay officers welcomed the information that the Revolutionary Movement Ordinance was likely to be strengthened by the inclusion of certain provisions for imposing civil disabilities," which would prohibit today's outlaw from becoming tomorrow's cabinet minister.[40]

The intended beneficiaries of the government effort to suppress the Congress, the Indian moderates, were also concerned about the effect on their own careers of a return to power of Congress. Very few Indians were taken into confidence regarding the government's political strategy, but among these were the Indian ministers of the three provincial governments which remained in office following the resignation of Congress ministries in 1939. At the conference of "provincial representatives" held at Simla on August 29 and 30, 1940, "The Ministers of all three Ministerial Provinces referred to the possibility that after the war or after the defeat of the Revolutionary Movement, the party responsible for it might be allowed to return to power. They asked whether any assurance could be given that history would not be allowed to repeat itself in this respect. The intentions of the Government of India on the one hand, and the difficulties, on the other, of any public announcement or assurance were explained to the conference."[41]

Sir A. Hope, governor of Madras, argued that the Congress were "an absolutely untrustworthy lot and it will cause immense resentment if we have any further truck with them."[42] And Sir Reginald Maxwell, recorded the viceroy, "is again urging on me that we should say that if Congress misbehave now, that is the end of them as a political party so far as we are concerned. Twynam [Sir Henry Twynam, governor of the Central Provinces] ... has begun to take the same line."[43] Amery accorded his endorsement for actions "to confound Congress, who are already sufficiently disunited over the country as a whole, and to strengthen all our supporters. I don't know how far in this matter you feel you have got to carry the whole of your Executive with you, but I should have thought you could make it clear to them that prompt action now, and the consequent burning of our boats as regards appeasing Congress, will not only strengthen their hands, but effectively put out of the picture any question of their being replaced by Congress nominees in the near future."[44] Linlithgow reflected on the difficulties of formally outlawing Congress in a letter to Twynam.

> Were we working a more autocratic system I have little doubt that we should be able to ... bluff our way through ... But the main difficulty ... is the practical difficulty when one is working with a democratic system such as ours of so to speak "outlawing" a major political party with a first-class machine and with unquestionably a very substantial degree of actual or potential support in the country. If one could be certain of getting away with it, well and good. But if having used the heavy weapon of outlawry we failed in our purpose the loss of face involved would be very great and our political defeat very serious. And so long as we are dealing with matters here under the ultimate control of Parliament, and so long

as, whatever the merits or demerits of the Indian case, a tiny group of left wingers such as Sorensen, etc., can without any fear of interruption ask questions in Parliament wholly misleading to those of us who know the facts but plausibly convincing to the audience at home, and so long as Parliament admits of being swept off its feet either by emotional waves or by the feeling that action of a particular type in India will have valuable repercussions in the Empire or outside the Empire, it is, as I see it, extremely hard to feel real confidence that we shall be left free to see through a policy such as I have now been talking about. Circumstances arise from time to time (1932 is a good example) when the course of events itself eliminates any risk of early Parliamentary reaction of the type that I have mentioned. But I gravely doubt, though I may be wrong, if that atmosphere prevails at home today. And if I am right in these hesitations then you would agree with me I think that the wise course is to play a more cautious hand than perhaps one's instincts may at all times altogether commend to one. Do not however think that my mind is in any way closed—very far from it.[45]

Linlithgow at this time felt he did not have the backing necessary to make an open declaration of his long-range intentions, but he tried to convey privately to his advisers, and through them to the Indian friends of British power, that long-range intentions were being pursued, even if perforce for the time being with great circumspection.

Assurances to civil servants and politicians that loyalty would be rewarded were coupled with an effort to give a "constructive lead" to moderate opinion by a demonstration that all reasonable Indian demands would be satisfied and that a British-led government could provide better government than Indians had been subjected to under two years of provincial Congress Raj. One problem which Maxwell reported from Bombay was that it was difficult to distinguish government policy sharply from that of the superseded Congress by reversing all Congress policies because "on the whole the legislative and administrative measures taken by the Congress Ministry have been beneficial."[46]

Noting Indian "anxiety . . . to contribute to the outcome of the war," the viceroy on June 5, 1940, expressed his hope that the establishment of a volunteer corps of Civic Guards would answer the widespread Indian desire "to give personal service of a voluntary character in connection with internal defence measures."[47] Three weeks later, on June 25, Sir Richard Tottenham, additional secretary in the Home Department, surveyed the effect of the viceroy's announcement, which had resulted in "The refusal both of the Muslim League and of the Congress to support the Civic Guard Movement; [and] the decision of Congress . . . to expand their own volunteer organisations." As Sir Richard noted, government-sponsored volunteer organizations were one thing, opposition-sponsored volunteer organizations quite another. "Surely the most dangerous feature of the [nongovernment volunteer] movement is the discipline and organisation that drill and training and the wearing of a uniform can impart, combined with the loss of prestige that Government must necessarily suffer by allowing the functions of their police or civic guards to be usurped by non-official agencies." Sir Richard was consequently forced to recommend the logical next step: suppression of competing volunteer organizations. As he concluded philosophically, "If there is to be war, it might as well be total war."[48]

On July 23 the viceroy's Executive Council approved the recommended policy of outlawing paramilitary volunteer organizations and on July 31 settled the details. On August 5 Sir Richard Tottenham issued from Simla a press communiqué explaining the new policy. He stated that "in regard to the great majority of these volunteer bodies it is impossible to suppose that they exist for any legitimate or peaceful purpose, and it must generally be assumed that they are being drilled either for communal conflict or for the purpose of supplanting the existing administration." The communiqué concluded by asserting that "The Government of India believe that the public at large will welcome and support the action . . . and they would emphasize that the Civic Guard must now be regarded as the only popular organisation available for the expression of the desire of all people of good intent . . . to serve their country in the present crisis."[49]

On August 19 Tottenham once again reviewed the situation. Press comment, he noted, had been characterized by a "lack of justice done to the Civic Guard Movement," which was often dismissed "contemptuously as a set of *jo hukums.*" He regretted the failure to recognize "the potential value of such a unifying movement which was intended not to suppress . . . the natural desire to supplement the existing official forces . . . in a time of national anxiety . . . but to guide it into the most practical and most truly national channels that are open to them in present conditions."[50]

Several reasons for the failure of the Civic Guard Movement are reflected in the experience of Bihar in 1942 with the formation of the government-sponsored National War Front. At an organizing meeting at Manbhum, reported the deputy commissioner, "the speakers read out their written speeches parrot-like and the movement is still-born and practically no response is forthcoming. At Dhanbad while the audience of 1500 persons attentively listened to the speech of the Provincial Leader and other local leaders, they dispersed with the shout 'Gandhiji-ki-jai.'" Many were reluctant to join the Front because "The impression still persists . . . that ultimately people enrolled in the Front will be sent to the actual battle fields." A further problem was that, apparently, "the poorer people demur to join [the Front's Village Defence Parties], because they have nothing to lose and there is no need for them to patrol the villages for the protection of the merchants and zamindars who profiteer or who live upon the cultivator. The majority of the members of the Village Defence Parties come from the smaller zamindars, the literate middle class and persons in some sort of service." Moreover, the War Front's "Grow More Food" campaign was resented because villagers felt that the chief obstacle to greater production was the arbitrary confiscation of their land, crops, and animals for military purposes.[51]

The Simla government felt that the nation's requirements had been recognized and met. As the experience with the Civic Guard and the National War Front demonstrated, however, government initiatives did not fare well when checked at every step by political organizations, including, preeminently, the Congress. Attempting to suppress any of the hydra-headed manifestations of the Congress, such as its competing volunteer corps, appeared to be self-defeating. True total war required tackling the phenomenon in its entirety, which was what the government hoped to accomplish by the Revolutionary Movement Ordinance.

The government's massive strategy for the total extinction of the Congress had one catch: it depended upon Congress striking the first blow by doing something vaguely "revolutionary" to which the government could react by calling into play its planned offensive. The government concluded that the moment had finally come in September 1940 when the Congress authorized Gandhi to undertake a campaign against the government. Gandhi then announced that he would initiate his campaign by asking Vinoba Bhave to give a speech in a village opposing all wars. Gandhi explained that Vinoba's special qualifications for undertaking this assignment included a fervent dedication to hand-spinning, about which he had written a textbook. The government, unable credibly to label this a revolution, were impotent, though many officials felt like Sir George Boag, who, Sir Reginald Maxwell reported, "obviously dislikes dancing to Gandhi's tune."[52] It was not until two years later, with the launching of the Quit India movement, that the government finally were confronted with something which might be labeled a revolutionary movement. At this time, the government attempted to implement the planned program of preemptive attack, but in the intervening two years innumerable complications had arisen. By not accommodating the government's desire for him to launch a rash attack, Gandhi had two years to build the basis of a genuine mass movement. The entry of the United States into the war and the presence of American troops on Indian soil had introduced American public opinion as a complicating factor. And the British home government had had time to interfere with the Indian government's admirably clear-cut plans as outlined in the original ordinance and manifesto.

There is no evidence that any Indian official within the small circle familiar with the government's intentions went beyond questioning tactics to question the basic desirability of smashing the Congress. The home government, however, proved to be softer on Congress. The war cabinet could not prevent Churchill from making speeches but felt that the implementation of Indian policy was too important to be left to the prime minister.

The need for cabinet action first arose when Secretary of State for India Amery was suddenly presented with a request for standby approval of the Revolutionary Movement Ordinance on September 11, 1940, in a telegram explaining that "you may not have yet received" the full text of the government's plan, sent by airmail some days earlier. Amery, however, refused to be panicked into action, and, after consultation with the war cabinet, began a protracted debate with the viceroy over the implications of his policy.

The viceroy was, to begin with, refused the standby approval he requested. He was told that he must seek cabinet approval before issuing the ordinance and that he must allow twenty-four hours for a decision to be taken. The secretary of state further pressed strongly the view that "if comprehensive action against Congress should become inevitable it would be desirable if possible for public confidence both here and abroad to represent reason for our action against Congress movement as their programme of obstruction of war effort and not their political aspirations." He noted that the ordinance was "primarily

directed against movement which however extreme is ostensibly political in character . . . I am only concerned that you should take into
consideration at all stages my preference from publicity point of view
that if conflict with Congress should arise, it should appear as an outcome of war necessity rather than as a political quarrel unrelated to
the war." Reporting the results of a cabinet discussion of September
16, Amery stated that the war cabinet would support the use of "all
necessary measures such as the Revolutionary Movement Ordinance
and . . . support firm action being taken against Congress leaders
the moment it was established that Congress was determined to embark
on a campaign of deliberate interference with conduct of the war."

Amery also carefully revised the viceroy's manifesto so as to remove
references to the "total extinction" of the Congress and to rewards
for loyal service. Amery emphasized that he did not wish to restrict
the government's freedom of action, that "the question of actual machinery to be used is largely a matter of convenience." He agreed "that
Ordinance would be most suitable instrument for dealing with a sustained emergency as soon as initial excitement has subsided and could
appropriately be promulgated at that stage." He felt strongly, however,
that "our *initial* action" should be justified in terms of war requirements,
keeping world public opinion in mind.[53]

From the viceroy's point of view, the secretary of state had completely
missed the point. The Indian government had decided after long
deliberations—to which the secretary of state had not been made a
partner—that the time for temporizing had passed. To be evasive and
circumspect about motives and intentions, and to escalate retribution
cautiously as the emergency developed, were precisely the techniques
which the government had rejected after full discussion. As Sir Richard
Tottenham commented regarding Amery's elimination of reference to
future rewards, "It may be impossible to give any definite guarantee
of future favours to those who support us, but unless we give some
hint to this effect, we shall not get the support that might otherwise
be forthcoming."[54]

The viceroy immediately protested Amery's suggestion that actions
against the Congress be justified in terms of defense requirements.

> We see no advantage and many disadvantages in starting action
> on a limited front by means of an *ad hoc* amendment of Defence
> of India Rules and then switching on to Ordinance powers for use
> on the whole front . . . To select a particular passage in resolution

in order to justify use of Defence Rules in first instance would imply
that other passages calling for general non-cooperation in order to
enforce political demands of Congress were not regarded as a definite
challenge to the authority of Government or that Government were
unwilling to take up such a challenge and this would be taken as
an indication that we still looked forward to making terms with Congress in the political field. Moreover in adopting such tactics we should
be electing to fight on ground chosen by Gandhi for propaganda
purposes and losing advantages of proclaiming at once the real character of the movement . . . To initiate action on an entirely new basis
would dislocate all our plans and lead to great deal of delay . . . and
the subsequent changeover from the Defence Rules to the Ordinance
would . . . produce impression that Government had been driven
on to fresh defences.[55]

The war cabinet remained adamant that they were only prepared
to back the viceroy in taking any concrete actions he considered necessary for the maintenance of public order and the safeguarding of the
war effort. The viceroy ultimately respected their wishes without changing his views or abandoning his determination to carry on his attack
on the Congress within the bounds prescribed by the war cabinet.
He interpreted their reservations narrowly, ignoring the long-range
implications of the secretary of state's telegrams that the war cabinet
did not wish him to prejudge India's political future. The viceroy felt
that their attitude "is but natural on the part of an overworked War
Cabinet, grappling from hour to hour with the tremendous emergencies
of a world war," and consequently "most reluctant to face a row in
India." They could not be expected to think through all the ramifications
apparent to one situated in Simla. The Indian government had to respect
their anxieties, but could not shirk their responsibilities. "Our business
is to do our best to see that appropriate steps are taken against a
revolutionary movement in time to check it before it gets out of hand."[56]

The Indian government proceeded with their plans for eradication
of the Congress on the assumption that the attitude of the home government reflected only caution, not disapproval. The official *History of
the Civil Disobedience Movement, 1940–41* noted that "It was, indeed,
a complicating factor that the Government of India had to bear constantly in mind that H.M.G. were naturally anxious to avoid 'serious
trouble in India' or a complete break with its most important political
party."[57] The Indian government were sufficiently intent on their course
to consider the wishes of Whitehall only a "complicating factor," not

a reason for a basic redirection of policy. In response to Amery's wishes, the Revolutionary Movement Ordinance was altered to eliminate the declaration of the Congress "as a whole" illegal; this was replaced with wording declaring only specified governing bodies of the Congress illegal. But when Nehru subsequently asked if he could be permitted to carry on the work of the National Planning Committee, of which he was chairman, from his jail cell, Sir Reginald Maxwell decided that the government had "no interest in the National Planning Committee which is merely a part of the Congress programme."[58]

The rigidity of the Indian government's anti-Congress stance was one reason for the war cabinet's decision to send their own emissary to India in March of 1942 in a last effort to settle with Congress in the wake of the Japanese sweep toward India's borders. The mission of Sir Stafford Cripps was a rerun in double time of the Montagu mission of 1917. In the third year of each World War, when British fortunes were at a low ebb, and India was becoming restive, a liberal cabinet member was sent to India to head off trouble by making promises of postwar progress. Montagu took six months and had a reasonable success in those more moderate, slow-paced days. Cripps spent three weeks in India and met with a sharp rebuff; lines were harder after his visit than before. Upon seeing the terms of the Cripps offer, Gandhi simply left town, leaving others to worry the ill-fated proposal to death. Linlithgow did not leave town, but he scarcely left the Viceregal Palace and also took no part in the negotiations; he was excluded by Cripps, who correctly perceived his hostility to any settlement with the Congress. Both parties most essential to the working of any agreement —Gandhi and Linlithgow—were convinced that negotiations could not be meaningful under the circumstances.

Montagu's purpose in coming to India in 1917 had been to placate public opinion in India during a war which did not directly threaten India. Cripps' chief purpose was to placate public opinion outside India—especially in the United States—by demonstrating that the government had made a reasonable effort to meet India's demands in the face of imminent invasion. Cripps' purpose in India was to call Gandhi's bluff. The Congress, in the view of the war cabinet, was trying to force the government's hand by insisting on a dictatorial control of India which might be wrested from a weakened British government forgetful of its obligations to others. The Congress claim to speak for all Indians was seen as a guileful device to wrest away more than could ever be rightfully theirs. Cripps was sent to India to call this bluff by indicating the government's disposition toward recognition of the right of "nonaccession" by the Muslims and the princes, if some measure of control were to be ceded to the Congress. It was hoped that once Congress had been clearly told they could not get their way by threats, Congress would knuckle under, become more reasonable, and help work out an agreed solution with Jinnah and the princes.

Cripps hoped to shock the Congress into acquiescence by making it clear that even British friends of the Congress were not willing to abdicate what they saw as their responsibilities. The war cabinet underestimated the depth of feeling of both Congress and the Muslim League. It was thought that it was possible to make the Congress more "reasonable" by threatening to set up Pakistan. It was further thought that once the Congress had become more reasonable, the threat of Pakistan would have simultaneously disappeared, since Jinnah would presumably be willing to cooperate with a reasonable Congress. The British government in the spring of 1942 saw both the Congress and the Muslim League as agitators in a political system in which ultimate authority and the power of initiative still remained in British hands. Cripps tried to manipulate the Indian parties from a position of strength which he did not possess. Gandhi and Jinnah called his bluff. What they sought was not in the power of the British to refuse.

With the failure of the Cripps Mission, the stage was finally set for a total confrontation. The Indian government still hoped in the summer of 1942 that, despite Whitehall's restrictions on the overtness with which they might operate, they would be able to achieve the desired result of smashing the Congress. Two years had passed, but the plan of operations remained the same. This called for swift preemptive action as soon as a definite threat could be verified. Within hours of the passage of the Quit India Resolution by the All-India Congress Committee meeting at Bombay on August 8, 1942, hundreds of Congress leaders, including Gandhi and the working committee, were arrested, and steps were taken to implement all the measures which formed part of the package plan for dealing with a revolutionary movement. Quick action was thought desirable to nip the movement in the bud. It was also seen as the only way of averting disaster, for this was to be the government's last stand.

In urging the importance of nipping revolution in the bud, the Indian government's telegram to the secretary of state of September 11, 1940 had argued that "Any delay . . . would in our opinion be fatal . . . Delay would be interpreted as weakness; would lose us support and would lead to greater trouble and wider repression later on. You are aware of the extent to which our military forces for internal security have already been depleted." In deciding to throw all their force behind an initial blow, the Government were frankly acknowledging their weakness and precarious hold on public opinion.[59]

The attraction of a preemptive attack has always been two-sided, appealing simultaneously to bravado and fear. It appeals to the desire to settle the matter quickly, and to the feeling of uneasiness that if not settled quickly, the matter will be settled unfavorably. A preemptive attack has always held a fatal fascination in precisely those circumstances in which it is likely to prove most disastrous.

A preemptive strike against a foreign power works only when a nation's military capability can be wiped out with one well-placed blow, and even then it is unlikely to work against a nation with the unlimited defense potential represented by the patriotism of ordinary civilians prepared to assume the burden of resistance when formal defenses fail. A domestic revolt may be nipped in the bud when the revolt is led by an unrepresentative minority who have not as yet succeeded in building wide support for their cause. Authorities may readily imagine that a revolt fits this pattern, since revolts are first articulated by small groups who appear to be unrepresentative. If this presumption is unjustified, an arbitrary move to arrest leaders may produce an instantaneous widening of revolt which is more intense, and more randomly destructive, than would have been the case had the leaders remained in active control of the movement.

The complex appeal of a preemptive attack corresponded well with the ambivalence of British official feeling about the Congress. Was Congress an incalculable menace or a contemptible irritant exploiting "to the utmost the nuisance value of intransigence"?[60] Would the Quit India movement succeed in forcing out the British, as the tsar had been toppled in the third year of World War I? Or was this disturbance only the death rattle of the Congress? The government feared one thing while wanting to believe another. The government, in any case, were not prepared to wait for the Congress to die a natural death because they recognized that their own attitude to the Congress was not identical with that of Whitehall or of the unpredictable Americans, who had to be taken into account now that American troops had been welcomed onto Indian soil. If the Congress were not decisively destroyed while the opportunity lasted, there was always a chance that it might fall into power after the war through the misguided generosity of external forces.

Official thinking vacillated between a confident assertion that the Congress was "sinking . . . still deeper into the bog in which they have landed themselves"[61] and a worried anxiety about the incomprehensible power which Gandhi seemed to hold over the Indian people. For decades the collapse of Congress had been foreseen as just around the corner. Lord Curzon had confided in 1900 his "belief that the Congress is tottering to its fall, and one of my great ambitions while in India is to assist it to a peaceful demise." By 1942, the metaphorical resources of officials had still not been exhausted. The Congress was now depicted as sinking into "a morass from which it was difficult to extricate itself. Its main object then was to avoid total immersion."[62] The governor of the Central Provinces, where Gandhi resided near Wardha, wrote to the viceroy that he considered Congress "an exploded force" and predicted that "any shot from Wardha . . . will go off at half-cock."[63] Gandhi's antiwar crusade showed "no immediate signs of degenerating into a mass movement." There was "no doubt that at the present moment Congress stock both in the districts and in Bombay City is lower than it has been for a number of years. I am told that even in Gujarat the attitude of the public towards Government officers is extremely friendly while elsewhere Gandhi caps and such like badges are being discarded."[64] At the beginning of 1942 the government were so satisfied with the drift of political events that they compiled the official, though "Strictly Secret" *History of the Civil Disobedience Movement 1940–41.* "So," concluded the *History,* "to all intents and purposes, fizzled out this latest, perhaps last and professedly most perfect, example of Gandhi's technique."[65]

Insofar as the Congress might be supposed to have been kept afloat over the years by the single-handed efforts of the incomprehensible Mr. Gandhi, this difficulty would be soon removed, it was thought, by the literal as well as political suicide of Mr. Gandhi. Since the beginning of the war the government had been braced to withstand an anticipated fast unto death and the expected riotous aftermath. The government had decided to let him die and were sufficiently convinced of Mr. Gandhi's irrationality to believe that he would play into their hands by in fact dying.

The official *History of the Civil Disobedience Movement, 1940–41* argued that Gandhi was basically motivated by a desire for attention; Gandhi "was content with his primary object of keeping Congress before the public eye." Gandhi's perverse childishness was further revealed by his insistence on overcom[ing] all opposition from his colleagues and . . . establish[ing] himself as the dictator of Congress policy." How such a determination to hoard all the glory for himself could be reconciled with the admission that he was a "trusted leader" with a "peculiar influence over the public mind" who was able to lead a movement when "the hearts of the people were not in it" could be explained only by the "ease with which many people in this country can be persuaded not to think for themselves."[66]

To keep himself in the public eye, the official *History* contended, Gandhi had disregarded his colleagues, chosen an unpopular cause, and advanced it in a dull manner; it is little wonder that officials predicted that such suicidal exhibitionism would lead next to a fast unto death, and that with Gandhi literally dead, the Congress would at last be politically dead.

Yet, several months after Gandhi's "last" movement had officially "petered out," the government were once again preparing for a massive showdown. Private discussions of Gandhi among British officials were punctuated with many brave words, but at the same time betrayed substantial unease that there might be more to the Gandhian phenomenon than they liked to admit. Gandhi figured frequently in British correspondence as "the Hitler of Indian politics,"[67] an appellation which, for all of its derisive contempt, contained no small element of grudging respect. "Knowing as we do his intense personal vanity and his anxiety also to keep Congress together," wrote Linlithgow on May 27, 1942, "he may well be prepared to take substantial chances in order again to consolidate his followers and to get the spotlight on to himself." But Linlithgow was reluctant to think that vanity would blind Gandhi to realities, for "the old man has lost none of his political skill with age. I shall be astonished if he moves unless he really feels that he has got sufficient degree of substantial support behind him . . . I think him still, as I have always thought him, the one man capable of uniting all the various threads of thought in Congress . . . Nehru may be a considerable orator and in many ways he has the qualities of a leader. But he is torn at all times by an internal conflict of ideals and he is too lacking in consistency ever in my judgment to be the sort of basis on which one could build with confidence."[68] It might be true that, as Amery believed, Nehru had "spun himself into a cocoon of his own perversion of history and diatribes against the British which blind him to all real facts. The type is not unfamiliar among nationalist intellectuals in other countries."[69] But Gandhi was impossible to label as a type or relegate to a shelf. Gandhi's "vanity" was the one basis for hoping that he might be led to destroy his own position by exaggerating his influence, but this was a frail hope, given the fact that Gandhi's "vanity" seemed so often to be matched by the "gullibility" of his followers.

The Congress would certainly be splintered, Linlithgow believed, if only Gandhi could be disposed of, or induced to dispose of himself. The war cabinet supplied what they hoped would be the solution: deportation to East Africa. Amery cabled his enthusiasm for the proposal, arguing that "Personally I believe dramatic effect of such an exercise of our authority might be very effective in breaking legend of Gandhi's power to defy Government and also that with distance interest in him will inevitably be less." Amery argued that deportation "has something of the same effect as decease. People forget all about them."[70] Brave words; but Linlithgow finally decided that Gandhi could not be deported precisely because of the public outcry this would provoke. Following Gandhi's arrest and internment in Bombay state, Linlithgow wrote to the governor of Bombay directing that "there should be a mild but very definite change in our attitude towards Gandhi and his complaints, and that he should be made to feel that he has damaged his reputation and reduced his status by what he has done. I think further privileges should be refused firmly but very politely."[71] Brave words; but at this same time Amery was cabling frantically, "By hook or crook we mustn't let him defeat us."[72]

The government hoped that they could act rapidly and forcefully enough to deter Gandhi's movement but their own advance forecasts, while underestimating the movement's potential, nonetheless predicted very serious trouble. In a letter drafted before the lightning arrests of August 9, and sent to the provinces on August 10, the home department catalogued the forms the movement might take, including "all suggestions which were not obviously fantastic." This was a formidable and relatively accurate list of thirty-six items, including such things as "Formation wherever possible of a parallel Government . . . General social boycott, particularly of individual Britishers, who are to be harassed in every possible way . . . Withdrawal of money from banks . . . Gandhi to declare himself a rebel, to disclaim British nationality and to fast unto death . . . Demolition of bridges . . . Incitement to Government servants including police and village servants to resign . . . Stopping of trains on railways by pulling of communication cords and any other non-violent means . . . Interference with telegraph and telephone communication including cutting of telegraph wires . . . [and] Mass ticketless travel on railways."[73]

The government's list of thirty-six items proved to be conservative in a number of respects. Rail communication was stopped in many areas by the removal of rails. In the category of "supplies" the government expected nothing more serious than the "picketing of liquor shops," while in fact a serious problem arose of denial of supplies to all government servants in many areas of the country. The government's miscalculation, however, was essentially one of degree. They did not fully anticipate the severity of the movement, but they certainly knew they would be in for a hard time. The government were not so much nipping a movement in the bud as they were flailing at the dark.

Two years after the initial controversy between the viceroy and the war cabinet regarding the proper method of dealing with a Congress revolution, the revolution broke out. The Revolutionary Movement Ordinance was updated and presented to the viceroy's Executive Council for ratification several days after the outbreak of the Quit India movement. Selected provincial officials had been informed of the contents of this ordinance more than two years previously; Council members—other than Sir Reginald Maxwell—were informed of its existence at the meeting at which they were expected to ratify it.[74] Despite certain "signs of doubt," the measure was approved, signed by the viceroy on August 12, and set up in type to be issued in the *Gazette of India Extraordinary*, but it was withheld pending the receipt of requests for it from the provinces. Such a request did come from the Central Provinces, but other provinces said that they could make do with powers available under the Defence of India Rules, if these could be used against the present movement. The dubious legality of using Defence legislation against a domestic uprising, which had seemed so inhibiting when discussed in the rarefied air of Simla, seemed inconsequential to governors faced with the practical problems of suppressing revolt. So long as they had the substantive powers contained in the ordinance, they could do without its preamble. Without a clear-cut mandate from the provinces, and bearing in mind the often-expressed unhappiness of the secretary of state, Sir Reginald Maxwell decided, with the concurrence of the viceroy, that the ordinance should not be issued.[75]

Sections of the ordinance were issued as amendments to existing laws and a memorandum was sent out stating that the policies to be followed in association with the ordinance were now to be followed independently of the ordinance. "Economic warfare" and the other measures to be implemented as part of the showdown with the Congress were still official policy. All the plans evolved over the past three years were brought into operation, but without the satisfyingly straightforward declaration of principle which had been intended to tie everything together and make the government's long range intentions clear to the public at large. In the end, the Congress was dealt with as a "defense" menace after all. The coming of the long-awaited crisis revealed that the central government in Simla alone felt that the Revolutionary Movement Ordinance was essential. Unlike the provincial governments, responding to local pressures, or the home government, responding to political pressures there, the Simla government saw the crisis as an opportunity to make a stand. When the chips were down, they discovered they were standing alone. The government were forced to back down and continue their policies in the old cautious, ambiguous way.

The provinces were not interested in a long-range statement of intentions because they were concerned simply with surviving from day to day. Nor did they feel the need for an elaborate statement of the powers whose use would be justified in suppressing a "revolutionary movement" because they preferred to rely on their own estimate of what emergency powers were necessary. Without bothering to inquire about the legal position, local officials took the law into their own hands and then sought to cover their actions after the fact. During the fall of 1942 the governments of Bihar and the United Provinces, where the uprising was most serious, urgently requested indemnity legislation to protect their officers in the taking of illegal actions against demonstrators. They sought an ordinance of a type for which there was no precedent in British Indian history. Indemnity acts had been passed in 1860 and 1919 to regularize actions already taken under martial law during the Great Rebellion of 1857, and in the Punjab at the time of the Amritsar Massacre. In 1942, however, martial law had not been declared, and the central government were requested to protect not only illegal actions already taken, but those which might be taken in the future. The customary wording of an indemnity act, moreover, exonerated actions taken by officials "in good faith"; now, an attempt was made to circumvent the question of whether or not the illegal actions of officials had been taken in good faith. The governments of Bihar and the United Provinces sought authorization to continue performing illegal acts, whether or not these might be held in a court of law to be malicious and excessive.

The illegal actions which the governments of Bihar and the United Provinces acknowledged had already been taken consisted primarily of "The taking of hostages; the destruction of property belonging to the rebels or their supporters; the calling in or seizure of arms or radio sets without waiting for the usual legal procedure; the forced employment of labour to repair sabotage and remove obstructions to communications; and the imposition of collective fines before the Collective Fines Ordinance was amended on August 19th to apply to the disturbances." The governor of the United Provinces, Sir Maurice Hallett, explained that, "For example, a relief party would make its slow way up a demolished railway track, mending as it went, and took hostages from the villages through which it passed as security against the cutting of the line behind . . . *Burning of Houses:* . . . In districts such as Ballia, the position was hopelessly out of hand. In one place I visited, the Tahsil, Seed store, Post Office and Police station had been sacked and burnt and a Congress Tahsildar [rent collector] installed. Yet when the relieving forces arrived, the chief miscreants had gone and had taken, in the great majority of cases, their families and belongings with them. They could not be arrested; they could not be made subject to a collective fine. An example was essential and at once. The ringleaders were absconding. Everyone knew them, and their houses; and in their absence, some example was necessary which the ordinary people understood as sensible justice, with the ruins of Government buildings as witness to what they had done." The houses of Congress absconders suffered the official wrath which could find no worthier target. "*Collection of Collective Fines:* . . . Collections were made at times before Government sanction was given. Collection was made at times without regular assessment, and was taken at times in kind at a valuation. All this was necessary as the essence was speed; but . . . the rough and ready immediate realization of collective fines . . . was not covered by law." Hallett also noted that while he felt that looting had not taken place, "the collection of collective fines in kind gives an obvious cover to such allegations."[76]

The burning of buildings and the imposition of collective fines were admittedly haphazard. Such acts, in the opinion of R.H. Niblett, district magistrate of Azamgarh, were also often motivated by a desire to punish general Congress sympathies rather than any definable act of rebellion. At Dohrighat a Harijan Ashram was burned because its leading spirit Swami Satyanand "was a Congressman; but, so far as I could discover, disapproved of the shape the movement had taken . . . Apart from a few servants, none of the inmates were over fourteen years of age. Among the buildings burnt here by the police was a library subsidized by the Rural Development Department. The house of Raghunath Singh of Bibipur, P.S. Kandhrapur, was sacked and burnt down by a police expedition. Raghunath Singh was undoubtedly one of the leading Congressmen in the district. But he had left the district before the trouble began; and there had been no act of sabotage in the near vicinity of Bibipur." The home village of Congressman Algu Rai Shastri, also in Azamgarh District, was severely punished. A house occupied by Shastri's relatives was burned and to realize an excessively harsh collective fine the authorities, among other things, "attached an elephant."

The campaign of what Magistrate Niblett called "official dacoity" (banditry) persisted long after the mass upheaval had subsided. It was argued that systematic destruction and confiscation were necessary to prevent a recurrence of disorder, but Niblett suspected that the real purpose was to attack the Congress as a political organization rather than to punish specific acts of lawlessness. Insofar as the persistence of Congress influence in any form was thought to be a potential source of violent opposition to British rule, any action intended to destroy Congress influence could be justified on the grounds of forestalling further violence. A deputy inspector general of police outlined to Niblett a policy of "the burning of Ashrams and houses of Congressmen" which he argued "was necessary, if trouble was not to recur. He added that these methods had the approval of Government. I pointed out that Martial Law had not been proclaimed; and such a course would not be justified. He then made it plain that he was determined to proceed on such a course. I replied that, if he was so determined, I could not prevent him; but he need not expect my consent. He retorted that he did not care whether I consented or not;

and that he would carry on as he had described. Finally, he said I was insulting him in describing his programme as official arson; and strode out of the room."[77]

Martial law was not declared because civilian officials continued in nominal—and often actual—command of operations to suppress the uprising. The actions taken were no less severe than would have been taken under martial law, but as the extraordinary measures were taken on the authority of civilian officials without a declaration of martial law, there was no precedent for exonerating them for exceeding their authority after the fact, let alone exempting their future actions from legal recourse, or eliminating the question of whether actions were taken in good faith. The indemnity acts which the governor general finally permitted the governments of Bihar and the United Provinces to pass indemnified only past acts done in good faith. Permission was refused to indemnify future as well as past acts, and the central government ultimately decided it was necessary to assert that they were indemnifying only acts done in good faith.

The desire of government officials to avoid the question of good faith reflected administrative distrust for what was called "the vagaries of the Indian Courts." This concern was incorporated in the acts finally passed in the stipulation that no suits could be brought against government officials alleging bad faith without the permission of the provincial government.

On August 11, 1942, Dewoo Ganpat, "a young man of twenty-two years of sound health and earning Rs. 35 per month . . . as a vegetable hawker near Byculla shouted a National Slogan" as a police lorry passed by. Two police subinspectors named Neville Cedric Pailin and Stanley Gilleit who were riding in the lorry "fired several shots at the deceased and shot him down." Dewoo Ganpat had been the sole supporter of his seventy-five-year-old father, who brought a suit against the Bombay government. "The jury empanelled by the Coroner of Bombay in connection with the inquest on the body of the deceased expressed an opinion that the Police had no cause to open fire . . . The Commissioner of Police stated that he carefully examined the facts of the case and that he proposed to take no action in the matter, as he holds that the firing was justified and that the opinion expressed by the jury was perverse."[78]

The Indian judicial system, from the lowest to the highest levels, including both Englishmen and Indians, had been demonstrating substantial reluctance to ratify the extraordinary actions taken by the government since the beginning of the war. The Special Criminal Courts Ordinance under whose authority thousands had been sent to jail was held to be invalid by the Calcutta High Court and this decision was subsequently upheld by the Federal Court.[79] Dozens of court decisions were handed down reversing administrative actions. The government, however, displayed an unrepentant indifference to the efforts by Indian courts to hinder their freedom of action and reissued ordinances—with slight revisions—as soon as laborious court proceedings had declared them invalid. In this, as in other ways, the government were acting consciously in a reckless fashion, attempting to hold the line for the moment, indifferent to the day when the world would be quieter and the government would find themselves standing alone amidst the shambles of their former legitimacy.

The Indian government were ultimately baffled by the subtlety of their own devices. They might still command sufficient police power to prevent their own "total immersion," to suppress overt hostility, and to hold the line in a garrison state under siege, but the methods of suppression employed signaled the end of Britain's legitimacy as a governing agency. The government might accomplish the momentary negative task of quelling revolt, but they were frustrated in their efforts to turn the confrontation to any constructive advantage. The events of the following months told a dismal story of governmental impotence. The effects of the Midnapur cyclone in the fall of 1942 and the Bengal Famine of 1943, which resulted in over a million deaths, were thought to have been aggravated by governmental obstruction of relief efforts. The government were not thought capable of responding with public spirit even to natural calamity. When the viceroy in these days traveled from city to city in his special train, a separate engine ran ahead to try the tracks, clearing the way across a hostile land.

Political initiative by an official autocracy is hampered by the very finality of the power it wields. Nominally, the British-Indian government during the war emergency could do anything; they consequently had to be very cautious not to intimate their intentions prematurely. The government wished to administer a crushing blow to the Congress, but righteous massive retaliation was difficult to unleash against Gandhi's subtle probing. The government wished to give firm assurance to their officials and political supporters that the government, rather than the Congress, held the keys to the future, but had to face the humiliation of discovering that their assurances were not altogether believed; practical evidence would alone alleviate the defeatist mentality. Practical steps, on the other hand, posed the risk that sympathy might redound to their opponents who could pose as victims of official persecution. The limitations constricting the government's power of implementation were not the sort they could advertise; these included official distrust of personnel, popular distrust of officials, and the veto power of the government in London. The government wished to pretend to omnipotence and hence could not appeal for sympathy on the basis of their difficulties, but they could not act with the assurance of omnipotence without exposing their weakness and inviting their downfall. The government were boxed in by pretensions; the Congress was free to use the daylight.

Foreign warfare has often been considered a unifying national experience; it is said that even tyrants when in domestic difficulties can recoup their fortunes by pursuing foreign adventures. National wars against foreign foes are usually thought of as providing a welcome relief from the bitterness of domestic political strife, providing a common denominator, a simple ultimate cause around which all can unite.

The truth of the matter is that foreign wars provide a welcome outlet for those fond of simple ultimate causes and an embarrassing interruption to others. War is always a weapon in the domestic battle, whether or not its manipulators are conscious of this. "War profiteers" exist in politics no less than in the munitions industry.

War is, furthermore, a double-edged political weapon. Since war is supposed to unite people around the nation's simple verities, it may bring into question the truth of those verities. The call for national unity may pose a tawdry contrast between rhetoric and reality. Following a call for the burying of differences, discrimination stands out in lurid relief. If patriotic offers of service are handled in a discriminatory manner, those scorned may react with extreme bitterness.

A war may aggravate internal animosities by its very claim to transcend them and accelerate the tempo of domestic change at a time when a moratorium on such change might have been presumed to be a necessity. It is easy for an elite to promise progress once the war is over. It is difficult for the disaffected to press for justice when any holding back on their part is readily branded as a comfort to the enemy.

The recent American debate over national priorities in the context of the cold war has followed the classic pattern of such confrontations. Those concerned with military preparedness argue that there is no point in improving American cities while they remain in danger of destruction by the enemy; opponents argue that if the cities are not improved, they will hardly be worth defending. Similarly, both World Wars were fought to make the world safe for democracy; opponents argued that unless the allied nations were first made truly democratic, the war effort would be needlessly hampered and its outcome of doubtful value for democracy. Referring to postwar prospects in 1942, Louis Fischer said to Gandhi, "It depends on the kind of peace we make." Gandhi replied, "It depends on what you do during the war."[1]

A debate over the priority of war or reform cannot avoid bitterness, given the height of emotions engendered by a war emergency, even though there may be no dispute over the ultimate necessity of the war itself. A more serious confrontation may result if opponents raise the question of the morality of the war involvement on any terms. This may be justified in terms of opposition to all wars, opposition to all wars of a certain sort, or a conviction that the nation is fighting on the wrong side of this particular war. In the latter case, sympathy for the enemy may be more than a loose accusation by chauvinistic extremists. Any sizeable opposition to any particular war is likely to have some participants motivated by each of these reasons. The freedom of speech permitted war opponents may also affect the types of arguments which are raised; a war involvement criticized on one ground may actually be opposed for more serious and hence more seditious reasons. Mild war critics are consequently liable, whether justly or unjustly, to suspicions of harboring more subtle motives than those they acknowledge.

The type of "reform" demanded by war opponents as a condition for war support, or as a guarantee against future mistaken involvements, also may range from a demand for an end to discriminatory treatment of troops of different races, to a demand for an immediate and total change of regime. Wars may result in revolution, sooner or later. Revolutions frequently come to power in the wake of war exhaustion. Such revolutionary regimes will probably take a very different view of the nation's war involvement, as reflected in the decision of the Bolsheviks in 1917 to make a mid-war peace settlement with Germany. The leaders of revolutions have not ordinarily been primarily identified as the leaders of antiwar agitations. War-related movements were critical, however, in the subsequent attainment of power by revolutionaries in such countries as Russia, Ireland, Yugoslavia, Indonesia, Burma, China, Vietnam, and India. In Russia, Yugoslavia, Indonesia, Burma, China, and Vietnam, the war-related movements developed in active war theaters.

Ireland and India are unusual in having experienced revolutionary antiwar movements while they were potential but not active theaters of war. The Easter Rebellion of 1916 and the Quit India movement of 1942 were integral parts of long-standing revolutionary movements and critical to their subsequent success.

Indian support for the British war effort in the First World War had been little more than a sporting proposition: Britain was fighting a war, so why not do the gentlemanly thing and help out with men and money? The war's direct impact upon India was largely economic. The British did seek to build up popular support for the cause and in this connection called upon the privileged classes to perform their appointed function as leaders of opinion. Some underground groups did collaborate with the enemy, but most nationalists demanded nothing more than a fair repayment for India's contribution to the war effort. The war made only a marginal impact on Indian politics, and it was only after the war that a serious confrontation developed.

The Second World War presented a direct threat of invasion; Bengal and Madras and other areas were bombed, and Indian territory was penetrated by the Japanese, aided by the forces of the provisional government of independent India. Indian political consciousness had, moreover, developed enormously in a direct line from the feeling of 1919 that India had been betrayed by British unwillingness to reward India's war services.

In 1939, Indians had once again been called to rally round the empire on the assumption that the only improvement in their lot they could expect was contingent upon the empire's strength. The war, after all, was being fought to safeguard freedom. Why, then, asked the Congress, had war been declared on behalf of Indians by a patronizing authority? The resignation of Congress ministries following the viceroy's Declaration of War was a protest against being forced to defend freedom. How could one wholeheartedly fight for the freedom of others when arbitrarily ordered to do so? When Churchill subsequently signed the Atlantic Charter declaring a purpose of the war to be the bringing of freedom to enslaved nations, and then stated that this did not apply to India, Indians saw this as confirmation of their worst suspicions.

In the course of his long career Gandhi had had to decide on two earlier occasions what course he should take in relation to the conduct of a war. In the Boer War, which occurred while Gandhi was in South Africa, he assisted the British but stated that "It must largely be conceded that justice is on the side of the Boers."[2] During World War I, he recruited soldiers to fight for the British Empire but also organized several local movements to protest economic exploitation. In each case, his decision was based on what he considered best for the movements with which he was then associated, considering the duties of citizenship and the merits of the war only in relation to this larger loyalty. Gandhi argued that Indians had an obligation to assist the British because "In every memorial we have presented, we have asserted our rights as . . . British subjects."[3] Whatever one thought of the merits of the war, one had an obligation to defend the state in which one had been claiming rights for so long.

In both the Boer War and World War I, demonstrations of Indian loyalty were handsomely received by the British, and handsome promises were made about the benefits Indians would consequently receive. In the Boer War, the discrimination practiced by the Boers against Indians—who were British subjects—was allegedly one reason the British were fighting. The British claimed to be fighting for "the rights of Indians." After the war, the discriminatory policy of the Boers was intensified under the British. In 1917, the British government committed itself to movement toward responsible Indian government following the war; after the war, the introduction of the repressive Rowlatt Acts quickly reversed the situation. The memory of these experiences was invoked by Gandhi in explaining his inability to conduct himself in the same loyal fashion in World War II. The beginning of this third war signaled the beginning of Gandhi's third great campaign.

The causes with which Gandhi involved himself are numberless; the organized campaigns, large and small, to which he devoted his full attention for a period would have to be counted in scores. All but three of these campaigns, however, were local or limited in some way to a person or a group or an issue. The three great national campaigns of 1919–1922, 1927–1932, and 1939–1943 stand out as events of major significance in all-India history as well as the Gandhian movement and in fact mark the generations of nationalist involvement. Each of these events served as a turning point in the lives of numerous people who were aroused to commit themselves to the service of radicalism by participation in these cataclysmic protests. Jawaharlal Nehru and Subhas Bose belonged to the class of 1919–1922; Aruna Asaf Ali to that of 1927–1932, and many leaders of Indira Gandhi's generation to that of 1939–1943.

The first campaign was born in the bitterness of disillusionment following World War I, when India's services were rewarded by repressive legislation and the gratuitous horror of the Amritsar massacre. At this time Gandhi took control of the Congress, drastically altered its organization and tactics, and announced a program designed to win immediate independence for India. The movement gathered momentum, and India was wracked by unprecedented excitement and activity. Amidst the upheaval, an incident of violence occurred and Gandhi suddenly called a halt to the entire movement. The young militants, such as Nehru, whom Gandhi had so aroused, were appalled that Gandhi should sacrifice a movement because of what they considered an unfortunate but eminently predictable accident. But Gandhi's indispensability was such that he left them no choice: when Gandhi called off the movement, it actually stopped. It is even possible that in calling off the movement when he did, Gandhi may have been more hardheaded than those who did not blink at bloodshed. There is some evidence that the movement was already disintegrating and that in stopping it as he did Gandhi was only snatching victory from the jaws of political defeat.

In the movement highlighted by the Salt March of 1930, Gandhi acted as a craftsman of politics, creating a major movement by the sheer genius of an unorthodox imagination. Gandhi had the precision of insight to see a revolution in a handful of salt.

The movement began in response to the appointment of the all-white Simon Commission in 1927, a signal that the next round of discussion of India's future would also be safely circumscribed. The movement ended in 1932 in total confrontation between a militant Congress and a stiff-necked viceroy, who arrested Gandhi and suppressed the movement. The intervening stages, highlighted by the Salt March and the second Round Table Conference, marked Gandhi's greatest personal ascendancy. During the march and the conference in London, Gandhi acted as he chose as the plenipotentiary of the Congress. Gandhi's sudden shifts, from defiance to cordial negotiations with Lord Irwin, from consultation in London to protest in India, were no longer a surprise. Gandhi's method still could prove dismaying, but there was a general recognition of Gandhi's talent for finding success in puzzling places and his capacity to anticipate public moods.

With the collapse of this second movement, however, it appeared that Gandhi might have been at last discredited. After his release from prison in 1934, Gandhi devoted his energies to his constructive program of village industries, Harijan welfare, and the rectifying of local injustices. Gandhi even resigned his membership in the Congress. Having set up his headquarters in the remote central Indian village of Sevagram, near Wardha, Gandhi made it clear that he did not wish to interfere where he was not wanted. With older Congressmen preoccupied with ministry-making, and with many younger activists attracted to the more militant leadership of Subhas Bose, it appeared that the seventy-year-old Gandhi might be left to end his days as a social worker.[4]

Gandhi was not disturbed by his apparent eclipse because he had long since learned his limits. He was prepared to bide his time because he realized that the sort of movement he could lead was possible only in periods of extreme stress, when people had grown tired of politicking and maneuvering for advantage, when people had had time to discover for themselves the futility of politics-as-usual. The outbreak of war in 1939 signaled the possibility that Gandhi might once again be wanted. The resignation of the Congress ministries put Congress in opposition, potentially poised for a campaign of the sort which only Gandhi could lead.

Grounds for Resistance

Congressmen opposed the war for many reasons. Some congressmen were concerned by Linlithgow's method of placing India in the war, some, like Gandhi, were pacifists, others felt that England's difficulty was India's opportunity, still others thought India was being asked to fight for an evil cause. Many were impressed by the Irish and Russian examples. Ireland had revolted from England during the First World War and remained neutral and ominously pro-Nazi during the Second. The Bolsheviks had taken unembarrassed advantage of the Russian government's wartime difficulties in 1917, and in 1939 entered into a nonaggression pact with Germany. Why should not India now oppose the war, suggested Congress Socialist leader Jayaprakash Narayan, and "utilize it to attain our own freedom"?[5] By the time England was in a position to dispose in an orderly fashion of India's claims for payment for loyal services rendered, England might once again be in a position to manage the negotiations to her own advantage.

The immediate past president of the Congress for the years 1938 and 1939, Subhas Bose, escaped to Germany and worked with the Axis against the British, making broadcasts from Berlin to India and raising armies from Indian prisoners of war in Germany and later in Singapore.

Those who took a less opportunistic, more ideological position were no more enthusiastic about the British war effort. Both socialists and communists were impressed by Soviet Russia's nonaggression pact with England's enemy. In early 1940 Nehru wrote to Gandhi his opinion that the war was a "purely imperialist venture on both sides . . . The British Government today is more reactionary and imperialist than it has ever been . . . The war and British policy grow more and more sinister every day."[6]

The reasons for which most congressmen opposed the British war effort were not Gandhian, but the possibility of a movement led by Gandhi seemed promising, even if Gandhi himself were to oppose the war only for reasons of his own. Gandhi was prepared to lead a general antiwar movement so long as it was conducted on his own terms, which meant beginning at the beginning. Instead of rushing into revolution Gandhi launched a series of tests of the bad faith of his opponents and the dedication of his supporters.

When Gandhi began the antiwar movement, he suggested to the British what their war aims ought to be by "assuming" these were their aims. His opposition to the war at this stage was based solely upon his opposition to all wars, a fact which he underlined by insisting that, insofar as he had any preference regarding the outcome of the war, he was sympathetic to the British, who had his "moral support." By its very nature, however, Gandhi contended, warfare made more difficult the attainment of the purposes which were used to justify it. Gandhi was unimpressed by the argument that the solution of little things such as Indian independence would be much simpler in the sane world sure to result from the war. He was unimpressed by the argument that mankind would have "realized" as a result of the war the irrefutability of the principles for which it was ostensibly being fought and be in an infinitely stronger position to implement justice, with the forces of injustice handily disposed of. On the contrary, Gandhi predicted the outcome of the war would parallel that of the *Mahabharata*, "the permanent history of man." Far from leaving strengthened the hand of a just victor, war would leave him prostrate. "The warring nations are destroying themselves with such fury . . . that the end will be mutual exhaustion . . . The victor will share the same fate that awaited the surviving Pandavas. The mighty warrior Arjuna was looted in broad daylight by a petty robber."[7]

When Gandhi finally launched an organized protest under the authority vested in him by the Congress in the fall of 1940, this first stage of formal protest turned out to be a carefully calculated campaign of "individual Satyagraha." This phase was also consciously restrained or "dull" as the government put it.

In 1930 Gandhi had personally inaugurated civil disobedience by picking up illegal salt from the shore at Dandi. In 1940 he chose to direct the initial stages of the movement from the background. As Gandhi explained, "A question has been asked why, if I attach so much importance to quality, I do not offer civil resistance myself. I have already said that unlike as on previous occasions I do not wish to do so for the very good reason that my imprisonment is likely to cause greater embarrassment to the authorities than anything else the Congress can do. I want also to remain outside to cope with any contingency that may arise. My going to jail may be interpreted as a general invitation to all Congressmen to follow suit. They will not easily distinguish between my act and speech."[8] Gandhi indicated his wish that this time the majority of congressmen should not court arrest, but rather should stay outside of jail to carry on work as long as they could, by deciding to stay out of jail himself as long as possible. Moreover, since events could force a modification of strategy at any time, continuous, intensive direction of the movement through its calculated stages by the "dictator himself" seemed more urgent than ever before.

While the government hoped that Gandhi would hurl all his forces against them at once, so that, once repressed, nothing would remain, Gandhi instead employed a form of symbolic guerrilla warfare. He developed his position slowly, in a manner which forestalled the possibility of massive retaliation and insured that no amount of physical force could refute the force of his arguments. Gandhi's intention was to build a movement which would ultimately acquire sufficient momentum to survive the elimination of its leaders, and this necessitated a slow process of education and careful restraint of premature confrontations.

He selected as the first three Satyagrahis individuals who would symbolize different reasons for opposing the government. Vinoba Bhave represented the absolute opposition to all wars which Gandhi himself shared. Jawaharlal Nehru followed Vinoba, to represent the opposition to Britain's "imperialist war" of pro-Soviet intellectuals. The third Satyagrahi was an unknown individual, one Brahma Dutt Sharma, designated to represent the common man. British police reports confirmed that Sharma was indeed "a very ordinary man, having no means of livelihood or any social position. He recently wrote a love letter to the daughter of one Hukam Chand, druggist of his village, which resulted in a quarrel." The speech for which he was arrested expressed, in addition to opposition to the war, very ordinary grievances; he complained that "the police would take out a cigarette from anybody's pocket, and would drink tea at other's expenses."[9]

Following these three carefully spaced acts of individual protest, Gandhi slowly expanded the movement. Increasing numbers of individuals were permitted to recite a set formula as follows: "It is wrong to help the British war effort with men or money. The only worthy effort is to resist all wars with non-violent resistance." They would then be arrested and sent to jail for short terms. For a year this procedure was followed with a gradually quickening tempo, until some 23,000 persons had been imprisoned. This form of symbolic protest having run its natural course, the movement was permitted to die out. The government were sufficiently confident that this "dull" movement represented the extent of Gandhi's capacity that when it receded, they released all Satyagrahis in a general amnesty and prepared the official *History* of the movement. While the government were summing up their report on how and why this movement had "petered out," Gandhi on December 5, 1941, was writing to Nehru, just released from jail, "It is nice to be able to write to you outside jail. But the pleasure is only momentary. For I cannot reconcile myself to these discharges. The discharges are a challenge."[10] Gandhi had thus decided to undertake a fresh protest two days before Pearl Harbor and long before the spectacular Japanese successes in Southeast Asia and the failure of the Cripps mission. While the government were concluding that Gandhi had exhausted his influence, Gandhi was already planning bigger things. Gandhi's tests had demonstrated that Indians were ready to move and the British were not. The public response to his limited campaign had indicated a desire for something more; the official response had indicated that something more was necessary.

Gandhi's new intention was to take a stand which would be authentically obstructive, which would compel something more than an optional response from the government. Gandhi had described his earlier policy toward the British war effort as one of "nonembarrassment," a symbolic protest which would not get in the way. Now his intention was reversed. The government had greeted his protests with amused indifference, thereby giving notice that symbolic remonstrance, being found genuinely noncoercive, would be cheerfully ignored. Having failed to provoke a voluntary response, Gandhi had decided to provoke an involuntary one. In a letter to Horace Alexander, of August 3, 1942, he recorded his "grave misgiving that those who are in authority do not want to part with India. With them it seems that to lose India is to lose the battle . . . I saw that some form of conflict was inevitable to bring home that truth to the British mind."[11]

The letters which British authorities seized from the Congress Socialist leader Jayaprakash Narayan when he attempted to smuggle them out of Deoli jail in the fall of 1941 give some indication of the growing urge for more extreme forms of protest which Gandhi's limited campaign had provoked among activists. In his letter to a fellow socialist, Jayaprakash spoke contemptuously of "this farce of Satyagraha" and advocated that to intensify their activities it was desirable for the Congress Socialists to enter into alliances with underground revolutionaries. A formal though secret merger with the Revolutionary Socialist party was discussed. It was even proposed to resort to the collection of funds by "the old method," a reference to forcible collection.

Jayaprakash's letters suggested that the anti-British sentiments of the majority of Congress Socialists had not been neutralized by the entry of the Soviet Union into the war as a British ally. During the period of the Russian-German treaty, communists had denounced the Allies as imperialists and worked together with other nationalists opposed to the British war. The German invasion of Russia turned the communists overnight into defenders of the British war as a people's war. The socialist-communist alliance split when it was necessary to choose between the relative priorities of Indian independence and defense of the Soviet Union. It soon became apparent that the communists had not been successful in carrying very many socialists with them in their precipitate reversal, which Jayaprakash considered "extremely childish."

"Our attitude," wrote Jayaprakash, "should be that we sympathize fully with Russia but are helpless to do anything about it." To assist the British simply because they were allied with Russia "would be a mistake . . . To continue this attack [on British imperialism] would itself be a service to Soviet Russia." Jayaprakash then proposed what he himself labeled a "political stunt." He suggested British officials be told that the Congress Socialists would assist in raising troops to be "sent directly to the Russian front, to be . . . commanded by the Russian forces."

Jayaprakash reported that he had made considerable progress among his fellow prisoners at Deoli in persuading communist sympathizers away from the party and in favor of carrying on a violent struggle in wartime against British rule. "Tilakraj, Richapal, Vatas (all very important members) are disgusted with the C.P. and have already decided that after going out they would advocate total separation from the C.P. . . . In any case, the majority of the Punjab comrades are definitely for leaving the C.P. consolidation after release." Jayaprakash concluded by mentioning that, not surprisingly, the attitude of communist leaders to his efforts to win their followers away was "extremely hostile."

Jayaprakash was busily planning new atrocities from his jail cell. At the same time, his mood suggested that nationalist unity might still be retrievable if Gandhi were to adopt a more aggressive stance. "We must have an illegal organisation and illegal activities," wrote Jayaprakash. "I have begun to feel very strongly that we must do something very spectacular at this moment . . . We cannot do anything big. But . . . we must do something to attract public notice and arouse enthusiasm among the youth. Do think of something." Jayaprakash felt that something had to be done which was more drastic than the symbolic war protest which Gandhi had sanctioned. If Gandhi continued his "farce," the radicals would have to carry on as best they could on their own. But, clearly, if Gandhi showed a lead they could follow, they would be back in harness in an instant. Jayaprakash, while denouncing Gandhi, was still "anxious to know" the news from Gandhi's headquarters at Wardha. "What are the general political prospects?"[12]

The government's official *History of the Civil Disobedience Movement, 1940–41* stated, optimistically, that Jayaprakash's letters had "cut the Mahatma to the quick."[13] Actually, their publication by the government in October 1941 was used by Gandhi as an opportunity for a clarification of his current position. "Frankly," he said, "all nationalist forces . . . are at war with the Government. And, according to the accepted canon of war, the method adopted by Jayaprakash Narayan is perfectly legitimate . . . [although] his method is harmful in the extreme, while a non-violent struggle is going on." Gandhi saw beyond Jaya-prakash's denunciation of himself, which according to the government's reckoning was all that Gandhi was concerned about, and recognized that his ire at Gandhi was a reflection of the dedication they shared. His methods were harmful at the moment, though, by implication, they might someday be in order.

Gandhi was thus considering escalating his confrontation with the government even before the Japanese began their swift advance toward India's borders. This new threat, however, provided new evidence of the need for quick action. In a speech in Gorakhpur on January 31, Nehru observed that "The satyagraha that was introduced has now been withdrawn . . . because Mahatmaji thought that some more far-reaching problems had cropped up than the individual satyagraha. Take for instance that bombs can fall over the city of Calcutta . . . If at that time we go to Calcutta and ask the residents to offer satyagraha it will be a useless thing." Nehru announced that the Congress would henceforth be concerned with building a country-wide network of civil defense volunteers "for defending our villages and cities . . . This organisation would be capable even of running the government."[14]

Throughout the spring Gandhi repeatedly criticized the British method of defending India from invasion. Gandhi sent his associate Mirabehn to Orissa in June to report on conditions there; she wrote that in the coastal areas villagers had been ordered "to immobilize their boats . . . Even for answering the calls of nature it is necessary to go in a boat. The villagers are in despair." In the canal districts, canals had been drained to prevent their use by the Japanese. "The working of the land has been all upset . . . When I look at these broad dry canal beds they strike me as more serviceable for bringing up tanks and other heavy equipment than they would be if full of water."[15]

Gandhi described receiving many letters indicating that the class of what he called "upper poor" were suffering extreme hardship due to the scarcity of grain arriving in cities.[16] Nor were the richer classes exempt; for the comfortable accommodation of foreign soldiers, the houses of wealthy Indians had been confiscated, and many motor vehicles had been "requisitioned."[17] Such inconveniences might have been tolerated as a part of a popular war effort; as reflections of British arbitrariness, they were insulting.

While Indian troops were sent abroad to fight for the empire, white troops, which were much more expensive to maintain, were sent to India—troops which could be used against a domestic uprising as well as for external defense. The British were preparing to hold their own, whether the defense of India was threatened by Japanese or by Indians. Under the threat of invasion, the British military authorities had instituted ruthless confiscatory measures, in the manner of a foreign army in disputed territory. No effective effort was made to enlist the willing cooperation of Indians, with the result that Indians were uncertain in what respects a Japanese occupation could be worse than the arbitrary destruction of their livelihood by British military authorities. From Bihar, the provincial chief secretary reported that, "Believing that Government intended to commandeer all standing wheat crops, cultivators in parts of the Northern districts are reported to have harvested the crop before it was time to do so."[18] A state of general excitement was aroused, in which everything was confused. Not knowing what to expect, and in any case indifferent to the fate of constituted authority, almost everyone was concerned simply with trying to protect himself and his family and friends.

With an unrattled grasp of bureaucratic prose, the chief secretary to the government of Assam reported that "The morale of the province has been put to a severe test by the [Japanese] raids of the 10th and 16th May on Imphal, and has not emerged well from it . . . *Prima facie* it appears likely that the number of persons who stuck to their posts after the second raid was in most departments exiguous, and the accounts of eye-witnesses show that a large and motley stream of labourers probably accompanied by demoralized subordinate officials has been passing down the road." The chief secretary, it would seem, had not left his desk to confirm the reports of eye-witnesses but nonetheless recognized demoralization when he saw it.[19]

Even more impressive than this response to a direct Japanese attack on a border town was the reaction to the Japanese advance reported from the interior province of Bihar. The chief secretary's Fortnightly Report for the first half of May 1942 was grim:

There is no improvement to report in the general public feeling. Defeatism and anti-British feeling encouraged by enemy broadcasts and by objectionable speeches are still pronounced. The unfavourable impression caused by the passage of trains through North Bihar containing sick and wounded from the Burma front is now likely to be strengthened by the unexpected return of labour which had only recently been recruited for the military roads in Assam. These labourers are returning in many cases with sores on their feet in a condition which shows that they have not been well cared for in the journey. And on their return the tale is spreading that many of them are victims of the Japanese air raids in Assam. Two incidents that have been reported during the fortnight illustrate the people's reluctance to go anywhere near the war zone and their continued fear at the proximity of soldiers. At Samastipur, five Indian engine-drivers who had been ordered to take their engines to Katihor for delivery to the Bengal & Assam Railway and to work them on that railway, refused together with their firemen and Khalasis [porters], to do so, and the engines had to be driven there by British foremen and drivers. At Mandar near Ranchi, the village tank was inspected by a military officer, whereupon some of the villagers promptly drained it for fear that troops might camp in the locality and harass the villagers. According to the District Magistrate of Gaya the general conclusion arrived at by the people is that the Japanese have succeeded in cutting off China from India and that the Burma road which was originally intended to be the lifeline of China has now become the line of Japanese invasion.[20]

Also from Bihar, word was received that "some Sadhus from Patna and Gaya . . . are believed to be responsible for the spread of anti-British rumours and pro-Japanese propaganda." This may have accounted for the report of the superintendent of police of Shahabad District that "many ordinary people believe the Japanese to be Hindus, and therefore, there is no need for any fear from a Japanese invasion."[21] The fact that people were less than receptive to reassurances that the British would hold their own is also suggested by the allegation made in December 1942 that the government "have placed an order with 'Bombay Garage' (Chinoy & Co.) for 10,000 *Dummy Aeroplanes* of wood; ostensibly they are to be distributed over Indian aerodromes to deceive the people that they have plenty of planes. The Japs will certainly not be frightened of the *British Dummy Planes.*"[22]

What Indians were witnessing on their own soil was minor in comparison to the experience of Malaya and Burma, the effects of whose evacuation Indians watched closely. At their meeting at the end of April 1942, the All-India Congress Committee charged that "The officials whose duty was to protect the lives and interests of the people in their respective areas . . . ran away from their post of duty and sought safety for themselves, leaving the vast majority of people wholly unprovided for. Such arrangements for evacuation as were made were meant for the European population."[23]

The evacuation of Burma presented a dismal picture of discrimination under stress. Harrowing tales were told of the division of refugees between those permitted to take the "White Road" and those forced to take the "Black Road," on which they were allegedly robbed by police and exploited mercilessly by opportunists along the route supplying cartage and food and water for exorbitant charges with police connivance. Many died along the way, and cholera stalked the refugee camps.[14]

Burma suggested the way in which Indians might be left to fend for themselves; Burma also suggested the probable result. "Burmese guerrilla bands are fighting for Japan against us," wrote W. M. Towler in the *Daily Herald* in an article entitled "Quislings in Burma." "Burmese snipers are picking off British soldiers. Burmese guides are leading Japanese patrols through the jungles. Burmese spies are giving away . . . information about our military dispositions. This should make us think."[25]

Indians were seeing proved before their eyes what nationalists had so long alleged: that Europeans thought of India as a place where a convenient living might be got, not as their own country. British officials evacuated Malaya and Burma; it would have been inconceivable to speak of "evacuating" England in comparable circumstances. India had been comfortably arranged to make life agreeable for those who administered India from isolated spots with pleasant climates. The administration were not prepared to provide leadership for a nation in crisis.

Following the Japanese air raids of April 6, 1942, on Vizagapatam, "the railways were practically paralysed and all the subordinate staff and labour fled from the place . . . All provision shops were closed and practically everyone deserted the town; the Port labour fled and so did the coolies employed on the construction of the new aerodrome."[26]

On the 11th of April the Madras government

> were advised by the local military commanders that intelligence had been received which made it appear that an invasion in force by the Japanese was likely to take place within a few days somewhere on the east coast of India at some point south of Masulipatam. The Government therefore decided that all Government offices which could be evacuated from Madras should be dispersed to towns further inland at once and they also issued a communique to the general public advising all those whose presence was considered not essential to leave the City as soon as possible. The Government offices were closed from Sunday April the 12th and ordered to

reopen a week later in the place to which they have been ordered to move . . . The Governor and his Advisers, the Chief Secretary and other Secretaries with skeleton staffs continued to work at Fort St. George. The effect of Government's decision to move their offices did far more than the advice in their communique to bring about an extremely rapid exodus and it is estimated that in the six days prior to and including the 14th of April some two lakhs [200,000] of people left the city . . . Even on the West coast there has been a tendency towards evacuation from the coastal towns into the interior. The District Magistrate of Malabar reports that there is a noticeable feeling that if it came to the worst the Japanese are not bad people after all and the District Magistrate is organising the Propaganda Sub Committee to combat this attitude.[27]

Surveying the Indian scene in the spring of 1942, Gandhi recognized that India was on the verge of chaos. The British government were in disarray, unable to control the people or defend the country. British defense efforts were, in fact, causing havoc and confusion. There was every reason to assume—as British intelligence assumed—that the Japanese advance across Asia would continue into Indian territory. It seemed inevitable that even if the Allies ultimately "won" the war, a sizeable portion of eastern India, if not the entire subcontinent, would come under Japanese control for a period of time. The Indian people were meanwhile reacting to the flight of their rulers with indifference and a desire to save their own skins by flight or accommodation with the new conquerors. Subhas Bose had joined with Britain's military foes as his proposed solution to the impasse; Gandhi felt under an obligation to give an alternative lead. Even if they failed, the Congress would then not be accused of having lain back supinely while Bose had been fighting for Indian independence. Gandhi felt that he must try to unite Indians around an Indian cause. He was unwilling to wait to see India conquered by the Japanese and then perhaps reconquered by the Allies, or to defer his hope for Indian independence until the "two foreign mad bulls" had settled their scores on Indian soil.[28] In the process, India would be physically wracked; more important, Indians would be humiliated by their passivity in permitting outsiders to arbitrate their fate. "It is not open to them to say that we must smother our consciences and say or do nothing because there is war," Gandhi asserted on July 25, 1942. "That is why I have made up my mind that it would be a good thing if a million people were shot in a brave and non-violent rebellion against British rule . . . Avowedly the different nations are fighting for their liberty. Germany, Japan, Russia, China are pouring their blood and money like water. What is *our* record?"[29]

On April 12 Gandhi's weekly *Harijan* reprinted the words of General G. N. Molesworth, deputy chief of the General Staff in India, regarding the way in which he expected a Japanese invasion would be met. "We shall hold vital places . . . but we cannot hold everyone," he commented. He consequently advocated educating "the masses to give the Japanese a great deal of trouble." Total surrender, he felt, would be "unworthy of our heritage . . . if we really feel India is worthy of having, we have got to see that we defend it."

It was an expert's opinion, concluded Mahadev Desai, that India could not be defended by violence. Indians did not have the sort of national spirit which Britishers had, or which President Roosevelt had hailed in America, "a tradition that goes back to Israel Putnam, who left his plough in a New England furrow to take up a gun and fight at Bunker Hill." Even if such a spirit had existed, "General Molesworth has frankly said, 'We cannot arm all.'" Desai suggested that if, as many military men had testified, superior weapons could never humble a determined people, if a nation's spiritual solidarity was its greatest military asset, then it was only reasonable to suppose that India's greatest military asset was the closest Indian approximation of such a national spirit, the spirit built up over twenty years by the Gandhian movement.

Gandhi's long-standing determination to pull out of the imperial system had, for example, stimulated many efforts to demonstrate that Indian villages could survive without the imperial structure resting on their backs. It was now also possible to demonstrate that autonomous villages had a unique defense capability. British plans for retreat proved that the urban-based imperial system could not, and did not care to, defend villages. The retreating army would confine itself to the defense of certain strategic enclaves, leaving villagers to their fate with a hearty slap on the back and a promise to return. Gandhi, without using the word "guerrilla," outlined a defense plan which, for all its apparent "madness," came very close to anticipating the dominant military phenomenon of the next thirty years. Gandhi proposed that the cities be evacuated to the greatest extent possible and that city-dwellers should settle in India's 700,000 villages and aid in the formation of self-help organizations. As he put it, "The seven hundred thousand dollars invested in the imperial bank of India could be swept away by a bomb from a Japanese plane, whereas if they were distributed among the seven hundred thousand shareholders, nobody could deprive them of their assets."[30]

Careful note was taken of the experience of resistance to Japanese invaders in China, where Japanese control of China's industrialized regions had stimulated a return to village industries in the interior.[31] Gandhi, furthermore, put his plan of village resistance into operation by sending "hundreds" of volunteers, including Mirabehn, to eastern India to instruct villagers in the method of resistance to the Japanese through noncooperation.[32] "Retreat itself is often a plan of resistance," Gandhi noted.[33]

The Morality of Violence

Gandhi now began systematically withdrawing the moral sanction of the British war effort he had extended at the beginning of the war. On May 18, 1942, he recalled that he "used to say that my moral support was entirely with Great Britain. I am very sorry to have to confess that today my mind refuses to give that moral support."[34] Now Gandhi suggested that "the Nazi power had risen as a nemesis to punish Britain for her sins of exploitation and enslavement of the Asiatic and African races."[35] "I do not say that the British are worse than the Japanese," he said, but, if Britain were not to free India, Britain did not "deserve to win." One should not forget that there were "powerful elements of Fascism in British rule." "Both America and Great Britain lack the moral basis for engaging in this war unless they put their own houses in order . . . They have no right to talk about protecting democracies and protecting civilization and human freedom, until the canker of white superiority is destroyed in its entirety."[36]

Gandhi thus summed up the import of the articles written in the preceding months for the *Harijan* by Mahadev Desai on "British and American Nazism." Despite the position of the Negro in America, the Americans "talk of democracy and equality! It is an utter lie," Desai quoted Gandhi as saying. The British, for their part, approved "a purely Nazi policy," the Southern Rhodesian Land Apportionment Act of 1941, which condemned "a million British subjects to restriction to a third of their own country and service-villainage in the rest of it for the benefit of a minority of 55,000 British subjects."[37] A month later, further evidence was published that "the American brand [of Nazism] is, if anything, worse than the British brand." Desai noted "the most ruthless prevalence of the colour bar there . . . No wonder that a 'Negro-man-in-the-street' wrote to the editor of a paper: 'When I read these things I am forced to wonder just how far removed is the brand of democracy that we practise from Fascism, Nazism, and barbarism.'"

As Gandhi withdrew the moral sanction he had extended to the British war effort, he also withdrew the moral opprobrium from violent resistance to it. The ever-present undercurrent of violence in the nationalist movement had preoccupied Gandhi even before his return to India in 1915. His important book *Hind Swaraj* was written on ship-board in 1909 on the way back from London where he had engaged in discussions with advocates of violence. *Hind Swaraj* is structured as a dialogue between an impatient revolutionary tempted by violence and Gandhi speaking as an "editor." This was Gandhi's manifesto, written long before he became the supreme leader of the nationalist movement, but at a time when violent methods seemed likely to become dominant, replacing constitutional agitation.[39]

During the first phase of Gandhi's active leadership, between 1919 and 1925, he again entered into strenuous debate with those eager to use violence. Violent methods, he argued, obstructed the road to independence. He succeeded at this time in persuading violent revolutionaries to suspend their activities to give his own novel techniques a chance. His movement was not only professedly non-violent; he called it off when unruly incidents occurred. Still unrepentant of the apparent failure of nonviolent revolution, he beat back the renewed challenge of the devotees of violence through the columns of his journal, *Young India*. In the issue of February 12, 1925, he published a letter from an advocate of violence, which contended that

Indian revolutionaries . . . suspended their activities so long simply to comply to your requests direct and indirect, and they went further. They actually helped you in the carrying out of your programme to the best of their abilities. But now the experiment is over and therefore revolutionaries are free from their promise, for, as a matter of fact, they promised to remain silent only for a year and no more.[40]

Gandhi rejoined that he had called off his movement because "the observance of non-violence was far below the required standard." He asserted that exponents of violence "have retarded the progress of the country."[41]

This exchange set the tone for many years. Gandhi and violent revolutionaries remained in touch and sympathetically appreciative of one another's intentions. The relationship suggested that of a father and a prodigal son. The fact that doubters continued to come to Gandhi with their objections to his methods was in itself emblematic of a father-son relationship. Absconding revolutionaries haunted the periphery of the Congress movement, making unannounced appearances after dark in the houses of respectable elders—incidentally suggesting the loneliness of their lives. The established leadership, for their part, were hard-pressed to match the glamour and popular appeal of such dramatic figures as Bhagat Singh, hanged for tossing a bomb into the Legislative Assembly in Delhi, or Chandrasekhar Azad, gunned down in an Allahabad Park. After 1925, the nationalist movement always had two sections. They were not opposed to one another in any formal sense, since underground activists operated in an isolated and sporadic manner. The two sections often seemed in fact and acted like natural allies, each performing a necessary, complementary task. It was risky for respectable leaders to advocate violence, even if they secretly approved of it. Violent revolutionaries, in turn, seemed to prize the shelter which association with Gandhian movements often provided. The activists of the two sections were individually well acquainted, and many were prepared to express private admiration for one another and for the importance of their activities. Gandhi, however, made a distinction. He never stopped talking with violent revolutionaries, but he never indicated an impression publicly or privately that their activities furthered the nationalist cause. "Use violence if you must," one individual recalls being told by Gandhi in the thirties, "but don't do it in connection with the Congress programme. Please set up your own organization."[42]

The emphasis changed, however, in the spring of 1942. Now Gandhi argued that under certain conditions the use of violence would not injure the national cause, however much he might prefer a different form of service.

Gandhi endorsed violent resistance without advocating it. When Gandhi gave advice it was never a simple matter. Gandhi ordinarily supplied a hierarchy of recommendations, starting with what he considered ideally preferable, and ending up with what he considered better than nothing. This made it easy for critics to present Gandhi as having contradicted himself. The official *History of the Civil Disobedience Move-*

ment, 1940-41 noted for example that Gandhi "continued, with his usual bland inconsistency, to confuse the issue between political objection to 'the war' and ethical resistance to 'war' as such and to harp at intervals on his professed desire to cause the minimum embarrassment to Government."[43]

To avoid such confusion Gandhi would have had to insist that as an objector to all wars he would have nothing to do with objectors to the "particular war" against the Axis. And yet, if general principles have any relevance at all, they must have relevance to particular cases. And, if moral men have any interest in efficacy, they must be willing to tolerate temporary recruits and partial conversions. Gandhi did not confuse his recommendations; he ranked them carefully from top to bottom, offering advice to those who were receptive whatever their level of dedication and sophistication.

Gandhi's use of ranked recommendations was explained in scholastic terms by Mahadev Desai. "Hindu moral philosophy—Gita ethics—" he wrote, "posits three gunas, *Sattwa, Rajas* and *Tamas. Ahimsa* belongs to the *sattwika* category, *himsa* belongs to the *rajas* category, and cowardice belongs to *tamas* category. Fearlessness, which may express itself in *ahimsa* or *himsa* according as a person is *sattwika* or *rajasa,* is the antithesis of cowardice. The one is the attribute of the brave, the other brings down man from man's estate. That is why cowardice has to be shunned at all costs."[44] Nonviolence, violence, and cowardice formed a hierarchy, and Gandhi had no qualms about making a positive recommendation that violence should be used by a man who was capable of choosing only between violence and cowardice.

Gandhi's mood and technique at this period are well illustrated by his discussion of the proper response to "criminal assaults." Discussing the response which women should make to assaults by Allied soldiers garrisoned in India, Gandhi began by suggesting that women "should leave the cities and migrate to the villages where a wide field of service awaits them. There is comparatively little risk of their being assaulted in villages." If a woman were in fact assaulted, her best defense would be the "flame of her dazzling purity." This would come naturally if women ceased "to tremble as they do today at the mere thought of assaults." "But," Gandhi conceded, "such faith or courage cannot be acquired in a day. Meantime we must try to explore other means." When attacked without warning a woman "may not stop to think in terms of *himsa* or *ahimsa*. Her primary duty is self-protection. She is at liberty to employ every method or means that comes to her mind in order to defend her honour. God has given her nails and teeth . . . So much for what a woman should do. But what about a man who is witness to such crimes? . . . If old, decrepit and toothless, as I am, I were to plead non-violence and be a helpless witness of assault on the honour of a sister, my so-called Mahatmaship would be ridiculed, dishonoured and lost. If I or those like me were to intervene and lay down our lives whether violently or non-violently, we would surely save the prey and at any rate we would not remain living witnesses to her dishonour."[45]

The wider relevance of such reflections was suggested by Gandhi's praise of Polish resistance to the German invaders. The violence employed by the Poles was condoned because it was defensive and spontaneous, like that employed by an assaulted woman. Gandhi explained that he was here referring to a situation in which "the weaker party does not make any preparation for offering violence for the simple reason that the intention is absent, but when he is suddenly attacked he uses unconsciously, even without wishing to do so, any weapon that comes his way."[16]

The potential relevance of Gandhi's writings on the propriety of the use of violence in self-defense to a full scale movement of the Congress had been indicated at the very outset of the limited campaign of Individual Satyagraha in the fall of 1940. On August 26, 1940, he wrote that "The policy of non-embarrassment was adopted on my initiative but it may not be allowed to be used to crush Congress." On September 6, 1940, he wrote "Congress restraint cannot be used for self-destruction," and at the meeting of the All-India Congress Committee of September 15 he suggested that he might go "to the Viceroy to ask him if the present situation does not place the Congress in danger of extinction."[47] In his climactic speech at Bombay on August 8, 1942, Gandhi explicitly applied the analogy of self-defense to the movement about to be launched. "If a man holds me by the neck and wants to drown me, may I not struggle to free myself directly?" In words reminiscent of his advice that one should not wish to remain alive as a passive witness to an assault on a woman, he said, "We shall either free India or die in the attempt; we shall not live to see perpetuation of our slavery."[48]

Gandhi had consistently opposed violence which he considered cowardly, such as the wreaking of havoc secretly by persons who refused to stay around to take the consequences of their actions. And he had consistently condoned as a last resort for those incapable of nonviolent resistance the repulsing by spontaneous violence of attacks by murderers, rapists, and the like. In 1942, Gandhi did not change his views; he simply added British rule to the list of criminal assailants against whom the use of violence in self-defense was permissible. "People have to protect themselves," Gandhi wrote in the *Harijan* of May 31, 1942, "against officials, against dacoits, [bandits], and possibly Japanese."

Gandhi had often stressed that his opposition to political violence rested in part on his conviction that a violent movement could never be a mass movement. Premeditated violence had to be secretive, the result of conspiracies entered into by small groups. "I hold that the world is sick of armed rebellions," he had once written. "I hold too that whatever may be true of other countries, a bloody revolution will not succeed in India. The masses will not respond. A movement in which masses have no active part can do no good to them. A successful bloody revolution can only mean further misery for the masses. For it would be still foreign rule for them."[49] He was prepared, he wrote, to use "the most deadly weapons, if I believed that they would destroy" the system of imperial rule. "I refrain only because the use of such weapons would only perpetuate the system though it may destroy its present administrators. Those who seek to destroy men rather than manners adopt the latter and become worse than those whom they destroy under the mistaken belief that the manners will die with the men."[50] In the summer of 1942, Gandhi concluded that the masses were ready for a fight and that the masses themselves were in a mood which brooked the use of violence. Deadly weapons, it seemed, might in fact destroy the system; violence would not this time leave the masses on the sidelines.

Gandhi was, moreover, impressed with the urgency of taking action in circumstances which all recognized constituted a critical moment in human history. If nonviolent struggle were to be proved fit only for summer soldiers, if Gandhi had to concede that people like himself had best keep their mouths shut during total war, his profoundest convictions would be turned into hypocrisy. Experiments in perfection were fine under laboratory conditions, but the real test came when action was called for in times of confusion and crisis. "I have waited and waited, until the country should develop the non-violent strength necessary to throw off the foreign yoke," Gandhi said. 'But my attitude has now undergone a change. I feel that I cannot afford to wait. If I continue to wait, I might have to wait till doomsday . . . That is why I have decided that even at certain risks, which are obviously involved, I must ask the people to resist slavery . . . The people have not my *ahimsa*, but my *ahimsa* should help them."[51]

Gandhi acknowledged the consequences of calling for a mass agitation given the present national mood in a letter to Mirabehn. Writing on May 23, he said, "'Our steps must be firm but gradual so that people may understand them so far as it is possible. A time must come when the thing may become beyond control. We may not purposely let it go out of control. Is this clear?"[52] "It is also now 'clear' what I meant when I said I was prepared to go to the extremest limit," Gandhi wrote in 1943, "is that I would continue the non-violent movement even though the government might succeed in provoking violence. Hitherto I have stayed my hand when people have been so provoked. This time I ran the risk because the risk of remaining supine in the face of the greatest world conflagration known to history was infinitely greater. If non-violence be the greatest force in the world, it must prove itself during this crisis."[53]

Gandhi even foresaw the crisis creating a situation in which the use of organized violence might be required. His thinking on this subject was contained in his suggestion that, if India became free, British and Indian troops might fight together against the Japanese. Suddenly filling a "gap" in his originally categorical "Quit India" demand, Gandhi announced that if the British quit India by terminating their political control, their troops might be permitted to stay to carry on the fight against the Japanese. Britishers considered this a cunning and patently hypocritical ploy to appeal to gullible American opinion. The British naturally asked, if Gandhi were sincere in his solicitude for the war effort, why did he encumber it with political demands? From Gandhi's point of view, however, principle was not a function of detail. The demand for withdrawal was just; an insistence that Britishers sub-sequently remove all their troops while fighting a world war with the Japanese would be violent. While India remained enslaved, the British war effort was indistinguishable from the Japanese. By holding India in subjection, the British had abrogated any right to claim a higher moral standing for their side. Gandhi was thus willing to see the British opposed, during the war, if necessary by violence. Once India had been freed, however, British troops might be permitted to remain to fight the Japanese because then the British would have reestablished a valid claim to moral superiority.

Gandhi considered that warfare was never desirable or very effective, but felt that if men engaged in warfare while sincerely trying to pursue good ends their opinions had to be respected. By freeing India, Englishmen would become men whose desires were worthy of respect by a person who refused to impose correct ideas on others by force. If Britishers still wished to continue fighting the Japanese after freeing India, they would have demonstrated that they were not fighting to keep India. "Whether without India Britain would have any reason to fight is a question I need not consider. If India is the stake and not British honour we should know."[54] If, after exonerating themselves by freeing India, Englishmen still wished to remain in India to fight the Japanese, it would be a violent act to prevent them from doing so. "I cannot all of a sudden produce in the minds of Britishers, who have been for centuries trained to rely upon their muscle for their protection, a belief which has not made a very visible impression even on the Indian mind."[55]

Gandhi, moreover, could not deny to Indians what he permitted Britishers. Gandhi said that he expected an independent India would also wish to fight the Japanese. "When India gets her freedom the probability is that I shall no longer be wanted by any party and everybody would be war-mad."[56] If Indians wished to defend their country—an admirable motive—by violence, their wishes would have to be respected by a believer in nonviolence. "I cannot oppose free India's will with civil disobedience," Gandhi replied to Edgar Snow's question as to whether he would oppose the use of armed force by an independent India, "it would be wrong."[56] If India were to resort to violence freely, if violence were a genuine expression of the popular will, Gandhi would not try to suppress it. Gandhi would have preferred to have India meet the Japanese with nonviolent resistance. Regrettably, "India has not yet demonstrated non-violence of the strong such as would be required to withstand a powerful army of invasion. If we had developed that strength we would have acquired our freedom long ago and there would be no question of any troops being stationed in India." The imperfect nonviolence which Indians had attained might be sufficient to make an impression on the "old occupant," subject to its cumulative effect over many years; it was not of sufficient vitality to halt a new invasion by the Japanese. "Thus we can disown the authority of the British rulers by refusing taxes and in a variety of ways. These would be inapplicable to withstand the Japanese onslaught. Therefore, whilst we may be ready to face the Japanese, we may not ask the Britishers to give up their position of vantage merely on the unwarranted supposition that we would succeed by mere non-violent effort in keeping off the Japanese."[58]

Gandhi was prepared to accept armed resistance against the Japanese by an independent Indian nation allied with a morally purified British nation if this were the desire of the majority. Many Britishers felt he had weakened his moral position in making this modification, and many Indians felt he had thereby diluted his demand. Actually, Gandhi was elaborating the logic of nonviolence; and, as some Indians realized, intensifying his threat. In condoning organized armed resistance against the Japanese, he was simultaneously condoning organized armed resistance against the British if they continued, as they seemed determined to do, on a course which made their cause morally indistinguishable from that of the Japanese. This was not Gandhi's wish. As he said, he could not lead the nation in an armed struggle. He would, however, stand aside if necessary and refrain from criticizing those who assumed command of an armed struggle. As a believer in nonviolence, he could not throttle the nation's will. If the nation chose a violent course, he was prepared to accept it. He was prepared to describe as nonviolence a spontaneous resort to violence in self-defense. He was also prepared, as an individual believer in nonviolence, to acquiesce in the use of organized violence by sincere men pursuing good ends, even though he could not approve of such violence or directly associate himself with its use. Whatever might be the consequences, and whatever might be the appeal of Gandhi's personal preferences, Gandhi was determined that India must now act for herself.

In analyzing the situation which Orissans were likely to face in the wake of a Japanese invasion, Mirabehn pointed out to Gandhi that there might be "a certain amount of rifles, revolvers and other small arms . . . left lying about unpicked up by the Japanese. If we do not make a point of collecting these things they are likely to fall into the hands of robbers, thieves and other bad characters . . . My instinct is to take them out to sea and drop them in the ocean." Gandhi replied that such a solution was "most tempting and perfectly logical.

It may be followed, but I would not rule out the idea of worthy people finding them and storing them in a safe place if they can."[59]

Planning Anarchy

British troops were rapidly retreating from Southeast Asia, evacuating civilians and troops in a highly discriminatory fashion. General Molesworth had announced that the British had in hand plans for the abandonment of at least some regions of India. All evidence indicated that the Japanese would be received by Indians with positive pleasure. It appeared likely that a Japanese-sponsored Indian government would soon set up its headquarters in eastern India. The kind of independent India for which Gandhi had been working for a generation might well be forestalled by liberation under entirely different auspices. In stark form, the options appeared to be that India might be left to herself or left to the Japanese. Gandhi's request that the British leave India to "anarchy" was his way of trying to avoid the second alternative.

"Hitherto," Gandhi wrote in the *Harijan* of May 24, "the rulers have said, 'We would gladly retire if we knew to whom we should hand over the reins.' My answer now is, 'Leave India to God. If that is too much, then leave her to anarchy.'" "My proposal is one-sided," Gandhi elaborated several weeks later, "i.e., for the British Government to act upon irrespective of what Indians would do or would not do. I have even assumed temporary chaos on their withdrawal."[60]

Gandhi said he preferred real anarchy, with its promise of a new birth, to the "ordered anarchy" of British rule. Gandhi did not personally advocate substituting Japanese for British rule, but pointed out that many other Indians would prefer such a change, and at any rate, Indians could not fight with the British to forestall it. Answering the protest of a friend who expressed his desire to help the British repulse the Japanese, Gandhi said, "You are labouring under a fallacy. Why do you say that the Japanese have no right to invade your country although it is in foreigners' hands? In the first place, the country is not yours while it is in others' hands. You cannot do what you like with it. The foreigners can and do. Secondly, if the Japanese have enmity against your master, they have every right to attack what your master possesses . . . The proper course for you is to ask the wrongful possessor to vacate your country . . . The British do not want your help on your terms . . . If, therefore, victory is achieved the British hold will be ever so much stronger than before. If they will not trust you now, there is no warrant for supposing that they will after victory. They will then ask you with greater force than now to produce the unity which cannot be produced whilst they are here."[61]

Gandhi's plan of anarchy echoed a popular sentiment and solved a dilemma. In 1857 the Great Rebellion had broken out amidst predictions that British rule had run its constituted course of one hundred years since the Battle of Plassey. In 1942 the second millennium of the Vikram era, used as the basis for the calendar in northern India, was coming to an end. In July, the attention of the government was drawn to a prediction by a blind *sadhu* of Muzaffarpur in Bihar that British rule in India would end "in three months and thirteen days." The report which reached the government had, however, omitted to mention the date on which this prophecy was made, which made somewhat more difficult the task of local officers who were, according to the report, taking "steps to scotch the rumour."[62] A couplet current in northern India at this time suggested that the year 2000 would herald the end of an era:

Jab lugega samvat bisa
Na rehange Musalman Isa[63]

"When the twentieth century comes to an end, neither Muslim nor Christian will remain." Most crudely this seemed to call for the expulsion of British and Muslim "foreigners" on this propitious date. The meaning it held for the sophisticated was more abstractly cataclysmic. The new millennium would be inaugurated by a great chaos in which all civilization as then known would be dissolved. All distinctions between individuals and communities would be obliterated and an entirely new age would be born. A popular expression in the literature of Indian revolutionaries had been the phrase, "Chaos is necessary to the birth of a new star."[64] Revolution and traditional millennialism came together in 1942.

Earlier in his career Gandhi had accepted the reformist argument that political independence must await the establishment of certain conditions, that political independence was the capstone of a structure of which a social transformation was the base.

I invite the attention of the revolutionaries [wrote Gandhi in 1925] to the three great hindrances to swaraj—the incomplete spread of the spinning wheel, the discord between Hindus and Musalmans and the inhuman ban upon the suppressed classes.[65]

Gandhi at this time thought of nonviolent struggle as an extension of the work of the social reformers. In 1942, however, he too spoke of the advantages of anarchy. The change reflected his growing concern over the likely result of the Hindu-Muslim split, given the imperial setting which permitted the British to play off communities against one another. Gandhi now felt that orderly evolution could not build the society he envisioned; this would be possible only after an interval of cleansing anarchy. The British proclaimed their inability to withdraw from India in an orderly fashion in the midst of a war emergency. Gandhi suggested that they withdraw in a disorderly fashion. The communal problem must be settled before withdrawal, argued the British; commitments must be honored. Gandhi replied that the communal situation was aggravated by the British presence and could not be settled so long as the British continued to make and honor commitments entered into as an external force dealing with Indian groups separately. Men would be brought together by stark necessity; only then could they create institutions suitable for the new world. Any order produced before the healing flood eliminated all distinctions would only perpetuate old divisions into the new order. The pristine, chaos-born order would be prevented from assuming its natural contours if the flood were not permitted to do its work first.

Gandhi had now abandoned his effort, stretching back to the Khilafat movement of the twenties, to form a united front of Hindus and Muslims which would speak with a single voice in demanding British withdrawal. The emergence of Jinnah, a Muslim leader with mass appeal who could also deal effectively with the British government, and the crystallization of the demand for Pakistan in the Muslim League resolution of 1940, had convinced Gandhi that the situation could not be retrieved by friendly persuasion. Gandhi recognized that, under these circumstances, an orderly British withdrawal could only proceed in a "Solomon-like" fashion; if two women claimed a child for their own, it would have to be cut in two.[66] The only way to avoid such fairness, Gandhi concluded, was for the British to leave India without making arrangements for succession. So long as the British remained, competing groups would not be "solid parties," because "they are often acted upon by the British power, they look up to it and its frown or favour means much to them. The whole atmosphere is corrupt and rotten . . . as soon as the vicious influence of the third party is withdrawn, the parties will be face to face with reality and close up ranks."

How could such a dereliction of responsibility be justified in the light of Britain's many solemn undertakings to insure Indian well-being? "It was wrong, I say, to possess India. The wrong should be righted by leaving India to herself."[67] It would be a further blot on the British record, Gandhi argued, if, after everything else she had done to India, she now attempted to withdraw with honor. The wrong of conquest would then be compounded by the wrong of face-saving retreat. "Honor" in such circumstances involved an effort to preserve a spurious façade of continuity, to paste a label of high purpose on the desire to make the best of a bad bargain. The slogan of orderly withdrawal is "Let us not recriminate; it might prove embarrassing." Lord Mountbatten's speeches as viceroy in 1947–1948 were, for example, published in a book entitled *Time Only to Look Forward.*[68] Attempting to judge in the name of honor what is the best alternative to a now discredited policy is only the perpetuation of arrogance by other means. Gandhi thus spurned British solicitude for devising ways to "soften" the impact of their withdrawal. The Quit India demand, he stated, "is a demand made upon Britain to do the right irrespective of the capacity of the party wronged to bear the consequences of Britain's right act. Will Britain restore seized property to the victim merely because the seizure was wrong? It is none of her concern to weigh whether the victim will be able to hold possession of the restored property."[69]

Withdrawal with continuity is possible so long as the withdrawing power honors commitments and does not abandon its allies. To the extent that such an effort involves a refusal to acknowledge that earlier commitments were misguided, and earlier policies had mischievous effects, to that extent will the determination to withdraw with honor become a determination to mar the future. The desire to preserve honor may result in narcissistic and dangerously destructive actions.

To preserve itself from the shock of recognition of failure, the retreating power may pose as a condition of withdrawal the partial salvaging of the beneficiaries of its former policies. The policy of nation-building in retreat becomes the policy of protecting enclaves. Retreat with honor preserves vanquished imperialism's self-respect by denying total victory to those to whom the field is abandoned.

To the argument from honor is appended the argument of common sense. Is not an orderly withdrawal and a settlement of the claims of all parties in the field the only solution feasible? This too is an argument advanced from an imperial vantage point. The withdrawal of imperial power is the end, from the imperial standpoint, a time for summing up and settling claims. But such a summing up and settling of claims is only the beginning from the point of view of those waiting their turn. The matter may be "settled" in the mind of the withdrawing power, but the settlement only inaugurates the struggle between rival claimants, disputing what is awarded and what is deserved. As Gandhi argued in the *Harijan* of July 20, 1947, three weeks before Independence Day, "Man had the supreme knack of deceiving himself. The Englishman was supremest among men. He was quitting because he had discovered that it was wrong on economic and political grounds to hold India in bondage. Herein he was quite sincere. It would not be denied, however, that sincerity was quite consistent with self-deception. He was self-deceived in that he believed that he could not leave India to possible anarchy if such was to be India's lot. He was quite content to leave India as a cockpit between two organised armies. Before quitting, he was setting the seal of approval on the policy of playing off one community against another."[70] In depicting the probable result of a partition of India, Gandhi predicted that "Each party will probably want British or foreign aid. In that case, good-bye to independence. The fight will then [employ] the usual way of violence. I dare not contemplate the actuality. I should not like to be its living witness."[71]

It is part of the rationale of an evolutionary conception of political development that a smooth transfer of power from one regime to another requires that real power should not be transferred until the moment when all is in order, constitutions written, and designated authorities ready and waiting. The difficulty is that when preparations for independence are made in this way, they will be made with reference to the reserved authority of the departing power, not as a direct exercise of sovereignty. A constituent assembly works with a notion of whom it must please—either a sovereign people or a reserved alien authority. Sovereignty must be transferred before a constitution is written—any other procedure is an exercise in manipulation, in the creation of new forms for disguising the perpetuation of old authority.

A representative assembly, whether gathered to write a constitution or for more routine business, cannot wield sovereignty. A representative assembly, in which all groups are represented but in which no one has ultimate responsibility, when not constrained by concern to please an external authority, will be able to reach agreement on routine matters of common interest—such as the passage of a budget—but not on matters of sovereignty. It is what might be called the deliberative fallacy to assume that a sovereign general will can emerge from negotiation among all interested parties. Representative assemblies can ratify or anticipate the will of others but cannot act unitedly on matters on which the interests of groups are basically at odds. An imperialist recommendation to a representative assembly to "Reach an agreement; then we will leave" is thus a way of forestalling departure. All agreements are reached under constraints. The placing together of autonomous groups in a colonial assembly without the constraint of power in the hands of one group is a guarantee of stalemate.

Like King Lear, the British in India announced an intention to depart and invited potential heirs to struggle for the largest portion of the inheritance. Each of India's major communities was encouraged to deal with a hypothetical future. It would have been foolish for responsible leaders not to have anticipated the worst, not to have striven, like good lawyers, to secure the best possible terms of settlement for those they represented. The difficulty stemmed from the fact that they were pleading for an inheritance before a dying invalid, not arguing before a judge over the terms of a will.

When asked what in fact the British might have done, Gandhi replied that they might have "asked either the Congress or the League to form the cabinet."[72] This solution suggested the solution Solomon actually intended in proposing to the two women that they divide the baby between them. Gandhi expected that whichever party was given full power would come to terms with the other, or face the threat of noncooperation by it, and that things could sort themselves out by a democratic process of nonviolent struggle once the rival claimants were left to deal with one another directly.

Such responses by Gandhi to the suggestion that he should "be constructive" have usually been dismissed as escapism, being utterly impractical. How could the "great Hindu leader" seriously propose an all-Muslim League government as anything more than a subtle snare? Actually, Gandhi's method of cutting the Gordian knot was much more practical than the endless floundering of negotiators tinkering with mechanisms. It was not only practical; it was tried and tested. In 1939, Gandhi had used precisely this approach when the Congress was badly split by the determination of Subhas Bose to come to an immediate showdown with the British.

Bose, contemplating the anxious international situation which was soon to lead to war, thought the moment opportune for a final struggle with the British. Gandhi, contemplating the internal condition of India, felt that the nation's mood was surly and that the Congress was not then psychologically prepared for a disciplined nonviolent confrontation. A difference of perspective on such a fundamental issue could not be evaded. Gandhi's solution was to give Bose free rein. He quickly discovered his inability to carry on by himself and resigned as president. Bose had been acting as if he had no use for those he termed the "Gandhites"; Gandhi, instead of opposing, told him to go ahead and exercise full power if he could. Gandhi's supporters, he informed Bose, "will not obstruct you. They will help you where they can, they will abstain where they cannot. There should be no difficulty whatsoever, if they are in a minority. They may not suppress themselves if they are clearly in a majority . . . I cannot, will not impose a cabinet on you . . . It would amount to suppression. Let the members exercise their own judgment. If you do not get the vote, lead the opposition till you have converted the majority . . . My conviction is that working along our lines in our own way we shall serve the country better than by the different groups seeking to work a common policy and common programme forced out of irreconcilable elements."[73] Gandhi's technique of nonviolent struggle was a form of democratic competition, which assumed that it was better to stand alone for one's convictions than accept a compromised position of power in the hope of "working from within."

It might be supposed that Gandhi's preference for letting one side have its way was intended as a device to eliminate all opposition. The result of offering all power to Bose was, of course, the garnering of all power for himself. The cant of consensus often serves as a convenient cover for coercion by a dominant elite. Gandhi was, however, actually prepared to let power go to either side. His willingness to act as a loyal opposition was so complete that it subjected him to another charge—of caving in and sacrificing his own cardinal principles. When in 1947 the Working Committee had committed themselves irrevocably to accepting Mountbatten's plan of partition, Gandhi dropped his uncompromising opposition and himself urged support for the plan, whose dire consequences he continued to expound. He acted in the same fashion between January and April of 1942 when the Japanese advance toward India, following the German attack on Russia, stimulated a temporary revival of interest on the part of Nehru and

Azad in a compromise settlement with Britain which might make possible Congress cooperation with the British against the Axis. Gandhi, already launched on the campaign which was to lead to the Quit India movement, and more sensitive than other Congress leaders to the country's uncompromising mood, had no interest in fishing for compromises which he considered would be unacceptable either to Indians or to the British government. Gandhi nonetheless urged acceptance by the All-India Congress Committee at Wardha in January 1942 of the Working Committee's Bardoli Resolution. Since "the resolution reflects the Congress mind," Gandhi refrained from asking for a test vote on a proposal which he considered "undoubtedly . . . a step backward."[74] During the subsequent visit of Sir Stafford Cripps to explore possibilities for compromise, Gandhi simply left town, telling Nehru and Azad to accept or reject the Cripps proposals according to their own discretion. Gandhi frequently accepted defeat with a plea for support for the victors and a clear indication of his intention to continue fighting against the proposals whose acceptance he urged. Nonviolence required that one abide by the wrong opinions sincerely held by others until they had been honestly persuaded to change their course.

"If there is a dispute between two boys over the ownership of an apple," Gandhi explained, "the non-violent way is to leave the apple for the other party to take, the latter well knowing that it would mean non-co-operation on the surrendering party's part."[75] In a fight, only cunning instincts were brought into play, and before it was over the apple might be trod upon or rotten. In a gamble, giving the apple to one's opponent, there was a chance that higher instincts might be invoked; absolute power of disposition provided a possibility that generosity might be the result and that a settlement might be arrived at without an exhaustion too great to permit its enjoyment.

Gandhi's call for anarchy was also his way of announcing that the attainment of the sort of freedom he envisioned would require a social rebirth. The social system of British imperialism was basically wrong, and every sign of its vigor in prosecuting the war was a sign of the urgency with which revolution was called for. If Indians volunteered for the British army, they did so only out of financial need—as evidenced by the fact that they were equally prepared to fight for the Japanese. "Slaves do not fight for freedom."[76] If Indians contributed funds, they did so only under subtle psychological coercions of which they might not even be aware. "No contribution made to a conqueror can be truly described as voluntary.''[77] If the viceroy's actions were cloaked by the presence of Indians on his Executive Council, so much the worse. "That you had the approval of your Indian 'colleagues,'" Gandhi wrote the viceroy, "can have no significance, except this that in India you can always command such services. That cooperation is an additional justification for the demand of withdrawal."[78]

Gandhi proposed the establishment of a new chaos-born order, free from the curse of vested interests demanding satisfaction for their loyal support of a discredited regime. Indians who had become part of the British system—princes, landlords, bureaucrats, soldiers, and police—were to be opposed with the violence permissible in self-defense, no less than British officials. The princes were doomed unless they voluntarily identified their lot with the people. "Will the princes march with the time or must they remain tied to the imperial chariot wheel?"[79] "In the villages . . . the peasants will stop paying taxes . . . Their next step will be to seize the land."

"With violence?" I asked.
"There may be violence, but then again the landlords may cooperate." "You are an optimist," I said.
"They might cooperate by fleeing," Gandhi said.[80]

The same test applied to princes and landlords would be applied to the Muslim League leadership.

"Do you think," I asked, "that the Moslems will follow you in your civil disobedience movement?"
"Not perhaps in the beginning," Gandhi said. "But they will come in when they see that the movement is succeeding."
"Might not the Moslems be used to interfere with or stop the movement?"
"Undoubtedly," Gandhi agreed, "their leaders might try or the government might try, but the Moslem millions do not oppose independence and they could not, therefore, oppose our measures to bring about that independence. The Moslem masses sympathize with the one overall goal of Congress: freedom for India. That is the solid rock on which Hindu-Moslem unity can be built."[81]

Gandhi was prepared to undertake the ultimate test of Jinnah's claim that only he could represent India's Muslims, the ultimate test of Jinnah's ability to survive his abandonment by his British patrons. Gandhi was convinced by now that Jinnah would only give up his demand for Pakistan "when the British are gone and when there is therefore nobody with whom to bargain."[82]

Gandhi predicted that he might be able to do something "very big, if the Congress is with me and the people are with me." And the people were with him "because, as I sense the mood of the country, everybody wants freedom—Hindus, Musalmans, untouchables, Sikhs, workers, peasants, industrialists, Indian civil servants, and even the princes . . . Things cannot go on as they have been."[83] Working together, they would "adopt such non-violent measures as would compel the Power to comply with the appeal" to withdraw.[84]

Interspersed amidst such optimistic hopes, however, were detailed anticipations of virtually every aspect of the movement and its mode of suppression. Gandhi urged the "whole of India to launch upon a non-violent struggle on the widest scale." He trusted that the struggle would be non-violent; "But even if I am deceived in this, I shall not swerve." "If the Government keep me free, I will spare you the trouble of filling the jails," he told the All-India Congress Committee, at once stating what he hoped would happen and what he expected in default of that. "Let the Government then shower bombs, if they like," Gandhi stated, though one wonders if he realized how nearly accurate this prediction would prove. He recognized, however, that the "hysterical outburst" which had greeted his announced intentions in America and Great Britain might be the "precursor" of the movement's suppression. This might "cow down the people for the moment, but it will never put out the light of revolt."[85]

Gandhi expected violence, but he also hoped to be in a position to check its spread. One questioner asked Gandhi to distinguish between his own policy and that of Nero, fiddling while Rome burned. "Will you also be fiddling in Sevagram after you have ignited the fire which you will not be able to quench?" Gandhi replied that "Instead of fiddling in Sevagram you may expect to find me perishing in the flames of my own starting if I cannot regulate or restrain them."[86]

In deciding to act, Gandhi had to withstand an avalanche of concerned disapproval. His "daughter" Mirabehn (actually the daughter of a British admiral) with whom he exchanged affectionate notes almost daily during this period, was upset by Gandhi's apparent willingness to countenance the use of violence. Nehru was distressed by actions which he felt might harm the Allied cause, with which he had become sympathetic now that the British and Americans were allied with the Russians and Chinese. Gandhi's oldest English friends, such as Horace Alexander and Agatha Harrison, tried to communicate to him the inability of English liberals to follow his logic from the vantage point of their war-beleaguered nation. Bertrand Russell announced that a lifelong devotion to Indian freedom could not prevent him from expressing his dismay at Gandhi's present plan.

The American press, which Gandhi had been sedulously cultivating all spring, was extemely harsh. *Life* contrasted Chiang Kai-Shek, "the fighting leader of Free China," with Gandhi, "the talking leader of subject India," and contended that "Gandhi has decided to leave India the football of destiny." The *New York Times* expressed concern that Gandhi might "do more harm to his people than Genghis Khan or any other of the long array of conquerors." Gandhi published all these arguments in the *Harijan*. "I know that the novelty of the idea and that too at this juncture has caused a shock to many people," he replied. "But I could not help myself. Even at the risk of being called mad, I had to tell the truth if I was to be true to myself."[87]

9

Spontaneous Revolution:

August 1942

In the early hours of August 9, 1942, only a few hours after the termination of the climactic session of the All-India Congress Committee in Bombay at which the Quit India Resolution was passed authorizing Gandhi to take whatever steps he considered necessary to force the British out of the country, and only shortly after the many leaders gathered there had returned to their residences, police began arriving at the door. When the wives of arrested leaders attempted to telephone others to spread the alarm, they discovered that all lines had been severed. Throughout the country local officials, responding to tele-graphed codewords such as "Pantaloon" and "Adolf," arrested other leaders who were not to be found in Bombay.[1] The government reported modestly that "The total number of arrests probably did not exceed a few hundreds." In the United Provinces alone, however, the number of persons placed in preventive detention on August 9 was 547.[2]

The special train which was to carry the government's prize prisoners to Poona and Ahmednagar departed from Bombay's Victoria Terminus at 7:18 A.M. on the morning of August 9, by which time 43 leaders had been collected from different parts of Bombay. Gandhi was in a subdued mood, but many others were in a high-strung condition. "An atmosphere suggestive of forced gaiety prevailed before the train's departure," reported F. E. Sharp, the deputy inspector-general of police who was in charge of the operation. The first difficulty arose, Sharp recalled, from the fact that "one young man G. G. Mehta of Bombay City had by mistake been allowed to seat himself in the compartment specially selected for myself. He refused to leave and had to be bodily carried by some constables into an adjoining compartment."[3]

Gandhi was taken from the train at Chinchwad for transfer to the Aga Khan palace near Poona. The members of the Working Committee were destined for Ahmednagar fort, and the train proceeded on through Poona station, where more trouble was encountered. The special train was supposed to race through Poona station without stopping. A shunting operation was underway, however, which forced the train to a stop. When interrogated later, the senior station master claimed "to be ignorant until a late hour of the fact that any Special Train was running and that he was not present when the train passed through." In retrospect Sharp was "very strongly" of the opinion that the Poona station masters were either idiots or undercover agents.

Though the urgency of providing an unobstructed passage for a special train from Bombay on this particular morning had not occurred to the Poona station masters, substantial numbers of other Poona residents had suspected that the arrested leaders might pass that way. "Those on the platform at once recognized Nehru and S. D. Deo," Sharp recounted, "and commenced to run up the platform amid cries of 'Jai' . . . Hardly had I alighted on the platform when to my surprise I saw Nehru with remarkable agility climbing through the corridor window on to the platform. He was about ten yards from me and rushed straight towards the crowd. I got in his way and asked him to stop, but he made no attempt to do so and hence I was constrained to stop him with outstretched arms. He struggled violently with me screaming at the top of his voice that the Police were making a lathi charge and he would not have it. I said I knew nothing of this and my orders were that he should not communicate with the public and he must please resume his seat in the train . . . He shouted to me . . . 'I don't care for your bloody orders.' He is a big man and was having a fair share of the struggle with me. At this moment a Sub-Inspector caught him round the waist and with help of two other constables . . . he was then overpowered . . . As proof of the violence of this short struggle the Superintendent Railway Police was kicked on the leg by S. D. Deo and also sustained a small scratch on his wrist and I myself am feeling the effects of a sprained finger." One of what would prove to be hundreds of thousands of acts of protest had ended.

"After my last night's speech, they will never arrest me," Gandhi had remarked shortly before the police arrived, combining in a phrase his reasonable expectation and his optimistic wish. Gandhi had spoken at unaccustomed length the night before, to leave his colleagues with a message in case he were to be arrested the next day, and possibly with the hope that his speech itself might forestall his arrest. The resolution adopted had noted that "A time may come when it may not be possible to issue instructions or for instructions to reach our people, and when no Congress Committee can function. When this happens, every man and woman who is participating in this movement must function for himself or herself within the four corners of the general instructions issued. Every Indian who desires freedom and strives for it must be his own guide." Gandhi had added his voice: "I confess there are many black sheep amongst us Congressmen," he said. "But I trust the whole of India to launch upon a non-violent struggle on the widest scale. I trust the innate goodness of human nature which perceives truth and prevails during a crisis, as if by instinct. But even if I am deceived in this, I shall not swerve." He gave his listeners a "mantra . . . : Do or Die . . . Let every man and woman live every moment of his or her life hereafter in the consciousness that he or she eats or lives for achieving freedom and will die, if need be, to attain that goal."[4] After his previous night's speech, Gandhi was ready for his arrest.

The possibility of mass arrests had been long anticipated. When asked in July 1942 if he expected the movement to collapse "if Government sent you and thousands of your followers to jail?" Gandhi replied, "On the contrary, it should gain strength if it has any vitality."[5] Word of the government's plan to arrest Gandhi and other leaders was received almost as soon as it was drafted. The government's provisional plan of attack was approved at a small meeting in the Home Department on Sunday afternoon, August 2. No one in the meeting, however, was of sufficiently humble status to dispatch the letter of instructions to the Bombay government; the letter was sealed and dispatched by a clerk who, several hours later, was closeted with the secretary of the Delhi Congress Committee. Asaf Ali, a member of the Working Committee and president of the Delhi Congress Committee, was informed of the letter's contents that evening and carried the word to the other members of the Working Committee gathering in Bombay. Other reports also reached the Congress president from Bombay police sources. Some members of the Working Committee were skeptical; the report itself might be a government ruse designed to force precipitate action. It was decided to make no move suggestive of knowledge of British intentions. The only practical use made of the advance warning was by the Delhi Congress Committee, who printed up posters announcing Gandhi's arrest and calling for a general strike to protest in advance of the event. They were consequently in a position to distribute these posters within thirty minutes of the announcement of the arrests, a feat which led Delhi magistrates to conclude that the Congress must be in possession of an immensely efficient modern press.[6]

While congressmen in Delhi and elsewhere were already beginning to act on their own responsibility, as provided for in the Quit India Resolution, the remnants of the Congress hierarchy still at large in Bombay were beginning to assemble. Maulana Azad, the Congress president, had called a meeting of Congress officials to meet at G. D. Birla's house early on the morning of August 9. Sadiq Ali, office secretary from the All-India Congress Committee headquarters in Allahabad, Pyarelal, Gandhi's secretary, and others met there, but the focus of the gathering remnants had shifted by mid-morning to Dhayabhai Patel's house, considered a less likely target of police inquiry. Mrs. Sucheta Kripalani, wife of the Congress general secretary, and others who might have been expected to know, were asked to reveal what the plans of the High Command had been; they could only say that, to the best of their knowledge, there were no definite plans. After much discussion a twelve-point declaration was drawn up, largely based on earlier Congress movements, calling for a nation-wide hartal (strike) and a nonviolent struggle to end British rule within two months. Government servants and soldiers were requested to resign rather than oppose the people's will, and students over sixteen were urged to leave school to participate in this climactic struggle. Some thirty people were drafted into service to make typed and handwritten copies of the plan for circulation to the All-India Congress Committee members who were still at large to carry back to their respective provinces. The statement was vague, but it gave a signal that the will to resist of those considered too unimportant to arrest was unshaken; the movement was to go on, in the manner Gandhi had contemplated for the period following his arrest, with every person acting on his own initiative and authority.

Tentative plans for a mass movement such as that called for in the twelve-point declaration had been circulating in different parts of India for several weeks prior to August 9. The plan disseminated by

the Andhra Pradesh Congress Committee on July 28, 1942, for example, had anticipated a gradual escalation through peaceful picketing
to active obstruction of roads and the cutting of telegraph wires. But
all these plans had been dependent upon Gandhi's final approval and
premised upon the continuance of a situation in which an open movement was still possible. As meetings of the survivors—secretaries,
wives, and sons—took place in the days following August 9, a gradual
sense of the need for a new sort of movement emerged. The Bombay
police had sealed bank accounts and seized Congress offices and files.
Any form of open movement seemed forestalled by the scope of police
action against the party's visible leadership and assets. The spontaneous mass outbursts and police retaliation throughout the country also
seemed to suggest that, whatever one might think of it, the nationalist
struggle had clearly entered a new phase.[7]

The survivors were motivated by what was known and what was
feared. It was not known for several weeks what had happened to
those arrested. It was thought that they might have been shot. The
report of the sudden death in prison from a heart attack of Mahadev
Desai fed this suspicion; Desai was a vigorous man in middle age,
and it was widely assumed that he had not died a natural death. It
was expected that news of more mysterious deaths would soon
appear.

Immediately following the arrests of August 9, Secretary of State
for India L. S. Amery made a series of statements on the B.B.C. and
to the American public. To justify extreme measures, Amery depicted
the threat in extreme terms. Basing his charges upon captured documents such as the Andhra circular of July 28, Amery described as the
firm intention of Congress conspirators what was in fact a tentative
outline of actions to be taken at a very advanced stage of a confrontation planned to begin much more modestly. The Congress leaders,
Amery contended, had planned to unleash an orgy of senseless
destruction of public property, cutting telegraph and telephone lines,
uprooting rail lines, and looting and burning post offices and banks.
It turned out to be a self-defeating justification. The menace Amery
depicted was what many Indians subsequently attempted to create.
What Amery said had been the Congress plan was accepted as the
Congress plan by indignant demonstrators groping for direction.
Many wanted to take extreme measures; Amery's charge gave them
an excuse for taking them in the name of the Congress. They wanted

to believe that such actions were legitimate and so were willing to accept Amery's credentials as an interpreter of Congress thinking. What Amery claimed to have prevented, he instead helped to bring about.

K. G. Mashruwala, who succeeded Mahadev Desai as editor of the *Harijan* for the two issues which could be brought out before police destroyed its files and equipment, played a key role in turning Amery's imputations into Congress policy. In the meetings which took place following the arrests of August 9 he was under considerable pressure to indicate some measure of approval of a movement which seemed destined to result in widespread destruction. His views were circulated in the final issue of the *Harijan*, dated August 23. The events which were in progress, he said, were a reflection of undisciplined violence, but "Much though I dislike the acts, I regret I am unable to condemn my people." Such acts had been willed by the British government by their removal of "the leaders and the organisation who could control the people." Since "those at White Hall and New Delhi" had become "insane" they had provoked a predictable response. For the future, Mashruwala argued that "Dislocation of traffic communications is permissible in a non-violent manner—without endangering life . . . Cutting wires, removing rails, destroying small bridges, cannot be objected to in a struggle like this provided ample precautions are taken to safeguard life . . . The non-violent revolutionaries have to regard the British power in the same way as they . . . would the Axis Power and carry out the same measures." Mashruwala thus formally dubbed the movement then underway a legitimate self-defense effort, to which all of Gandhi's theoretical writings on self-defense could be properly applied.

In subsequently expressing a certain amount of regret for the role he had played at this time, Mashruwala described how he "was thrown off my guard by no less a person than Mr. Amery himself. The speech which he made shortly after the arrest of the leaders on August 9th, 1942, gave me the first information of the items of a possible programme . . . I was desired to examine that programme . . . I have to say that . . . instead of analysing the programme made known by Mr. Amery by a mere intellectual process, I should have looked for light to the higher guide within me."[8]

Whatever the effect of Amery and Mashruwala may have been, the days and weeks which followed produced an unprecedented assault on the symbols and sinews of government. Everywhere the targets were rails and roads, telegraph and telephone communications, and government buildings and personnel, just as Amery had foreseen. The targets chosen were, however, logical enough given the intensity of feeling and the universal sense that the final crisis was at hand. The instinct was to destroy or capture everything the government thought valuable enough to protect. Gandhi had taught that the emblems of India's "development" were the tentacles by which she was strangled. Communications and transport in this crisis had only one purpose: to facilitate repression. The anarchy of which Gandhi spoke—an India without British law and order—the village self-sufficiency of which he spoke—with localities cut off from the wider world—were experiments Indians were now willing to make. And, while the advocacy of sabotage was a new experience for Gandhians such as Mashruwala, the perpetration of sabotage was not so new to many "black sheep," who now swung into action. For years the more radical nationalists had occupied their idle hours sketching the layout of strategic installations and devising crude explosives. While Amery was wrong to ascribe a desire for violence to the Congress High Command, there were many in the Congress who had been making the plans he alleged.

A flood of underground leaflets and radio broadcasts emerging from local headquarters across the country tried to spell out a program of Gandhian insurrection. One set of instructions read:

> (1) Declare yourselves free men and your village a free village . . .
> (4) Establish a panchayat in your village. The panchayat will be your Government . . .
> (5) Wherever you are well-organised, take peaceful possession of the Thanas, courts, and other Government buildings in your area. Those who resist your possession should be confined in suitable places. They shall be our prisoners and should be properly housed and properly fed.
> (8) Disorganise the communication whose sole use today is to suppress us. Take care that you take or injure no life.[9]

Another circular warned against letting "grains fall into the hands of the police. Keep them where they cannot find them." Villagers were urged to "Pay the landlord who is with you just enough rent to maintain himself and his family. Pay nothing to the landlord who is an ally of the Government . . . Do not keep paper money with you. It is a fraud. Soon it will lose all value and buy nothing. Convert paper money into goods while there is yet time."[10] A third asserted that "The credit of British Government has almost disappeared in India, as gold and silver have been taken to England and there is shortage of copper coins as well. Paper currency is in full swing. The villagers should be advised verbally and through leaflets not to send their grain to the market, as grain is being sent out of India for military purposes, and also is stored in Cantonments for emergency purposes . . . Carts carrying grain to the market should be stopped, if they do not listen to the advice given."[11] An appeal addressed to businessmen urged them to "Think of the unsoundness of Indian currency" and "talk about it among friends."[12]

The implicit purpose of the movement was to destroy the structure of British India, all the components of a developed society which made it possible for a handful of Englishmen to live above the level of subsistence of the Indian villager. The purpose was "the deliberate snapping of the artificial link of slavery between the villages and the cities. Let not this deliberate atomisation be confused with the gradual falling asunder of a country through decay. The deliberate breaking of the imperialist unity forced on a country presupposes strength and vigour. The strength that can consciously break up a vast country into its numberless villages can also put them together into a new symphony of health and beauty."[13]

The demolition of communications and the collapse of the currency would be no hardship for the masses. "As for the masses they can even travel on foot. The Government has not built Railways or roads for their benefits. It builds Railways or roads for the transport of Government officials and troops from one place to the other. Where are Railways and roads to be found in villages? Again, crores [tens of millions] of Indians have always remained half fed. Even before the beginning of the movement there were many persons who could not get grains, salt, fuel and other such things. They will, therefore, be able to anyhow bear these difficulties for a couple of months, but how will Government officials and troops carry on who consume eggs, butter and loaf only? They will have to face ruin in a couple of months." The moral was clear: "You are perfectly within your right to put out of action the system of communication, whether roads or railways or postal and telegraphic services . . . through which the police and the military and civil officials maintain their stranglehold on you."[14]

While the goals of the movement were everywhere the same, the tempo, and consequently the techniques, varied from region to region. In the first days there were scattered hartals, burnings, marches, and protests everywhere. In Bihar, this rapidly grew into a mass insurrection of equal intensity in cities and rural areas. On August 10, a partial hartal was observed in Patna and demonstrations occurred throughout the province. On August 11, crowds raided the Secretariat and Assembly buildings in Patna, and the sabotage of communications was in full swing everywhere.

"The thoroughness" of the sabotage, observed Sir T. Stewart, governor of Bihar, "had to be seen to be believed. Telegraph poles complete with their full equipment of wires were pulled over and branches of trees a foot and over in diameter were chopped down. This was not the work of five minutes or an hour but nevertheless no information came into headquarters that this wholesale destruction was going on." The entire state was in chaos. Beginning on August 12, "Patrol trains with troops moved both East and West . . . removing road blocks, breaking up opposition and extricating Europeans with the result that Patna and the road to the East for about 27 miles was reasonably secured." At Futwah, however, on the 13th, two RAF officers were dragged from a train and killed. "With rail, telegraph and telephone communications out of order we lost immediate touch with other districts," wrote the governor, "except Gaya with which we at an early date established a daily shuttle service by 'Tiger Moth' planes belonging to the Bihar Flying club." On the 14th, the first of several attacks by military aircraft armed with machine guns was made on crowds dismantling railroad tracks and bridges at Kajra. From Dehri-on-Sone it was reported that "official residences of all [were] burnt by mob" on August 14. At Bihta on the 15th "40 wagons of British troops rations" were burnt. On the 17th the government reported "All traffic on B. & N. W. Railway dislocated." At Narayanpur on the 18th, a military aircraft crashed. The pilot was killed in the crash; the rest of the crew, reported the governor, were "killed by mob." On the 19th it was "Reliably reported that saboteurs in certain areas have taken trains and driven them." On the 21st, the vital Tata Iron and Steel works at Jamshedpur were shut down by a complete strike; the workers, led by the subordinate supervisory staff, "Openly stated they will not resume work until a National Government has been formed." Several thousand workers returned after a few days but the supervisory staff kept the plant closed down entirely until September 3d. By the 22d of August the "evacuation process" for "the European planting community" had begun, according to Governor Stewart, "and meantime I have asked the military authorities to arrange for extensive air reconnaissance over the danger area." On August 24 it was reported that an "Officer and four men of the Yorks and Lancs Regiment killed at Marhowrah near Chapra were apparently overcome after some 40 people had been killed by their fire."[15] On August 26 there was a complaint that the "Disappearance of railway technical staff [was] holding up repairs." On the 30th a five-hundred foot breach in a railway embankment twenty miles east of Mansi was discovered. On September 3d, town police went on strike in Jamshedpur. On the 4th, six hundred prisoners in the Bhagalpur central jail mutinied and "murdered and burnt" the deputy superintendent and several other jail employees. On the 7th, at Champaran, "Troops seized stores of spears, bows, arrows, pepper, syringes and nitric acid." On the 9th, it was reported from Darbhanga that "during period of disturbances all police stations except five in district [were] attacked and in most cases records and furniture burnt." On the 10th, word came that the breach east of Mansi was "now 700 ft." On the 11th, 5,000 copper miners struck at Mushabanai. On the 15th, at Losarhi, "Troops . . . opened fire at 2 mobs, which successively attacked them with spears and other weapons, killing 9 including the chaukidar [night watchman] who led one of the mobs." In Ranchi district, during the first half of October, "police on two occasions had to disperse parties who had assembled armed with bows and arrows with the intention of raiding a dak [mail] bungalow and destroying mission houses."

In Bihar, disturbances were so widespread that the provincial government were not even aware of the situation in different regions until many days later. Villagers attacked rail lines miles from the nearest city. Almost everyone contributed: "Spears and other weapons are being manufactured by village blacksmiths from fish-plates and other pieces of metal taken from Railway lines." Unarmed crowds overpowered troops and took control of trains. Strikes were led by owners and foremen, joined by C class apprentices and sweepers. Tribes took up their bows and arrows. Crowds attacked prisons; prisoners attacked their guards; 205 policemen defected. The "usual police and C.I.D. sources of Information . . . had dried up." The government were reduced to retaliating from the air; all other avenues were cut off.

By October, Bihar's jails were crammed with 27,000 prisoners, double their rated capacity. "In August there were 163 dacoities [bandit raids] in the Province against a triennial monthly average of 46 . . . In several cases of an essentially criminal nature the dacoits shouted political war cries such as 'Swaraj Ho Gaya' [Independence has come] or "Gandhiji-ki-jai" [Victory to Gandhi]." For September, "265 dacoities were reported against a triennial average of 41.2 for this month." As police stations throughout the province were reestablished, it was clear that the movement was not over; it was simply going underground. When, on November 9, Jayaprakash Narayan escaped from Hazaribagh central jail in a party of "six political prisoners, five of whom are of an extremely dangerous type," officials knew that sabotage activities could be expected to continue indefinitely.[16]

The movement in Bihar was more immediate, spontaneous, and intense than elsewhere, but in many parts of the country localities erupted in a similar fashion. In the entire eastern half of the United Provinces, the situation rivaled that in Bihar, though in this region there is more evidence that the movement first took hold among urban and intellectual elements who then carried the message of revolution to the countryside.

In the first few days following August 9, the pattern in the United Provinces was one of urban disorder, instigated primarily by students. In Allahabad on August 12 "students attacked the district officer and had to be fired on . . . girl students were placed in the forefront of the procession . . . Immediately afterwards a well-planned attack was made on the Kotwali [police headquarters], which was isolated by road blocks and extensive damage was done." At Hardwar on August 19, "students of the Gurukul and Rishikul broke loose and with the help of *Mela* [religious festival] pilgrims took over the town for a short period looting a post office [of] Rs. 2,500, burning railway buildings, invading police out-posts and destroying police uniforms. The Deputy Superintendent of Police was dragged from his car, taken into a house and beaten by Rishikul students to within an inch of his life . . . His munshi [clerk-translator] was also beaten nearly to death." Such outbursts quickly gave way, however, and students began dispersing as their college hostels were closed by police orders.

"Practically everywhere the students of the principal colleges after doing what damage they could locally have gone off in parties to see what damage they can do in neighbouring towns and in the rural areas."[17]

"On August 14th a passenger train flying a Congress flag arrived full of students from Benares" in Ballia, and shortly thereafter the entire eastern region was out of control. Students, cooperating with groups who had been preparing for armed struggle for some time, organized large raiding parties in rural areas. At a raid on Saidraja station it was noted that "Though the attackers were numerous they were not a mob but advanced in some sort of formation and when repulsed carried off their dead in bullock carts." At Madhuban in the Azamgarh district "The rebel force came up from three directions and then combined in due order to carry out the assault. They were armed with spears and lathis [sticks] and were assisted by two elephants." From August 14 "Detailed reports from the Eastern disturbed area . . . ceased to be available, but deterioration . . . was obviously rapid." Ballia was completely cut off for ten days. "Unfortunately in most places in the Eastern area, there was a rapid collapse of morale. Police stations were captured and guns taken . . . In the disburbed area the rebels are everywhere accompanied by large crowds of villagers with an organising core of students and agitators." Individuals who were properly trained and equipped were sent aloft to clip telegraph lines with wirecutters and protective gloves. Often, however, the aroused villagers simply tossed ropes over the wires and pulled them down, poles and all, occasionally with the assistance of elephants.[18]

In western India the pattern of disorder was again somewhat different. Urban dislocation in Ahmedabad and Bombay was severe and prolonged. Disturbances in these cities, largely stimulated by students, continued almost unabated for months. In Bombay, bomb explosions became almost daily occurrences. When activity spread into the countryside around Bombay, it was in a distinctly methodical fashion. Here, sabotage was sophisticated and persistent. Slow to get underway, sabotage activities once started were conducted with such careful preparation and deliberation that the government were relatively helpless to combat them. Disorderly disturbances in Bihar and the United Provinces were finally curtailed by a show of orderly force; in Bombay, police retaliation was more often foreseen and hence forestalled. The number of bomb explosions in Bombay province far exceeded the number in the rest of India combined. Through December 1943, 447 bomb explosions were recorded in Bombay, against a mere 8 in Bihar. Damage in many categories was greater in Bihar than in Bombay, but in Bihar the damage was more often done by unarmed crowds attacking troops and demolishing buildings with only the simplest of tools (see tables 1 and 2).

In Ahmedabad, where Gandhi's influence was strong, the movement had a unique degree of coherence. The Congress controlled the mills of Ahmedabad, owners and workers alike. The owners took the initiative in closing the mills, which remained completely shut down for several months. Thousands of workers left the city. The city was immobilized by an organized campaign which declared each day in turn to be a strike to commemorate a different cause or hero. There was Professor Bhansali Day, Mahadev Desai Day, Chimur Atrocities Day, and so forth, and every now and then, when invention ran thin, an all-purpose Martyrs Day would be resorted to. Even after five months of protest in Ahmedabad, on January 10, 1943, "The Police were stoned by crowds on sixteen different occasions, and one policeman was slightly injured."[19]

In Bombay city, where labor was divided between Congress and the pro-war communists, and in Poona and other surrounding towns, the students took the lead in causing sustained urban turmoil. Unlike Bihar, where an earthshaking mass uprising carried everything before it, uprooting every stationary object in sight, in Bombay city, in a movement led by students who were reluctant to raze the city altogether, the protest was more selective and symbolic—but no less intense. Wild street warfare raged for several days, with crowds attacking with stones and bottles, police retaliating with bullets and "tear smoke." Police opened fire on the crowds in Bombay on twenty-six occasions on August 10, killing sixteen persons. On August 11, the police fired thirteen times, killing six.

For several months, school and college attendance remained no more than 10 to 20 percent. Students were on the rampage, and not a day passed without a spate of violent incidents. Students did not tear up rail lines, but they boarded trains, broke windows, pulled alarm chains, and ripped open cushions in first class compartments. At Dadar station on August 10, "Benches, iron bars and sleepers were thrown across the permanent way . . . At Marine Lines some students lay across the railway track disorganising train services for some time." On Au-

Table 1. Statistics Connected with Congress Disturbances for the Period Ending 31 December 1943, by provinces

Category	Madras	Bombay	Bengal	United Provinces	Punjab
Government servants (excluding those of the central government)					
Police					
Number of occasions on which police fired	21	226	63	116	1
Number of casualties inflicted, fatal	39	112	87	207	—
Number of casualties inflicted, nonfatal	86	406	149	458	—
Number of casualties suffered, fatal	—	6	5	16	—
Number of casualties suffered, nonfatal	91	563	180	333	—
Number of defections from police	1	6	—	2	—
Other government servants					
Number of attacks on other government servants, fatal	—	1	—	3	—
Number of attacks on other government servants, nonfatal	19	50	14	141	—
Number of defections from other government services	—	3	—	9	—
Damage to property (excluding central government property)					
Number of police stations or outposts etc. destroyed or severely damaged	5	46	4	42	—
Number of other government buildings destroyed or severely damaged	50	318	95	45	2
Number of public buildings other than government buildings, e.g., municipal property, schools, hospitals, etc., destroyed or severely damaged	57	152	58	37	4
Number of important private buildings destroyed or severely damaged	11	38	29	3	5
Estimated loss to government	Rs.225192	845410	171876	363366	1000
Estimated loss to other parties	Rs.916025	563581	55391	102778	105000
Cases of sabotage					
Number of bomb explosions	17	447	51	60	—
Number of bombs or explosives discovered without damage	35	738	106	157	1
Number of cases of sabotage to roads	32	78	57	84	—
Number of cases in which collective fines imposed	41	73	20	7	—
Amount of collective fines imposed	Rs.1034359	817950	605503	3176973	—
Number of sentences of whipping inflicted	295	17	2	1252	—
Number of arrests made	5859	24416	4818	16796	2501
Number of local authorities superseded under Defence Rule 38 B or otherwise	27	19	11	7	—

Source: National Archives of India, Home File No. 3/52/43 Poll. (I).

Bihar	Central Provinces	Assam	North-West Frontier Province	Orissa	Sindh	Delhi	Coorg	Total
96	42	4	1	9	—	22	—	601
166	45	15	3	69	—	20	—	763
508	181	19	13	111	—	10	—	1941
26	8	—	—	1	1	—	—	63
342	256	17	52	26	90	62	—	2012
205	2	—	—	—	—	—	—	216
4	2	—	—	—	—	—	—	10
87	39	—	—	13	—	1	—	364
4	—	—	5	—	—	—	1	22
72	29	4	—	5	—	1	—	208
103	41	64	1	25	—	4	1	749
92	45	66	—	8	2	4	—	525
119	2	61	—	2	1	2	—	273
354720	424840	284582	200	46459	1904	15456	120	2735125
495231	167270	194847	—	33598	2932	370376	245	3007274
8	10	10	1	—	50	—	10	664
218	18	9	1	—	13	11	12	1319
169	7	43	—	4	—	—	—	474
16	3	1	—	—	5	—	7	173
2660765	344595	339487	—	27750	—	—	—	9007382
340	282	—	—	9	—	—	—	2562
16202	8753	2707	2339	2806	3689	90	860	91836
3	35	—	—	5	—	1	—	108

Table 2.   Statistics Connected with the Congress Disturbances for the
Period Ending 31 December 1943, Central Departments

Railways

Number of railway stations destroyed or severely damaged	332
Number of cases of serious damage to tracks since 1 October 1942[a]	411
Number of cases of serious damage to rolling stock	268
Number of derailments or other accidents resulting from sabotage	66
Estimated loss to railway property	Rs:52,00,000

Post and Telegraph Department

Number of P. & T. offices, suboffices, etc. destroyed or severely damaged	945
Number of cases of destruction or serious damage to other property (telegraphs and telephones)	12,286

Military

Number of occasions on which military fired	68
Number of casualties inflicted, fatal	297
Number of casualties inflicted, nonfatal	238
Number of occasions of firing from air	5

Source: National Archives of India, Home File No. 3/52/43 Poll. (I).

[a]"Damage to track" was so widespread before 1 October 1942 and varied so greatly in extent that it is impossible to give detailed figures. The cost of such damage was approximately Rs.9 lakhs, compared to which the damage done in the cases recorded since October 1942 is almost negligible.

ust 14 at Bordi, "some six hundred boys obstructed the train by standing on the track."

A major student target was clothing which marked an individual as a government servant or an Anglicized Indian. Numerous cases were reported of "rowdy urchins . . . molesting pedestrians clad in European dress," or "indulging in petty acts of mischief, like the burning of hats." On September 11 at Dadar, "some boys and girls accosted pedestrians, relieved them of their hats and ties and burnt them."

Students were also in the lead in initiating the second phase of the insurrection, a form of rural mass action which was sufficiently distinctive to be eventually dubbed in underground circles as "the Karnatak pattern." This consisted of carefully organized attacks by large bands of unarmed or crudely armed villagers. Several of the original incidents of this type were the work of students, but the pattern quickly became established throughout the countryside where it continued almost unchecked until the end of the war in 1945. It was difficult for student guerrillas to hold together, and students soon melted into the countryside where they continued to work from their home villages. Villagers accepted the encouragement of students and older underground workers, but made "the Karnatak pattern" their own. Carefully coordinated lightning attacks would be made by groups often numbering several hundreds who would be back tending their fields by the time the police arrived. The object was to cause as much damage as possible in a brief time, and the emphasis was thus on dislocation rather than demolition, on barricading train tracks rather than ripping them up. Small groups of specialists in sabotage were also at work around Bombay, performing the tasks which required more skill and fewer people, but it was the technique of coordinated mass action by ordinary villagers which formed the most remarkable feature of the Karnatak pattern.

On August 18, a group of thirty-four students from Baroda were discovered at Adas station "lurking behind a hedge in a field. It appears that they were planning to board the train without tickets. The police party, who challenged them, was attacked with stones. One student rushed at the head constable with a clasp knife, while two others assaulted a constable whereupon an armed party of five standing behind opened fire. In all seven rounds were fired, which resulted in immediate death of three and serious injuries to six. Eleven others received minor injuries." On August 31, "A bus, conveying some detenus from Vengurla to Malwan, was held up by a crowd of about 500 students. They stoned the bus and some of them let off the air from the tyres."

By the end of August, students as a separate force were being replaced by organized villagers. At Chikhodra, on August 28, "when the Police made a lathi charge on some male demonstrators, drums were beaten, and out rushed about 200 Patidar women, armed with 'dharias' [scythes] 'vansis' [bamboo poles] and sticks." On September 9, a coordinated attack involving two columns approaching from different directions was made "on the Faduj Kacheri [courthouse] . . . The . . . attack was planned, as practically every person in the crowd of two thousand was armed with some weapon or other." On the same day at Kumta, "A Mamlatdar's peon, who was sent out by the Mamlatdar [deputy revenue collector] to ask the mob to disperse, was severely belaboured."

On September 10,

a mob, armed with dangerous weapons, marched on the town of Mahad in an attempt to loot the Treasury and burn the Post Office . . . In the early hours of morning, the mob started on its march and a couple of miles from Mahad they came upon a Circle Inspector, an Aval Karkun [government head clerk] and a "Pattewalla" [messenger] who were travelling in a bus. The mob halted the bus, and forced the Circle Inspector and Aval Karkun under threat of burning them alive, to wear Gandhi caps. The Aval Karkun was also made to carry a Congress flag at the head of the procession. When they reached the Post Office, some members of the mob broke it open and burnt the greater part of the records, and other property in it, valued at Rs. 300 to 400 . . . A Sub-Inspector, hearing the tumult, came out alone to see what was happening. He was immediately tied with ropes and made to join the procession. An unarmed police party, who encountered the mob later, were severely belaboured and four of the party, who fell to the ground, were trampled upon, and the rest were left to lie by the roadside, bleeding profusely, while the mob continued its march. When the march grew menacing and the rioters charged at the Police, the latter opened fire, and the Aval Karkun was unfortunately hit and killed, as he and four other Government servants, whom the mob had roped in, were used by the processionists as a shield against any frontal attack by the Police . . . The Mamlatdar of Mahad, who came out of his house, was also roped in by the mob and made to join the procession . . . That the whole affair was deliberate and preconcerted was evident from the fact that telegraphic communications all over the District had been dislocated and roads leading to the town were blocked or damaged.

On November 5, "A gang of about 100 persons armed with spears, 'dharias' etc. and with their faces masked, went about in villages of the Jalalpore Taluka indulging in incendiarism and other destructive activities . . . Simultaneously another gang of 30-35 was operating near Sisodra . . . From Sisodra they proceeded to Munsad, and on the way burnt a wooden bridge . . . The mango grafts of a Police patel [village sheriff] were cut."

On January 16, "a goods train dashed against a large boulder on the track near Belgaum." On the 19th, "a train collided against a bullock cart, filled with rafters, placed on the track at a level crossing between Usra and Jekot stations." On the 20th, while land revenue was being collected at Tolgi "some 100 saboteurs, who had mingled themselves among the villagers, suddenly sprang upon the Police Guard and the village officers in the chavdi [police post], and disarmed the Police of their arms and ammunition . . . Rs. 2,305 (the total amount of land revenue collected) were stolen by the saboteurs." On the 23d, "the village chavdi at Yedravi was set on fire by a gang of about fifty saboteurs, who also destroyed the standing crops of the Police Patil."[20]

This sampling of the thousands of incidents which occurred around Bombay in the months following August 9 reveals a pattern of entrenched warfare against which the government were helpless. Armed with homemade spears, captured muskets, and coconut shells filled with acid, villagers throughout the region were prepared to try their hand at organizing a local raid.

The British government's official statistics on the extent of the disturbances (see tables 1 and 2 above) are no doubt somewhat conservative—it was occasionlly alleged by nationalists that not 1,000 but 50,000 Indians had been killed by British firing—but there is no reason to suppose that the relative picture they present is inaccurate. These figures confirm the dominance in the movement of Bihar, the United Provinces, and Bombay and reveal the moderate but significant strength of the movement in Madras (where it was opposed by Rajagopalachari) and in Assam, Bengal, Orissa, Delhi, and the Central Provinces. (In Assam, in October, in a blending of modern and traditional forms of protest, "while a Sub-Deputy Collector in Kamrup was proceeding on tour to hold a revenue sale, he was obstructed by some boys lying down in front of his elephant and he did not proceed."[21]) The movement was also strong in the North-West Frontier Province, where figures reflecting violence and destruction are not a valid indicator, and in certain princely states for which figures are not available. The movement had no appreciable strength in Punjab and Sindh.

Regional variations suggest something about the attitude of locally concentrated communities. In Sindh, many persons were already participating in the activities of the militant Muslim sect, the Hurs. In Punjab, the Muslim and Sikh communities had strong traditions of military service and remained largely uninvolved. Even in areas where the movement was most intense, however, there were groups and parties which held back, either skeptical or flatly opposed.

The Quit India movement was instigated by the Congress but it could not be ignored by non-Congress groups. Gandhi had frankly stated that he intended to test the capacity of Muslim League leaders to hold Muslims in line. Other parties too saw the Quit India movement as a challenge to their ability to maintain a separate independence in the face of such a potentially popular crusade which might sweep all before it, leaving opposition leaders without followers. In addition to the Muslim League, the tempest threatened to uproot the communists, the Hindu Mahasabha, the Sikhs, the Untouchables, and the Kisan [peasant] Sabhas. During the nationalist movement, groups and parties were more sharply distinguished one from another at the level of leadership than at the level of membership; many had been members of Congress as well as of the Muslim League, communist party, or Hindu Mahasabha. A difference of opinion on an issue such as participation in the Quit India movement, however, necessitated a test of primary loyalty.

The attitude of the Hindu Mahasabha was sympathetic but aloof. Sikh and Untouchable leaders were noncommital or critical. Communist leaders were too committed to the British war effort for international reasons to succumb to the temptations of action politics, though Congress leaders did try to convert P. C. Joshi, the communist general secretary. Among student communists, however, many who were less impressed with considerations of international policy joined the Congress movement.

A telegram from the Home Department to the secretary of state for India dated September 5, 1942, noted that the "Communist Party of India remains doubtful factor. Its official policy is still pro-war and such influence as it possesses [over?] labour has been exercised on the right side in several cases, but behaviour of many of its members proves what has always been clear namely that it is composed far more of anti-British revolutionaries than of genuine believers in communist creed. Tactics of disturbances and many illegal pamphlets circulated in support of them have had distinctly communistic flavour."[22] In legalizing the communist party and releasing many communists in July 1942, the British government had been hopeful that the communists would give the Congress more trouble than they gave the government, but the British had no illusions about the loyalty of communist leaders or the sympathies of the communist rank and file. The many socialists whose socialism was frankly more nationalist than international—those associated with Bose's Forward Bloc and with the Congress Socialist party—found no difficulty identifying their efforts completely with the wide-open Quit India movement, and in the end took virtual charge of the movement.

The Muslims were, as always, the biggest question mark. The Quit India movement, in providing a demonstration that Indian nationalism had developed beyond the point at which any Indian group was prepared to support any British initiative to sustain their rule, also provided a demonstration of the real situation existing between the Hindu and Muslim communities at this critical stage. British authority collapsed, and with it the British ability to protect the minorities from majority tyranny. In this situation of virtual anarchy, Indian communities, as Gandhi had anticipated, were free to deal with one another without the artificial intervention of the British as a third party. The real relationship existing between the two communities was finally put to the test which had figured in hypothetical rhetoric for so long. The result was conclusive—but unexpected.

The remarkable thing about Hindu-Muslim relations during the Quit India movement is that nothing remarkable happened. The predictions of congressmen, Muslim Leaguers, and British officials were all belied. Hindus did not terrorize Muslims; but neither did the Muslims join in the struggle. Most Muslims kept aloof, offering support neither to the nationalist uprising nor to their supposed British benefactors.

In report after report on the local course of the uprising, the entry under the heading "communal" was the single phrase "Nothing to report." Muslims almost everywhere acted with the same unanimity displayed by nationalists; they remained strictly neutral. Since their conduct was not identified in nationalist eyes as pro-British, their neutrality provoked no adverse reaction. In fact, in certain places Muslims participated in the movement incognito—not wishing to help the British, though reluctant to identify themselves publicly as Muslims with the Congress.

The absence of communal violence was so marked as to appear slightly sinister in the eyes of Lord Linlithgow. He saw evidence of Congress strategy in the fact that the disturbances had not followed the "normal" course into communal excess; the "absence of communal trouble," wrote Linlithgow, "must be put down largely to disciplined abstention from interference with Muslims."[23]

From the United Provinces it was reported that "Muslims have kept severely aloof from the movement and Muslim quarters remained quiet . . . the Congress have made no attempt to embroil them . . .

Each of the two major communities have been behaving almost as if the other did not exist . . . In fact Hindu clerks going to work in Cawnpore preferred to do so through the Muslim quarters, where for the last 10 years they have been afraid to show their faces." The one exception to the embroilment of United Provinces students in the movement was at Aligarh where the vice-chancellor, "Dr. Sir Zia-uddin Ahmad, has . . . kept his students completely aloof from the movement." The government of the United Provinces considered it likely, however, that "the violence of [the Quit India movement] and its organization have made a very deep impression on Muslims."[24]

In Delhi, differences arose in the approach to the movement of spokesmen of the Muslim League and the pro-Congress Jamiat-ul-Ulema-i-Hind, which "at its Working Committee meeting in Delhi on the 17th [of August] and succeeding days adopted a resolution expressing sympathy with the Congress cause but at the same time denouncing the acts of violence."[25] The Muslim members of the Jamiat-ul-Ulema-i-Hind engaged in genuinely "Gandhian" demonstrations only, staging open protest marches. During October, a war of words developed between the Muslim factions of Delhi. "On each of the three Fridays of the fortnight meetings with audiences ranging from two to four hundred have been held in the Fatehpuri Mosque and at these speakers have condemned the present Congress movement and appealed to Muslims to remain aloof from it. Each Friday meetings with audiences of similar size have been held in the Jama Masjid under the joint auspices of the Majlis-i-Ahrar and the Jamiat-ul-Ulema-i-Hind; at that on the 16th October Government was criticized for not providing facilities for Haj pilgrims."[26]

On October 31, in a "communal incident," three persons, two Muslims and one Hindu, were killed while engaging in what appeared to be an "attempt to sabotage railway property. Investigation has revealed that two of the three were known railway coal thieves."[27]

The main efforts of Muslim League leaders in the fall of 1942 were devoted to urging Muslims to continue their abstention from the Congress movement on the one hand, and on the other to urging the government to exempt Muslims from schemes of collective responsibility. The Bombay government reported that "All Muslim inhabitants, members of the Scheduled Castes, Government servants, and those who helped the Police in the course of investigation of the offences are generally exempted from these collective fines. Muslim inhabitants were not exempted in Baramati town as there was evidence of Muslim complicity in the acts of sabotage at that place."[28]

In a telegram dated September 5, 1942, the governor of Bihar confided to Lord Linlithgow the mixed emotions he felt regarding the proper treatment of Muslims:

> Representatives of Muslim League have claimed that the Muslim community should be exempted from liability to contribute to any collective fine which may be imposed on Patna city or elsewhere," he wrote, "on the ground that they kept strictly aloof from all mischievous activities. The facts are substantially as stated, though Muslim bad characters have also taken part in disturbance, but my own first reaction was that an attitude of complete aloofness differs little from one of acquiescence in a campaign of destruction and interference with Civic rights and amenities and that Muslim community should pay like the others: otherwise basic idea of collective fine disappears. I instructed my officers accordingly. On the other hand it now appears that elsewhere in Bihar Muslims have taken an active part in restoring order and communications and, while it is possible to exempt Muslims in particular localities where assistance has been given, insistence on a general rule that Muslims must pay with the rest may (a) have an adverse effect on those who have co-operated, and (b) set Muslim League by the ears not only in Bihar but elsewhere. I confess I do not like sacrificing conviction to expediency but have no particular desire or indeed leisure to take on a fight with the League at present moment, much less embarrass other Governors or Governments. I am inclined therefore if Your Excellency agrees to go considerable way to meet Muslim claim and to make community liable only when there is reason to believe they were actively involved as in certain places they are said to have been.

Lord Linlithgow replied two days later that he agreed that "it would be well to go slow, or even desist altogether from realising fines from Muslims." The Muslim League was given a grudging exemption because the government did not want to add to their own difficulties. But the Muslim League was as anxious to demonstrate its independence of the government as of the Congress. In November, the Bihar Muslim League protested "against Muhammadans being included in collective responsibility schemes for safeguarding communications."[29]

The Quit India movement provided the first real test of the Muslim League's presumption to speak for the Muslim majority. The result was convincing evidence that most Muslims did think of themselves as unrepresented by the Congress movement and were prepared to act as a separate force, despite dispersal over the entire map of India. The electoral dominance which the League attained in Muslim constituencies for the first time in the elections of 1946 may be said to have been foreshadowed in this spontaneous demonstration by most Muslims of a sense of separation in the test which Gandhi ordained—the test of anarchy.

Organization

The August Uprising was spontaneous; no preconceived plan could have produced such instantaneous and uniform results. Congressmen with organizational experience who remained at large after August 9 had, however, been moving quickly to assemble the rudiments of a new underground organization. Funds were collected and a network of contacts was established throughout the country, so that some coordination might be possible behind a screen of pseudonyms, falsified addresses, and midnight movements. An "All-India Congress Committee office" operated secretly for a time from room number 30 on the second floor of Patladhis Mala, No. 69/87 Cathedral Street Bombay, and later shifted to room number 16 on the second floor of Govind Building, Kehtwadi Main Road, Bombay. These rooms served as a makeshift office for a staff composed of a coordinator, an accountant, a typist, and a peon. A substantial correspondence flowed in and out of the office. "Sometimes we used to post about 200 envelopes a day." An elaborate system of cover addresses made it possible to continue operating in this fashion without detection. The office channeled communications from underground workers seeking to contact one another and collected news of the movement's progress for cyclostyled distribution. The basic office staff remained the same, though there were numerous rotations in personnel. The holders of the different offices were given code names, which were assumed by whoever happened to be functioning in a given capacity at a given time. The office head, who coordinated activities across the country, was called Kikaji; this role was usually taken by Sadiq Ali, relieved by B. K. Keskar, Dwarkanath Kachru, and others. The office accountant was called Ramesh; a number of different people in succession bore this name. In this way, communications were sustained despite the risk of arrest and the need for undertaking unexpected journeys; important messages were sent by courier.

In addition to the code names attached to office functionaries, several code names were also regularly used by certain individuals. Thus, Sucheta Kripalani was known as Dadi or Behan Ji; Baba Raghavdas as Didi; Ram Manohar Lohia as Doctor; Aruna Asaf Ali as Kadam; and Achyut Patwardhan as Kusum.[30]

The Bombay office called itself the "A.I.C.C. office," but it exercised no real authority. From time to time cyclostyled messages would appear bearing various imposing headings, that of the "A.I.C.C." or the "Central Congress Directorate." Such bodies did exist, but they were fluctuating and self-appointed. While communications were sustained among prominent underground workers in different parts of the country, and a series of meetings took place in Delhi, Benares, Calcutta, and Bombay, no sustained coordination or direction was possible. The meetings were marked by an exchange of views between people working separately, committed to differing policies. Regional leaders, in turn, had to rely on local volunteers, and anyone with an idea was encouraged to try it out. If a student—or a professor—arrived to spend the night with a suitcase full of explosives, his host would wish him well, even if he personally abstained from his violent schemes.

Radhe Shyam Sharma, professor of chemistry at Benares Hindu University and warden of the Birla Student Hostel—an abrupt man with a hawk's eyes and pride—had suddenly found himself, like many others, unexpectedly underground. On August 9, Professor Sharma and his colleague Dr. Kaushalya Nand Gairola had raised the standard of revolt on campus. The university gates were closed and Benares Hindu University was declared free Indian soil. The university military training corps was declared the army of free India. Students took processions into town and succeeded in raising the Congress flag over government buildings while the police looked on. Police firing did occur in several places, and one student was killed and others seriously injured.[31]

At 5 A.M. on August 19 the university was finally occupied by British and Australian troops. On the eve of the seizure, Sharma and Gairola urged the students who had not already done so to proceed to their homes and continue the struggle from there. Gairola and Sharma by this time had Rs. 5,000 bounties on their heads. Gairola held a Vienna degree and was alleged on this basis to have Nazi sympathies. Sharma had no previous record of shady associations, but British police files quickly began recording the exploits of "the notorious ex-professor . . . Radhe Shyam and his gang of U.P. terrorists."[32]

The students and their leaders managed to escape arrest at the time the university was occupied with the active assistance of virtually all the city's respectable inhabitants and a certain amount of sympathetic advance warning from Indian police officials. Absconders hid in the backs of houses deep in the impenetrable small lanes of the old city and set out on foot for home. Rail traffic and all forms of communication had by now been effectively cut off.

After his escape from the campus, Professor Sharma walked on foot the seventy miles to Allahabad, with the shaven head and saffron robes of a sadhu. From Allahabad he reached his native Gwalior and then went to Delhi where he made contacts with other revolutionaries. Once established in Delhi, the professor of chemistry soon became a specialist in the manufacture of explosives.

As useful as Sharma's knowledge of chemistry were his contacts in his home region, the princely state of Gwalior, conveniently close to Delhi. The princely states had traditionally been thought exempt from the hazards of political radicalism because the princes were able to deal with agitators without bothering about public opinion or legal proprieties. Many Englishmen had envied the ease with which the princes had dealt with troublemakers. Recent years had seen much of this change, and the princely states not only were themselves no longer exempt from turmoil, but were aggravating instability elsewhere. The Congress had developed, either directly or through parallel organizations, legions of sympathizers in the princely states. The greater casualness of law enforcement in the princely states was beginning to be used by nationalists against authority, rather than by authority in dispatching agitators. The stringent proscription of firearms imposed on Indians in British India, for example, did not exist in the princely states, and this now provided militants with a convenient source of weapons.

Professor Sharma's chief supplier of explosive material was a Gwalior forest contractor who had access to dynamite for earth-moving work. Shells were supplied by a Gwalior ironmonger. Professor Sharma's traffic in such commodities was facilitated by the military themselves. Army officers traveling with bulky suitcases were not viewed suspiciously by the police, and many silent sympathizers remaining nominally in British service provided such assistance. Professor Sharma tested his pilot bombs in a second princely state, in the arid hills near

Jaipur. Bombs were placed underground and detonated from a distance.

Professor Sharma was arrested on New Year's Eve, December 31, 1942. He had avoided detection for months by shifting his disguise from that of a sadhu to that of a Muslim maulana, with beard and cap, and by shifting daily between twenty-five separate residences. He was arrested while approaching one of his ammunition dumps. Two weeks later, follow-up raids were made on two other dumps, rented rooms in Bazaar Sita Ram and in Karol Bagh, where the police unearthed "186 gelignite sticks, 183 detonators, 1,200 feet of fuse, 30 lbs. of gunpowder, 46 empty cast iron containers designed for bombs, 3 incendiary or explosive bombs, large quantities of chemicals and some documents." A number of bombs were thrown by the British into the Jumna river, where they exploded. This so astonished the authorities responsible for disposing of the bombs that several munitions experts were sent to interview Professor Sharma in prison to attempt to ascertain why they had not been deactivated by contact with water. The professor declined to reveal this professional secret.

Professor Sharma also recalls being urged to divulge the whereabouts of others. He was kept awake for long periods and placed in an especially damp riverside cell of the Red Fort. He was told that Aruna Asaf Ali had been arrested and had already confessed. He was shown her purported confession which did contain certain accurate details. He was even presented with a copy of the *Hindustan Times* with the headline "Detenu's Mother Dies." Sharma was asked if he wished to attend to his mother's last rites; he said he did. Then he was informed that he would be permitted to do so only after he had divulged certain information, and he rightly suspected the entire affair was a ruse.[33]

Professor Sharma's adventures suggest many of the reasons for the success of the underground movement. Professor Sharma was not a professional revolutionary. He had had no previous experience with the use of pseudonyms and sabotage. Once underground, however, he was able to draw freely upon the normal resources of a respectable professional background. The people he had known in ordinary times did not disown him now. The effectiveness of underground workers such as Professor Sharma, who, following his release from prison, resumed the teaching of chemistry at Benares Hindu University, depended upon the support of thousands of ordinary people continuing in ordinary occupations.

In Bombay, equipment for the transmitters of the underground Congress radio station was supplied by the respectable firm of Chicago Radio and Telephone Company Ltd., and the transmitters were assembled and reassembled after each shift to a new secret location by skilled technicians supplied by the same company. It was only through such sophisticated assistance from respectable sources that the amateurs who actually manned the microphones were able to function. The chief announcer was a young girl who "was, prior to her arrest, reading for the M.A." Usha Mehta, reported the police who arrested her, "is obviously an ardent Congress woman, but had not come to notice before in this connection." Usha Mehta was slight girl with large, intense eyes and a startlingly rich voice. For some time she had been meeting every Sunday with a group of fellow students interested in promoting Hindi as the national language. Her parents were, however, somewhat suspicious about the motives which brought this group together. Her father, a judge in British service, said to her, "I don't care what you do with your life, but please finish your studies first." When Gandhi was arrested, Usha told her father that her studies would have to wait; the nation had to be freed now. Usha moved out of her father's house and went underground, shifting regularly from one rented room to another to escape police detection; her mother, however, always knew where she was. Acting with the cooperation of her fellow Hindi enthusiasts, Usha decided to establish an illegal radio station, and within a couple of weeks, by the end of August 1942, they were on the air. Any initiative, no matter how farfetched, seemed to catch fire. An inexperienced girl with a crazy idea found people ready to offer her money and equipment. Once launched on the airwaves, she was sought out by more people, including Dr. Ram Manohar Lohia, who supplied funds for an even larger transmitter which ultimately carried Usha's defiant message from her Bombay back room all the way to Calcutta and Madras. For three months, news of the progress of the revolt, supplied from secret contacts, and the recorded voices of Gandhi and other leaders were beamed across India, to the consternation of British officials who roamed the streets of Bombay in a "detection van," trying to track down the signal. Usha was ultimately caught in the act through information supplied to the police by one of the technicians on whom the technologically uninitiated Usha had to rely. Before August 9, Usha Mehta, like Professor Sharma, had been a respectable member of the academic community; after August 9, she had suddenly become a fabled heroine, broadcasting sedition each night from "somewhere in India."[34]

The fact that all Indians formed a class in British India is reflected in the degree to which, in 1942, the word "underground" expanded to include virtually the entire nation. The main sources from which activists were drawn, according to one underground circular, were: "a) Such Congress and other political workers as are still out and active; b) Students and teachers; c) Strikers and dismissed workers from factories; d) Workers of social welfare institutions; e) The better type Sadhus and Fakirs."[35] Even more significant than this diversity of activists was the fact that, for the first time, the sophisticated, Anglicized class indicated that however much they might dislike the Congress they could no longer stand with the government in opposing the Congress.

Sir T. Stewart, governor of Bihar, commented caustically on the fact that "*Moderate* opinion climbed the fence as soon as there was firing. The Elder Statesmen had no doubt that the firing, if not entirely justified, was yet done in good faith but they would have been failing in their duty if they did not tell us that the younger generation believed that the firing was deliberate murder . . . There is, too, a certain amount of resentment amongst the intelligentsia in that they have had to undergo certain inconveniences in these days of stress and say that a B.O.R. on picket duty sometimes fails to distinguish between an advocate of the High Court and a possible saboteur. The Bar have been tricky and have tried to jockey the Chief Justice into closing the Courts." Sir C. P. Ramaswamy Aiyar resigned from the viceroy's Executive Council, expressing a desire to meet with Gandhi, although the real reasons for his resignation were dissimulated in the public announcement. The viceroy complained that he could not "quite make out what is moving C.P. unless it is the general Hindu sensitiveness to this sort of business. But I am astonished that anyone of his political experience, etc., should want to make this formal approach to Gandhi . . . This development on the part of a man whom we should all of us have regarded as completely dependable and solid is a lamentable commentary on the strain with which we will be faced were we to agree to an Indian Home Member."

The British were beginning to wonder whether they could trust *anyone*; and with good reason. Indians high in government service were explicitly and constructively cooperative with terrorists, even if not publicly so. Mrs. Aruna Asaf Ali, while absconding, traveled from city to city in aircraft requisitioned for military purposes, with the assistance of sympathetic pilots such as Biju Patnaik, later chief minister of Orissa. Mrs. Sucheta Kripalani, while absconding, often stayed with her cousin, an I.C.S. officer stationed at Patna; when on one of her trips she was arrested at his house, he "got into a lot of trouble"—with Indians. Many absconders moved with remarkable freedom across the country, receiving the passive support of government officials, the financial support of government contractors, and shelter from respectable devotees of nonviolence.[36]

Without Gandhi, everyone acted on his own authority and interpreted Gandhi according to his own lights—and desires. Gandhi's name was quoted freely on fugitive leaflets, and his vague general instructions were placed at the head of detailed plans for sabotage. Various rumors spread about to the effect that Gandhi had sanctioned train derailments if only a red warning flag were waved, or that Gandhi drew the line only at murder. Abdul Ghaffar Khan, one of the few prominent congressmen not arrested on August 9, devised an ingenious solution to the problem of "Gandhian" sabotage. Ghaffar Khan was prepared to sanction cutting wires and removing rails if the perpetrator immediately reported his crime to the police. He explained that "This would add to the moral courage of the worker and set an example of uprightness and bravery to the people and also save them from being victims of harassment and suspicion."[37] Few, however, acted on this advice.

"We took Gandhi's statement that anarchy was better than slavery and said, all right, then we will have anarchy," one former revolutionary recalls. Another considered Gandhi's nonviolence his "dhar," or shield, permitting him to engage in violence with greater impunity than would have been possible in a frankly violent campaign.[38]

Jayaprakash Narayan took greater pains to think through his position. He argued in the first of his letters written after his escape from prison in November 1942 that a violent struggle could not be Gandhian, but that it might still be considered legitimately a Congress struggle. Jayaprakash noted the longstanding differences between Gandhi and the Congress Working Committee on questions of national defense. "The Congress has stated repeatedly," he wrote, "that if India became free, or even if a national government were set up, it would be prepared to resist aggression with arms. But, if we are prepared to fight Japan and Germany with arms, why must we refuse to fight Britain in the same manner? The only possible answer can be that the Congress in power could have an army, whereas the Congress in wilderness has none. But supposing a revolutionary army were created or if the present Indian army or a part of it rebel, would it not be inconsistent for us first to ask the army to rebel and then to ask the rebels to lay down arms and face British bullets with bared chests?"[39]

Jayaprakash justified armed revolt against British rule by employing, as Gandhi himself had done, an analogy between what was sanctioned for use against the Japanese and what would be sanctioned for use against the British, if they proved themselves no better than the Japanese. Jayaprakash recognized that Gandhi was not himself prepared to lead or advocate armed revolt, but that Gandhi had been prepared to let other congressmen resort to arms if all else failed.

The fact that congressmen resorted to violence did not in itself violate the guidelines Gandhi had laid down. Much less Gandhian than the violence of the movement was the general enthusiasm with which so many Indians greeted the prospect of a Japanese invasion. Gandhi wanted to see the British kicked out of India, so it was said, and consequently Britain's enemy was India's friend. The Indian National Army, composed of Indians sworn to loyalty to the British who were now fighting against the British, might thus be viewed in Jayaprakash's terms as men who had answered the Gandhian call to leave British employment and the Congress call to fight with arms against the aggressors, the intruding British. For most Indians, the response to tales of Indian National Army prowess, of the daring of Subhas Bose, and the reverses of the British at the hands of the Germans and Japanese was simply one of gratifying excitement. Bose dared to do what many had wished: to flee the country and fight on the side of Britain's enemies. His escape from Calcutta house arrest and travels to Germany through Russia, and thence to Singapore by submarine, were profoundly exciting to Indians frustrated to be immobilized in the midst of a world-wide crisis. Indians listened eagerly to the regular radio broadcasts in Hindi from Berlin at eight each evening. One person, a student in 1942, recalled the elation with which the announcement was received at Benares Hindu University that the Nazis had enough bombs to submerge the British Isles under ten feet of water.[40]

Gurdip Singh of Jhabal Kalan had plenty of time to devote to savoring enemy broadcasts while imprisoned in the Punjab:

Yogi Ram Nath had his private Radio set which was daily switched on for receiving broadcasts from Berlin, Rome, Tokyo and

Saigon . . . We were much interested in the Saigon broadcast from which we learnt that Indian National Army comprising about a lakh [100,000] soldiers was formed among the Indian war prisoners in the Jap occupied countries. This army was announced to be ready for an attack on India to liberate her from the British clutches. We heard the speeches of Rash Behari Bose and S. C. Bose and also the accounts of the Bangkok Conference which affected my mind in as much that a movement was started ex-India for the freedom of motherland . . . In the beginning the enemy propaganda was not much liked by the Congressites and throughout so by the two communists. When the Congress took steps towards launching C.D. [civil disobedience] movement the interest in the enemy broadcasts was very much increased.[41]

At the height of the disturbances in Bihar, the government reported that "Enemy broadcasts . . . are freely listened to everywhere . . . Agitators in Muzaffarpur district are said to have circulated the rumour that aircraft seen coming over . . . belonged . . . to the Germans and Japanese and were carying Indian political leaders."[42]

The enthusiasm with which protestors greeted news of Japanese advances probably suggests little more than the degree to which their actions grew from desperation. Some activists attempted to coordinate their efforts with a prospective invasion, while others concentrated their hopes on a new and larger mass uprising. In both cases, they were reflecting anxiety about the effect of their own unaided underground activities. Most underground workers acted as drastically as they did precisely because they were convinced that British rule would last and last for endless decades to come, and such a prospect was unbearable. At whatever cost, with whatever prospect of success, some gesture had to be made indicative of resentment at British intransigence. Those who persisted in underground activities did so to demonstrate that the spirit of resistance would not die. As individuals wearied of a furtive life and "dropped out" by submitting to arrest, they were making individual decisions which contained very little sense that they were letting down the side. They were not betraying a collective enterprise with a chance of success; they were only terminating their individual witness. Little or no resentment was felt by those who persisted against those who were no longer "with us."

The mood of underground workers was also expressed in a widespread preoccupation with the threat of rape. Rape always accompanies the chaos of warfare, resulting from military bravado or the desperation of sick and vengeful men. The incidence of British rape at the time of the Quit India movement cannot account, however, for the pervasiveness of Indian anxieties. The British and their allies, it was held, were everywhere indulging in rape with phenomenal determination. Agitators had long portrayed British exploitation of India's resources in metaphors of sexual violation, to suggest British contempt for all standards of civilized conduct, and to induce Indians to respond to a political challenge as they would to a family insult. With an added access of anger, natural British propensities would, it was feared, inevitably engender unprecedented atrocities.

The dread of rape of an oppressed majority may be as pervasive as that of their oppressors, though it originates in different anxieties. A ruling race suffers from fears that those who are in other respects powerless and inferior may possess greater sexual energy and resentment sufficient to direct their energies against the ruler's wife. What is unknown—the secret resources of those victimized—feeds on what is repressed—one's awareness of one's own limitations. The greater one's reluctance to come to terms with one's own guilt and inadequacy, the greater one's estimate of the menace of others. It is necessary to decry what one hates to admit one wants. The oppressed man, in contrast, fears that his oppressor may prove as aggressive sexually as he is in other ways. The oppressed man assumes that his oppressor must be powerfully attracted by those he seeks to control. Contemptuous of their sensitivities, he is not indifferent to their charms. Rape seems a natural consequence when longing is unleashed by resentment, in retribution for the oppressed man's refusal to continue his ritualized propitiation of the aggressor. After the initial defiance of a tense but familiar relationship one becomes painfully conscious that things are never so bad that they might not get worse. Fear of sexual assault by an insatiable oppressor reflects a horrified sense of how much one has risked in throwing over a settled tyranny of limited brutality. The underground vision of Britishers as uncontrollable rapists was an expression of the agonized desperation of those who nonetheless persisted in defiant rebellion.

The desperation of the underground movement is further suggested by the fact that even those who claimed to be working for the rapid attainment of full independence had almost no notion of what might happen once victory had been achieved. The condition of independence was as dimly imagined as a future life, and virtually no thought was given even in abstract terms to the proper sort of government for a free India. Revolutionary governments of various sorts were established in different parts of the country, but these were clearly extraordinary arrangements for extraordinary circumstances. "Panchayat Raj" (village self-government) was declared in some regions as a conscious offering to Gandhi on the occasion of his arrest, with an emphasis on mass participation in spontaneous decisions. Police stations were captured and arrangements for tax collection and courts were extemporized. Such governments lasted only a few weeks.

Other governments were evolved in connection with the later underground phase of the movement, governing at night areas which the British nominally controlled during the day. These were the sinews of the underground movement, providing shelter, communication, and funds for roaming revolutionaries. Both of these forms of government were expressions of the movement, not intended seriously as prototypes of government for settled times.

The ultimate goals of the underground revolutionaries were vague. The main differences within the movement were on questions of method. With the waning of spontaneous mass activity, the need for active stimulation and direction was clear. The responsibility for making a conscious decision regarding the type of action which should be planned and advocated could thus no longer be evaded. As the thinking of individuals began to clarify, groups began to emerge which represented a commitment to turning the movement in one direction or another. Alternative plans were formulated, but no one group or plan ever became dominant. The movement remained too fugitive and scattered for any one group to feel that they could afford to dissociate themselves from colleagues espousing different methods. No one was prepared to betray an old associate over a difference of opinion about the proper method of pursuing the common goal.

The thinking of underground workers gravitated toward one of three main points of view. One group, represented most notably by Jayaprakash Narayan, wanted to see the movement substantially reorganized into a disciplined guerrilla effort in which violence would be systematically employed. A "centrist" group, consisting primarily of the Congress socialists who had taken a major responsibility in coordinating activities during the fall, were prepared to carry on in a roughly similar fashion in the future, providing encouragement to resistance efforts spontaneously undertaken by volunteers in different parts of the country. The third group, the "Gandhians," including those such as Sucheta Kripalani and Sadiq Ali who had been closely associated with the Congress organization before August 9, were beginning to feel that secret activities should be either given up altogether or at least made more "Gandhian" by concentration on "constructive" activities.

The mentality of the most militant activists is well illustrated by a pamphlet the police unearthed at Nasik and also found later circulating in Punjab entitled "A.B.C. of Dislocation." In it was set forth an elaborate plan for the formation of a nation-wide guerrilla force, to be called Azad Dastas (Free Bands) in evocation of the name of the Azad Hind Fauj (Free Indian Army, or Indian National Army) advancing through Burma. The guerrillas were to be organized on a model of democratic decentralization: "There are 250 districts in British Occupied India. In a district of average size 250 Azads might be organized in five Jathas of 50 Azads each. [The district] should further be divided into 25 Dastas of ten Azads each. It is suggested that every member of the Dasta should have the sur-title Azad added to his name; so that, if his name is Sher Singh he should be known as Sher Singh Azad. In this manner our Azad would mean the same as the Spanish 'guerrilla' or the Russian 'Partisan.'"[43]

Each group of ten Azads was to elect a leader, who would then be given unquestioning loyalty. A special effort was to be made to induce policemen and soldiers to desert in order to become Azads. An Azad Subedar would coordinate activities at a provincial level, as would an Azad Ziladar for each district, chosen from the five Jathedars in each district.

The Azad bands were to seek contributions of food and clothing from the local population of the area in which they operated. It was noted that "There are a million sadhus in our country who do not work and are yet fed by the people"; the Azads "shall only be a sixteenth of this number." Azad Dastas were also encouraged to "loot mail bags, small post offices . . . and other stores of the usurpers." The document added, "It should be mentioned here that it would be inadvisable for our Dastas to get mixed up with professional dacoits or other criminals." The caution to be chary of criminal ties was well advised; leading nationalists were often approached by dacoits with offers to supply funds through armed robberies.[44]

The Azad Dastas were urged to make their headquarters in jungle areas, but not to disregard the possibility of operating even in populous

areas "when they are firmly rooted among the mass of our people."
The Azad Dastas were thought of as a supplement to the "main part
of our Revolution . . . an open rebellion of the whole people
. . . Their continuous conflict with the enemy will keep up and
radiate the spirit of resistance and also be a training to the people
in general in the acts of resistance." The Azad Dastas would inspire
and guide the masses at large when they once again rose as they had
in August 1942, thereby insuring a momentum which would carry them
on to total victory. The Azad Dastas would also be preparing the ground
for an easier victory by gradually bringing about "the atomization of
the country" advocated by "the A.I.C.C. Radio." Atomization meant
the "breakup of the artificial shackles of unity imposed upon the country." It meant "not only . . . the putting out of action of rails and
roads that coil round the country like a black serpent and collect its
blood in central reservoirs," but also "the much vaster effort of putting
out of action the relation between village produce and city manufacture
and the system of currency and taxation . . . This action in August
–September was the work of the masses, who instinctively knew that
the rails and roads were the vipers that sucked their blood and made
the rule of the foreigners possible. The intensity of the mass upsurge
having declined for the time being, the cutting up of these vipers is
now the work of our Azad Dastas, which have their roots among the
masses and draw their sustenance and sanction from them."

The pamphlet then offered some practical advice regarding methods
of looting and dislocation. Azads were advised that "It takes half-
an-hour to saw an average telegraph pole." When cutting wires, one
should bear in mind that "if the hands are wrapped in dry cloth no
shock will ever be felt." With regard to railways, it was noted that
"Rails can be cut with a hacksaw; it takes 45 minutes to do that. Cut
a portion, say a foot long, and leave it in place so that the damage
may not be apparent to a driver; this will derail a train. Another method
is to remove fish-plates . . . The nuts are unscrewed by a suitable
spanner, universal spanner or pipe-tongs." Railway engines could best
be put out of commission "with the cooperation of railway men. Special
attention should be paid to it and our Labour Department should be
asked to help."

Electric railways, it was advised, could be best damaged by cutting
with a hacksaw "the legs of corner towers . . . of pylons that carry
the overhead lines . . . CAUTION: Take care that the overhead lines

do not fall upon or touch the body as the towers fall; else you will die."

With reference to industrial sabotage, as in the case of the sabotage of railway engines, the method advised was to befriend workmen who would themselves know how best to dislocate the operation in which they were engaged.

The instructions regarding the manufacture and use of incendiaries and explosives were given in elaborate scientific detail, reflecting painstaking experimentation by specialists such as Radhe Shyam Sharma, as well as careful study of "Military Pamphlet No. 7 of 1940" and the recommendations of the "U.S. Bureau of Mines."[45]

The Nasik document is noteworthy for the practicality of its advice. It advocated the avoidance of heroics and suggested that the blowing up of big bridges be attempted only by highly trained specialists. The emphasis was on the sort of destruction which could be accomplished with a minimum of training and dexterity by small groups equipped with simple tools. The document was also ideologically modest. The activities of the guerrilla bands were understood as a contribution to the initial Gandhian objective of a spontaneous popular uprising. The destruction of means of transport and communication was thought of as facilitating the attainment of the Gandhian objective of village autonomy. The guerrillas were encouraged to think of themselves as part of the wider Congress movement and as persons who might assist the masses in technical ways but should not impose upon them their own will or ideas.

There is no evidence that this blueprint for a nation-wide loosely-associated network of guerrilla bands was anywhere implemented in the precise form described, although Jayaprakash Narayan, whom the British suspected to be the prime author of the "A.B.C. of Dislocation," in fact did devote some months to the establishment of a camp for the training of guerrillas across the Indian border in Nepal. As a model for the efforts of the thousands of underground agents spread throughout the country, however, the plan had considerable significance.

The bulk of underground workers seem to have assumed that the movement could only hope to carry on in the same old random way. On July 12, 1943, the Bombay police seized a copy of a cyclostyled letter addressed to the Bihar Provincial Congress Committee stating that "sabotage of Karnatak pattern is approved by Central Directorate of Congress. Please note. (Signed.) Prabhat, Office Secretary." This document represented the considered opinions of the "centrist" faction who sought to perpetuate the movement by drawing on past experience. Based on recent developments around Bombay, the document sent to Bihar explained that "Targets chosen are mostly small and always belong to Government and are mostly in villages. For instance, Mail Runners, Mail Buses, small post offices, post boxes . . . dak bungalows, village records . . . small culverts, railroads, roads, etc." Such activities were carried out without elaborate training or equipment by villagers who continued their customary activities "unless they become so marked as to be declared absconders by the police . . . Invariably the villagers have acted as screens and shelters to active workers."

In contrast to the recommendations of the "A.B.C. of Dislocation," the "Central Directorate" advocated that dislocation be carried on normally by ordinary villagers in their spare time. Furthermore, "Non-killing and non-injury to human life is strictly enjoined . . . No question of arms, therefore, arises." When arms had been seized from the police in Karnatak, the letter stated somewhat wishfully, they had simply been "dumped safely away." "Most of the raids were surprise raids by small groups carried out surreptitiously. But not a few were open, by broad daylight, by big numbers sometimes consisting of from 30 to 150 persons from round about villages. It has been kept in view that these raids are not ends in themselves. They are meant to lead to mass action or mass upheaval one day. Therefore open action is always preferable."

The "Central Directorate of Congress" advocated a program of widespread but part time harassment by ordinary villagers taking care to avoid injury to human beings. This program shared with the proposal for violent guerrilla action an assumption that the ultimate objective was a second spontaneous mass uprising on the pattern of August 1942. The viewpoint attributed to the "Central Directorate" seems to have been shared by such leaders as Aruna Asaf Ali, Ram Manohar Lohia, and Achyut Patwardhan.

A distinctive "Gandhian" faction within the underground movement began to take definite shape only in the wake of Gandhi's fast begun on February 10, 1943. The fast reminded many underground workers of the extent to which they had departed from Gandhi's path. In the shadow of the fast, the glamour of the underground life paled. Sucheta Kripalani decided that she must see Gandhi even if this meant surrendering herself to the police. She communicated her desire to an Indian

I.C.S. officer, H. V. R. Iengar, additional secretary, Home Department, Bombay, who arranged for her to visit Gandhi in Poona and to depart without being arrested. Gandhi was delighted—and surprised—to see her. He inquired about her health but made no reference to her underground activities, a fact which she interpreted to her profound relief as indicating Gandhi's approval of her right to continue underground if she so desired.[46]

Gandhi was not inclined to exert pressure on underground workers to surrender themselves if they themselves wished to continue their activities. Gandhi's fast had nonetheless had the effect of reminding many people of Gandhi's importance to them. The prospect of his death had inevitably stimulated sobering reflection on the morality of their own activities, as judged by Gandhi's standards. They began asking themselves questions, on Gandhi's behalf.

In the weeks following the fast, Gandhi's presence began to tell in the underground movement. In March, Sadiq Ali confided to an office assistant "that Gandhi had not expressed dissatisfaction or otherwise with what individuals were doing as he had told them they could act as free men, but as far as he himself was concerned, he disapproved of secret methods and activities involving violence. Sadiq Ali then said that he himself felt that Gandhi was right and so decided to go to the U.P. to do constructive work."[47]

With Sadiq Ali's departure the Bombay "A.I.C.C." office soon ceased to function. Sadiq Ali's abandoned office assistant reported that he "used to hear that the more extreme members of the High Command, viz. Ram Manohar Lohia, Aruna Asaf Ali, Jai Prakash and Achyut had a separate machinery of their own and conducted their own affairs irrespective of our propaganda activities."

Sadiq Ali was arrested in April 1943. (He had been arrested once before but had been released shortly thereafter, as the police had failed to determine his identity.) Other underground workers who shared his current thinking decided to meet in Benares on May 23 "to consider the probabilities of doing constructive programme in the present circumstances . . . Mrs. Kripalani, Baba Raghavdas, Dwarkadas Kachru, Mrs. Asaf Ali and some others whose names were not disclosed to me were to go . . . As far as I know Mrs. Asaf Ali was the only non-Gandhite representative in the meeting." Baba Raghavdas was informed of the date and place of the meeting by courier who met him "on the Bathing Ghat near Howrah Bridge on the 19th May, 1943.

When in Calcutta he is invariably to be seen on the Bathing Ghat, between 7 A.M. and 9 A.M. and that is the time and place for meeting contacts."[48]

It was decided at Benares that an attempt should be made to carry on "constructive work" from underground. The leaders for whom there were warrants would remain hidden; but the activities they planned would be public demonstrations in the Gandhian tradition. Such a "half-Gandhian" procedure was difficult to implement and not altogether satisfying. Increasingly, Gandhian activists began consciously or unconsciously to will their own arrests; Mrs. Kripalani, for example, greeted her arrest while visiting at the house of her I.C.S. cousin as a welcome release from a wearisome and increasingly unsatisfactory existence.[49]

All underground workers—not simply the "Gandhians"—were strongly influenced by Gandhi. The perspectives of each of the three major underground groups were based on interpretations of Gandhi's teachings. All were committed to ending British rule by a genuine mass uprising; none had succumbed to the temptation of attempting to institute a new autocracy which, for the masses, would still mean "foreign rule." And, beyond mere intellectual debts, all were bound to Gandhi by intense ties of personal respect and affection which made them anxious for Gandhi's approval and distraught to think of India deprived of his presence.

Meaning

Gandhi's twenty-one-day fast, begun on February 10, 1943, marked a turning point in the "aboveground" evolution of the movement as well as in its underground phase. As the spontaneous fury of the movement began to subside, to be replaced by calculated sabotage, Gandhi once again inserted himself into the situation in the only way now open to him, through fasting. The fast produced a startling effect on the government, on world opinion, and on non-Congress Indian opinion, as well as upon underground workers.

Until he decided to fast, Gandhi had been totally secluded by the government. Prominent moderates such as Rajagopalachari were not permitted to see him. His letters to the viceroy, including one of September 23 in which he referred to "deplorable destruction" by "people wild with rage to the point of losing self-control," were not released because he suggested that "the Government goaded the people to the point of madness."[50] The government were prepared to publicize a statement of repentance or an assertion of the culpability of perpetrators of violence, but as Gandhi refused to supply such a statement, his views were suppressed entirely.

The news of Gandhi's decision to fast, however, could not be suppressed, for the government did not wish to be blamed if he died as a result. The news of his decision produced such an extraordinary upheaval in Britain and America, as well as among Indians of all shades of opinion, that the government were forced to provide an elaborate explanation of their conduct, including the tardy release of the correspondence which had taken place between Gandhi and the viceroy.

The fast brought to a head the dissatisfaction with the government of those who had not entirely approved of the Quit India movement but nonetheless felt that Gandhi and the Congress had a positive contribution to make and should not be treated as common criminals. Gandhi in politics might be viewed as a rival; Gandhi in prison in danger of death could only be viewed as a national asset.

The fast made "the Indian problem" headline news in the British and American press. In India, the fast was much more than a news story; it was a call to arms. Throughout 1942 Gandhi had acted as a partisan. He had swept along the hesitant Nehru and Azad and landed them all in jail. The moderates were then compelled to swing into action. Their previous role as a friendly voice of caution to extremists had run its course; now intensive mediation was called for, with the threat of a fast forcing the pace. The moderates were now compelled to press the government on behalf of the extremists, whereas before they had tried to exert restraint on extremists. In going to prison, and then launching his fast, Gandhi had forced them into a more active, implicitly a more nationalist, role. By taking an intransigent stand, Gandhi had forced others into the role of mediator on his behalf.

The "moderates" of 1943 included any Indian who was neither in prison nor an absconder: academics such as S. Radhakrishnan and communists such as Ranadive; industrialists such as J. R. D. Tata and aristocrats such as the Maharajkumar of Vizianagram. All these and many others were brought together in February 1943, in a common effort to force the viceroy to release Gandhi unconditionally. Three hundred prominent figures led by Tej Bahadur Sapru and M. R. Jayakar gathered in Delhi at a two-day "All-India Leaders' Conference" on February 19 and 20 to petition for Gandhi's release; the government's response was a brief note from the viceroy's secretary stating that "No new factor has emerged since" February 10, a pointed rebuke to the three hundred leaders for having considered their opinion potentially a "new factor."[51] Also included among the events which failed to qualify as a "new factor" were the resignations on February 17 of three Indian members of the viceroy's Executive Council in protest against the goverment's indifference to the fast. The government had decided to accept the risk that Gandhi might die, and plans had been made to handle the popular protests which were expected to follow his death. Gandhi's death was not an acceptable cost in the eyes of the members of the Executive Council who resigned. Arresting Gandhi was a way of expressing disapproval of what he had done; letting him die would have been to express disapproval of what he was. At this point, three Indian members of Council had to acknowledge their differences with British officials.

The widespread popular anxiety about Gandhi's physical condition, and the efforts of leaders to focus the pressure of public opinion on the government, intensified long-standing grievances against government efforts to control the press. On February 13 a group of American journalists, including Herbert Matthews of the *New York Times*, and correspondents of the Associated Press, United Press, *Time*, *Life*, the *New York Herald Tribune*, *Chicago Tribune*, and *Chicago Daily News*, addressed a letter to the viceroy complaining that "Despatch after despatch has been ruthlessly cut by censors. We are not allowed to mention even the names of certain personalities. Worst of all, concrete facts, some of which have been reported in the Indian press, are kept from the American public."[52] News of Gandhi's physical condition could not be suppressed altogether, but the government did what they could to reduce its impact. In Delhi, for example, the *Hindustan Times* was ordered not to print headlines regarding the fast "extending over a width greater than that of two columns of the usual width" or in type "exceeding one-fifth of an inch in overall height."[53] Readers of the *Hindustan Times*, it was hoped, would not be left with the impression that the fast was a matter of great consequence in the eyes of the paper's editor—Gandhi's son Devadas.

The government's press policy had gone through several cycles over the past two years. While Gandhi was preparing the Quit India movement, the government had retaliated with an almost equally strenuous public relations effort. In the propaganda war which raged before August 9, both Gandhi and the government had engaged in the practice of "liberating" documents. The British published the letters which Jayaprakash Narayan had tried to smuggle out of jail in the fall of 1941 because it was thought they would embarrass Gandhi. The government also published unofficial minutes of meetings of the Congress Working Committee which , so the government explained, had been "recovered in a . . . police search," which exposed the degree of dissension which existed in the Congress inner circle. The minutes revealed that Nehru had initially agreed with the government's official contention that Gandhi's activities were implicitly pro-Japanese.[54] Gandhi, for his part, printed in the *Harijan* under the heading "Amazing Disclosures," and with a sardonic comment that the government would no doubt thank him for publicizing their activities, two secret letters in which the government outlined an active policy of instigating anti-Congress feeling. The letters included, among other things, details of slanderous cartoons which non-Congress papers might be encouraged to produce and a list of organizations which might be approached by local government officials with encouragement to denounce the Congress.[55]

The arrests of August 9, and the outbreak of open, not merely verbal, warfare between the government and the Congress, produced a new press policy. The press were warned that "the editor of any newspaper who supports or encourages the mass movement . . . or who opposes the measures taken by Government to avert or suppress that movement, will be guilty of an offence against the law. Moreover, it is undeniable that the publication of factual news, both by the selection of events reported and by the manner in which they are displayed, can do even more to advertise, and thus support, the movement than editorial comment thereon." It was ordered that facts published were to be "derived only from recognized and responsible sources," in other words, from government, or from correspondents registered with the government.[56]

Newspapers were compelled to feature war news from abroad; brief references to derailments, bomb explosions, and police firings in major cities were hidden in inside pages. Linlithgow was nonetheless far from mollified. On August 17 he complained that "The Press has been a great nuisance, and I have been continually conscious that we were not doing enough to curb the flood of news." Many newspapers, including fourteen of the sixteen Calcutta papers, ceased publication altogether to express sympathy with the Congress and opposition to the stringent controls under which they were expected to operate. Linlithgow, however, suspected that this suspension might be a result, not of patriotism, but of bribery. "Either they are altruistic in a high degree, or . . . they have received financial assistance in some subterranean way, for the loss to a paper like the *Amrita Bazar Patrika* with a circulation of 45 to 50 thousand must be very substantial." Ironically, the most strenuous newspaper criticism of the government during the crucial days of August 1942 appeared in one of the two papers which was not closed down, the British-owned *Statesman*. Linlithgow was incensed but felt that indirect pressure was the only response in this case; with the cooperation of Amery in London, he succeeded in persuading the newspaper's British owner to fire the *Statesman's* troublesome editor, Arthur Moore, who was "allowed to leave preparatory to retirement on full emoluments"—effective August 17, 1942.[57]

By cutting off news coverage of the movement the government sought to insure its rapid suppression. It is often assumed that sensational news coverage is responsible for translating a local incident into a widespread uprising. But as the Quit India movement was not nipped in the bud by the arrest of thousands of leaders, because it was not simply the creation of those leaders, so the movement was not stalled for want of media coverage. The arrest of leaders only made things worse; such was also the result of the denial of news coverage.

Wild rumors sped in the place of accurate information. People craved to hear something and would listen to anything. The truth could not have been worse than what was readily believed—that Bengal had fallen and Mahadev Desai had been shot in detention and fifty thousand unarmed Indians had been gunned down and so on endlessly. During Professor Bhansali's sixty-three day fast to protest government inaction regarding the Chimur atrocities, his death was reported many times and riotously protested; actually, he did not die at all.

Major nationalist newspapers had ceased publication following August 9 to protest government censorship, but several were able to use their equipment to produce illicit publications, such as the booklet "India Ravaged" which recounted numerous British atrocities. Enemy broadcasts from Germany, Tokyo, and most notably from Japanese-controlled Saigon were eagerly followed for information on Indian affairs. An official of the B.B.C. reported after a visit to India that

"Nine large stations batter at India every night. They are all powerful and offer good reception, and with technical proficiency in programme presentation, they combine a very fair understanding of the spirit of the peoples to whom they are broadcasting all over India . . . The usual question when an Indian buys a wireless set, I was told by big dealers in Bombay, is 'Can I hear Germany and Japan on this?''' News broadcast from the underground Congress radio stations was more accurate, but these stations were makeshift, fugitive arrangements broadcasting less than an hour a day with weak signals which could not match that from Saigon. The greatest significance of the underground stations lay in their defiance of police detection; the very fact of their existence, the very fact that their signals emerged each evening was inspiring. The main means of communication, however, were hurriedly duplicated broadsides, posters plastered in public places, and word of mouth. The government's assumption that people would only know what they read in the controlled newspapers was disastrously disproved.[58]

Gandhi's fast, and the impossibility of suppressing news concerning it, forced the government back to the offensive. The government had informed Gandhi that they "would be very reluctant to see you fast."[59] Having failed to dissuade him, they sought to induce him to fast outside of prison, by accepting a temporary release. Gandhi replied that if his releasse were unconditional, he might not fast; if his release were only for the duration of the fast, he could just as easily abstain from food in prison as out of prison. The government then publicized their willingness to let Gandhi fast outside of prison to forestall charges that they had hastened his death. Referring to Gandhi's willingness to abandon his fast if released unconditionally, Linlithgow derided the fast as an attempt to "find an easy way out" of prison. The viceroy, while doubting Gandhi's motives, also offered an exegesis of Gandhi's principles. "I regard the use of a fast for political purposes," he wrote, "as a form of political blackmail (himsa)."[60]

The actual reason for Gandhi's preparedness to abandon his fast upon his unconditonal release was the reverse of that supposed by the government. The government presumed that Gandhi craved his release for selfish reasons, just as he hoped to gain it by devious means; Gandhi, on the other hand, would have considered his unconditinaal release a mark of "penance" by the government, an   admission of the questionable propriety of having arrested him in the first place, and as such precisely the sort of gesture which he had announced might induce him to terminate his fast.

Gandhi's fast represented in several respects an "escalation" in accordance with his general sense of the climactic nature of this movement. He had never before fasted to exert pressure on a viceroy. Ordinarily, the targets of his fasts had been Indians, persons who held him in high personal esteem. Gandhi had always attempted to establish a direct personal relationship with the political authorities with which he dealt, in keeping with the highly personal idiom he preferred. Through personal interviews and idiosyncratic letters, Gandhi had sought to impress his personality on a succession of viceroys. Gandhi even at this juncture, however, did not make an exaggerated estimate of the esteem in which he was held by the viceroy. For the purpose of eliciting some sign of governmental contrition for their responsibility for the disturbances, Gandhi chose a long but limited fast, of twenty-one days, which raised the possibility but not the certainty of his death—he was then seventy-three years old and suffered from high blood pressure. If he survived, as he desired to do, he would not have to seek ignominious expedients to bring his fast to a close before a clear victory was won.

As it turned out, Gandhi had calculated correctly in suspecting that the moment for a direct fast against the British viceroy had come at last. Linlithgow, after all, had been in India longer than any viceroy since Curzon, and, in his way, Linlithgow was devoted to Indian interests and had surrounded himself with Indian advisers on his Executive Council. Though he gave little public indication, Linlithgow was indeed shaken by the fast and induced by it to undertake an act of defiance of Churchill.

The approaching fast overwhelmed the ordinary business of the government of India. Linlithgow "deluged" the war cabinet with telegrams, and at a critical moment convened his Executive Council for a three-hour meeting at 12:30 A.M. Expecting Gandhi to die, Linlithgow steeled himself for the abuse which he knew would follow Gandhi's death. In the Executive Council he noted "there is a percentage which hates the idea of his dying to their discredit . . . And I am very much afraid that the old man (to whom incidentally I give full marks for his reply, which was a masterpiece of the usual type!) will force us to face up to that issue. If he does, I may have very serious trouble."[61]

Gandhi the prisoner had forced the viceroy into post-midnight conferences with his advisers and brought the ordinary business of government to a halt. "We are not masters of the time-table in this matter," grumbled Linlithgow.[62] On February 8, the secretary to the governor of Bombay attempted to deliver to Gandhi the prisoner a letter from Sir Richard Tottenham. He arrived at Gandhi's "detention camp" at 6 P.M. "It was a day of silence and he gave me a written note asking me to call again at 9 P.M. As Mr. Gandhi observes old time, this meant 10 P.M. Accordingly I called on him at 10 P.M."[63] Gandhi was once again calling the tune.

Under strong pressure from his Council, Linlithgow decided to release Gandhi for the duration of his fast. Churchill, however, was appalled by this suggestion, asserting his conviction that "this our hour of triumph everywhere in the world was not the time to crawl before a miserable little old man who had always been our enemy."[64] Linlithgow was ordered not to release Gandhi, but Linlithgow decided to defy Churchill, cabling in defense of his action the argument that "No wise skipper . . . would choose to put the helm over hard in weather like this."[65] As it turned out, Gandhi took Linlithgow off the hook by declining to be released, but Linlithgow had for the first time demonstrated a conviction that Gandhi might be more salient to the viceroy of India than was the British prime minister. Some months later, Linlithgow again sought to accommodate Gandhi in defiance of the cabinet, when Gandhi attempted to contact Jinnah. On this occasion Linlithgow commented, "I am not sure whether Daniel had the advantage of Cabinet advice before entering the lion's den, but like him I am concerned to get out alive."[66]

Gandhi's fast continued with unbroken rigor for ten days, when at the point of death he was persuaded to limit his fast to the extent of taking a limited amount of liquid nourishment for the remainder of the twenty-one days. Gandhi had previously described his fast as a fast "to capacity," had made it clear he did not wish to die, and, following his minimal concession to human frailty, referred to his ordeal as a "fraudulent fast." All that could have been accomplished by the fast had been accomplished, and now his main concern was staying alive while maintaining the basic contours of his initial resolution to fast for twenty-one days. As Gandhi's determination to stay alive even at the sacrifice of his initial regimen became clear, a wave of gloating relief surged through the British government. The "old rascal," commented Churchill, had once again been exposed as a master of "bluff and sob-stuff." "We have exposed the Light of Asia—Wardha version—for the fraud it undoubtedly is: a blue glass with a tallow candle behind it!!" rejoiced Linlithgow. "The old man has done . . . neither more nor less than one of these reducing fasts which people used to do at Champney." Linlithgow, who had himself "wobbled" under Gandhi's challenge, now censured the behavior of the governor of Bombay on this score: "Even Lumley himself has not been free from one or two qualms," Linlithgow wrote to Amery, "and you will have noticed a wobble which I did not think a very good one when a few days ago he gave support to the suggestion that we should send someone down with evidence to try and satisfy Gandhi that our case was really watertight. That suggestion . . . I was not for a moment prepared to consider, and I am only a little surprised that Lumley should have thought that possible . . . But one has of course to make allowances for the additional nervous tension and strain in the case of people who are on the spot, in the very Gandhian atmosphere of Bombay city and Gujarat; and in Lumley's case, too, for the fact that he is at the end of a very heavy Governorship of 5½ years during which he has had no relaxation whatever and in the course of which he has had to face a number of trying and difficult decisions."[67] After the fact, Linlithgow, himself at the end of an even longer term as viceroy, was trying to forget the strain he had felt as a man on the spot.

By fasting Gandhi sought to raise the question of responsibility for the events following August 9 and the related question of the meaning which was to be placed on these events in planning India's future. Three days after the fast commenced, the government took up the challenge by rushing out a pamphlet on *Congress Responsibility for the Disturbances, 1942–43*. Its concluding words asserted that "only one answer can be given to the question as to who must bear the responsibility for the mass uprising and individual crimes which have disgraced and are still disgracing the fair name of India. That answer is—the Indian National Congress, under the leadership of Mr. Gandhi."[68] The government outlined a vigorous indictment, on the basis of which they hoped that they would not be blamed if, under the circumstances, they let Mr. Gandhi die.

The government referred to evidence they possessed linking Gandhi with violence—evidence which, however, could not be made public.

The evidence in the government's possession consisted of the published texts of Gandhi's writings in the *Harijan* and intelligence reports that individual congressmen had engaged in violent acts after August 9.

That congressmen were fully implicated in the disturbances which followed August 9 was clear. The government, to maintain their own self-respect, had further to contend that the disturbances were not worse because of the arrests of August 9. In order to contend that these arrests were not miscalculated, it was necessary to argue that the arrests had forestalled even worse disorders, that the disorders were only an attenuated version of what was to come anyway. In this view, the disorders were not provoked by the arrests, but were what remained of Gandhi's prearranged plan.

Had Gandhi remained free, the consequences might have been equally serious for British rule, but events would certainly have developed differently. The events of August can be said to have been anticipated by Gandhi—if he were to be arrested. It is impossible to say that Gandhi wanted events to develop in this way, or that he actively planned the strategy of those who protested his arrest. Maulana Azad, the Congress president, states in his autobiography that he conferred with regional Congress leaders regarding the possible methods of protesting the arrests of Gandhi and others. The use of violence in these protests, wrote Azad, "was what I had anticipated and to some extent even advised and discussed with our workers." Azad made it clear that so long as the government "allowed us to function, the movement must develop strictly according to Gandhiji's instructions. If, however, the Government arrested Gandhiji and other Congress leaders, the people would be free to adopt any method, violent or non-violent, to oppose the violence of the Government in every possible way."[69] Linlithgow wrote to Gandhi on February 5, 1943, that the Congress on August 8 had "declared a 'mass struggle' . . . appointed you as its leader and authorized all Congressmen to act for themselves in the event of interference with the leadership of the movement . . . There is evidence that you and your friends expected this policy to lead to violence; and that you were prepared to condone it, and that the violence that ensued formed part of a concerted plan, conceived long before the arrest of Congress leaders."[70] Linlithgow's statements, taken separately, were roughly accurate, but the cumulative impression that the inevitability of this course of events reflected Gandhi's will and desire was misleading, as was the implication that Gandhi's theoretical writings on self-defense, and Azad's general discussions regarding what might be done "in the event of interference with the leadership" constituted a "concerted plan." Gandhi launched a movement which, it was known, might become violent if the government insisted. Linlithgow sought to contend that Gandhi had willed his own arrest and wished for the result of his arrest, which would have absolved the government of any responsibility for unduly aggravating events by the arrests of August 9. Linlithgow suggested that Gandhi must have known that he would not be listened to. Gandhi may have suspected that he would not be listened to, but he had never before discounted the possibility of a change of heart, and had not done so in this instance.

"I have a grouse with you," Gandhi had objected to a questioner in the spring of 1942 who was pressing Gandhi to concede that the movement he had called for would result in violence. "Why should you shove all the blame on to me for all that may happen by reason of my taking action for the discharge of an overdue debt?"[71] A nonviolent leader was responsible, Gandhi suggested, for wishing that the status quo be changed. He should not, however, be intimidated by accusations that his actions would result in violence. In Gandhi's view, responsibility for such violence would lie with those who made it inevitable, the British government, if by arresting him they made it impossible for him to exert a restraining influence. Gandhi had often accepted responsibility for the excesses of agitators not even remotely known to him and attempted through fasts and other techniques to control their actions and, failing that, had been prepared to terminate agitations altogether. If he was arrested, however, he felt that responsibility for subsequent disorders should rest with the government. He had never been interested in fashioning a movement in which excesses were impossible because in such a movement independence of judgment would have been impossible. Failures or excesses were to be dealt with when they materialized, not before. Notwithstanding his reputation for calling off movements when they became violent, Gandhi had a strong stomach and was prepared to accept a high degree of bloodshed and disorder as a predictable part of nonviolent revolution. "I have before me a list of 20 civil resistance movements beginning with the very first in South Africa," Gandhi wrote to the government on July 15, 1943. "I do recall instances in which popular frenzy had broken out resulting in regrettable murders. These instances of mob-violence, though bad enough, were but a flea-bite in proportion to the vast size of this country."[72]

As Gandhi realized, individuals indulging in violence in periods of cultural transition may not be criminals. The reason that "excess and riot follow repression and suppression when the moral restraints are lifted," suggests Erik Erikson, is "precisely because of the autocratic and blind nature of these restraints."[73] Gandhi had undertaken to free individual Indians as well as the Indian nation, and accepted the likelihood of a period of individual psychological anarchy before a freely accepted self-discipline was substitued for the oppression of compliance with externally-imposed standards.

Linlithgow called Gandhi's fast "a form of political blackmail." A nonviolent action may seem to be a form of blackmail employed by men hypocritically disclaiming responsibility for the effects of their own incendiarism. This is a valid charge if nonviolent agitators indulge in insinuations that if nonviolence fails, violence will follow, thereby suggesting that it is in the self-interest of officials to deal with them rather than wait to face more militant protesters. They are saying, "We are better than the people behind us; if we are rejected, they may take over. We are your friends, it is in the interest of both of us to agree to terms before it is too late." Such a utilization for nominally nonviolent purposes of the threat of violence if demands are not met was not in keeping with Gandhi's style, which was to recommend nonviolent action to all, and to suggest to those intent on violence that they proceed with their violent acts immediately if they felt they should.

Gandhi did not say, I am nonviolent, but if you don't settle with me, others may come who will use violence. Gandhi said, Your system must go, and if I were convinced that violence were the only way to end it I would use violence myself. Gandhi was a nonviolent revolutionary, not a person using nonviolence for strategic, limited ends. A constitutional agitator differs with violent revolutionaries with regard to both ends and means; Gandhi differed with violent revolutionaries only with regard to means, and in this respect only conditionally.

Gandhi thought it unreasonable for the British government to blame him for all the violence which followed his arrest, when they prevented him from exerting a controlling influence. The British, for their part, found it difficult to appreciate the advantages of a controlled insurrection against their rule. The unexpected vehemence of the protest against the arrest of Gandhi and the Working Committee did give the British occasion to wonder if things might not have been better if the more responsible congressmen had been left free. One local experiment along these lines was made whose results were not reassuring. In Ballia district in the eastern United Provinces, when events seemed to be totally out of control, the district magistrate decided "to create an atmosphere of non-violence" by releasing Congress leaders, including Cheetu Pande, chairman of the District Congress Committee. "The immediate effect of this action was that these persons formed a procession and accompanied by a large mob held a meeting, at which they made no attempt to restrain their followers, with the result that the houses of some Government officials, a title holder, and a doctor were looted. On the following day, August 20th, the mob started looting the railway goods sheds . . . On the 22nd the Chairman of the District Congress Committee announced that in future all complaints should be brought to him and not to the Government authorities."[74]

The conduct of Cheetu Pande was not a very good indicator of what Gandhi would have done. Presumably, a better indicator of the role Gandhi might have played if he had remained free was in the conduct of Khan Abdul Ghaffar Khan, the "Frontier Gandhi" who maintained good order and a nonviolent atmosphere in the raids and demonstrations in the North-West Frontier Province.[75] On the frontier, demonstrators were beaten with *lathis*, rather than shot, and the government engaged in practical jokes, such as the mixing of purgatives in the food of demonstrators who were "inflated with poisoned tea,"[76] rather than firings from the air.

The truth of the matter was that the government were helpless. Arresting people caused turmoil; releasing people also caused turmoil. The Quit India movement demonstrated that Indians wanted British rule to end now—whether or not Indians or Britishers were ready. And this time the government did not miss the point. The success of the Quit India movement was reflected in the guarded yet decisive recognition by British officials surveying the wreckage of empire that they could no longer exert influence to control the course of events. The Congress, which had been supposed to be on its last legs, had paralyzed the country. An acknowledgment that in openly defying the law India's most important political organization was supported by general public opinion would be in effect an acknowledgment that the government could no longer govern. Behind the public accusations of Congress responsibility for the disturbances lay precisely such an acknowledgment.

In the early days of the movement, when demonstrators were first testing their strength, government officials spoke confidently of the initial protests as an encouraging sign of the movement's weakness and predicted a quick return to normal. In the spring of 1943, when the movement was seriously demoralized and reduced to a furtive symbolic defiance, officials were speaking gloomily of the movement lasting indefinitely; they saw no sign that the intensity of sabotage might abate. What had happened in the course of these few months was the appearance for the first time in the history of Britain's relations with India of a widely shared defeatist mentality. Officials abandoned the tendency to see every new protest as an indication of the growing weakness of the Congress, every outburst of opposition as the movement's "death rattle." While Churchill exulted that "the number of white troops in that country is larger than at any time in the British connection," officials in India questioned whether this was a reassuring gauge of the imminence of final victory over the Congress. Officials in India had abandoned the tendency to label Congress leaders as unrepresentative, to contend that the "vast silent majority" were still with the government. After several weeks' experience of the Quit India movement, officials began recording—and forwarding to their superiors—the opinion that this movement was a movement of "the people," that there was no way of denying the fact that saboteurs had the backing of the people at large.

From Bihar it was reported that "The public as a body remained apathetic and their attitude was far from helpful . . . In brief the authorities could rely on practically no cooperation from the general public . . . There was general sympathy of the Hindu public with the ultimate object of the Congress movement though not necessarily with the means employed."[77]

Similar sentiments were voiced by the government of the United Provinces. "Few Hindus probably approve of the action which has been found necessary to maintain order," noted the "Fortnightly Report . . . for the First Half of August." "There were many who began to believe that the Congress promise that they would paralyze Government in a week would be fulfilled and who did not wish to be on the losing side. With one or two notable exceptions little help has been received from people from whom help might have been expected."[78]

From Bombay it was noted that "The last C.I.D. [Criminal Intelligence Division] report says, 'Mention has previously been made of the almost insuperable difficulty of obtaining evidence against those persons who are committing acts of sabotage . . . It is the common experience of the Police today that the ordinary villager will not bear evidence against Congress workers either because he is afraid to do so or because he is in tacit sympathy. C.I.D. officers have met with a general conspiracy of silence.'" Commentng on the C.I.D. report, the Bombay government acknowledged that "There is little disposition on the part of the general public to regard saboteurs and bandits as anti-social and criminal elements of society." Two weeks later, the report from Bombay cautioned that "It is not be be expected . . . that the movement will collapse quickly . . The tracking down of saboteurs who work secretly and get about at night over the countryside is a matter that requires much patience; particularly when the general population is sullen and unhelpful."[79]

The seriousness of the situation was immediately apparent. Explaining why it had gotten out of hand to such an extent was more difficult. Since the conduct of the war with Japan was uppermost in the minds of British officials, the first possibility considered was that the Quit India movement might be attributable to a pro-Japanese conspiracy. The Quit India movement had drastically crippled the British war effort at a time when India was in imminent danger of foreign invasion. There was first of all the fact that the equivalent of fifty-seven battalions of British troops had had to be employed in sixty different places to quell domestic uprisings, with the resultant "loss of six to eight weeks' training in certain field army formations and training units."[80]

In addition to the disruption of communication with the threatened eastern region, the movement had also caused a breakdown in the supply of essential comodities to the troops. A "minimum 50 percent of aerodrome construction and building projects [were] retarded four to six weeks due to shortages of coal, cement, bricks and labour difficulties [and the] loss to date of 10 percent of annual steel production due to Tatas strike."[81] In Kashmir, a factory producing parachute silk was burned.[82] Forty-five percent of India's production of khaki was halted by strikes; the production of leather goods was cut by 50 percent. The troops were also affected, the Supply Department reported, by the fact that "The premier cigarette producing concern—The Imperial Tobacco Co., with its factories in Calcutta, Bombay, Bangalore and Saharanpur—is likely to experience considerable delay in their deliveries. Their Monghyr Factory which is the source of their supply of all cigarette paper and other printed material is reported to have been seriously damaged. No communication with the factory has however been possible so far." Gandhi would no doubt have been interested to learn that the government considered that "The most serious factor of the movement" as it affected military requirements" is the closing down of the Ahmedabad Calico Mills and Messrs. Hathi Singh & Co., who are the chief producers of sewing cotton." The government had reserve stocks of cloth on hand, but sewing thread was nowhere to be found. An army might survive without tobacco; but not without thread.[83]

Who could have caused such havoc, other than the enemy? The government, prompted personally by Churchill, sought for some months to secure evidence of fifth column activity by the Japanese. On September 14, 1942, Churchill wrote to Amery, "Please let me have a note on Mr. Gandhi's intrigues with Japan . . . The note should not exceed three pages of open typescript." The reply Churchill received did not exceed three lines: "The only evidence of Japanese contacts during the war relates to the presence in Wardha of two Japanese Buddhist priests who lived for part of 1940 in Gandhi's Ashram"[84]

Linlithgow briefly entertained a suspicion that Indian "big business" might be the connecting link between Congress and the Japanese. "Civil disturbances and interruptions of production such as have occurred," he observed, "are not in themselves favourable to 'Big Business' and it is therefore necessary to look for ulterior motives. There is, or has until recently been, a widespread belief among Hindus in this country that we shall not be able to keep the Japanese out of India. This belief has no doubt given rise to a fear among millowners and others that if India becomes the scene of warfare their plant and machinery will run the risk of being destroyed . . . A further and even more important possibility is that there is a clique of financiers in India who, taking a leaf out of Japan's book, and even possibly with Japanese assistance, are endeavoring to use the Congress organisation and the political ferment which it has brought about to establish for themselves a position of financial domination in India comparable to that obtained by the 'Big Four' in Japan . . . If these surmises are true it may well be the case that 'Big Business' is the *fons et origo* of the recent disturbance and the real link between the Congress and Japan . . . It is quite possible that only Gandhi and his intimates are aware of the exact place which the Congress political programme occupies in working out much larger designs . . . I contemplate that a stage might be reached when we could strike against the Birla brothers and other leading financiers engaged with them in the conspiracy."[85] The picture was lurid indeed, but it seems to have been little more than a passing suspicion. Linlithgow soon acknowledged that the movement was essentially a Congress movement: antigovernment, not specifically antiwar, and not coordinated with a Japanese advance. The movement was strongest in Congress-dominated areas and it was only coincidental that these were also areas through which passed the British lines of supply to the eastern war front. No effort was made to disrupt the Bihar coal mines, for instance, which were vital to the war effort.

Explaining the Quit India movement as a new manifestation of Congress strength required that one try to understand the underlying sources of that strength. "Even allowing for the bad reputation of Bihar as a train wrecking area, I have been surprised at the scale and nature of the preparations and of the interference with railway traffic, etc., there," Linlithgow confessed. "I cannot but ask myself whether the local authorities in Bihar ought not to have had their ears a little closer to the ground—or alternatively, to the extent that this business may be spontaneous, whether it ought not to be possible to get some clearer impression than I at any rate have at the moment of the underlying causes of this agitation which bubbles up at regular intervals in the district round Patna, Arrah, and Dinapore."[86]

Searching for an explanation, Linlithgow turned to Sir Maurice Hallett, currently governor of the United Provinces, and a former governor of Bihar. Hallett supplied Linlithgow with a detailed analysis of the background of Congress influence in Bihar and the eastern United Provinces. "My views might be summed up," he wrote, "by saying that the trouble was facilitated by the fact that there were bad landholders and bad District Officers."[87] The regions which experienced the most convulsive disorders, Hallett argued, were ones where the Congress had been successful in seeking to alleviate tenant grievances. Especially during the period when Congress ministries held office in Bihar and the United Provinces, from 1937 to 1939, the Congress had developed a strong following in rural areas plagued by oppressive landlords. The success of the Congress in politicizing these areas had in turn taken its toll of the administration. The civil servants who had been effective in these areas were ones willing to cooperate with the Congress; others had resigned or sought employment elsewhere. In the United Provinces, British officers had sought to leave the Congress-influenced eastern region for the relatively quieter western half. In the months immediately preceding the Quit India movement, Hallett had in fact sent British officers he trusted to posts in the eastern region, because of the growing importance of this area in the wake of the Japanese advance, but these officers were ineffective in trying to quell disturbances in areas they were still unfamiliar with.

As Hallett observed, the Quit India movement was successful in large measure because in a crisis Congress leaders could draw upon a reservoir of goodwill built up over a number of years. But Hallett was frank in admitting that he had not expected that the Congress would unleash a movement of this sort. "I anticipated a somewhat fatuous attempt at the forms of civil disobedience which have taken place during previous years."[88] Building on earlier movements, the Congress had raised the level of conflict to a new level. Calling for a movement in which everyone would think and act for himself, the Congress had launched a movement which could not be suppressed by the arrest of thousands of leaders. Calling for the use even of violence in what would be a final showdown with the British, the Congress had succeeded in crystallizing the feeling of desperation of the vast majority of Indians. The Congress had gambled—and won. Linlithgow came to feel that "had we not struck as swiftly and as decisively as we did we might have found ourselves faced with an extremely awkward situation, wholly revolutionary in character, well organised by people working underground and deterred by no considerations of non-violence or the like."[89] For the moment, the government had held. In the future, however, they acted on the assumption that the Congress was not a party which could be manipulated from a position of strength; that the Congress was not a party which would antagonize public opinion by a resort to revolutionary defiance of the "legitimate" British government. The Congress had finally been recognized as not merely a party of troublesome agitators, but a sovereign force. The government still wished to continue to hold the line for the duration of the war, but began to talk and plan for the postwar period on the assumption that the Congress now held the upper hand.

The change following August 1942 was first and foremost one of mood, the fact that, as Chief Justice Sir Maurice Gwyer put it, "so many Englishmen in India have ceased to believe in themselves or indeed in anything else."[90] British officials were reluctant to state the obvious, but the implications of a shift in perspective were clearly imbedded in the details of policy discussions of a range of sensitive issues.

Before the Quit India movement, for example, British concern for the future victimization of loyal Indian officials had resulted in the extending of "assurances" that the Congress was not to be the destined beneficiary of British withdrawal. When the issue of victimization was reviewed in the wake of the Quit India movement, the emphasis had shifted. Guarantees were held to be useless, since they could not be enforced. An effort was now made to make the best of the situation by means of arguments which implied that things might not be so bad for Indian officers after all under an independent Indian regime. Sir Reginald Maxwell suggested that loyal Indian officials were not resented by Congress politicians because it was understood that they did not love their masters, but only needed the money. Sir Richard Tottenham argued that future victimization was more likely to follow communal lines than to reflect resentment over past actions taken by officials against their countrymen.[91] Linlithgow expressed his belief that "reflection on the part of potentially disloyal officers would show that disloyalty to one master is not necessarily a good recommendation for employment by another, however opposed politically." It was hoped that Indian officials would be loyal in form, but it was accepted that, as Maxwell put it, "our officials . . . must naturally in considering their future prospects look towards the rising rather than the setting sun. The one thing quite certain that they have to go upon is that we shall not be here to employ or protect them in the future . . . and we cannot reasonably expect our servants to do more for the present Government than their duty actually requires . . . I think there is no use in embarking on any line of propaganda unless we believe it. It is merely a matter of speculation to say that the power of the Congress is on the wane unless and until we have in sight some other movement arising in the country which can offer a serious challenge to it: that may yet come but I doubt whether there is time for it before constitution-making begins."[92]

The existence of "a good deal of pretty strong pro-Congress feeling" among the Hindus in the Indian Civil Service was now described as "inevitable."[93] The governor of Bihar reported that "certain Indian officers of the I.C.S. consulted [Chief Secretary] Godbole as to whether they might put in a 'round robin' to Government for the release of Gandhi. Godbole reported this at once, but did not disclose the names."[94] Godbole was formally loyal to his superiors—but had drawn a line which his superiors would not be permitted to cross.

Moderate non-Congress politicians who had once seemed a promising countervailing force were now derisively shoved aside. "These
weakkneed moderates" were labeled contemptuously "the first cousins
of Congress." "None of them count for a row of pins," Linlithgow
exclaimed resentfully. The "so-called Moderates . . . have done
nothing to help us, and I am not a bit concerned about their feelings
in the present circumstances . . . they are wholly unrepresentative."
"The so-called 'leaders' have no following," agreed Sir Maurice Hallet,
"and it is very right to use inverted commas when that expression
is used."[95]

"The moderate elements in this country . . . are excellent publicists
but otherwise negligible," observed Linlithgow. "Hindu opinion is substantially behind Congress, and Muslim opinion behind Jinnah."[96] The
chief remaining ground for political optimism appeared to be the possibility of evolution *within* the Congress, and the emergence of "a new
set of leaders for Congress" who would alter the "negative and sterile
concepts of Gandhi and his 'Yes-men.'"[97] Then there was the wan
hope that the British by surrendering might be able to accomplish what
they had failed to accomplish by force, that since "Congress hitherto
has been held together mainly by hatred of British rule [it] may lose
its cement when that comes to an end."[98]

It was now assumed in New Delhi that the Congress would win
any election in which they were permitted to participate, since Congress
"possess the only effective vote-catching machine in India."[99] It was
further assumed that new initiatives taken by the government to
strengthen non-Congress alternatives would backfire. Sir Maurice
Gwyer put it in the strongest possible terms when he wrote Linlitgow
that "I think no one can deny that every act of the British Government,
and even every act which can be imputed to them, however falsely,
is regarded as inspired by malevolence and cunning and as part of
a hedgehog system of fortification which Great Britain is supposed
to be building round herself so as to avoid having to transfer the tiniest
fragment of political power."[100] Amery and Linlithgow had abandoned
their enthusiasm for demonstrating the adequacy of strong government,
and now spoke only of the possibility of salvaging the "federal" principle
of the constitution of 1935. Amery in particular was attracted by the
thought that an American-style executive might be acceptable in India:
if the parties were given control of a legislature, would it not be possible
at least to prevent them from taking direct control of the executive

as well? Both Amery and Linlithgow had switched to a policy of calculated retreat. Linlithgow, a few months earlier, had considered the idea that Britishers might remain in India as technical specialists after power had been acquired by Indian politicians a contemptible and cowardly thought. Now, he began to stress Britain's defense capability as a useful trump card, suggesting that it might be possible for Britain to offer to provide defense services to an independent Indian government in return for the retention of certain privileges in British hands.[101] The temporary continuation of the status quo was now seen as the *best* Britain could hope for; all the alternatives under consideration involved degrees of capitulation to Indian demands.

Amery in fact could think of nothing more useful to do than to begin second-guessing where the British had failed. "Looking back," he wrote to Linlithgow "one can never help regretting that we did not keep Kashmir after the Sikh Wars and use it for the large scale settlement both of old British Officers and soldiers and also for Anglo-Indians . . . Possibly it has been a real mistake of ours in the past not to encourage Indian Princes to marry English wives for a succession of generations and so breed a more virile type of native ruler."[102]

Churchill had not changed. Churchill continued to disparage any talk which implied that Britishers should "keep our word about being kicked out in due course."[103] But when Churchill had delivered one of his dramatic orations at the height of the Quit India movement, Linlithgow had considered it a good tonic for Indian malcontents; in March 1943, when informed that Churchill had decided *not* to speak on India, Linlithgow exclaimed "Thank goodness!"[104] Linlithgow had enough things to worry about without having to handle the Indian response to a new Churchillian outburst.

Linlithgow realized that in using main force to suppress a revolutionary insurrection he had lost his legitimacy and gained in return only a temporary respite. "Great material injury and inconvenience has been caused to the leading fomenters of the rebellion and to their more prominent supporters," he observed in a letter to Hallett. "I should have thought myself that it would be some considerable time before the effects of the methods which we adopted died away."[105] Linlithgow knew, however, that it would be only a matter of time "before the political storm breaks again."[106]

In a public speech of December 7, 1942, Linlithgow expressed "keen and deep regret" at having had to deal with "an uprising . . . of great gravity and great severity . . . To the sorrow of all of us who care for the good name of India those disturbances were disfigured by very shocking cases of brutality and violence. And a grievous feature of them is the use to which designing men endeavoured to turn, and indeed succeeded in many cases in turning, the young enthusiasm, the intelligence, and the lack of experience of the student community. Those who diverted those young men, young men of such promise, with their future just opening before them into the dangerous paths of civil tumult and disorder, carry an immense responsibility to India, and to the ardent and generous youth which they have led astray."[107] Linlithgow's words conveyed a genuine sense of sorrow. Nothing he said, moreover, suggested a conviction that the situation could be salvaged. The government's will, their zest for new initiatives, had been shattered. The Congress bore "an immense responsibility" precisely because it had succeeded in gaining its objective.

Gandhi was released in 1944 because the government feared that his death would soon follow the deaths in detention of Gandhi's secretary, Mahadev Desai, and Gandhi's wife, Kasturba. Gandhi had refused to accept a conditional release at the time of his fast in 1943; the government therefore set no conditions for his release on this occasion in their eagerness to insure that he would in fact spare them the embarrassment of dying in a British prison.

The government's willingness to release Gandhi unconditionally was also a sign of the changing times. The war situation was less tense, and the Quit India movement seemed at last to be losing strength. And Linlithgow had been replaced as viceroy by the unassuming soldier Lord Wavell, who accepted as inevitable a role for the Congress in India's future.

Gandhi devoted the first months of his freedom to assessing the meaning of the Quit India movement, in terms of his original intentions, his basic principles, and his current hopes for India's future. While attempting to heal the wounds the movement had left, he sought to apply its lessons. Gandhi's new effort to negotiate with Jinnah at this time, for example, reflected his awareness that Jinnah had proven himself equal to the challenge to his ability to speak for the Muslim majority which Gandhi had mounted in 1942.

During the Quit India movement, Jinnah had kept Muslims apart despite the collapse of British authority without which many congressmen thought he could not survive. As the movement subsided, Jinnah had moved quickly to consolidate his gains. The Muslim provincial ministries which had remained in office during the war had been headed initially by non-Congress notables, regionally prominent aristocrats not dependent upon the support of any national party, the sort of men Britishers had hoped would be the beneficiaries of India's political liberalization. Many were dedicated nationalists who had held aloof from direct action politics, still hopeful that a mutually satisfactory settlement with the British could be worked out. Abandoning the search for a middle way to orderly independence confronted them with an unwelcome choice. In a context of total confrontation between the Congress and the government it was difficult to remain neutral. The chief ministers of Bengal and Sindh were dismissed when they lost the confidence of their governors as a result of very moderate demonstrations of nationalist feeling. Muslim moderates found themselves being ruthlessly categorized as either pro-Congress or pro-government; most Muslim moderates faced with this dilemma found themselves increasingly drawn into the militant Muslim League.

The British were now forced to rely heavily on the support of the Muslim League, which, as a power unto itself, was difficult to control, but which was at least clearly opposed to the Congress. With the British government eager for his cooperation, Jinnah brought pressure on the regional Muslim leaders who had been trying to avoid taking sides. The League offered a powerful national focus toward which non-Congress Muslim notables were induced to orient their attention. Between 1943 and 1945, the prospect of the survival of British rule being no longer credible, all the predominantly Muslim provincial ministries felt the effects of strong Muslim League pressure. At the beginning of the war, provincial ministers who enjoyed British patronage had been free to pursue a somewhat independent course on party questions. By the end of the war, most Muslim ministers had come to terms with the Muslim League, the only bastion which seemed capable of surviving the Congress tide. For the continuance of a semblance of Indian cooperation, the British were forced to rely on Jinnah's patronage, which Jinnah bestowed because it provided the opportunity to consolidate the League's control over Indian Muslims.

Perceiving all this, Gandhi still hoped to prevent the partition of India, but he now realized that this could not be accomplished by disregarding Jinnah. Gandhi initiated the "Gandhi-Jinnah talks" despite the objection of many congressmen still intent on pursuing the earlier policy of open defiance. Gandhi recognized that much had happened in two years; the movement he had launched had served its purpose, creating new conditions which had to be analyzed from a fresh perspective.

While asserting that the Quit India demand remained a valid statement of policy, Gandhi refrained from resuming command of the Quit India movement. His authority as leader of the movement, as conferred by the All-India Congress Committee resolution, he explained, had lapsed at the time of his imprisonment and could not be automatically resumed after his release. Millions of people had accepted the challenge of acting on their own, and authority could not have been drawn back into his person without another protracted period of preparation.

The millions who had acted on their own were, however, anxious to know what Gandhi thought of the way in which they had employed their freedom. Gandhi did not endorse the manner in which the movement had been carried on, but neither did he condemn it. Gandhi criticized the nationalists who had lapsed from nonviolence in a sympathetic manner. He applauded their motives (for the Quit India Resolution still stood); he applauded their courage; he asserted that their movement had furthered the nationalist cause. Violent resistance was, he said, on balance a positive contribution, but it was nonetheless regrettable in that it was a much weaker contribution than could have been made by the use of pure nonviolence. Gandhi refused to assist the government in opposing the continuation of violence because he felt he could not "be reformer and informer at the same time."[108] He hoped that violent revolutionaries might profit from their mistakes; he was not interested in helping the government profit from their mistakes.

Gandhi anticipated and implicitly sanctioned—both before and after the fact—the mass outbursts which followed the arrests of August 9. His initial comment, when informed of their extent, was an expression of surprise that they had not been even more severe. The August uprising had been a remarkably close approximation of Gandhi's description of the conditions under which violence might be "almost nonviolent." Large masses of people, after severe provocation and acting on a sudden impulse, had openly taken the law into their own hands. Gandhi's main concern was with the secretive nature of the underground movement which followed the first upheavals. Causing injury to others' persons and property was not necessarily violent according to Gandhi's thinking. Such injury, when the result of a spontaneous open effort of self-defense, was compatible with an adherence to nonviolence. What made many of the events which followed the August uprisings violent in Gandhi's eyes was their covert, premeditated nature. Gandhi held that members of the underground movement were nobly motivated but that their idealism would have been much better expended in public defiance of the government. Much of Gandhi's energy in the months following his release was consequently devoted to efforts to persuade those who were still underground to reveal themselves. Hearing that Aruna Asaf Ali was in poor health, he sent her a letter. "I have been filled with admiration for your courage and heroism," he wrote. "I have sent you messages that you must not die underground. You are reduced to a skeleton. Do come out and surrender yourself and win the prize offered for your arrest. Reserve the prize money for the Harijan cause."[109]

Gandhi's letter to the absconding Aruna found its mark. "Your precious words reached about a fortnight ago," she replied. "Throughout these twenty-two months you have been very close to me. In moments of my anguish and distress I found myself recalling your image. I can now understand the fascination of image worship. Your tender and warm appreciation of what I have done has over-whelmed me . . . I have been a stranger to you all these years . . . All unbeknown to yourself you have liberated many a captive soul—Need I say more?" Aruna told Gandhi that she would willingly give herself up if he desired that she do so on political grounds; if he were motivated only by concern for her personal comfort, she felt she must refuse. On June 30, 1944, Gandhi replied:

> Pria Putri [Dear Daughter] Aruna,
>   . . . I consider myself to be incapable of asking anyone much less you, of doing anything that would hurt your pride   This struggle has been full of romance and heroism. You are the central figure . . . I do not want you to surrender unless you feel that it is the better course. I have brought myself to regard secrecy as a sin in the application of Non-violence. But it cannot be followed mechanically . . . You must therefore be the best judge of what is proper . . . This I promise, I will not judge you, no matter what you do.

Aruna replied, on August 2, 1944, "I will now go into voluntary inaction for a while . . . I shall now have to busy myself quelling the 'storm.' After that I shall try and take a course of electric massage . . . Why have you this magic of stirring hearts, stimulating minds and soothing the troubled waters of the soul?"

Aruna's letters suggested the degree of authority which Gandhi possessed even for those who consciously departed from his principles. During the period of Gandhi's imprisonment, individuals such as Aruna had felt that they must decide for themselves on a course of action. If Gandhi said that they must act according to their own judgment, they must do so even when their judgment led them to conclude that a Gandhian strategy was impossible. "We undertook individual responsibility for such alternative forms of defensive actions as were organized or practised," Aruna wrote to Gandhi, indicating that Gandhi's parables on the legitimacy of violence employed in self-defense had in fact been the basis on which underground workers rationalized their activities. The exercise of independent judgment which Gandhi permitted was the assurance Aruna required that her activities would not be disapproved by Gandhi. When Gandhi's release made communication possible, Gandhi's help was sought as those underground tried to find a way out of the impasse of fugitive defiance.

Gandhi's letters found Aruna "somewhere in India" and induced her to abandon sabotage. Aruna came secretly to see Gandhi. But the British never found her, and she remained at large until the warrant for her arrest was canceled after the war. Carrying on her successful defiance of British authority while Congress prisoners were beginning to be released was, however, a difficult task. The movement to which she had contributed so much had run its course. What should she do?

On March 23, 1945, Aruna again turned to Gandhi. "Every country, and every generation leaves in the wake of gigantic movements a band of vagrants, disowned and disinherited," she wrote. "Like driftwood caught in stagnant waters, rootless, banished from all spiritual moorings . . . that is how one feels these days. There was a time when we of the August revolt thought and felt like Gods . . . For the first time we feel broken . . . We know ours is the voice of lost souls that championed a lost cause . . . Will you not restore to us our faith in life? We need it even more for dying."[110]

10

Aftermath

The Quit India movement was, as Lord Linlithgow observed in a telegram to Churchill, "by far the most serious rebellion since that of 1857."[1] The upheavals of 1857 and 1942 were in fact parallel in a number of respects. Both eradicated British authority in large areas of the country; both were most intense in many of the same areas of northern India. The differences between these two events mark the extent of the changes which had occurred over ninety years. In 1857, British rule was a struggling, makeshift affair and was challenged by the traditional social groups whose positions were being gradually eroded. The rebellion was indiscriminately xenophobic and backward-looking. The rebellion was a last stand by groups which would never again be in a position to challenge British rule. The British, moreover, were moved by the challenge to strengthen their rule, responding with renewed determination to remove the conditions which made the rising possible. In 1942, British rule was apparently impregnable; pulling British authority down by a spontaneous uprising was a much greater feat —a feat accomplished entirely without the aid of regular military forces, which in the rebellion had been supplied by mutineers from British service and the armies of several princely states. In 1942, the British Indian army and police were vastly more efficient and better disciplined forces, and the rebels were all raw amateurs. The Quit India movement was not begun or ended by the military; the movement was a violent expression of political forces whose resources included much more than the strength of arms, and which would not disappear if physically crushed. The rebels, having positive goals, employed violence symbolically, with discrimination, and hoped that some of their opponents could be persuaded to join them. The British, formally triumphant, responded to the movement with an awareness that no new effort could establish British rule on a solid footing. The seemingly similar outbursts of popular fury of 1857 and 1942 had opposite results. One led to an even firmer imposition of British rule; the other, though superficially a more futile effort, brought British rule to an end. Behind the shouting and the bloodshed, intellectual forces were at work which in 1857 left the rebels demoralized and the British more determined than ever. In 1942 the renewed clash had left the victorious British demoralized and the defeated rebels more determined than ever. Between the first outburst and the second, a revolution had taken place.

In the Quit India movement, the Indian revolution reached its climax. The revolution, conceived as an open rebellion against an apparently invincible regime, had presumed that success would be measured, not by the content of British offers, but by the strength and clarity of Indian will. Indians would be free when they acted as free men, without reference to British desires, when the appeals for generosity of the moderates and the opposition-defined defiance of the reactionaries were replaced by a confident indifference to the continuing British presence. India declared herself to be already independent, and in India's will to act independently the revolution had triumphed.

In 1942, communication between New Delhi and London was almost instantaneous; two hours was sufficient for the delivery of an urgent telegraphic message. Yet India and Whitehall were still very distant in a psychological sense, and the exchanges which took place between the viceroy and the war cabinet in London during this decisive year were characterized by a peculiarly discontinuous quality. For a brief moment at the height of the crisis of August 1942 unanimity reigned, and determination in both capitals was strong. At other times, when a mood of confidence dominated in one capital, dark pessimism dominated the other. Six months before the Quit India movement, at the time the Cripps Mission was initiated, New Delhi was brimming with confidence, while the war cabinet thought compromise might be necessary; after the Quit India movement, the war cabinet became curiously heroic, while New Delhi was demoralized. This progression of moods was, moreover, not merely random; it led straight to the manner in which Britain vacated India in 1947.

When the Quit India movement first began to take definite shape in the summer of 1942, its import had been perceived with clarity in both London and New Delhi. Linlithgow and Amery both spoke forcefully to the effect that this was in fact a final showdown which would decide once and for all whether British or Congress presumption would be shown up. On July 15, 1942, Amery asserted that "After all, we are dealing with people who are more and more advancing the claim to be considered as the alternative Government of India and ingeniously fortifying that claim step by step. At some point or other we have got to make it quite clear that *we* are the Government of India and that the claim is a bubble to be pricked."[2]

A showdown had been welcomed, its import in the short- and long-run clearly perceived, and the extent of Congress vindication acknowledged. Such clarity was possible for British officials in the heat of the moment when directly engaged in battle. With the crisis past and the issue decided adversely, clarity receded. In New Delhi, the British failure to attain total victory was only indirectly acknowledged as tantamount to total defeat. In London, a recognition of the truth was not repressed; in London, the failure of earlier predictions led to a new effort at clarification which was not hampered by an embarrassed sense of reality.

Churchill, with his usual capacity for the bold depiction of alternatives, stated the problem simply as a choice between cutting and running or standing and ruling. The alternatives under serious consideration in the war cabinet in the aftermath of the Quit India movement were (a) to impose on India a heavy new bill for services rendered during the war and then clear out altogether, or (b) to engage in a grand scheme of majestic politics involving direct appeals to Indian peasants and workers over the heads of the "unrepresentative" bourgeois Congress.

On September 15, reported L. S. Amery, "Winston harangued us at great length about the monstrous idea that we should spend millions upon millions in the defence of India, then be told to clear out, and on top of it all owe India vast sums incurred on her behalf . . . Winston's idea apparently being that . . . we should draw up a supplementary bill against India which may equal if not exceed the accumulated sterling balances!" At the war cabinet meeting of August 31, on the other hand, "Winston began one of his usual curious monologues about India, treating the present trouble as completely disposed of and as evidence of the fact, which he has always insisted upon, that Congress really represents hardly anybody except lawyers, money-lenders and the 'Hindu priesthood.' From this he rambled on to the suggestion that it would really pay us to take up the cause of the poor peasant and confiscate the rich Congressman's lands and divide them up. Others

chipped in, more particularly Bevin, with demands for social reform."[3]
Significantly, Churchill's heroics on the Indian question were suddenly of great interest to his more liberal colleagues. Cripps in fact composed a "Note" dated September 2 giving a detailed proposal for reform from above:

> 16. If the British Government could enlist the sympathy of the workers and peasants by immediate action on their behalf, the struggle in India would no longer be between Indian and British upon the nationalist basis, but between the classes in India upon an economic basis. There would thus be a good opportunity to rally the mass of Indian Opinion to our side.
> 17. It is most important that the Indian workers and peasants should realise that it is a British initiative which is working for them against their Indian oppressors; this would entail a proper publicity service in India.[4]

Even the cautious Amery seemed to have been affected by the general enthusiasm. After disparaging Churchill's exaggeration, Amery admitted that "As a matter of fact, I am not sure that the time has not come . . . for a much bolder social policy."[5]

In the privacy of the cabinet, Churchill spoke with equal drama of the strategy of cut-and-run and that of stand-and-rule, but it was clear that his instinct lay in the direction of the more heroic course. His instinct was out of place; he had, however, stated the alternatives with greater abruptness than the government of India were capable of. Linlithgow and his advisers were too painfully implicated in the Indian situation to permit a forceful penetration to the core of their dilemma. They too preferred a grand manner, but felt at the same time the utter impossibility of undertaking such a course. Before the Quit India movement, the viceroy had been eager to move ahead to scatter the Congress and rally the moderates, but had been restrained by a realization that his actions were subject to being overruled by a cabinet which included Cripps and Attlee. After the Quit India movement, the viceroy was forced to shift his apprehensions in the opposite direction. Now the greatest obstacle to grand new initiatives did not seem to be parliamentary timidity, but Indian intransigence. Before the Quit India movement, his concern had been whether Parliament would back him up. Now the viceroy's chief concern was that the cabinet and British public opinion in general would not fully grasp the seriousness of his situation and the difficulty he would face in merely holding on to power, let alone undertaking new initiatives.

The "gravity and extent" of the disorders "we have so far concealed from the world for reasons of military security," Linlithgow cabled, with the result that "opinion at home may think . . . this business has not been so serious as, in fact, it has."[6]

The persistence of popular support for the Congress now appeared to be a "most intractable problem."[7] The British could not circumvent the Congress by direct appeals to the masses; the masses, to the extent to which they were not controlled by the Congress, were even more hostile to the British than the Congress. Churchill had posed the necessity for a sharp break with the status quo in order to force the issue in one direction; the consequence was to force the issue in the other direction. Churchill said "Rule or get out." The viceroy was unable to do either. Churchill's heroics forced the British to choose, and the viceroy informed them that one of their supposed options was now closed.

The wrenching events at the war's end registered the changes which had been wrought during the war. Churchill's now exclusively Conservative government concluded that their election prospects might be enhanced by a rapprochement with Congress leaders and sanctioned the calling of the Simla Conference, for which Nehru, Azad, and other Congress leaders were released from prison. The Simla Conference of June 1945 was as abortive as Churchill's election bid, but, as Azad has observed, the conference "marks a breakwater in Indian political history. This was the first time that negotiations failed, not on the basic political issue between India and Britain, but on the communal issue dividing different Indian groups."[8] For the first time, the British made no effort to take creative advantage of India's diversity. Divisions did not thereby disappear. The conference nonetheless signaled the fact that, even before the decisive Labour victory of July 1945, the British, having failed to create a political India to accord with the hierarchical pomp of the just-completed capital city, were now eager to quit.

The released Congress prisoners were everywhere greeted by jubilant throngs. The massive indignation expressed at the British effort to stage treason trials for Indian officers who had fought with the Japanese further indicated the meaning which Indians intended to give to the wartime era. It quickly became apparent that the British not only could not influence the future course of Indian politics, but could not even insure law and order for the time being. Indians in British service, many of whom had been secretly sympathetic during the Quit

India movement, were now openly so. Maulana Azad noted that,"Wherever I went during this period, the young men of the Defence forces came out to welcome me and express their sympathy and admiration without any regard for the reaction of their European officers." In Calcutta "a large gathering of constables and head constables surrounded my car. They saluted me and some touched my feet. They all expressed their regard for Congress and said that they would act according to our orders."[9] The Naval Mutiny of February 1946 demonstrated that the Congress were already the de facto rulers of the country. Twenty ships in the Bombay harbor, as well as all the shore batteries, were taken over by Indian sailors, training their guns on the white troops rushed to Bombay to recapture the harbor. "Almost all of the Royal Indian Navy's 75 or more ships and 20 shore batteries on the subcontinent were affected."[10] Only Congress intervention brought the strike to an end. The Congress secured guarantees against victimization from the British and reassured the sailors that only technicalities now remained before their formal assumption of power. The Congress had the loyalty of the public and the services to command, and the British were given only a brief respite to honor their promise to depart.

Gandhi's demand that the British should unilaterally Quit India was in fact the demand on which the British government acted in 1947. And the basis for their withdrawal was, to a considerable extent, an acceptance of Gandhi's demand that India be left to anarchy. The initial announcement of withdrawal was unconditional and time-bound; Britain would go by June 1948, whether a "stable" window-dressing regime had been manufactured in the meantime or not. If no national government had been agreed upon by that date, the government proposed to hand over sovereign power to the several provinces. This might in fact have occurred and ushered in a period of loose federalism comparable to the immediate postrevolutionary American situation under the Articles of Confederation, had Wavell remained viceroy.[11] Wavell drew up a plan of staged military withdrawal from India, called by the inspired title "Operation Ebbtide," but could make no headway in forming a stable national government. Lord Mountbatten's sudden arrival, and his sudden decision to settle things on the basis of the establishment of two successor states, to be free within a matter of weeks, represented a temporary return of the British zeal for a departure premised upon a "settlement" rather than anarchy.

The letter of instructions Prime Minister Attlee gave Mountbatten in 1947 urged him to work out a settlement which would preserve Indian unity *if possible*; British dedication to unity was no longer a device for postponing Indian independence, but merely an expression of nonbinding preference. The important part of Mountbatten's charge was that he should work out a settlement acceptable to the parties concerned. The "parties concerned" were the Congress and the Muslim League. The parties whose interests were now to be sacrificed if necessary included the princes, the Sikhs, and the Untouchables—all those groups which, along with the Muslims, Churchill had been fond of enumerating as the "composite majority" that supported British rule. Discretionary power to protect the weak which the British had for so long insisted on retaining in their own hands as a check on party tyranny was no longer an issue. "Sovereignty" had passed into Congress hands and the British realized that they would have to act fast if they were to persuade the sovereign Congress to make any concessions whatsoever before their formal power lapsed.[12] The development of Muslim consciousness in the years since 1940 had made the Pakistan demand one whch would have had to be dealt with by any Indian ruler. There was no necessary reason, however, why it had to be dealt with before British withdrawal. The only justification for doing so involved an assumption that the British would deal with the demand more justly than a successor government, which would, nonetheless, have to live with the situation which the British would leave after making a settlement. Mountbatten stated that his first consideration in urging a quick settlement was that this "would be likely to make for lasting goodwill between the United Kingdom and the successor Governments in India";[13] Mountbatten said nothing of the relationship likely to exist between the successor governments themselves. Sovereignty was handed over to two successor regimes, in recognition of the need for politically effective control of the tense situation in the country. The details of the partition scheme were withheld pending the working out of a just settlement by British authority. The two new governments were thus given full responsibility without full authority. As a result, neither government was satisfied with the settlement or prepared to defend it. Nothing was settled except the fact that arbitrary direct power had been transferred to two new governments.

Significantly, much better success resulted from British handling of the Sikhs, Untouchables, and princes, where anarchy was once again the order of the day. These groups were simply abandoned. The leaders of the Muslim League and the Congress were men whose goodwill was worth having, in Mountbatten's opinion, while other groups remained as negligible as the Muslim League and the Congress had themselves once seemed. "The Provincial Muslim and Provincial Sikh political leadership," Mountbatten commented, "was in the hands of unbalanced and seemingly unintelligent men."[14] Minorities were no longer to be protected; they were told to look for protection to the new sovereign power. The princes were treated no differently; they were told that they were now free, as British paramountcy had simply lapsed. The British announcement that the princes should now consider their solemn covenants with the British scraps of paper had the effect which Gandhi had anticipated: the princes, faced with hard realities and deprived of the opportunity of maneuvering for advantage which an external power provided, quickly came to terms. Where trouble persisted, it was a consequence of the partition of the subcontinent and the opportunity to maneuver with reference to a new third party.

The abandonment of the princes to the fond clutches of the totalitarian Congress was, as Tory statesmen pointed out, dishonorable. It dishonored the memory of a mistaken policy from which the nation now wished to dissociate itself. It dishonored the attempt to sustain vestiges of a mistaken policy for the purpose of coddling the national myth that mistakes could never have been made. It damaged the nation's credibility, shaking the world's faith that Britain would continue to uphold the same mistaken policy in other areas. It made possible, on the other hand, fresh thinking about the nation's place in a changed world, and a healthy acceptance of the nation's limitations and fallibility. Britain only learned to live with the world after she gave up the idea of conquering it.

11   Gandhi's Future

At the moment when the British government finally accepted Gandhi's demand that they quit India, Gandhi was ignored by his oldest associates. "The Working Committee is with me and not with you," Mountbatten, pleased with his success in inducing the Working Committee to accept his plan of partition, is reported to have remarked to Gandhi. In reply Gandhi said, "Yes, the Working Committee is with you, but the people are still with me." The Congress leadership had left Gandhi, but Gandhi had not left his post.

The nationalist movement by 1947 had succeeded in altering the lives of millions of individuals who, in fighting for a cause, had also shaped the basis for a new society. Yet, as in other self-fulfilling revolutions, the political implications of these individual changes were difficult to assess. It would be some time before the degree to which Indians had come to think of themselves as a coherent nation would be apparent. The crises of independence, moreover, had left India's new rulers little time for reflection. The instinct of harried men was to grasp what tools of power lay at hand to restore order as quickly as possible, postponing Gandhi's advice to a more convenient occasion.

Among Indians in general, as well as among their leaders, a decline in revolutionary ardor had set in. Even transformed individuals cannot live forever in a state of exaltation. Revolutions change patterns of behavior, but they cannot permanently change human nature. Once a new plateau is reached, normal human concerns reappear. The revolution was over for the time being, and none too soon for some.

With the attainment of independence nationalists either announced their goals attained and turned their attention to less revolutionary matters or resolved to pursue their goals by other means. Politics-as-usual claimed the bulk of nationalists of all stripes, leaving only a handful of activists still determined to pursue revolution in opposition to the new structure.

Gandhi, and the Indian revolution, had reached a point which Eamon de Valera, and the Irish revolution, had reached in comparable circumstances following the First World War. Ireland had been declared independent of Great Britain during the Easter Rebellion of 1916, in the midst of the war. The Rebellion of 1916 had been forcibly put down, but a negotiated settlement declaring most of Ireland independent was made shortly after the war's end. This settlement, made with a section of the rebels of 1916, provided for the partition of Ireland along religious lines. The motive force of Irish nationalism was in large part Catholicism; the British had proclaimed for many years their inability to grant Irish independence because of the impropriety of subjecting Protestant Ulstermen to the tyranny of the Catholic majority. When independence could no longer be avoided, a northern enclave was cut away to honor the British insistence on justice for the minority, which had been used for so long to forestall the granting of independence on any terms.

The supreme leader of the 1916 uprising, Eamon de Valera, refused to accept the partition of Ireland, and broke bitterly with those former colleagues who did accept partition, who consequently became the new Republic's first constitutional leaders. De Valera declared that "An Ireland in fragments nobody cares about." He stated that "We cannot admit the right of the British Government to mutilate our country, either in its own interest or at the call of any section of our population . . . if your Government stands aside, we can effect a complete reconciliation." He argued that "true friendship with England can be obtained most readily now through amicable but absolute separation. The fear, groundless though we believe it to be, that Irish territory may be used as the basis for an attack upon England's liberties, can be met by reasonable guarantees not inconsistent with Irish sovereignty."[1]

When de Valera failed to prevent members of his own movement from accepting Irish independence on terms which he could not accept, he took his cause into the wilderness and plunged his country into civil war. He ultimately emerged victorious, as the leader of a more fully independent country, but was unable to undo the partition.

An analysis of the Irish experience, written by Mahadev Desai, was printed in the *Harijan* of August 2, 1942, a week before the Quit India movement was launched. As Desai pointed out, the parallels were uncanny. Britain was once again insisting upon the importance of protecting minorities and the impossibility of acting in a way which would

—allegedly—give a foothold to the enemy in wartime. Desai hoped that Indians might improve upon the Irish example by using less violence and attaining quicker and fuller success. The prospect that the parallel would continue on into the postwar years and even past independence was not cheering, but the possibility could not be overlooked. When the war ended, India, like Ireland, was partitioned, although Gandhi, like de Valera, remained unalterably opposed.

Within the limits which circumstances permitted him, Gandhi modified the Irish example. Most significantly, he loyally supported the Congress leaders who voted to accept independence with partition to which he remained in principle opposed. Gandhi, like de Valera, launched a new campaign to bring the ideal for which independence had been sought closer to reality. But Gandhi was a different man, and an older man, and this was reflected in the way he set out on his self-appointed mission.

The nationalist movement had never been Gandhian, and it was less so at the end than at the beginning of the Gandhian era. Gandhi's very success in encouraging other strong leaders to develop themselves had placed in positions of leadership men confident of the need to differ with Gandhi on specific issues. On October 5, 1945, Gandhi had addressed a letter to Nehru concerning "the difference of outlook between us . . . I have said that I still stand by the system of Government envisaged in *Hind Swaraj*. These are not mere words. All the experience gained by me since [1909] when I wrote the booklet has confirmed the truth of my belief." Nehru replied flatly that "It is many years since I read *Hind Swaraj* . . . But even when I read it twenty or more years ago it seemed to me completely unreal . . . It is thirty-eight years since *Hind Swaraj* was written. The world has completely changed since then." Gandhi replied characteristically that "It would not matter if ultimately we might have to agree to differ so long as we remained one at heart as we are today."[2] Gandhi had always welcomed as followers persons of diverse views, but the attainment of independence brought home to Gandhi just how few of his followers adhered to his views in their entirety. Gandhi the revolutionary had designated Nehru the socialist as his "political heir," but Gandhi also sensed, as Nehru moved closer to the acquisition of formal power, that Nehru now needed to be pushed in a somewhat more revolutionary direction.

If even Gandhi's "political heir" was not "Gandhian," what compulsion need less prominent followers feel? Worship is a convenient way to avoid taking something seriously. Gandhi's elevation in popular esteem kept pace with a sense of his irrelevance. Gandhi spoke of himself in 1947 in his characteristic idiom as a "back-number."[3] He was well aware from a much earlier date that he was destined to suffer the fate of other prophets, more doted on than understood. Periodic obeisance relegated Gandhi away from intrusion into ordinary concerns. Many followers failed to recognize that servile adoration was not perfect service.

How does one cope with the prospect of becoming a figurehead? Many leaders have seen themselves quietly eased onto the image shelf with others whose names are ritually invoked. The temptations are to lapse into querulous vindictiveness, imposing petty servilities on those who pretend to major deference, or to succumb to a self-deluding sense of gratification at signs of superficial adulation. A dangerous third alternative is to demonstrate personal integrity publicly by gambling with easy honor and charting a new course in the wilderness. King Lear in abdicating chose the first route; many secretly bitter men, the second. Gandhi, like the disappointed Lear, chose to set out on a new quest.

Gandhi could not readily disown the new government, headed by Nehru and Patel, long his close associates. Nor could he resist the call to alleviate the anguish of the transition by attempting to calm communal passions and ease the lot of refugees in the wake of the partition. Gandhi's energies in his last months were devoted almost exclusively to relief work. In thus absorbing himself, however, he was acting as a man postponing a major decision. Woven throughout his many pleas for compassion are intimations of the way in which he was moving. For Gandhi was cautiously preparing to launch a new revolution.

Gandhi refused to associate himself with the festivities of independence. Three different government officials asked him for a statement in honor of August 15, 1947, suggesting that "if he did not give any message to the nation, it would not be good." He replied that he "had run dry . . . There is no message at all. If it is bad, let it be so." Repeated requests from the B.B.C. for a similar statement were also rejected, Gandhi commenting, "They must forget that I know

English."[4] Gandhi observed the day by fasting. He had planned to be in rural Noakhali on August 15 but had been detained in Calcutta. Gandhi discouraged the celebration of the Hindu festival of Diwali several months later, refuting the suggestion that it should be celebrated with special observances because it was the first Diwali after independence.[5]

On his birthday, Gandhi expressed a wish to die. "He said that many friends had hoped he would live to be 125 but he had lost all desire to live long, let alone 125 years."[6] This was on October 2. On January 14, 1948, two weeks before his assassination, he returned to this theme:

> Before I ever knew anything of politics in my early youth, I dreamt the dream of communal unity of the heart. I shall jump in the evening of my life, like a child, to feel that the dream has been realized in this life. The wish for living the full span of life, portrayed by the seers of old and which they permit us to set down at 125 years, will then revive.[7]

Gandhi believed that he had two choices following the attainment of independence: to die as a failure or to undertake an arduous new crusade. He could imagine dying at once, or beginning again like a child, like a man with fifty years more to live.

Gandhi used the phrase "passive resistance" to describe the movement which had ended with the attainment of independence. The phrase recurred repeatedly in his writings and speeches in the last six months of his life. "The proper term" for what India had been practicing for the last thirty years, he wrote in the *Harijan* of July 13, 1947, a month before independence, "was passive resistance. Passive resistance was a preparation for the active resistance of arms." A week later he wrote that "Passive resistance, unlike non-violence, had no power to change men's hearts. The consequences they knew but too well. The Swaraj of their dreams was far off."[8] This theme, sounded even before independence, recurred frequently in his speeches to the daily prayer meetings in Delhi.[9] Without regretting the past or indulging in recrimination, Gandhi was firmly putting the nationalist movement behind him and dissociating himself from those who claimed power from their participation in it. During the movement itself, Gandhi had spoken repeatedly of his dissatisfaction with the quality of the movement but had insisted that it was necessary to forge ahead and hope for improvement. Now that the movement was over, Gandhi pronounced its epitaph. "Gandhi proceeded to say [to a visitor of August 30] that it was indeed true that he had all along laboured under an illusion. But he was never sorry for it. He realized that if his vision had not been clouded by that illusion, India would never have reached the point which it had done today."[10]

Gandhi had once observed that he had purchased his third-class ticket all the way to the holy city of Hardwar, where the Ganges broke out of the Himalayas, while most others in his movement had purchased their tickets only up to Delhi.[11] Now, Delhi had been reached and only Gandhi was left on the train. Gandhi trenchantly disposed of Congress Raj by noting the "dishonesty of the many who can mould public opinion [and the] obstinate refusal of sufferers to learn from their sufferings."[12]

Now that the burden of subjection had been lifted," he noted, "all the forces of evil had come to the surface . . . But what remained to be done was to marshall all the forces of good."[13] He suggested that the vote be given to eighteen-year-olds and denied to those over fifty.[14] Political power, he felt, was best entrusted to those hoping for a better future, rather than to those intent on denying their irrelevance by imposing the past on the present.

Gandhi's new program was his old program applied to the conditions of independence. India's new rulers were not to be permitted to lapse into the pattern of their former masters.[15] Panchayat Raj institutions were to become the new focus of government—whether or not they were recognized as such in law—because centralized institutions could not serve the individual needs of millions of people. The villager was to be taught that "he is no longer a serf born to serve the cities and towns of India but that he is destined to exploit the city dwellers for the advertisement of the finished fruits of well-thought-out labours." Labor was to "realize its dignity and strength. Capital has neither dignity nor strength compared to labour."[16] And, India and Pakistan were to be reunited, in spirit if not in a technical sense. Gandhi spoke of India's 700,000 villages, including those of both countries in his reckoning. He spoke of his eagerness to go to Pakistan to ease communal tensions there as he had done in India. Gandhi confronted urban communal violence in Calcutta and Delhi and everywhere struggled to control the growing hatred between India and Pakistan.

Gandhi went to Noakhali—a rural area of Bengal soon to become a part of Pakistan—to demonstrate his conviction that communal hostility would have to be controlled in one village before it could be controlled on a national or international level. He was sympathetic with the problems of those who had set themselves on the firing line of day-to-day administration in the capital cities, but he restlessly groped beyond. Going from the capital to a village and setting out to learn Bengali at the age of seventy-seven was not an escape from responsibility; it was an escape from trivia. In the capital, Nehru and Patel wrestled with the crisis of the moment; in Noakhali, Gandhi was molding the shape of the future. His intensely personal experiments with the quality of his continence, in a village, with his grandniece, were the preoccupations of a man with his eye on the future, indifferent to his "position" in the context of past achievement.

Gandhi's final proposal, on which he was working at the time of his death, to turn the Congress into a Lok Sevak Sangh, or People's Service Organization, was his way of finally cutting his organizational ties with those who had moved into positions of authority. The gesture was largely symbolic. Either Nehru and others would have insisted on the retention of the Congress name, or they would have established a new party under a new name. In either case, the point would have been made that Gandhi had severed his ties with an organization now devoted primarily to the gaining of office.

Gandhi's break with his oldest co-workers was not an expression of bitterness, though he did feel some bitterness. His frequent references to his "disillusionment" were meant in an almost technical sense, for he was working out a destiny which he had known was inevitable. He had predicted that the "National Government" to be set up after independence would be a "mixture," with all elements of the nation having "a voice in the government of the day." In addition, he hoped that "a strong party representing true non-violence will exist in the country."[17] Gandhi was perhaps disillusioned to discover how many of his close followers preferred to join the national government instead of his "party representing true non-violence," but the path he had embarked upon as the leader of an independent organized conscience of the nation involved no repudiation of the new national government, but simply his recognition that it had indeed begun to follow the policies he had long anticipated it would follow. "A goal ceases to be one, when it is reached," he said in Delhi on January 14, 1948.[18] Now that a national government had been established he was charting out a new goal. Gandhi had departed, even though for the moment he was riding in an empty train.

Selected Bibliography
Notes   Index

Selected Bibliography

PRIVATE PAPERS
Gandhi Papers. Gandhi Memorial Museum. New Delhi.
Linlithgow Papers. India Office Library. London.
Nehru Papers. Nehru Memorial Museum. New Delhi.
Rajendra Prasad Papers. New Delhi.

GOVERNMENT AND PARTY RECORDS
All-India Congress Committee Papers, Indian National Congress. Nehru Memorial Museum. New Delhi.
Mansergh, Nicholas, ed. *The Transfer of Power, 1942–7*. 3 vols. published to date. London: Her Majesty's Stationery Office, 1970——.
Proceedings of the Government of India: Home (Political), 1939–1945. National Archives of India. New Delhi.
"Report on the Civil Disturbances in Bihar, 1942." Political and Secret Library. India Office Library. London.

NEWSPAPERS AND PERIODICALS
Harijan (Ahmedabad), 1939–1942.
Hindustan Times (New Delhi), 1939–1942.
Statesman (Calcutta), 1939–1942.
Times of India (Bombay), 1939–1942.

BOOKS AND ARTICLES
Alexander, Horace. *Gandhi Through Western Eyes*. Bombay: Asia Publishing House, 1969.
Achebe, Chinua. *No Longer at Ease*. London: Heinemann, 1966.
Altbach, Philip G. *Student Politics in Bombay*. Bombay: Asia Publishing House, 1968.
Azad, Maulana Abul Kalam. *India Wins Freedom*. Bombay: Orient Longmans, 1959.
Aziz, K. K. *The Making of Pakistan*. London: Chatto & Windus, 1967.
Bailyn, Bernard. *The Ideological Origins of the American Revolution*. Cambridge, Mass.: Harvard University Press, 1967.
—— *The Origins of American Politics*. New York: Alfred A. Knopf, 1968.
Banerjea, Surendranath. *A Nation in the Making*. Bombay: Oxford University Press, 1963.

Barnouw, Erik, and S. Krishnaswamy. *Indian Film*. New York: Columbia University Press, 1963.

Birla, G. D. *In the Shadow of the Mahatma*. Calcutta: Orient Longmans, 1955.

Blake, William. *The Portable Blake*. New York: Viking Press, 1955.

Boardman, Eugene Powers. *Christian Influence Upon the Ideology of the Taiping Rebellion, 1851–1864*. Madison, Wis.: University of Wisconsin Press, 1952.

Bolitho, Hector. *Jinnah, Creator of Pakistan*. Karachi: Oxford University Press, 1969.

Bonarjee, N. B. *Under Two Masters*. Calcutta: Oxford University Press, 1970.

Bondurant, Joan. *Conquest of Violence*. Berkeley: University of California Press, 1965.

Bose, Nirmal Kumar, and P. H. Patwardhan. *Gandhi in Indian Politics*. Bombay: Lalvani Publishing House, 1967.

Bose, Nirmal Kumar. *My Days with Gandhi*. Calcutta: Nishana, 1953.

_____ ed. *Selections from Gandhi*. Ahmedabad: Navajivan Publishing House, 1968.

Bose, Subhas Chandra. *An Indian Pilgrim*. Bombay: Asia Publishing House, 1965.

Broomfield, J. H. *Elite Conflict in a Plural Society*. Berkeley: University of California Press, 1968.

Campbell-Johnson, Alan. *Mission with Mountbatten*. London: Robert Hale, 1951.

Casey, Lord. *Personal Experience: 1939–46*. London: Constable & Company Limited, 1962.

Chandra, Bipan. *The Rise and Growth of Economic Nationalism in India*. New Delhi: People's Publishing House, 1966.

Chatterji, Jogesh Chandra. *In Search of Freedom*. Calcutta: Firma K. L. Mukhopadhyaya, 1967.

Cheng, J. C. *Chinese Sources for the Taiping Rebellion, 1850–1864*. Hong Kong: Hong Kong University Press, 1963.

Danzig, Richard. "The Announcement of August 20th, 1917," *The Journal of Asian Studies*, November 1968.

Das, Durga. *India from Curzon to Nehru and After*. London: Collins, 1969.

Datta, K. K. *History of the Freedom Movement in Bihar*, vol. III: *1942–1947*. Patna: Government of Bihar, 1958.

Devanesen, Chandran D. S. *The Making of the Mahatma*. New Delhi: Orient Longmans, 1969.

Dey, Lal Behari. *Recollections of Alexander Duff and of the Mission College Which He Founded at Calcutta*. London, 1878.

Eckstein, Harry, ed. *Internal War*. New York: Free Press of Glencoe, 1964.

Engels, Frederick. *The Peasant War in Germany*. Moscow: Foreign Languages Publishing House, 1956.

Erikson, Erik H. *Childhood and Society*. New York: W. W. Norton, 1963.

_____ *Gandhi's Truth, On the Origins of Militant Nonviolence*. New York: W. W. Norton & Company, 1969.

_____ *Identity, Youth and Crisis*. New York: W. W. Norton & Company, 1968.

_____ *Insight and Responsibility*. New York: W. W. Norton & Company, 1964.

_____ *Young Man Luther*. New York: W. W. Norton & Company, 1962.

Fanon, Frantz. *Black Skins, White Masks*. New York: Grove Press, 1967.

_____ *The Wretched of the Earth*. London: MacGibbon and Kee, 1965.

Fischer, Louis. *A Week with Gandhi*. London: George Allen & Unwin, 1943.

_____ *The Life of Mahatma Gandhi*. London: Jonathan Cape, 1962.

Friedrich, Carl J., ed. *Revolution*. New York: Atherton Press, 1966.

Frykenberg, Robert. *Guntur District, 1788–1848*. Oxford: Oxford University Press, 1965.

Fuchs, Stephen. *Rebellious Prophets*. Bombay: Asia Publishing House, 1965.
Gandhi, Manubahen. *The Lonely Pilgrim*. Ahmedabad: Navajivan Publishing House, 1964.
Gandhi, Mohandas K. *An Autobiography*. Ahmedabad: Navajivan Publishing House, 1958.
———— *An Autobiography, The Story of My Experiments with Truth*. Boston: Beacon Press, 1959.
———— *Bapu's Letters to Mira, 1924–1948*. Ahmedabad: Navajivan Publishing House, 1959.
———— *Delhi Diary*. Ahmedabad: Navajivan Publishing House, 1960.
———— *Gandhiji's Correspondence with the Government, 1942–44*. Ahmedabad: Navajivan Publishing House, 1957.
———— *Gandhiji's Correspondence with the Government, 1944–47*. Ahmedabad: Navajivan Publishing House, 1959.
———— *Satyagraha in South Africa*. Ahmedabad: Navajivan Publishing House, 1961.
———— *The Selected Works of Mahatma Gandhi*. 6 vols. Ahmedabad: Navajivan Publishing House, 1968.
———— *To the Students*. Ahmedabad: Navajivan Publishing House, 1965.
Geertz, Clifford. *Agricultural Involution*. Berkeley: University of California, 1963.
Ghosh, K. K. *The Indian National Army*. Meerut: Meenakshi Prakashan, 1969.
Glendevon, John. *The Viceroy at Bay: Lord Linlithgow in India 1936–1943*. London: Collins, 1971.
Gopal, Ram. *Lokamanya Tilak*. Bombay: Asia Publishing House, 1956.
Grier, William H., and Price M. Cobbs. *Black Rage*. New York: Basic Books, 1968.
Gunther, Frances. *Revolution in India*. New York: Island Press, 1944.
Hardinge of Penshurst, Lord. *My Indian Years, 1910–1916*. London: John Murray, 1948.
Hartz, Louis, *The Founding of New Societies*. New York: Harcourt, Brace and World, 1964.
———— *The Liberal Tradition in America*. New York: Harcourt, Brace, 1955.
Hodson, H. V. *The Great Divide*. London: Hutchinson, 1969.
Horsburgh, H. J. N. *Non-Violence and Aggression*. London: Oxford University Press, 1968.
Huntington, Samuel P. *Political Order in Changing Societies*. New Haven: Yale University Press, 1968.
Hutchins, Francis G. *The Illusion of Permanence: British Imperialism in India*. Princeton: Princeton University Press, 1967.
India, Government of. *Congress Responsibility for the Disturbances 1942–43*. New Delhi: Government of India Press, 1943.
India Ravaged. Published secretly by *Indian Express*, Madras, 1943.
India Unreconciled. New Delhi: Hindustan Times Press, 1944.
Irschick, Eugene G. *Politics and Social Conflict in South India*. Berkeley: University of California Press, 1969.
Johnson, Chalmers. *Revolutionary Change*. Boston: Little, Brown, 1966.
Joshi, P. C. *Communist Reply to Congress Working Committee's Charges*. Bombay: People's Publishing House, 1945.
Kartini, Raden Adjeng. *Letters of a Javanese Princess*. New York: Alfred A. Knopf, 1920.
Karve, D. D. *The New Brahmans*. Berkeley: University of California Press, 1963.
Keer, Dhananjay. *Veer Savarkar*. Bombay: Popular Prakashan, 1966.
Khanna, R. N., ed. *Gandhi's Fight For Freedom, 1942*. Lahore: Allied Indian Publisher, 1944.

Kissinger, Henry. "The White Revolutionary: Reflections on Bismarck,"
    Daedalus, Summer 1968.
Kopf, David. *British Orientalism and the Bengal Renaissance*. Berkeley: University
    of California Press, 1969.
Lawrence, Peter. *Road Belong Cargo*. New York: Humanities Press, 1964.
Linlithgow, Marquess of. *Speeches and Statements*. New Delhi: Bureau of Public
    Information, Government of India, 1945.
Lipset, Seymour Martin. *Revolution and Counterrevolution*. New York: Basic Books,
    1968.
——— *The First New Nation*. Garden City, N.Y.: Doubleday, 1967.
Lothian, Sir Arthur Cunningham. *Kingdoms of Yesterday*. London: John Murray,
    1951.
Lutfullah. *Autobiography*. London: Smith, Elder, 1857.
McCully, Bruce. *English Education and the Origins of Indian Nationalism*. Gloucester,
    Mass.: Peter Smith, 1966.
Majumdar, R. C. *Struggle for Freedom*. Bombay: Bharatiya Vidya Bhavan, 1968.
Mannoni, O. *Prospero and Caliban*. New York: Praeger, 1956.
Mehta, Ashoka, and Achyut Patwardhan. *The Communal Triangle in India*.
    Allahabad: Kitabistan, 1942.
Menon, K. P. S. *Many Worlds*. London: Oxford University Press, 1965.
Menon, V. P. *The Transfer of Power in India*. Bombay: Orient Longmans, 1957.
Michael, Franz. *The Taiping Rebellion*, vol. I. Seattle: University of Washington
    Press, 1966.
Miller, Perry. *Orthodoxy in Massachusetts, 1630–1650*. Boston: Beacon Press, 1959.
Mill, John Stuart. *Autobiography*. New York: American Library, 1964.
Mitra, Bejan, and Phani Chakraborty. *Rebel India*. Calcutta: Orient Book Co., 1946.
Molesworth, G. N. *Curfew on Olympus*. Bombay: Asia Publishing House, 1965.
Montagu, E. S. *An Indian Diary*. London: William Heinemann, 1930.
Moon, Penderel. *Gandhi and Modern India*. London: The English Universities
    Press, 1968.
Moore, Barrington, Jr. *Social Origins of Dictatorship and Democracy*. Boston: Beacon
    Press, 1966.
——— "Revolution in America?" *New York Review of Books*, 12 (January 30, 1969).
Mountbatten, Earl. *Time Only to Look Forward*. London: Nicholas Kaye, 1949.
Mukerjee, Hiren. *Gandhiji: A Study*. New Delhi: People's Publishing House, 1969.
Nanda, B. R. *Mahatma Gandhi*. London: George Allen & Unwin, 1959.
Narayan, Jaya Prakash. *Towards Struggle*. Bombay: Padma Publications Ltd., 1946.
Nehru, Jawaharlal. *A Bunch of Old Letters*. London: Asia Publishing House, 1969.
——— *The Discovery of India*. Bombay: Asia Publishing House, 1964.
Nelson, William H. *The American Tory*. Oxford: Clarendon Press, 1961.
Niblett, R. H. *The Congress Rebellion in Azamgarh, August–September 1942*. Allaha-
    bad: Superintendent, Printing and Stationery, Uttar Pradesh, 1957.
Pal, Bipin Chandra. *Memories of My Life and Times*, vol. I. Calcutta: Modern Book
    Agency, 1932. Vol. II. Calcutta: Yugayatri Prakashak, 1951.
Parikh, Narhari D. *Sardar Vallabhbhai Patel*. 2 vols. Ahmedabad: Navajivan Pub-
    lishing House, 1953.
Polak, Millie Graham. *Mr. Gandhi: The Man*. Bombay: Vora & Co., 1949.
Prasad, Amba. *The Indian Revolt of 1942*. Delhi: S. Chand, 1958.
Pyarelal. *Mahatma Gandhi—The Last Phase*. 2 vols. Ahmedabad: Navajivan Pub-
    lishing House, 1965.
Ramusack, Barbara. "Indian Princes as Imperial Politicians, 1914–1939," unpub.
    Ph.D. diss., University of Michigan, 1969.

Rao, M. B., ed. *The Mahatma, A Marxist Symposium.* Bombay: People's Publishing House, 1969.

Richey, J. A., ed. *Selections from Educational Records, Part II, 1840–1859.* Calcutta: Bureau of Education, India, 1922.

Rudolph, Lloyd I. and Susanne H. *The Modernity of Tradition.* Chicago: University of Chicago Press, 1967.

Ruskin, John. *Unto This Last,* in *The Works of John Ruskin,* vol. XVIII. London: George Allen, 1905.

Sahai, Govind. *42 Rebellion.* Delhi: Rajkamal Publications, 1947.

Sayeed, Khalid bin. *The Political System of Pakistan.* Boston: Houghton Mifflin, 1967.

Schram, Stuart. *Mao Tse-Tung.* New York: Simon & Schuster, 1966.

Schwartz, Benjamin. *In Search of Wealth and Power.* New York: Harper & Row, 1969.

Seshachari, C. *Gandhi and the American Scene.* Bombay: Nachiketa Publications, 1969.

Seth, Harilal. *Gandhi in Arms.* Lahore: Hero Publications, 1943.

Singh, Darbara. *Indian Struggle 1942.* Lahore: Hero Publications, 1946.

Sitaramayya, Pattabhi. *The History of the Indian National Congress.* 2 vols. Bombay: Padma Publications, 1947.

Slade, Madeleine ("Mirabehn"). *The Spirit's Pilgrimage.* London: Longmans, 1960.

Tagore, Rabindranath. *Nationalism.* New York: Macmillan, 1917.

Taub, Richard. *Bureaucrats Under Stress.* Calcutta: Firma K. L. Mukhopadhyay, 1969.

Tendulkar, D. G. *Abdul Ghaffar Khan.* Bombay: Popular Prakashan, 1967.

———— *Mahatma,* vol. VI: *1940–45.* New Delhi: The Publications Division, Ministry of Information and Broadcasting, 1962.

Toye, Hugh. *Subhash Chandra Bose.* Bombay: Jaico Publishing House, 1966.

Tucker, Robert C. "The Theory of Charismatic Leadership," *Daedalus,* Summer 1968.

Ward, R., and D. Rustow. *Political Modernization in Japan and Turkey.* Princeton: Princeton University Press, 1964.

Weber, Max. *The Theory of Social and Economic Organization,* trans. A. M. Henderson and Talcott Parsons. New York: Free Press, 1965.

Wilcox, Wayne. *Pakistan: The Consolidation of a Nation.* New York: Columbia University Press, 1966.

Wolpert, Stanley. *Morley and India, 1906–1910.* Berkeley: University of California Press, 1967.

Woodruff, Philip. *The Men Who Ruled India,* vol. I: *The Founders,* vol. II: *The Guardians.* London: Jonathan Cape, 1955.

Wilkinson, Rupert. *Gentlemanly Power: British Leadership and the Public School Tradition.* Oxford: Oxford University Press, 1964.

Yajnik, Indulal. *Gandhi as I Know Him.* Bombay: G. G. Bhat, no date.

Notes

1. INTRODUCTION

1. Alexis de Tocqueville, *The Old Regime and the French Revolution*, trans. Stuart Gilbert (New York: Anchor, 1955).

2. See Samuel P. Huntington, *Political Order in Changing Societies* (New Haven: Yale University Press, 1968) and Seymour Martin Lipset, *The First New Nation* (Garden City, N.Y.: Doubleday, 1967). In his essay, "Revolution and Counterrevolution" (chapter 2 of his book of the same title; New York: Basic Books, 1968), Lipset makes a comparison of the effect of the revolution in the United States with the effect of the counterrevolutionary tradition in Canada, but does not extend it, as might well be done, into a comparison of the American-Canadian experience with one revolution with the experience of other societies with other revolutions.

2. THE IMPERIALIST'S DILEMMA: UNEQUAL PARTNERS

1. See Lloyd I. and Susanne H. Rudolph, *The Modernity of Tradition* (Chicago: University of Chicago Press, 1967), part III.

2. Chinua Achebe, *No Longer at Ease* (London: Heinemann, 1966), p. 75.

3. J. A. Richey, ed., *Selections from Educational Records, Part II, 1840–1859* (Calcutta: Bureau of Education, India, 1922), pp. 385, 375, 374, 375.

4. Bipan Chandra, *The Rise and Growth of Economic Nationalism in India* (New Delhi: People's Publishing House, 1966).

5. For a study of the effects of the exploitative development of Indonesia see Clifford Geertz, *Agricultural Involution* (Berkeley: University of California Press, 1963).

6. Erik Barnouw and S. Krishnaswamy, *Indian Film* (New York: Columbia University Press, 1963), p. 11.

3. THE IMPERIALIST'S DILEMMA: THE LIMITS OF LIBERALIZATION

1. Samuel H. Beer, *Modern British Politics* (London: Faber & Faber, 1965).

2. See Samuel P. Huntington, *Political Order in Changing Societies* (New Haven: Yale University Press, 1968), chap. 1, for a different approach.

3. Bankim Chandra Chatterjee, *Abbey of Bliss (Ananda Math)*, trans. Nares Chandra Sen-Gupta (Calcutta: P. M. Neggi, no date); Charles Baron de Montesquieu, *Persian Letters*, trans. J. Robert Loy (New York: Meridian, 1961).

4. Pattabhi Sitaramayya, *History of the Indian National Congress*, vol. I, *1885–1935* (Bombay: Padma Publications, 1947), p. 34.

5. E. S. Montagu, *An Indian Diary* (London: William Heinemann, 1930), pp. 288, 388, 363.

6. Richard Danzig, "The Announcement of August 20th, 1917," *Journal of Asian Studies*, November 1968, p. 20.

7. *Ibid.*, p. 35.

8. Stanley Wolpert, *Morley and India, 1906–1910* (Berkeley: University of California Press, 1967), p. 195.

9. Danzig, "Announcement of August 20th, 1917," p. 25.

10. Montagu, *An Indian Diary*, p. 55.

11. Wolpert, *Morley and India*, p. 220. Morley was referring to the question of liquidating India's profitable opium trade with China.

12. The words are those of the then Viceroy Lord Hardinge of Penshurst in *My Indian Years, 1910–1916* (London: John Murray, 1948), p. 51.

13. Montagu, *An Indian Diary*, p. 174.

14. *Ibid.*, p. 243.

15. Wolpert, *Morley and India*, p. 139.

16. Commonwealth Relations Office Library, Mss. Eur E 264/2, quoted in Barbara Ramusack, "Indian Princes as Imperial Politicians 1914—1939," unpub. Ph.D. diss., University of Michigan, 1969, p. 86.

17. Montagu, *An Indian Diary*, p. 5.

18. Nicholas Mansergh, ed., *The Transfer of Power, 1942–7* (London: Her Majesty's Stationery Office, 1971), II, 837.

19. Hardinge, *My Indian Years*, pp. 10–11.

20. *Ibid.*, p. 122.

21. Montagu, *An Indian Diary*, p. 16.

22. Mansergh, ed., *Transfer of Power*, II, 299.

23. See Richard Taub, *Bureaucrats Under Stress* (Calcutta: Firma K. L. Mukhopadhyay, 1969), chap. 11.

24. Rupert Wilkinson, *Gentlemanly Power: British Leadership and the Public School Tradition* (Oxford: Oxford University Press, 1964).

25. John Whitney Hall, "The Nature of Traditional Society: Japan," in R. Ward and D. Rustow, *Political Modernization in Japan and Turkey* (Princeton: Princeton University Press, 1964), p. 32.

26. Philip Woodruff, *The Men Who Ruled India*, vol. II, *The Guardians* (London: Jonathan Cape, 1955).

4. THE NATIONALIST'S DILEMMA: COPING WITH THE WEST

1. See, for example, Iltudus Prichard, *The Chronicles of Budgepore* (London: W. H. Allen, 1893).

2. See Robert Frykenberg, *Guntur District 1788–1848* (Oxford: Oxford University Press, 1965).

3. Lutfullah, *Autobiography* (London: Smith, Elder, 1857), p. 375.

4. See, for example, Peter Lawrence, *Road Belong Cargo* (New York: Humanities Press, 1964), and O. Mannoni, *Prospero and Caliban* (New York: Praeger, 1956).

5. Lal Behari Dey, *Recollections of Alexander Duff and of the Mission College Which He Founded at Calcutta* (London, 1878), quoted in Bruce McCully, *English Education and the Origins of Indian Nationalism* (Gloucester, Mass.: Peter Smith, 1966), p. 44.

6. See K. P. S. Menon, *Many Worlds* (London: Oxford University Press, 1965).
7. Subhas Chandra Bose, *An Indian Pilgrim* (Bombay: Asia Publishing House, 1965), pp. 82–83, 99. The experience of youthful Indians coping with Westernization has been richly documented. Indian leaders customarily wrote their autobiographies *before* assuming public office, thereby supplying a considerable amount of material concerning their formative years. Long jail terms are a natural stimulus to autobiography. Materials on which to base other forms of literary exercise are difficult to come by, and the very fact of incarceration stimulates interest in producing an apologia, to satisfy oneself as well as to communicate with one's followers and one's captors.
8. Narhari D. Parikh, *Sardar Vallabhbhai Patel* (Ahmedabad: Navajivan Publishing House, 1953), I, 22.
9. Bipin Chandra Pal, *Memories of My Life and Times*, vol. I (Calcutta: Modern Book Agency, 1932), 200; vol. II (Calcutta: Yugayatri Prakashak, 1951).
10. Mohandas K. Gandhi, *An Autobiography* (Ahmedabad: Navajivan Publishing House, 1958), pp. 7 ff.
11. Pal, *Memories of My Life and Times*, I, 196.
12. *Ibid.*, I, 394 ff.
13. Gandhi, *An Autobiography*, pp. 63–66.
14. Pal, *Memories of My Life and Times*, I, 149.
15. Surendranath Banerjea, *A Nation in the Making* (Bombay: Oxford University Press, 1963), pp. 30–31.
16. See Menon, *Many Worlds*, p. 68.
17. See David Kopf, *British Orientalism and the Bengal Renaissance: The Dynamics of Indian Modernization, 1773–1835* (Berkeley: University of California Press, 1969).
18. Raden Adjeng Kartini, *Letters of a Javanese Princess*, trans. Agnes Louise Symmers (New York: Alfred A. Knopf, 1920), pp. 29, 39, 43–44.
19. See Bipan Chandra, *The Rise and Growth of Economic Nationalism in India* (New Delhi: People's Publishing House, 1966).
20. Alan Campbell-Johnson, *Mission with Mountbatten* (London: Robert Hale, 1951), p. 69.
21. Eugene Irschick, *Politics and Social Conflict in South India: The Non-Brahman Movement and Tamil Separatism* (Berkeley: University of California Press, 1969), p. 106.
22. Hector Bolitho, *Jinnah, Creator of Pakistan* (Karachi: Oxford University Press, 1969), pp. 49–50.
23. William H. Grier and Price M. Cobbs, *Black Rage* (New York: Basic Books, 1968).
24. Erik Erikson, *Young Man Luther* (New York: W. W. Norton, 1962); Bose, *An Indian Pilgrim*, chap. 7.
25. *Ibid.*, pp. 60 ff.
26. For a full account of the various types of cargo cults see Peter Lawrence, *Road Belong Cargo* (New York: Humanities Press, 1964).
27. See Stephen Fuchs, *Rebellious Prophets* (Bombay: Asia Publishing House, 1965).
28. J. C. Cheng, *Chinese Sources for the Taiping Rebellion, 1850–1864* (Hong Kong: Hong Kong University Press, 1963), p. 77. See also Eugene Powers Boardman, *Christian Influence Upon the Ideology of the Taiping Rebellion, 1851–1864* (Madison, Wis.: University of Wisconsin Press, 1952) and Franz Michael, *The Taiping Rebellion*, vol. I (Seattle: University of Washington Press, 1966).
29. Bose, *An Indian Pilgrim*, pp. 54–55.
30. Har Bilas Sarda, *Life of Dayanand Saraswati* (Ajmer: P. Bhagwan Swarup, 1946), pp. 5, 6, 12, 17.

5. THE REVOLUTIONARY SOLUTION

1. See Harry Eckstein, "On the Etiology of Internal Wars," *History and Theory*, 4 (1965), 133–163. See also Harry Eckstein, ed., *Internal War* (New York: Free Press of Glencoe, 1964).

2. John Adams to Hezekiah Niles, 1818, quoted in Bernard Bailyn, *The Ideological Origins of the American Revolution* (Cambridge, Mass.: Harvard University Press, 1967), p. 160.

3. Samuel P. Huntington, *Political Order in Changing Societies* (New Haven, Conn.: Yale University Press, 1968), pp. 266 ff.

4. John Stuart Mill, *Autobiography* (New York: New American Library, 1964), pp. 112, 113.

5. Huntington, *Political Order*, p. 125.

6. *Ibid.*, p. 115.

7. William H. Nelson, *The American Tory* (Oxford: Clarendon Press, 1961), p. 90.

8. *Ibid.*, pp. 87–88.

9. See Bernard Bailyn, *The Origins of American Politics* (New York: Alfred A. Knopf, 1968).

10. See Louis Hartz, *The Liberal Tradition in America* (New York: Harcourt Brace, 1955).

11. The argument made here about the American revolutionaries parallels to some extent the argument Perry Miller has made regarding the first founding act of will by the Puritan colonists. Miller demonstrates that the Puritan settlers of Massachusetts also failed to perceive the nature, extent, and effect of their own radical act. They were "Non-separating Congregationalists" who separated themselves by 3,000 miles from the Church of England in order to do as they wished while still considering themselves not separated from the Church of England. Like the revolutionaries, they saw their first task as an old one, to create a body which would be a legitimate component of the Church of England, although altogether different. They failed to perceive the true requirements of the new society they had founded and just how new that society was. The result was the creation of an anomalous situation—orthodoxy in Massachusetts—which could not last, which bore no relation to practice or necessity, but which was nonetheless eminently logical. It was no less revolutionary because it was apparently and in intention traditional. See Perry Miller, *Orthodoxy in Massachusetts, 1630–1650* (Boston: Beacon Press, 1959).

12. For a discussion of the relevance of caste to democratic functioning see Lloyd I. and Susanne H. Rudolph, *The Modernity of Tradition* (Chicago: University of Chicago Press, 1967), part I.

13. Quoted in Ram Gopal, *Lokamanya Tilak* (Bombay: Asia Publishing House, 1956), p. 145.

14. See Bailyn, *The Origins of American Politics*, and his *The Ideological Background of the American Revolution*.

15. Dhananjay Keer, *Veer Savarkar* (Bombay: Popular Prakashan, 1966), p. 26.

16. *Ibid.*, pp. 35, 67.

17. Rabindranath Tagore, *Nationalism* (New York: Macmillan, 1917), pp. 16, 17, 60, 61.

18. William Blake, *The Portable Blake* (New York: Viking Press, 1955), pp. 12, 411, 463, 566.

19. Frederick Engels, *The Peasant War in Germany* (Moscow: Foreign Language Publishing House, 1956), pp. 72, 18.

20. See Barrington Moore, Jr., *Social Origins of Dictatorship and Democracy* (Boston: Beacon Press, 1966). See also his "Revolution in America?" *New York Review of Books*, 12 (January 30, 1969), 6–12.

21. See Louis Hartz, *The Founding of New Societies* (New York: Harcourt, Brace and World, 1964), and Seymour Martin Lipset, *Revolution and Counterrevolution* (New York: Basic Books, 1968).

22. See Wayne Wilcox, *Pakistan: The Consolidation of a Nation* (New York: Columbia University Press, 1966) for an account of Pakistan's belated attack on the problem of the princely states.

23. Quoted in Melvin Richter, "Tocqueville's Contribution to the Theory of Revolution," in Carl J. Friedrich, ed., *Revolution* (New York: Atherton Press, 1966), 111.

24. M.K. Gandhi, *Satyagraha in South Africa* (Ahmedabad: Navajivan Publishing House, 1961), p. 92.

6. GANDHI AS A REVOLUTIONARY LEADER

1. B. R. Nanda, *Mahatma Gandhi* (London: George Allen & Unwin, 1959), p. 199.

2. Stuart Schram, *Mao Tse-Tung* (New York: Simon & Schuster, 1966), pp. 30–31.

3. Mohandas K. Gandhi, *An Autobiography, The Story of My Experiments with Truth* (Boston: Beacon Press, 1959), pp. 82–83.

4. *Ibid.*, p. 68.

5. *Ibid.*, p. 79.

6. See Benjamin Schwartz, *In Search of Wealth and Power: Yen Fu and the West* (New York: Harper & Row, 1969); and the Introduction by Louis Hartz, who explores many of the consequences of cultural borrowing outlined here. A contemporary example of this phenomenon is the popularity of Ayn Rand in underdeveloped countries as a "typical" spokesman of capitalism. Historical examples of borrowing would include John Calvin borrowed by Scotland, John Locke by the United States, Karl Marx by China and Russia—and other countries—and Rousseau, like Calvin a Genevan, by France.

7. Gandhi, *An Autobiography*, pp. 298–299.

8. John Ruskin, *Unto This Last*, in *The Works of John Ruskin* (London: George Allen, 1905), XVIII, 20–21. Gandhi was also influenced by two other Western eccentrics—Tolstoy and Thoreau.

9. N. K. Bose, ed., *Selections from Gandhi* (Ahmedabad: Navajivan Publishing House, 1968), p. 64.

10. *Ibid.*, p. 66.

11. Story related by Gandhi's interrogator, Ronald Duncan, New Delhi, February 2, 1970.

12. N. T. Katagade, "Pundalik," in D. D. Karve, *The New Brahmans* (Berkeley: University of California Press, 1963), pp. 268–273.

13. Max Weber, *The Theory of Social and Economic Organization*, trans. A. M. Henderson and Talcott Parsons (New York: Free Press, 1965), p. 363.

14. Katagade, "Pundalik," pp. 248–249.

15. D. G. Tendulkar, *Mahatma* (New Delhi: Publication Division, Ministry of Information and Broadcasting, Government of India, 1962), VI, 128; from the *Harijan*, July 26, 1942; and Indulal Yajnik, *Gandhi as I Know Him* (Bombay: G. G. Bhat, no date), p. 52.

16. Robert C. Tucker, "The Theory of Charismatic Leadership," *Daedalus*, Summer 1968, p. 746.

17. Gandhi, *To the Students* (Ahmedabad: Navajivan Publishing House, 1965), p. 19.

18. Gandhi, *Satyagraha in South Africa* (Ahmedabad: Navajivan Publishing House, 1968), p. 64.

19. Yajnik, *Gandhi*, p. 138.

20. Gandhi, *Satyagraha in South Africa*, pp. 50–52.

21. National Archives of India (N.A.I.): Home File No. 3/25/40 Poll. (I), New Delhi.

22. Henry Kissinger, "The White Revolutionary: Reflections on Bismarck," *Daedalus*, Summer 1968, pp. 888–889.

23. N.A.I.: Home File No. 3/33/43 Poll. (I), telegram No. 2427, dated March 27, 1943.

24. Erik Erikson, *Gandhi's Truth* (New York: W. W. Norton, 1969), p. 368.

25. Gandhi, *Gandhiji's Correspondence with the Government, 1942–44* (Ahmedabad: Navajivan Publishing House, 1957), p. 151.

26. Bose, ed., *Selections*, p. 123.

27. *Ibid.*, p. 177.

28. See Erikson, *Gandhi's Truth*. Gandhi first tackled Marx's *Das Kapital* while imprisoned at the age of seventy-four. He encountered Freud even later in life. At the age of seventy-seven he wrote in a note to his secretary, N. K. Bose, "What is Freudian philosophy? I have not read any writing of his. One friend himself a Professor and follower of Freud, discussed his writings for a brief moment. You are the second." Letter dated March 19, 1947, in N. K. Bose, *My Days with Gandhi* (Calcutta: Nishana, 1953).

29. Nanda, *Mahatma Gandhi*, p. 293.

30. Gandhi, *Gandhiji's Correspondence*, p. 43.

31. Millie Polak, *Mr. Gandhi: The Man* (Bombay: Vora & Co., 1949), p. 90.

32. Gandhi, *Satyagraha in South Africa*, p. 266.

33. Bose, *My Days with Gandhi*, p. 139.

34. *Ibid.*, p. 177.

35. Quoted in Lloyd and Susanne H. Rudolph, *The Modernity of Tradition* (Chicago: University of Chicago Press, 1967), p. 245. Gandhi's attitude toward his family and the relation of this to his public career are explored at length by the Rudolphs in *The Modernity of Tradition*, as well as by Erikson in *Gandhi's Truth*. For an elaboration of the argument that Gandhi acted with violence in repressing natural desires, see Erikson, part III, chap. 1. A *sadhu* is an ascetic.

36. Bose, *My Days with Gandhi*, p. 181.

37. Hugh Toye, *Subhash Chandra Bose* (Bombay: Jaico Publishing House, 1959), p. 25.

38. See Narhari Parikh, *Sardar Vallabhbhai Patel* (Ahmedabad: Navajivan Publishing House, 1953), vol. 1.

39. Yajnik, *Gandhi*, p. 9.

40. Interview, Indulal Yajnik, December 22, 1969.

7. QUIT INDIA: OFFICIAL VIOLENCE

1. Marquess of Linlithgow, *Speeches and Statements* (New Delhi: Bureau of Public Information, Government of India, 1945), pp. 199–200.

2. Sir Arthur Lothian, *Kingdoms of Yesterday* (London: John Murray, 1951), p. 107.

3. *India Unreconciled* (New Delhi: The Hindustan Times, 1944), p. 43.

4. Nicholas Mansergh, ed., *The Transfer of Power, 1942–7* (London: Her Majesty's Stationery Office, 1971), II, 156, 533, 830–831.

5. Government of India, *Gazette of India Extraordinary* (New Delhi), August 8, 1942.

6. Mansergh, ed., *Transfer of Power*, II, 274, 876, 213.

7. *Ibid.*, II, 329.

8. *Ibid.*, II, 630.

9. *Ibid.*, II, 403.

10. Hector Bolitho, *Jinnah, Creator of Pakistan* (Karachi: Oxford University Press, 1969), p. 96.

11. Significantly, this prediction was borne out following the partition. When Jinnah finally succeeded in establishing Pakistan he became her governor-general and governed in a viceregal manner. Nehru became prime minister of India, helping to establish Indian politics on the domestic English model of a ceremonial head of state with effective power lodged in a parliamentary prime minister. Jinnah helped pattern Pakistan's political development on the model of imperial British India, with an autocratic chief executive standing at the head of an administrative bureaucracy. See Khalid bin Sayeed, *The Political System of Pakistan* (Boston: Houghton Mifflin, 1967).

12. Mansergh, ed., *Transfer of Power*, II, 257, 913, 810.

13. *Ibid.*, II, 11.

14. *Ibid.*, II, 350. Letter, Amery to Linlithgow, 7 July 1942.

15. *Ibid.*, II, 210, 124.

16. *Ibid.*, II, 139.

17. *Ibid.*, II, 455. Amery's mention of "cat-and-mouse" tactics was made with reference to the proposal to release Gandhi during his fast and to rearrest him as soon as he stopped fasting.

18. *Ibid.*, II, 427.

19. *Ibid.*, II, 566.

20. *Ibid.*, II, 661.

21. *Ibid.*, II, 579, 870, 854.

22. *Ibid.*, II, 808, 752.

23. *India Unreconciled*, p. 501.

24. Mansergh, ed., *Transfer of Power*, II, 190, 920.

25. *Ibid.*, II, 813.

26. *Ibid.*, II, 261, 547–548; letters, Linlithgow to Amery.

27. *Ibid.*, II, 547, 873.

28. *Ibid.*, II, 112.

29. National Archives of India (N.A.I.): Home File No. 3/16/40 Poll. (I).

30. N.A.I.: Home File No. 3/13/40 Poll. (I), letter from Maxwell to the Viceroy's Private Secretary, dated April 25, 1940.

31. N.A.I.: Home File No. 6/13/40 Poll. (I), labeled "Most Secret (Keep in Almirah)."

32. N.A.I.: Home File No. 3/15/42 Poll. (I).

33. N.A.I.: Home File No. 6/8/40 Poll. (I).

34. N.A.I.: Home File No. 13/4/40 Poll. (I), letter from Hallett to Maxwell, dated October 10, 1940.

35. *Ibid.*, letter from Maxwell to Hallett, dated November 4, 1940.

36. N.A.I.: Home File No. 3/31/40 Poll. (I), "Extract from Secret Report from H.E. the Governor of U.P. to H.E. the Viceroy, No. U.P. 92, dated April 23, 1941."

37. N.A.I.: Home File No. 3/13/40 Poll. (I).
38. *Ibid.*
39. N.A.I.: Home File No. 3/31/40 Poll. (I), "Extract . . . April 23, 1941."
40. N.A.I.: Home File No. 3/13/40 Poll. (I), Civil disabilities, however, were ultimately not included in the Revolutionary Movement Ordinance.
41. *Ibid.*, Appendix V.
42. Mansergh, ed., *Transfer of Power*, II, 443.
43. *Ibid.*, II, 213.
44. *Ibid.*, II, 380–381.
45. *Ibid.*, II, 233–234.
46. N.A.I.: Home File No. 3/13/40 Poll. (I).
47. Linlithgow, *Speeches and Statements*, p. 244.
48. N.A.I.: Home File No. 74/340 Poll. (I).
49. *Ibid.*
50. *Ibid. Jo hukms* are roughly equivalent to what in English are called "Yes-men."
51. N.A.I.: Home File No. 18/5/42 Poll. (I), "Fortnightly Report from the Government of Bihar for the Second Half of May, 1942"; Home File No. 18/7/42 Poll. (I), "Fortnightly Report from the Government of Bihar for the Second Half of July, 1942."
52. N.A.I.: Home File No. 3/31/40, dated February 24, 1941.
53. N.A.I.: Home File No. 3/16/40, telegrams dated September 18, 1940, September 13, 1940, September 18, 1940, September 17, 1940, September 18, 1940, September 13, 1940.
54. *Ibid.*, Appendix VII to Notes.
55. *Ibid.*, telegram dated September 15, 1940.
56. *Ibid.*, comment by Linlithgow, dated October 1, 1940.
57. Government of India, *History of the Civil Disobedience Movement, 1940–41*, a "Strictly Secret" document printed for official distribution.
58. N.A.I.: Home File No. 3/31/40 Poll. (I).
59. N.A.I.: Home File No. 3/16/40 Poll. (I).
60. Government of India, *History*.
61. N.A.I.: Home File No. 3/16/40 Poll. (I).
62. Government of India, *History*.
63. N.A.I.: Home File No. 6/13/40 Poll. (I), letter dated August 12, 1940; N.A.I.: Home File No. 3/25/40, letter dated January 29, 1941, from the Government of India to all Chief Secretaries.
64. N.A.I.: Home File No. 3/31/40 Poll. (I), statement of Sir Reginald Maxwell.
65. Government of India, *History*.
66. *Ibid.*
67. Mansergh, ed., *Transfer of Power*, II, 196, 376; III, 457.
68. *Ibid.*, II, 135, 213.
69. *Ibid.*, II, 455.
70. *Ibid.*, II, 596, 455.
71. *Ibid.*, II, 683.
72. *Ibid.*, II, 770.
73. N.A.I.: Home File No. 3/15/42 Poll. (I).
74. *Ibid.*
75. N.A.I.: Home File No. 25/1/42 Poll. (I).
76. N.A.I.: Home File No. 3/42/42 Poll. (I), letter from Hallett to Maxwell, dated October 21, 1942.
77. R. H. Niblett, *The Congress Rebellion in Azamgarh* (Allahabad: Superintendent, Printing and Stationery, 1957), pp. 49–50, 44, 47.

78. N.A.I.: Home File No. 3/42/42 Poll. (I), letter from the Government of Bombay to the Home Department, Government of India, dated January 16, 1943.

79. *Ibid*.

8. QUIT INDIA: GANDHI'S ANSWER

1. Louis Fischer, *A Week with Gandhi* (London: George Allen & Unwin, 1943), p. 33.

2. Mohandas K. Gandhi, *Satyagraha in South Africa* (Ahmedabad: Navajivan Publishing House, 1961), p. 72.

3. *Ibid.*, p. 72.

4. For an account of Gandhi's full career see B. R. Nanda, *Mahatma Gandhi* (London: George Allen & Unwin, 1959).

5. National Archives of India (N.A.I.): Home File No. 43/96/41 Poll. (I).

6. Nehru to Gandhi, January 24, 1940, and February 4, 1940, Nehru Papers, Nehru Memorial Museum, New Delhi.

7. D. G. Tendulkar, *Mahatma* (New Delhi: Publications Division, Ministry of Information and Broadcasting, Government of India, 1962), VI, 60.

8. N.A.I.: Home File No. 3/18/40 Poll. (I), "Cutting from the Hindustan Times," dated October 16, 1940.

9. N.A.I.: Home File No. 3/18/40 Poll. (I).

10. Gandhi to Nehru, December 5, 1941, Nehru Papers.

11. Horace Alexander, *Gandhi Through Western Eyes* (Bombay: Asia Publishing House, 1969), pp. 204–206.

12. N.A.I.: Home File No. 43/96/41 Poll. (I).

13. Tendulkar, *Mahatma*, VI, 12.

14. Hallett to Linlithgow, February 17, 1942, translation of report of Nehru's speech, Linlithgow Papers, vol. 105, India Office Library.

15. *Harijan*, July 12, 1942.

16. *Ibid*.

17. N.A.I.: Home File No. 18/4/42 Poll. (I), "Fortnightly Report from the Government of Bihar for the First Half of April 1942."

18. *Ibid*.

19. N.A.I.: Home File No. 18/5/42 Poll. (I), "Fortnightly Report from the Government of Assam for the First Half of May 1942."

20. *Ibid.*, "Fortnightly Report from the Government of Bihar for the First Half of May 1942."

21. N.A.I.; Home File No. 18/4/42 Poll. (I), "Fortnightly Report from the Government of Bihar for the First Half of April 1942"; "Fortnightly Report from the Government of Bihar for the Second Half of April 1942."

22. N.A.I.: Home File No. 3/19/43 Poll. (I), "A.I.C.C. News Bulletin No. 18," dated December 25, 1942.

23. Tendulkar, *Mahatma*, VI, 79.

24. File No. B-126, "Troubles and Difficulties in the land route from Burma to Chittagong via Prome and Akyab," Nehru Papers.

25. *Harijan*, July 12, 1942.

26. N.A.I.: Home File No. 18/4/42 Poll. (I), "Fortnightly Report from the Government of Madras for the First Half of April 1942."

27. *Ibid*.

28. *Harijan*, July 5, 1942; the words of a questioner.

29. *Ibid.*., August 2, 1942.

30. Tendulkar, *Mahatma*, VI, 97.
31. *Harijan*, May 17, 1942.
32. See Madeleine Slade ("Mirabehn"), *The Spirit's Pilgrimage* (London: Longmans, 1960).
33. Tendulkar, *Mahatma*, VI, 69
34. *Ibid.*, p. 86.
35. *Ibid.*, p. 76.
36. *Ibid.*, pp. 94, 106, 100, 87.
37. Mahadev Desai, "British and American Nazism," *Harijan*, February 15, 1942.
38. Mahadev Desai, "Evidently a Long War," *Harijan*, March 22, 1942.
39. M. K. Gandhi, *Hind Swararj* in *The Selected Works of Mahatma Gandhi*, ed. Shriman Narayan (Ahmedabad: Navajivan Publishing House, 1968), vol. IV.
40. Quoted by Manmathnath Gupta in "Gandhi and the Revolutionaries During 1925," in M. B. Rao, ed., *The Mahatma, A Marxist Symposium* (Bombay: People's Publishing House, 1969), p. 98.
41. *Ibid.*, p. 104.
42. Interview, Radhe Shyam Sharma, December 11, 1969.
42. Government of India, *History of the Civil Disobedience Movement, 1940–41*, a "Strictly Secret" document printed for official distribution.
44. *Harijan*, April 5, 1942.
45. *Harijan*, March 1, 1942.
46. M. K. Gandhi, *Gandhiji's Correspondence with the Government, 1942–44* (Ahmedabad: Navajivan Publishing House, 1957), p. 141.
47. N.A.I.: Home File No. 3/16/40 Poll. (I), "Copy of a Telegram from Gandhi to Carl Heath, London, dated the 26th August, 1940"; "Copy of a Telegram from Gandhi, Wardha, to Carl Heath, Friends House, Euston Road, London, dated the 6th September 1940"; "The Associated Press of India (Inland News Telegram), Bombay, September 15, 1940."
48. Tendulkar, *Mahatma*, VI, 167, 161.
49. Gupta, "Gandhi and the Revolutionaries," pp. 101–102.
50. N. K. Bose, ed., *Selections from Gandhi* (Ahmedabad: Navajivan Publishing House, 1968), pp. 64–65, from *Young India*, March 17, 1927.
51. Tendulkar, *Mahatma*, VI, 92.
52. M. K. Gandhi, *Bapu's Letters to Mira* (Ahmedabad: Navajivan Publishing House, 1959), p. 336.
53. Gandhi, *Gandhiji's Correspondence*, p. 140.
54. *Harijan*, July 19, 1942.
55. *Ibid.*, July 5, 1942.
56. *Ibid.*, August 9, 1942.
57. Tendulkar, *Mahatma*, VI, 125.
58. *Harijan*, July 19, 1942; July 5, 1942.
59. Nicholas Mansergh, ed., *The Transfer of Power, 1942–7* (London: Her Majesty's Stationery Office, 1971), III, 419, 421.
60. *Harijan*, June 14, 1942.
61. *Ibid.*, May 17, 1942.
62. N.A.I.: Home File No. 18/7/42 Poll. (I), "Fortnightly Report from the Government of Bihar for the Second Half of July 1942."
63. Interviews, Viswanath Sharma and Ananda Krishna, December 11, 1969.
64. Gupta, "Gandhi and the Revolutionaries," p. 93.
65. *Ibid.*, p. 102.
66. I Kings 3: 23–27.

67. *Harijan*, June 21, 1942.

68. Earl Mountbatten, *Time Only to Look Forward* (London: Nicholas Kaye, 1949).

69. *Harijan*, July 19, 1942.

70. N. K. Bose, *My Days with Gandhi* (Calcutta: Nishana, 1953), p. 248.

71. Tendulkar, *Mahatma*, VI, 74–75.

72. *Harijan*, May 24, 1942.

73. Gandhi to Bose, March 30, 1939, Nehru Papers; Gandhi to Bose, April 10, 1939, Rajendra Prasad Papers, New Delhi.

74. Tendulkar, *Mahatma*, VI, 41.

75. *Ibid.* p. 74.

76. Fischer, *A Week with Gandhi*, p. 92.

77. *Harijan*, May 17, 1942.

78. Tendulkar, *Mahatma*, VI, 176.

79. *Ibid.*, p. 142.

80. Fischer, *A Week with Gandhi*, pp. 90–91.

81. *Ibid.*, pp. 92–93.

82. *Ibid.*, p. 104.

83. Tendulkar, *Mahatma*, VI, 90, 99.

84. *Harijan*, May 17, 1942.

85. Tendulkar, *Mahatma*, VI, 166, 161, 163, 140.

86. *Ibid.*, p. 130.

87. *Harijan*, July 26, 1942; August 2, 1942; May 31, 1942.

9. SPONTANEOUS REVOLUTION: AUGUST 1942

1. The code word "Pantaloon" was recalled by a former member of the I.C.S. posted in Bombay. According to the "Report on the Civil Disturbances in Bihar, 1942" (Library, Political and Secret Department, F. 204 India Office Library) the Bihar government used the code word "Adolf" to order the arrest of congressmen on the more important "A" list and "Benito" to order the arrest of those on the less significant "B" list.

2. Government of India, *Congress Responsibility for the Disturbances, 1942–43* (New Delhi: Government of India Press, 1943), p. 21; National Archives of India (N.A.I.): Home File No. 18/8/42 Poll. (I), "Fortnightly Report from the Government of U.P. for the Second Half of August, 1942."

3. N.A.I.: Home File No. 3/21/42 Poll. (I).

4. D. G. Tendulkar, *Mahatma* (New Delhi: The Publications Division, Ministry of Information and Broadcasting, Government of India, 1962), VI, 151, 166, 161.

5. *Harijan*, July 26, 1942.

6. Interview, Jugal Kishore, March 20, 1970. See also Maulana Abul Kalam Azad, *India Wins Freedom* (Bombay: Orient Longmans, 1959), p. 83.

7. Nicholas Mansergh, ed., *The Transfer of Power, 1942–7* (London: Her Majesty's Stationery Office, 1971), II, 557–558. Interviews, Sadiq Ali, March 16, 1970, Jugal Kishore, March 20, 1970, Sucheta Kripalani, January 21, 1970. For the text of the twelve-point program, see *August 9th, 25th Anniversary* (New Delhi: All-India Congress Committee, 1967).

8. Pyarelal, *Mahatma Gandhi, The Last Phase* (Ahmedabad: Navajivan Publishing House, 1956), I, book one, 337–338, n. 1.

9. N.A.I.: Home File No. 3/19/43 Poll. (I), "All-India Congress Committee Instruction No. 7, To Peasants, Multiplied by the Council of Action. Bengal P.C.C., 13/9/42."

10. *Ibid.*, "All-India Congress Committee, Instruction No. 12, To the Peasants of India."

11. *Ibid.*, "Circular issued by the Organiser, War Council, U.P. Congress."

12. File No. G-26, 1942, "Appeal No. 4, To the Businessmen," All-India Congress Committee Papers, Nehru Memorial Museum, New Delhi.

13. *Ibid.*, "A.I.C.C. Appeal to Students No. 3."

14. N.A.I.: Home File No. 3/19/43 Poll. (I), "Vandemataram, Circular No. 8, Bihar"; "All-India Congress Committee, Instruction No. 12, To the Peasants of India."

15. Mansergh, ed., *Transfer of Power*, II, 787–788, 777, 789, 795.

16. N.A.I.: Home File Nos. 18/8/42 Poll. (I)—18/11/42 Poll. (I), "Fortnightly Reports from the Government of Bihar," August–November 1942; N.A.I.: Home File No. 3/30/42 Poll. (I), "Provincial Summary of Events Connected with the Disturbances for the period of 9th August–14th September, 1942, in Bihar."

17. N.A.I.: Home File Nos. 18/8/42 Poll. (I)—18/10/42 Poll. (I), "Fortnightly Reports from the Government of U.P.," August–October 1942.

18. *Ibid.*

19. N.A.I. Home File No. 3/15/43 Poll. (I), "Calendar of Events Connected with the Civil Disobedience Movement, 1943."

20. *Ibid.*

21. Mansergh, ed., *Transfer of Power*, III, 189.

22. *Ibid.*, II, 906.

23. *Ibid.*, III, 76.

24. N.A.I.: Home File No. 18/8/42 Poll. (I), "Fortnightly Report from the Government of U.P. For the First Half of August 1942"; "Fortnightly Report from the Government of U.P. for the Second Half of August 1942."

25. N.A.I.: Home File No. 18/8/42 Poll. (I), "Report from the Government of Delhi for the Month of August 1942."

26. N.A.I.: Home File No. 18/10/42 Poll. (I), "Fortnightly Report from the Government of Delhi for the Second Half of October 1942."

27. *Ibid.*

28. N.A.I.: Home File No. 18/9/42 Poll. (I), "Fortnightly Report from the Government of Bombay for the First Half of September 1942."

29. Correspondence between the governor of Bihar, Sir T. Stewart, and Lord Linlithgow printed in Mansergh, ed., *Transfer of Power*, II, 908–909, 916. For the November protest, see N.A.I.: Home File No. 18/11/42 Poll. (I), "Fortnightly Report from the Government of Bihar for the First Half of November 1942."

30. N.A.I.: Home File No. 3/70/43 Poll. (I), the "confessions" of a clerk in the "A.I.C.C." office.

31. Interview, Surya Narayan Rao, December 10, 1969. Rao was hit by three bullets at this time.

32. N.A.I.: Home File No. 3/6/43 Poll. (I); File No. 3/66/43 Poll. (I).

33. Interview, Radhe Shyam Sharma, December 11, 1969; N.A.I.: Home File No. 3/6/43 Poll. (I).

34. N.A.I.: Home File No. 3/44/43 Poll. (I); interview, Usha Mehta, June 12, 1970.

35. N.A.I.: Home File No. 3/19/43 Poll. (I), "All-India Congress Committee, Instruction No. 11."

36. Mansergh, ed., *Transfer of Power*, II, 790, letter from Sir T. Stewart to Lord Linlithgow, August 22, 1942, and telegram from Linlithgow to Amery, August 16, 1942; interviews, Aruna Asaf Ali, October 31, 1969, Sucheta Kripalani, January 21, 1970.

37. D. G. Tendulkar, *Abdul Ghaffar Khan* (Bombay: Popular Prakashan, 1967), p. 353.
38. Interviews, Radhe Shyam Sharma, December 11, 1969, Viswanath Sharma, December 12, 1969.
39. Jayaprakash Narayan, *Towards Struggle* (Bombay: Padma Publications, 1946), pp. 25–26.
40. Interview, Ananda Krishna, December 12, 1969.
41. N.A.I.: Home File No. 44/37/43 Poll. (I).
42. N.A.I.: Home File No. 18/9/42 Poll. (I), "Fortnightly Report from the Government of Bihar for the First Half of September 1942."
43. N.A.I.: Home File No. 3/64/43 Poll. (I).
44. Interview, R. R. Diwakar, February 5, 1970.
45. N.A.I.: Home File No. 3/64/43 Poll. (I).
46. Interview, Sucheta Kripalani, January 21, 1970.
47. N.A.I.: Home File No. 3/70/43 Poll. (I).
48. *Ibid.*
49. Interview, Sucheta Kripalani, January 21, 1970.
50. *India Unreconciled* (New Delhi: The Hindustan Times, 1944), pp. 173, 122; the latter phrase is from his letter of January 29, 1943.
51. *Ibid.*, p. 197.
52. N.A.I.: Home File No. 33/4/43 Poll. (I).
53. *Ibid.*
54. Government of India, *Congress Responsibility*, Appendix I, pp. 42–46.
55. *Harijan*, August 23, 1942.
56. *India Unreconciled*, pp. 135–136.
57. Mansergh, ed., *Transfer of Power*, II, 742, 698.
58. *Ibid.*, III, 197; N.A.I.: Home File Nos. 37/1/43 Poll. (I) and 3/44/43 Poll. (I).
59. *India Unreconciled*, p. 126, letter from Sir Richard Tottenham, February 7, 1943.
60. *Ibid.*, pp. 123–124, letter from Lord Linlithgow, February 5, 1943.
61. Mansergh, ed., *Transfer of Power*, III, 640.
62. *Ibid.*, III, 621.
63. *Ibid.*, III, 641.
64. *Ibid.*, III, 632. The words are Amery's version of Churchill's remarks.
65. *Ibid.*, III, 622.
66. *Ibid.*, III, 999.
67. *Ibid.*, III, 744, 746.
68. Government of India, *Congress Responsibility*, p. 41.
69. Azad, *India Wins Freedom*, pp. 81, 90.
70. *India Unreconciled*, pp. 122–123.
71. Tendulkar, *Mahatma*, VI, 130.
72. M. K. Gandhi, *Gandhiji's Correspondence with the Government, 1942–44* (Ahmedabad: Navajivan Publishing House, 1957), p. 139.
73. Erik H. Erikson, *Gandhi's Truth* (New York: W. W. Norton, 1969), p. 251.
74. N.A.I.: Home File No. 18/8/42 Poll. (I), "Fortnightly Report from the Government of U.P. for the Second Half of August 1942."
75. See Tendulkar, *Abdul Ghaffar Khan*, pp. 338–360.
76. N.A.I.: Home File No. 3/19/43 Poll. (I), "Translation of Cyclostyled Pamphlet in Pushtu, Published by the 'Markaz-I-A'Alia.'"
77. Appendix E, "Report on the Civil Disturbances in Bihar, 1942," Political and Secret Department Library, F. 204, India Office Library.

78. N.A.I.: Home File No. 18/8/42 Poll. (I), "Fortnightly Report from the Government of U.P. for the First Half of August 1942."

79. N.A.I.: Home File No. 18/10/42 Poll. (I), "Fortnightly Report from the Government of Bombay for the First Half of October 1942"; and "Fortnightly Report from the Government of Bombay for the Second Half of October 1942."

80. Mansergh, ed., *Transfer of Power*, II, 935.

81. *Ibid.*, II, 935.

82. *Ibid.*, II, 905.

83. File No. G-26, 1942, "Secret Report of the Government Belonging to the Supply Department," October 1942, All-India Congress Committee Papers.

84. Mansergh, ed., *Transfer of Power*, II, 961, 978.

85. *Ibid.*, III, 190.

86. *Ibid.*, II, 740.

87. Hallett to Linlithgow, August 24, 1942, Linlithgow Papers, vol. 105, India Office Library, London.

88. Hallett to Linlithgow, August 18, 1942, Linlithgow Papers, vol. 105.

89. Mansergh, ed., *Transfer of Power*, II, 740.

90. *Ibid.*, III, 95.

91. *Ibid.*, III, 161.

92. *Ibid.*, III, 291, 157.

93. *Ibid.*, III, 942.

94. *Ibid.*, III, 765.

95. *Ibid.*, III, 708, 877, 789, 877.

96. *Ibid.*, III, 16.

97. *Ibid.*, III, 161.

98. *Ibid.*, III, 849.

99. *Ibid.*, III, 849.

100. *Ibid.*, III, 838.

101. *Ibid.*, III, 543.

102. Amery to Linlithgow, October 1, 1943, Linlithgow Papers, vol. 12. Amery thought that in the present circumstances it might be desirable to resettle the Anglo-Indians in the Andaman and Nicobar islands, in order to make "an effective coherent community of them."

103. Mansergh, ed., *Transfer of Power*, III, 1003.

104. *Ibid.*, III, 870.

105. Linlithgow to Hallett, July 13, 1943, Linlithgow Papers, vol. 106.

106. Linlithgow to Amery, March 16, 1943, *ibid.*, vol. 12.

107. *India Unreconciled*, p. 94.

108. Pyarelal, *Mahatma Gandhi, The Last Phase*, I, 42.

109. *Ibid.*, p. 36, letter dated June 9, 1944.

110. Text of Aruna Asaf Ali—Gandhi correspondence, Nehru Papers, Nehru Memorial Museum.

10. AFTERMATH

1. Nicholas Mansergh, ed., *The Transfer of Power, 1942–7* (London: Her Majesty's Stationery Office, 1971), II, 853.

2. *Ibid.*, II, 391. See also pp. 631–632.

3. *Ibid.*, II, 874–875.

4. *Ibid.*, II, 884.

5. *Ibid.*, II, 875.

6. *Ibid.*, II, 853, 911.

7. *Ibid.*, II, 964.

8. Maulana Abul Kalam Azad, *India Wins Freedom* (Bombay: Orient Longmans, 1959), p. 110.

9. *Ibid.*, p. 126.

10. Philip G. Altbach, "The Bombay Naval Mutiny," *Opinion*, July 27, 1965, and August 31, 1965.

11. The period of the Articles of Confederation was suggested as a model for British withdrawal from India by Franklin Roosevelt in a telegram to Churchill in 1942, reprinted in Mansergh, ed., *Transfer of Power*, I, 409–410.

12. For Attlee's letter, see H. V. Hodson, *The Great Divide* (London: Hutchinson, 1969), pp. 545–547.

13. *Ibid.*, p. 551.

14. *Ibid.*, p. 550.

11. GANDHI'S FUTURE

1. Mahadev Desai, "Ireland—A Comparison and Contrast," *Harijan*, August 2, 1942.

2. Dorothy Norman, ed., *Nehru, The First Sixty Years* (London: The Bodley Head, 1965), II, 177–181.

3. M. K. Gandhi, *Delhi Diary* (Ahmedabad: Navajivan Publishing House, 1960), p. 39.

4. N. K. Bose, *My Days with Gandhi* (Calcutta: Nishana, 1953), pp. 254–255.

5. Gandhi, *Delhi Diary*, p. 153.

6. *Ibid.*, p. 56.

7. *Ibid.*, p. 337.

8. Bose, *My Days with Gandhi*, p. 270n.

9. Gandhi, *Delhi Diary*, pp. 276–277 and throughout.

10. Bose, *My Days with Gandhi*, p. 271.

11. N. K. Bose and P. H. Patwardhan, *Gandhi in Indian Politics* (Bombay: Lalvani Publishing House, 1967), p. 37.

12. Gandhi, *Delhi Diary*, p. 153.

13. Bose, *My Days with Gandhi*, p. 271.

14. N. K. Bose, ed., *Selections from Gandhi* (Ahmedabad: Navajivan Publishing House, 1968), p. 115.

15. Gandhi, *Delhi Diary*, p. 68.

16. *Ibid.*, p. 376.

17. Bose, ed., *Selections*, p. 189; *Harijan*, June 21, 1942.

18. Gandhi, *Delhi Diary*, p. 337.

Index

"A.B.C. of Dislocation," 251–254
Achebe, Chinua, 305
Adams, John, 74–75, 308
Africa, 65–66
Ahimsa, 123–127, 200–201, 203
Ahmad, Sir Zia-uddin, 238
Ahmadiya, 70
Aitchison Commission, 26–27
Aiyar, C. P. Ramaswamy, 245
Akhnaton, 72
Alcoholic beverages, 112
Alexander, Horace, 189, 215
Ali, Sadiq, 220, 240, 251, 255, 315
Altbach, Philip, 319
Ambedkar, B. R., 101
America, United States of, 156–157,
    164, 167, 169, 203, 257–258, 275
American Revolution, 4, 75–77, 79–83,
    87, 88, 96–100
Amery, L. S., 147, 150, 168, 260, 264,
    271, 311, 316, 317, 318; on Cyril As-
    quith, 41; on Congress, 145, 149, 160;
    on Revolutionary Movement Or-
    dinance, 164–166; on Quit India
    movement, 221–223, 283–285; on
    post-war India, 275–276
Andhra, 221
Anglo-Indians, 18–19, 135, 276, 318
Aristotle, 74
Asaf Ali, Aruna, 183, 241, 243, 245,
    254–255, 280–281, 316, 318
Asaf Ali, M., 219
Asquith, Cyril, 41
Assam, 192, 193, 235, 313
Athens, 87
Attlee, Clement, 142, 285, 288, 319
Aurobindo, Sri, 68, 91
Australia, 241
Azad, A. K., 213, 220, 257, 265–266,
    286–287, 315, 317, 319
Azad, Chandrasekhar, 199
Azad Dastas, 251–253

Bailyn, Bernard, 82, 88, 308
Balfour Declaration, 32
Banerjea, Surendranath, 59–60, 307
Bangladesh, 99
Barnouw, Eric, 305
Baroda, Gaekwar, 37
Beer, Samuel, 24, 305
Benares, 241, 255, 256
Benares Hindu University, 119, 241,
    243, 247
Bengal, 182, 235, 260, 278, 295, 315;
    famine of 1943, 178; partition of, 47,
    48, 71; renaissance of, 60–61
Bentham, Jeremy, 8–9, 89
Besant, Annie, 119–120
Bhagavad Gita, 91, 127, 200
Bhandarkar, Professor, 122
Bhansali, Professor, 229, 260
Bhave, Vinoba, 163, 187
Bihar, 207, 312, 313, 314, 315, 316, 317;
    and Gandhi, 134, 274; and the Na-
    tional War Front, 162–163; and In-
    demnity legislation, 174–177; and a
    Japanese invasion, 192–193; and the
    Quit India movement, 225–229,
    231, 235, 245, 248, 253–254, 269,
    272; and the Muslim League, 239
Birla, G. D., 134, 220, 270
Birsa Munda, 70
Bismarck, Otto von, 22
Black Americans, 4, 75, 81, 96, 97,
    100–103, 197–198
Blake, William, 93–94, 308
Boag, Sir George, 164
Boardman, Eugene Powers, 307

Bolingbroke, Viscount, 88
Bolitho, Hector, 307, 310
Bolivia, 103
Bombay, 161, 168, 263, 264, 316, 318, 319; and the Quit India movement, 177, 217–221, 228–229, 230, 232–235, 238, 240–241, 243–244, 253–255, 261, 269–270; and the Naval Mutiny of 1946, 287
Bose, Nirmal Kumar, 129, 132, 310, 314, 315, 319
Bose, Rash Behari, 248
Bose, Subhas Chandra, 53, 67, 68, 183, 236, 307, 310, 315; and Gandhi, 133, 137, 211–212; and Axis powers, 185–186, 195, 247–248
Burke, Edmund, 64, 93
Burma, 103, 192–194, 251, 313

Calcutta, 41, 51, 53, 178, 191, 241, 244, 256, 259, 270, 287, 294, 295
Calvin, John, 309
Campbell-Johnson, Alan, 307
Canada, 98–100
Canning, Lord, 48
Cargo cults, 70
Central Provinces, 170, 231, 235, 247
Ceylon, 51, 134
Chamberlain, Austen, 38
Chandra, Bipan, 305, 307
Chapekar brothers, 91
Charisma, 114–119
Chatterjee, Bankim Chandra, 31, 305
Chelmsford, Lord, 33–35, 37–39, 42, 140
Cheng, J. C., 307
Chiang Kai-shek, 142–143, 216
Chimur atrocities, 229
China, 44–46, 76, 86, 95, 98–99, 116, 119, 193, 196, 197, 309
Chou En-lai, 86
Christ, 20, 69, 70
Christianity, 11–12, 51, 70–71
Churchill, Winston, 41, 141–143, 151–152, 164, 182, 262–264, 269, 271, 276, 282, 284–286, 317, 319
Civic Guards, 161–163
Civil War, American, 87
Cobbs, Price M., 307
Communists, Indian, 147, 148, 189–190, 229, 236, 248
Comte, Auguste, 107

Congress, Indian National: and Gandhi, 121–122, 133–135, 184–185, 187, 199, 201, 211–215, 279–281, 290–296; and World War II, 139–140, 182, 185–186, 193, 195, 211–212; British official views of, 140–145, 147–150, 153–154, 167–172, 273–278; and the Revolutionary Movement Ordinance, 154–161, 163–166, 173–174; volunteer bodies, 162; and the Quit India movement, 175–179, 217–257, 259–261, 264–273, 280–281
Cripps, Sir Stafford, 144, 151, 167–168, 188, 213, 283, 285
Cromwell, Oliver, 119
Cuba, 103
Curzon, Lord, 47, 48, 170, 262

Danzig, Richard, 306
Das, C. R., 133
Dayanand, Swami, 56, 72–73, 307
Delhi, 37, 219–220, 235, 238, 241–242, 257–258, 294–295, 316, 319
Deo, S. D., 218
Desai, Mahadev, 196, 197–198, 201, 221, 222, 229, 260, 277, 291–292, 314, 319
Deshpande, Gangadharrao, 114
Dey, Lal Behari, 51–52, 306
Diwakar, R. R., 317
Dostoevski, Fyodor, 113
Duncan, Ronald, 309
Dutch, 1, 62

Easter Rebellion, 182, 291
Eckstein, Harry, 308
Education, 7–16, 51–59
Education Despatch of 1854, 12–14
Engels, Frederick, 94, 308
English Revolution, 79, 96
Erikson, Erik, 7, 119, 126, 267, 307, 310, 317

Fanon, Frantz, 65
Fischer, Louis, 181, 313, 315
France, 1, 4, 5, 31, 75, 76, 79, 86, 87, 88, 97, 103
Freud, Sigmund, 126–127, 310
Friedrich, Carl J., 309
Frykenberg, Robert, 306
Fuchs, Stephen, 307

Gairola, Kaushalya, 241
Gandhi, Devadas, 258
Gandhi, Indira, 183
Gandhi, Kasturba, 130, 131, 277
Gandhi, Mohandas K., 141, 145, 146,
    150, 157, 163, 164, 178, 307, 309,
    310, 311, 313, 314, 315, 317, 318, 319;
    as a young man, 55–58, 105–106;
    and reaction, 90–91, 94–95; and
    Martin Luther King, Jr., 100–101;
    and Ruskin, 108–110; on "civili-
    zation," 111–112; on conversion,
    112–113; and charisma, 114–119; style
    of, 119–122; tactics of, 122–132; and
    followers, 132–136, 184–185; and
    Quit India movement, 136–138,
    217–223, 227, 229, 234, 235–236,
    238, 258–259, 268; official views of,
    124, 170–173; on British war efforts,
    181, 182–183, 185–189, 190–191,
    195–197; on violence, 197–206,
    265–267; on anarchy, 206–216, 287,
    289; 21-day fast by, 256–258, 261–
    264, 274; and Japanese contacts,
    271–272; upon release from prison,
    1944, 277–281; last days, 290–296
Ganpat, Dewoo, 177
George III, 88
George V, 37, 65
Germany, 98, 143, 156–157, 181, 185–
    186, 189, 196, 201, 212, 246, 247, 248,
    260–261
Ghana, 103
Gilleit, Stanley, 177
Godbole, Y. A., 274
Gokhale, G. K., 56, 64, 65, 122, 128,
    146
Gopal, Ram, 308
Greece, 99
Grier, William, 307
Guevara, Che, 103
Gujarat, 86, 170, 228–229, 264
Gupta, Manmathnath, 314
Gwalior, 242
Gwyer, Sir Maurice, 273, 275

Haileybury, 45
Hall, John Whitney, 306
Hallet, Sir Maurice, 157–159, 175–176,
    272–273, 275, 276, 311, 312, 313, 318
Hardinge, Lord, 41–42, 306
Harischandra, 55, 56

Harrison, Agatha, 215
Hartz, Louis, 83, 308, 309
Heath, Carl, 314
Hind Swaraj, 111, 121, 125, 198, 292
Hindu Mahasabha, 147, 148, 236
Hitler, Adolph, 86, 171
Hobbes, Thomas, 89
Ho Chi Minh, 86
Hodson, H. V., 319
Holland, 1, 62
Hope, Sir A., 160
Hopkins, Harry, 142
Hung Hsiu-ch'üan, 70–71
Hunter, Lord, 126
Huntington, Samuel P., 4, 76, 77, 80,
    81, 305, 308
Hyderabad, 100

Iengar, H. V. R., 255
Indemnity Acts, 174–177
Indian Civil Service, 42–47, 53, 59–60,
    133, 214–215, 246, 255, 256, 274
Indian National Army, 247–248, 251
Indonesia, 1, 103, 181
Ireland, 96, 98, 100, 135, 181–182, 185,
    291–292, 319
Irschick, Eugene, 307
Irwin, Lord, 41
Israel, 99

Jallianwallah Bagh, 126, 159, 174, 184
Jamiat-ul-Ulema-i-Hind, 238
Japan, 98; traditional government of,
    44–46; military advance toward
    India of, 143, 182, 188, 191–197,
    202–206, 246–248, 259, 260–261,
    270, 271–273, 286
Jayakar, M. R., 257
Jinnah, Mohammed Ali, 101–102,
    145–147, 168, 208, 214, 275, 277, 278,
    307, 310
Jordan, 99
Joshi, P. C., 236

Kachru, Dwarkanath, 240, 255
Kartini, Raden Adjeng, 62, 307
Karve, D. D., 309
Kashmir, 270, 276
Katagade, N. T., see Pundalik
Keer, Dhananjay, 308
Keskar, B. K., 240

Khan, Khan Abdul Ghaffar, 246, 268, 317
King, Martin Luther, Jr., 100–101
Kishore, Jugal, 315
Kissinger, Henry, 124, 310
Kopf, David, 307
Korea, 98
Kripalani, Sucheta, 220, 241, 246, 251, 254, 255, 256, 315, 316, 317
Krishna, 69
Krishna, Ananda, 314, 317
Krishnaswamy, S., 305

Lawrence, Peter, 306, 307
Lawrence, T. E., 32
Lear, King, 211, 293
Lenin, 86
Linlithgow, Lord, 141, 185, 310, 311, 312, 313, 316, 317, 318; opinion of Gandhi of, 124, 261–267; Gandhi's opinion of, 128; opinion of Congress of, 144, 147, 154–161, 237; opinion of Muslim League of, 147, 237, 239; on political future of India, 147–154, 274–277, 285; and Revolutionary Movement Ordinance, 154–161, 164–167; on C. P. Ramaswamy Aiyar, 245; on press, 259–260; on complicity with Japan of Indian business, 271–272; on Quit India movement, 282–283
Lipset, S. M., 4, 305, 309
Locke, John, 309
Lohia, Ram Manohar, 241, 244, 254–255
Lok Sevak Sangh, 296
Lothian, Sir Arthur, 141, 310
Lumley, Sir Roger, 264
Lutfullah, 51, 306
Luther, Martin, 67, 86, 87, 307

Macaulay, T. B., 12, 48
McCully, Bruce, 306
Machiavelli, Niccolo, 71–72, 89
Madras, 182, 194–195, 235, 244, 313
Mahabharata, 186
Malaya, 1, 193, 194
Mandeville, B., 89–90, 92
Manning, Cardinal, 106
Mannoni, O., 306
Mansergh, Nicholas, 306, 310, 312, 314, 315, 316, 317, 318, 319

Mao Tse-tung, 86, 105, 116, 309
Marx, Karl, 77, 107–108, 111, 309, 310
Mashruwala, K. G., 222–223
Matthews, Herbert, 258
Maxwell, Sir Reginald, 155–156, 158–161, 164, 167, 174, 274, 311, 312
Medicine, 111–112
Mehta, G. G., 217
Mehta, Usha, 244, 316
Melbourne, Lord, 89
Menon, K. P. S., 53, 307
Michael, Franz, 307
Midnapur cyclone, 178
Mill, J. S., 3, 78–79, 107, 308
Miller, Perry, 83, 308
Milton, John, 107
Minto, Lord, 27, 33, 35–36, 41–42
Mirabehn (Madeleine Slade), 191, 197, 203, 205, 215, 314
Molesworth, General G. N., 196, 206
Montagu, Edwin, 32–37, 39, 42, 49, 140, 167, 306
Montesquieu, Baron, 31, 88, 305
Moore, Arthur, 260
Moore, Barrington, Jr., 96, 309
Moplas, 102
Morley, Lord, 27, 33, 35–36, 287
Mountbatten, Lord, 209, 212, 288–290, 315
Mudaliar, Sir Ramaswami, 151–152
Muhammad, 115
Münzer, Thomas, 94
Muslim League, 102, 147, 148, 161, 168, 208, 211, 214–215, 236, 238, 239, 240, 278, 288, 289
Muslims, 97, 135, 168, 207, 275; before British, 30, 31; and Pakistan, 98, 100–102, 145, 208, 277–279; Churchill on, 143; and Quit India movement, 214, 235–240
Mussolini, B., 105

Nair, Sankaran, 37
Nanda, B. R., 309, 310, 313
Naoroji, D., 146
Narayan, Jayaprakash, 185, 189–190, 227, 246–247, 250, 253, 255, 259, 317
National War Front, 162–163
Naval Mutiny, 287
Nawanagar, Maharaja, 151–152
Nehru, Jawaharlal, 101, 183, 213, 286, 310, 313, 315, 318, 319; on communalism, 83–84; Linlithgow on, 171; and

Gandhi, 184, 259, 292–293, 296; on
    World War II, 186, 187, 191; and Quit
    India movement, 218, 257
Nelson, W. H., 308
Nepal, 253
Nero, 105, 215
News, regulation of, 258–261
Newton, Isaac, 93, 94
Niblett, R. H., 176–177, 312
Nigeria, 103
Niles, Hezekiah, 308
Nivedita, Sister, 91
Noncooperation, 123
Norman, Dorothy, 319
North-West Frontier Province, 235,
    268

Orissa, 191, 205, 235, 246

Pailin, Neville Cedric, 177
Pakistan, 98, 99, 100, 102, 143, 146, 147,
    168, 208, 214, 295, 310
Pal, B. C., 54, 58, 59, 307
Pande, Cheetu, 268
Parikh, Narhari, 307, 310
Parsis, 146, 153
Patel, Dhayabhai, 220
Patel, Sardar Vallabhbhai, 53–54, 118,
    133–134, 293, 296, 307
Patel, Vithalbhai, 53–54
Patnaik, Biju, 246
Patwardhan, Achyut, 241, 254–255
Pearl Harbor, 139, 188
Philippines, 2
Pincutt, Frederick, 105–106
Plato, 46
Polak, Henry, 108, 128
Polak, Millie, 128, 310
Poland, 139, 201
Prasad, Rajendra, 315
Prichard, Iltudus, 306
Princes, 34, 36–38, 41, 99, 135, 152,
    168, 214–215, 276, 288–289
Pundalik, 113–114, 116–117, 242, 309
Punjab, 190, 235, 247, 251
Pyarelal, 220, 315, 318

Radhakrish'nan, S., 257
Raghavdas, Baba, 241, 255
Rajagopalachari, C., 235, 256
Ramusack, Barbara, 306
Ranadive, B. T., 257
Rand, Ayn, 309

Rand, Plague Commissioner, 91
Rao, Surya Narayan, 316
Rape, 200–201, 202, 248–249
Rebellion of 1857, 30, 153, 155, 174,
    207, 282–283
Revolutionary Movement Ordinance,
    154–158, 163–167, 173–174, 312
Richter, Melvin, 309
Ripon, Lord, 48
Roberts' Rules of Order, 3
Robespierre, 86
Roman Empire, 85
Rome, 86, 87
Roosevelt, Franklin, 142–143, 196, 319
Roosevelt, Theodore, 101
Rousseau, Jean Jacques, 86, 94, 120,
    129, 309
Rowlatt Acts, 159, 183
Roy, Raja Ram Mohan, 68, 69
Rudolph, L. I., 305, 308, 310
Rudolph, S. H., 305, 308, 310
Ruskin, John, 108–113, 309
Russell, Bertrand, 216
Russia, 76–78, 97, 136, 143, 169, 181,
    185, 186, 189, 196, 212, 247, 309

Salt March, 110, 184
Sapru, Tej Bahadur, 257
Sarda, Har Bilas, 307
Satya, 123–126
Satyagraha, 117, 123, 124, 129, 187–188,
    189, 191, 201
Satyanand, Swami, 176
Savarkar, V. D., 91, 308
Sayeed, Khalid bin, 311
Schram, Stuart, 309
Schwartz, Benjamin, 309
Scindhia, 37
Shakespeare, William, 107
Sharma, Brahma Dutt, 187–188
Sharma, Radhe Shyam, 241–244, 253,
    314, 317
Sharma, Viswanath, 314, 317
Sharp, F. E., 217–218
Shastri, Algu Rai, 176
Shivaji, 91
Shravana, 55, 56
Sikhs, 102, 135, 215, 235, 236, 276,
    288–289
Simla Conference, 286
Simon Commission, 184
Sindh, 235, 278
Singh, Bhagat, 199

Singh, Gurdip, 247–248
Sitaramayya, Pattibhi, 306
Slade, Madeleine, see Mirabehn
Smith, Adam, 89
Snow, Edgar, 204
Socialists, 185, 189, 236–237, 250
Solomon, King, 208, 211
South Africa, 101, 108, 121–122, 128,
  135, 182–183, 266, 309
Sparta, 90
Spencer, Herbert, 107
Stalin, 86
Steel, Flora Annie, 64
Stephen, James Fitzjames, 48
Stewart, Sir T., 225–226, 239, 245, 274,
  316
Swaraj, 123, 227
Swift, Jonathan, 89

Tagore, Rabindranath, 92–93, 308
Taiping Rebellion, 70–71
Tata, J. R. D., 257
Taub, Richard, 306
Tendulkar, D. G., 309, 313, 314, 315,
  317
Thoreau, Henry, 109, 309
Tilak, B. G., 87, 90, 91, 122, 308
Tocqueville, Alexis de, 3, 5, 75–76,
  100, 305
Tolstoy, Leo, 309
Tottenham, Richard, 156, 161–162, 165,
  263, 274, 317
Towler, W. H., 194

Toye, Hugh, 310
Tucker, Robert C., 119, 310
Turkey, 99
Twynam, Sir Henry, 160

United Provinces, 315, 316, 317, 318;
  and Indemnity Legislation, 174–177;
  and Quit India movement, 217,
  227–228, 235, 241–242, 255, 268–269,
  272; and Muslims, 237–238
Untouchables, 101, 135, 176, 185, 215,
  236, 238, 280, 288
Usman, Sir Mahomed, 151

Valera, Eamon de, 291, 292
Vietnam, 98–99, 181
Vizianagram, Maharajkumar, 257
Voltaire, 93

Walpole, Robert, 88
Washington, Booker T., 101
Wavell, Lord, 277, 287
Weber, Max, 114–119, 309
Wilcox, Wayne, 309
Wilkinson, Rupert, 44, 306
Willingdon, Lord, 40, 141
Wolpert, Stanley, 306
Women, 123–124, 200–201
Woodruff, Philip, 306

Yajnik, Indulal, 118, 135–136, 309, 310
Yugoslavia, 181